America's Anchor

America's Anchor

*A Naval History of the
Delaware River and Bay,
Cradle of the United States Navy*

KENNARD R. WIGGINS, JR.

McFarland & Company, Inc., Publishers
Jefferson, North Carolina

LIBRARY OF CONGRESS CATALOGUING-IN-PUBLICATION DATA

Names: Wiggins, Kennard R., author.
Title: America's Anchor : A Naval History of the Delaware River and Bay, Cradle of the United States Navy / Kennard R. Wiggins Jr.
Description: Jefferson, North Carolina : McFarland & Company, Inc., Publishers, 2019 | Includes bibliographical references and index.
Identifiers: LCCN 2018054293 | ISBN 9781476671970 (softcover : acid free paper) ∞
Subjects: LCSH: United States—History, Naval. | United States. Navy—History. | Delaware River Estuary—History.
Classification: LCC E182 .W54 2019 | DDC 359.009749—dc23
LC record available at https://lccn.loc.gov/2018054293

BRITISH LIBRARY CATALOGUING DATA ARE AVAILABLE

ISBN (print) 978-1-4766-7197-0
ISBN (ebook) 978-1-4766-3435-7

© 2019 Kennard R. Wiggins, Jr. All rights reserved

No part of this book may be reproduced or transmitted in any form or by any means, electronic or mechanical, including photocopying or recording, or by any information storage and retrieval system, without permission in writing from the publisher.

Front cover image of an East prospect of the city of Philadelphia, from the Jersey Shore, 1754 (Miriam and Ira D. Wallach Division of Art, Prints and Photographs: Print Collection, New York Public Library)

Printed in the United States of America

*McFarland & Company, Inc., Publishers
Box 611, Jefferson, North Carolina 28640
www.mcfarlandpub.com*

To my friend William H.J. Manthorpe, Jr.

Acknowledgments

This is not my first book. I started my writing career with several relatively simple illustrated histories significant more for their images than for the writing. My last book was more of an exercise in writing and organizing my material but was still on a relatively modest scale. The book you hold is a much more ambitious project that required far more research and organization than my previous efforts. I learned a great deal from the many people who made contributions to this project both large and small. As the scope grew, so too did the generosity of those who helped make this possible.

Foremost is a gentleman of great passion, scholarship, and knowledge. Retired navy captain William H.J. Manthorpe, Jr., freely shared his extensive archive of notes, material, and naval lore in helping to lay the foundation for this tale. He remained very interested in this project throughout and advised me every step of the way. One could want no more from a collaborator. I treasure Bill's friendship and I respect his intellect.

My research took me to the Philadelphia Independence Seaport Museum, the Naval History and Heritage Command Library at the Washington Navy Yard, the National Maritime Museum and Library in Hampton Roads Virginia, the Norfolk Naval Museum, the Delaware State Public Archives, the University of Delaware Library, the Delaware Historical Society, the Delaware Military Museum Library, and the Hagley Museum Library in Wilmington, Delaware. It is a joy to do research in these places, where the staff is unfailingly knowledgeable and helpful.

Many individuals contributed to the production of this book. Thanks to Richard Gillis for the loan of maritime topics from his personal library; to Kim Burdick and my wife, Liz Wiggins, for proofreading my manuscript; to Thomas Reed for reading and reviewing the manuscript and offering interesting and informed new perspectives; and, of course, to Bill Manthorpe for his many contributions.

Table of Contents

Acknowledgments	vi
Preface	1
Introduction	3
One. Delaware River and Bay Maritime Heritage	5
Two. Creating an American Navy	20
Three. Maintaining American Sovereignty and Independence	51
Four. Years of Peace and Development	80
Five. The Civil War	107
Six. Years of National Expansion, 1865–1914	131
Seven. The Great War, 1914–1918, and through 1925	163
Eight. World War II	194
Appendix 1: Delaware Valley Sailor and Marine Medal of Honor Recipients	223
Appendix 2: Delaware-Built Civil War Vessels	239
Appendix 3: Post–Civil War, Wilmington-Built Ships, 1871–1917	249
Appendix 4: Ships of World War I from Delaware Shipyards	255
Chapter Notes	259
Bibliography	273
Index	277

Preface

It can be vexing for an author who sets out to write a book and—after much research, thought, organization, and rewriting—an entirely different product emerges. Books seem to take the author in directions he had never anticipated. In researching my last book, *Delaware in World War I*, I came across the story of the battleship USS *Delaware* and learned that there had been five previous ships named *Delaware*, each of which had a fascinating ship's history. The more I researched these ships, their captains, and their crews the more interested I became. So I resolved to write a book on them.

Then a friend and colleague, William H.J. Manthorpe, Jr., a retired navy captain, in correspondence revealed that he had just such a project already underway. His intent is to have an anthology of ships' histories and the men who sailed those ships ready for the launching of the next USS *Delaware*, a submarine, scheduled to deploy in 2019. I collaborated to a very minor degree with Bill on his book, sharing my research. In turn Bill generously shared with me his research, particularly on Cape Henlopen and Lewes, about which he had written in his book, *A Century of Service: The U.S. Navy on Cape Henlopen, Lewes, Delaware, 1898–1996*. Bill is something of a local legend as a researcher, writer, and speaker, and he had amassed a great deal of unpublished local naval history. He graciously agreed to share his extensive resources with me. His contribution has been invaluable in laying the foundation for the volume you hold here.

Again, the target kept moving. I started to write a book about significant military ships and sailors of Delaware. However, the navy was not the only military service to sail. The forerunner of the United States Coast Guard, the Revenue Service, was also a factor in local waters, and sometimes privateers as well. My topic area grew. Delaware waters are the pathway to the important port of Philadelphia. These waters reach from the Delaware Capes off Delaware and New Jersey to a large watershed in southeastern Pennsylvania and beyond. My scope widened to include trade, shipbuilding and navigation, and marine infrastructure such as lighthouses, canals, and range lights. It was very difficult to keep this topic corralled. It refused to obey. I tried to avoid venturing into a general discussion of *maritime* history and remained focused on the *naval* history of this geographic area of interest. However, to provide context and understanding it is necessary to go a little off topic from time to time, and I hope the reader will find these detours worthwhile. My aim was to offer a broad and complete understanding of the role of the Delaware estuary in the defense of our nation and in the development and progress of the United States naval components. The waterways of the Delaware spawned a disproportionate number of naval heroes and sailors.

I have tried to offer the background necessary to understand this narrative of ships and men, enlightened by the tales of numerous sailors and naval heroes, many of whom have been previously unknown to the general public. Therefore my tale jumps from notable ships to notable men and their deeds, in times of peace, war, and the continuum between. I have selected ships' histories that represent this area and that are representative of their times, offering a sample of naval activities, missions, and customs. I've attempted to offer a large overall story of the progress of the United States Navy, whose cradle lies between the shores of the Delaware, as told through the words and deeds of Delaware River and Delaware Bay ships and sailors.

The Delaware estuary is truly "America's Anchor."

Introduction

I'm in the research library at the Independence Seaport Museum in Philadelphia gazing out a large window onto an esplanade filled with tourists, children, and other passers-by. I'm looking south along the shore of the Delaware River. The museum is a little north of the site of the original Philadelphia Navy Yard in the Southwark district of the city.

The gray-green river here is calm and glassy on this summer day, sparkling with reflected sun. There are food vendors and a marina filled with pleasure craft, as well as the proud Spanish-American War veteran USS *Olympia*, Admiral Dewey's flagship at the Battle of Manila. Alongside it is the somber submarine USS *Becuna*, a veteran of World War II. Farther downriver the majestic tall ship *Moshulu*, now festooned with ferns as a floating restaurant, is tied alongside the quay. She is the world's largest square-rigged ship still afloat, built on the river Clyde in Glasgow in 1904. Directly across the river is the huge battleship USS *New Jersey*, another World War II veteran now berthed in nearby Camden. Without much difficulty, from this spot one will see working tugs, barges, container ships bound for exotic locales, lighters, tankers, freighters, and patrol craft passing up and down the river. Although the sight is rare now, in days past one would also see the occasional warship, whose purpose this book attempts to make clear. This riverfront and these historic vessels are chapters in a much larger story. The water in which they float is connected to the rest of the world. Indeed, it covers over two-thirds of the globe. The river here in Philadelphia and the bay below are pathways to the continents and seafaring nations and cities of the world. "The Sea is one" is a term used by mariners—a statement of both opportunity and threat.

The seas are a barrier to invasion by foreign enemies as they are also an avenue of approach. The Swedes, the Dutch, and the English successively used this most direct path to conquest on the shores of the Delaware. The great distances of the world's oceans offer a measure of insulation and security. They provided a barrier to our enemies during the world wars. However, geography by itself is not enough. It must be augmented by active defenses in the form of a navy. Britain prevailed on the sea as our enemy during the Revolution and during the War of 1812. Dewey's *Olympia* prevailed in 1898 and the *New Jersey* in 1945, providing a telling illustration of this important point. The great ocean also provides a trading route to enable commerce. Even before the War of Independence, Philadelphia was the premier commercial center in the colonies. This entrepreneurial city built ships along the shores of the Delaware and exported these ships and the goods they carried to England and Europe. The area handsomely profited by sea trade with the combatants during the Napoleonic Wars. Shortly after the Revolution,

Pennsylvanians and Delawareans were trading regularly with the Chinese and other Asian nations. For a brief period, whaling was another activity based on Delaware shores. All this commerce drew the attention of pirates, hostile rivals, and those who desired to plunder America's goods and impress her seamen. On a sea of anarchy, one needs friends and protection, hence another reason for a strong navy emerged to protect U.S. trade routes, vessels, and seamen from predation by enemies.

A navy is not just a collection of ships. Men are required to man the vessels, and the men must be organized, trained, and led. A navy needs onshore infrastructure for supply and repair, construction facilities for building, navigation aids for maneuvering, and canals, bridges, lighthouses, and other infrastructure. It requires doctrine and tactics to make the best use of the resources at hand, and situational awareness of its surroundings through scouting and observation.

In thousands of ways great and small the Delaware River Valley was the nursery that provided these men and women and these resources. Their sinew and toil built a navy manned by trained and disciplined sailors led by dedicated and visionary officers. This is their story.

One

Delaware River and Bay Maritime Heritage

The seal of Pennsylvania depicts a plow and sheaves of wheat below a sailing ship, symbolizing the state's maritime heritage. The Delaware state seal likewise depicts a sheaf of wheat, an ear of corn, and a cow, flanked by a farmer and a militiaman. Above it all sails a ship symbolizing Delaware's maritime heritage. Trade, shipbuilding, and fisheries were all a part of Pennsylvania's early history, especially the "three lower counties" that would later comprise Delaware. It owes its very existence to ships of exploration and settlement as well as ships of war. The wheat, corn, and beef wouldn't have made it to market without the ship bottoms to carry them.

Today most residents of the Delaware River Valley, its watershed, and the shores of this great estuary pay their waterway little heed. It goes unnoticed except when one crosses it on any of the majestic bridges that span the river. Any thought given to it at all might be by a ferry passenger or a sportsman who fishes its waters in the broader reaches of the bay or canoes the upper river. However, at one time it was the area's only link to the outside world, a vital artery of transport, trade, and communication. It was how farmers got their goods to market, and its tributaries powered mills for manufacture. The Delaware River and Delaware Bay also provided a gateway to Europe.

It still does all those things, but in a less visible way. Individual destinies are no longer personally linked to the river in ways they once were. Maritime activity is no longer at the center of lives here as it once was. The water that earlier was the primary link that joined our common destiny is perceived as no more significant than the rails, airlines, highways, power grid, or Internet.

Exploration

The first English explorer of the Eastern Seaboard, John Cabot, managed to miss the Delaware estuary in his explorations. The Delaware Bay was first sighted by Henry Hudson on the *Half Moon* in 1609, and he failed to venture much farther than the mouth of the bay, wary of its shoals and currents. He called it the South River and what later became the Hudson River was called the North River. A year later Samuel Argall, an English sailor sailing the pinnace *Discovery*, found his way into Delaware Bay when taking refuge from a storm. He named the bay for Lord de La Warr, the governor of Virginia. In 1616 Dutch navigator Cornelius Hendrickson, aboard the *Onrust*, sailed up the bay and proceeded up the river, mapping three tributaries between 38 and 40 degrees latitude.[1]

Another Dutch explorer, Cornelius Mey, captain of the *Blyde Boodschap* (Glad Tidings), gave the name Cape Cornelius (later Henlopen) to the cape at the southern mouth of the bay and his last name to the corresponding cape on the tip of New Jersey.[2] Only one of his dubbings stuck.[3]

Settlement

In December 1621 the Dutch West India Company was incorporated, and in 1623, three years after the landing of the Pilgrims at Plymouth, the first settlement on the shores of the Delaware was made by Cornelius Mey, who built Fort Nassau, near Gloucester, on the eastern bank. However, it was abandoned after three years, the first known permanent European-built structure in what would become the state of New Jersey.[4]

Besides the places already named, there were settlements at Swedesboro, Upland (now Chester), Manaiung (Manyunk), a handsome little fort of hickory logs at the mouth of the Schuylkill, Wiccacoa (Passyunk), Shackamaxon (Kensington), and elsewhere in the Delaware River Valley. Three Swedes subsequently owned the tract included in the ancient limits of Philadelphia, which they exchanged with Penn for a tract near the city containing 820 acres.[5]

The first European settlement in Delaware was called Zwaanendael, founded by a Walloon merchant named Samuel Godyn, with Peter de Vries as his captain, on what is now Lewes Creek in the spring of 1631. Its purpose was to establish a whaling station as well as to open the area to agriculture. They arrived aboard the *Walvis* (Whale) commanded by Captain Peter Heyes. A second expedition the following year learned that Zwaanendael had been vanquished by native Americans, and the nascent colony was subsequently abandoned.[6]

The first permanent settlement on the Delaware was by the Swedes, who arrived in 1638 aboard the vessels *Kalmar Nyckel* (Key of Kalmar) and *Vogel Grip* (Bird Grip). They debarked at a ledge of rocks on the Christiana River at Wilmington. Although they struggled to establish a toehold in the new world as they vied with Dutch and English foes, they had established themselves upon a great water highway that gave them easy access across the river as well as along its length. Wilmington predates Philadelphia by a half century and Baltimore by a century.[7]

The broad reach of the Delaware estuary was mostly flanked by marshy wetlands. With the Atlantic Ocean at one end and Philadelphia at the other end, it served as the interstate highway of its day. But people are more apt to live and work on secondary roads. Settlement took place on the few places where the topography was elevated, usually upstream in places like Philadelphia and Camden but also at points in Burlington, Bordentown, Wilmington, New Castle, and Lewes. Civilization would take root on upstream tributaries, giving rise to Salem, Milford, Dover, and Christiana. The waters that feed the estuary offered a resource for the entrepreneur. For the farmer and the fisherman the countless tributaries on both sides of the river offered access to nature's bounty. For the miller and sawyer these streams and creeks offered a source of power to grind wheat, cut wood, and make cotton and paper products. Although the very earliest European settlers on the shores of the Delaware were Dutch, their actual control lasted only fifteen years.

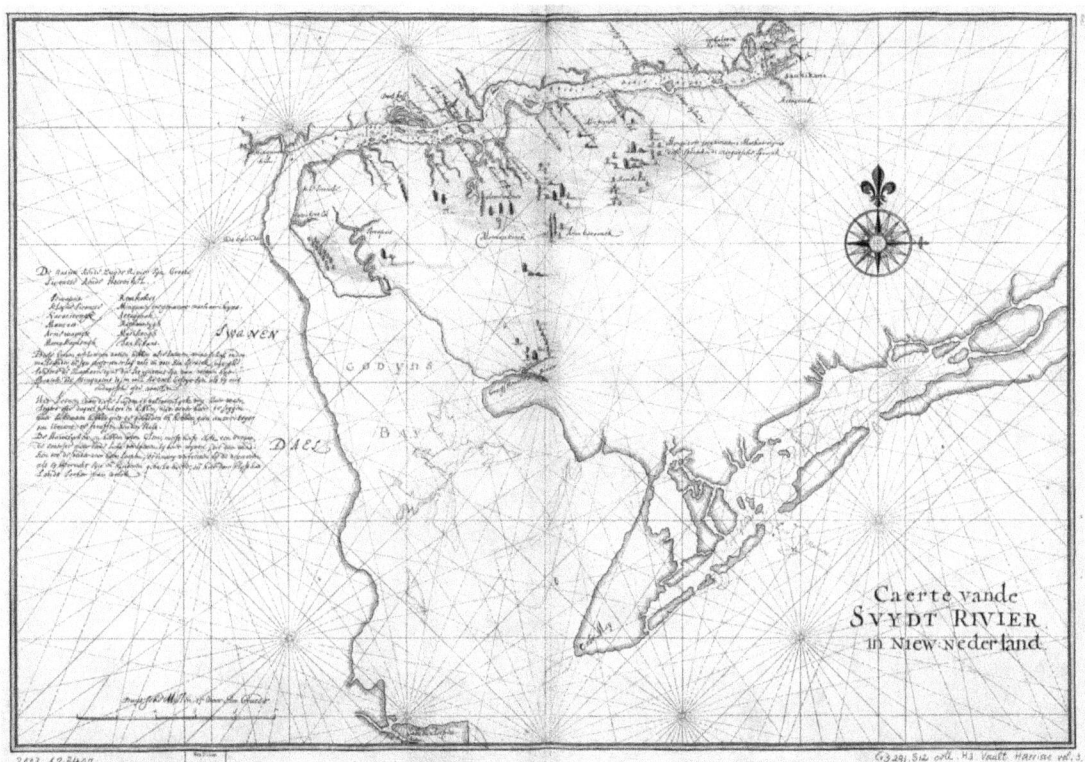

A map of South River in New Netherland. This pen-and-ink and watercolor map from around 1639 shows the South (Delaware) River, Delaware Bay, and the adjoining coasts. This region was part of the colony of New Netherland, which was established by the Dutch in 1621 and ruled by them until it was seized by the British in 1664. The map shows settlements and geographical features, with water depths in soundings. The text on the left side of the map contains a description of the Native American tribes living in the region (attributed to Joan Vinckeboons, 2003623407, Library of Congress, Geography and Map Division).

They were followed by the Swedes, who for seventeen years maintained their sway. New Sweden, a settlement of about 1,000 Swedes and Finns, was a string of settlements from just below the Christina River to Philadelphia along the west shore of the river.[8]

With the end of the Thirty Years' War and the Treaty of Westphalia in 1648, European nations began to compete for empire. Sweden, with a strong king, was fully engaged in defending the territory of its empire in Central and Eastern Europe. Free from Spain, the United Netherlands began its rise as a commercial and maritime power, intent on developing and extending its colony of New Netherlands beyond New Amsterdam. Great Britain wanted to extend its colonial presence in America to block the French to the north and Spanish to the south. To support larger colonies all these powers needed ports with well-sheltered harbors on the estuaries of rivers that provided access to the sea for the export of the products of the colony, the movement of government officials and investors, and the import of goods. In 1654 John Rising, the Swedish governor in Christina (near Wilmington) had seized a nearby Dutch Fort at New Castle, Fort Casimir. On August 31, 1655, the Swedes had formed the first recorded militia in the colony to defend themselves.[9]

Swedes summoning Dutch Fort Casimir (New Castle) to surrender, 1654 (Art and Picture Collection, New York Public Library).

In what would be among the first of many naval actions to follow in the watershed, the Dutch, led by Peter Stuyvesant, brought the largest naval armada yet seen on the Delaware to bear on the Swedish forces. The seven Dutch vessels included the *Waag* in the van, followed by *Abrams Offhandle* mounting four guns, the *Hollanse Tuijn, Prinses Royael, Hoop, Liefde*, and *Dolphin* all carrying cannon, along with several hundred armed soldiers. Landing between the two Swedish strongholds at Forts Casimir (New Castle) and Christina (Wilmington) they promptly avenged the loss of Fort Casimir and conquered all of New Sweden. In the process they killed cattle, poultry, and swine, and pillaged and plundered the territory.[10]

In 1658 the Dutch reestablished a small trading post near their earlier settlement that was augmented by Mennonite settlers. It was destroyed in 1663 when the Dutch vanquished the English Duke of York, who "in 1670 granted patents for land along the Whorekil creek to a number of Dutch and English families and set land aside for a town about one mile south of the inlet."[11] In 1670 the residents were given authority to build a

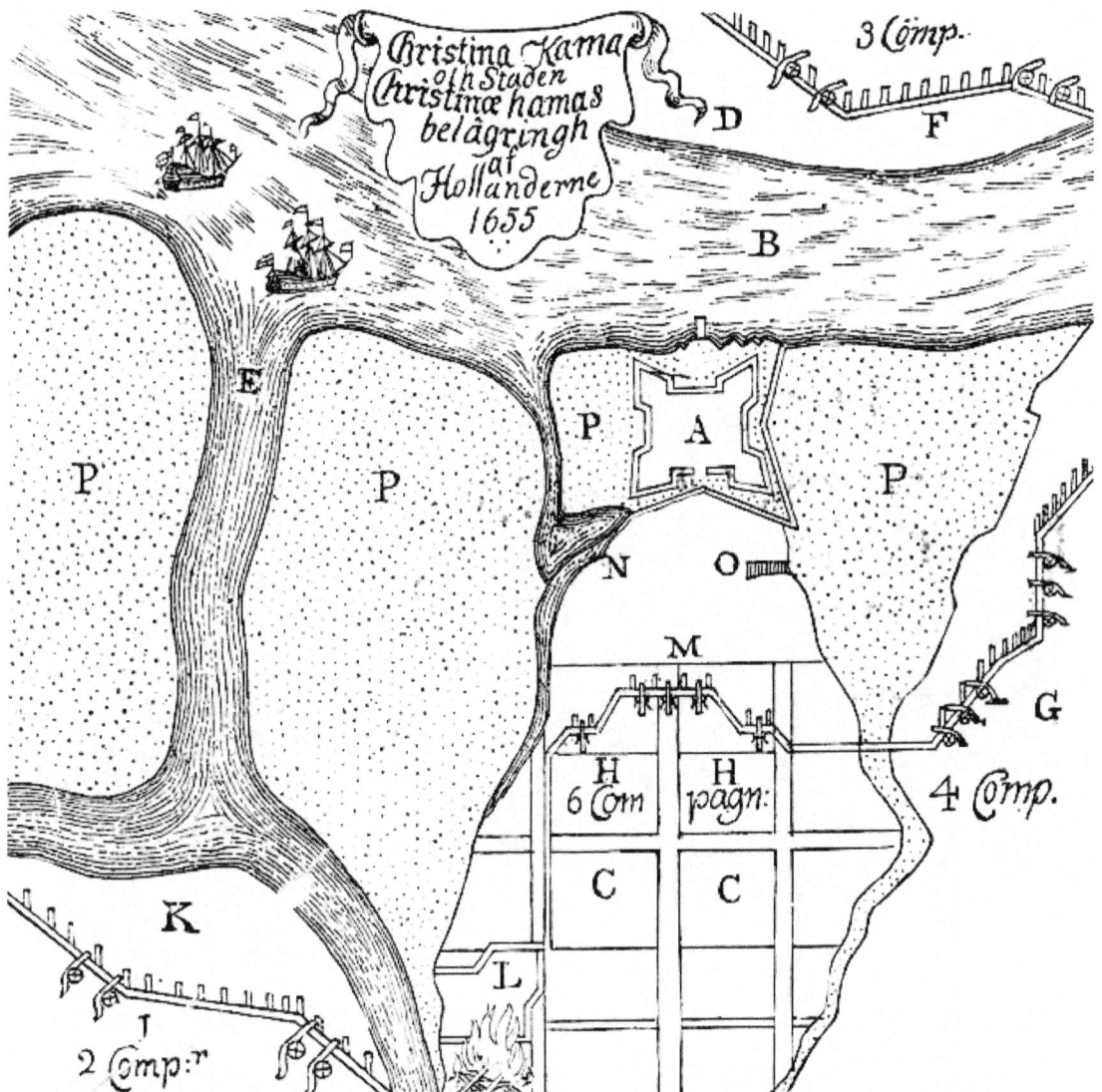

Map of the siege of Swedish Fort Christina (Wilmington), 1655 (New York Public Library).

defensive brick blockhouse west of town where they could take shelter in case of attack.[12] They certainly needed it. In 1673 the area was plundered and burned by the forces of Lord Baltimore[13] as one of the first steps in what, after William Penn received his grant in 1682, would become a century-long dispute over the territory that is now Delaware. The Dutch, vanquished in another part of the world by English arms, were forced to relinquish their holdings in the New World under the guns of a British fleet, and the government passed to the English Duke of York, who yielded his supremacy to William Penn in 1682.[14]

What is known today as Delaware was originally the three lower counties of Pennsylvania Province, established by the Quaker William Penn under a grant from the British crown. New Castle had been the port of entry and the administrative center for the colonial

Evacuation of Fort Christina (Art and Picture Collection, New York Public Library).

settlements until Penn changed the orientation toward his new town of Philadelphia. Arriving in New Castle aboard the *Welcome* in 1682, he sailed upstream, stopping at Upland (Chester) before reaching the confluence of the Schuylkill River and the Delaware. It was at this confluence that he established a town that eventually became Philadelphia and the legal center for the western bank of the Delaware River colony. Pennsylvania was snugly established upstream from the Delaware estuary far from rival threats in French Canada and Spanish America. A tavern, the Blue Anchor, was already doing business there when Penn arrived and began to lay out a grid of streets between the Delaware and Schuylkill rivers, a settlement dominated by peaceful Quakers. The merchants and tradesmen of Philadelphia openly despised the polyglot people of New Castle. The Quakers had a distrust of their multicultural downstream cousins who practiced freedom of religion.[15] Despite the artificial political divisions of the colonies, the thing that most united those in the area was the Delaware River and Bay. At this time of few usable roads, the main highway of trade, communication, and culture was via this common watery artery and its tributaries. However, it was not without its difficulties.

The landing of William Penn in Philadelphia, 1682, standing onshore greeted by large group of men and women, including Native Americans (Jean Leon Gerome, artist, 2004669764, Library of Congress).

Pirates and Privateers

The three lower counties were more exposed to depredation from Spanish and French pirates who repeatedly raided its vulnerable coasts. Despite the thin veneer of civilized society, this was still largely a lawless frontier. Attracted by the relative prosperity of the growing colony, a criminal element began to take advantage of the access the water provided. These rogue colonists were soon joined by foreigners and strangers who could make their escape to a foreign country with the booty they had stolen. They gained ever greater resources and easily outmanned and outgunned the local freeholders who opposed these raids. These freebooters, brigands, and privateers were a plague on the coastal colonies. The protected pacifist Quaker authorities in Philadelphia were disinclined to resist, and so matters were mostly left in the hands of the individual shipowners to take defensive measures. To complicate matters, the crown, being short of resources, authorized privateers to engage with the enemy during the many struggles for colonial dominance in the New World, often reflections of similar struggles in the Old World. It could be quite difficult to sort out the legitimate from the unlawful, the legal privateer from the pirate. For those who had resources, the pirate could often purchase pardon from the authorities, often turning around and beginning anew.

The first recorded pirate excursion was in 1653 when the New Amsterdam pirate Thomas Baxter raided Dutch settlements and took refuge among the English. The Dutch retaliated in kind. By 1687 events had accelerated with more and bolder expeditions on the Delaware shores that came to the attention of the crown. Sturdier enforcement on the one hand and forgiveness on the other lessened the threat for a time. But by 1698 the pirate threat grew once again. A sloop captained by a French pirate named Canoot arrived off Lewistown (Lewes) with fifty brigands who promptly plundered almost every house. All money and valuables found were taken away.[16]

The following year a laden brigantine named *Sweepstakes* at anchor off New Castle, bound for England, was carried off by brigands with crew and cargo. In 1696 the Council of Pennsylvania was called by Governor Markham to consider charges, made by the Lords of Trade, against Philadelphia for encouraging the pirate Avery. This man, one of the most noted freebooters of his day, a native of England, had at the age of 20 entered the *Duke*, a vessel fitted out by merchants of Bristol, for Spanish service. With others he mutinied, secured the vessel, and was made captain.[17] Lewes was raided by pirates or French privateers in 1698, 1703, and 1709.[18] The infamous Captain Kidd was a visitor to Lewes. During 1707–1709 a number of Philadelphia-bound or -based vessels were taken at sea on the approaches, and there were also raids once again on Lewistown and New Castle.[19]

During Queen Anne's War in November 1706 the assembly of the lower counties, at the suggestion of the governor, authorized the erection of a fort at New Castle to collect a duty. This duty was one-quarter pound of powder per ton for residents of the river and a half-pound for all others, excepting warships. The authorization and construction the next year was to provide the necessary powder for defense of the river. The duty was, however, highly unpopular in Philadelphia among the shipping merchants, and eventually the requirement lapsed over local objections.[20]

On Sunday, July 12, 1717, Spaniards from a captured pilot boat went ashore on the plantation of Edmund Liston, about four miles from Bombay Hook, near Woodland Beach. Armed with pistols, guns, and cutlasses they rifled Liston's house, taking even furniture and clothing, a Negro woman, her two children, and a Negro girl. They then clapped a pistol to Liston's breast and compelled him to accompany them to the plantation of James Hart, who, observing their approach, secured his doors and with a gun offered resistance.

Blackbeard the Pirate, **Edward Teach, 1725 (2007 677050, Library of Congress, Rare Book and Special Collections Division).**

The Spaniards fired upon Hart, and—after they wounded his wife and threatened to burn his house—he surrendered and his home was looted. In the evening of the same day the brigands also captured the pilot boat of one John Aries.[21]

The pirate Edward Teach, known as "Blackbeard," bought supplies in Philadelphia and, supposedly using Blackbird Creek as his hideout, captured vessels off the capes and plundered Lewistown. The Quakers of Philadelphia were uninterested in resisting piracy downstream. Blackbeard was finally killed in 1718 after a bloody fight with a man-of-war sent by the governor of Virginia.[22] During the summer of 1722 shipping on the Delaware was sorely crippled by a pirate brigantine cruising off the Delaware Capes. Trade was for a time entirely cut off. The *Pennsylvania Gazette* of July 26 states that for one week no vessels had entered except a sloop that had sailed for St. Christopher's; however, being thrice taken and plundered by pirates, she was obliged to return. A favorite and most successful ruse of these corsairs was to enter the Delaware Capes under English colors and signal for a pilot, who upon approaching was captured. The pilot boat was then manned and stationed within the capes; incoming vessels were then met and easily captured through this innocent-looking guise.[23]

The lower counties' demand for protection led to the establishment of a separate legislature and a militia at the turn of the eighteenth century, which ultimately led to an independent state in 1776. Depredations by sea would continue infrequently in one form or other until the conclusion of World War II.

Shipbuilding on the Delaware

The shipbuilding industry on the Delaware had its beginnings on Cooper's Island (later Vandever's Island) directly across the Brandywine River from Fort Christina, where Lauris the cooper and Persson the shipbuilder were plying their crafts when Governor Printz arrived in 1643. Printz built at Christina a "beautiful large boat" of 90 or 100 tons that for lack of the final fittings from Sweden seems never to have been completed.[24] Governor Printz commissioned sailing vessels in New Sweden in 1644, and Claas Claason and Thomas the carpenter constructed two small keel boats: "We have not been able to put into execution our plans concerning the keel boat which we have had in mind to build here, the reason being that two of the carpenters have been sick almost the whole year and one man alone has not been able to do such heavy work. Then the savages set a fire on the island in the night and burnt part of the material which had been sawed and cut for the boat."[25]

When the Dutch prevailed against the Swedes in 1655 they were the first to introduce African slaves to the colony. Along with slaves, one of the first things the Dutch imported was a shallop in knocked-down condition. A shallop is a broad-beamed, flat-bottomed, shallow-draft river boat propelled by oars or sail.[26] Six years before he founded Philadelphia, Penn had helped shipwright James West develop a small shipyard in 1676 along the Delaware riverfront at what later became Vine Street in the city of Philadelphia. Meanwhile, Penn recruited Welsh, Irish, Scots, and English Quaker craftsmen who were involved in shipbuilding in Bristol, England, and more fully along the Thames River, a great center of ship construction and merchant houses.[27] Shipbuilding activity along the Delaware River increased in the mid 1680s. Along with building canoes, shallops, sloops, yachts, and barges for local use, the first Dutch and Swedish colonists built vessels for coastal trade. Dr. Benjamin Bullivant, a traveler who visited New Castle in 1697, noted that the townsmen were actively engaged in shipbuilding.[28]

Most of the early American vessels were small, ranging from 20 to 200 gross tons. The oyster boat evolved from the Indian log canoe, and the sloop and shallop were derived from European models. In its earliest form, the American shipbuilding industry relied on the availability of cheap timber to produce vessels sold primarily in the British ship market. This extractive abundance continued into the eighteenth century and the American shipbuilding industry experienced phenomenal growth. Little was needed to open a shipyard: a sloping riverbank, a stock of timber, and the necessary tools and men to do the job. New yards sprang up from Maine to the Chesapeake Bay, and by the third quarter of the century the industry seemed firmly rooted along the entire north Atlantic coast. Ship sizes grew slightly in the 1700s. From an average size of about 50 tons in the 1600s, average tonnage increased to about 150. The demand for vessels proved so great that many British buyers frequently supplied North American builders with ironware, cordage, and sails for ships under contract. By 1774 colony-built ships accounted for an astonishing one-third of the British tonnage.[29]

Delaware remained economically tied to its larger neighbor to the north. The seaport of Philadelphia was the largest city in the colonies, largely thanks to the Delaware estuary and its strategic central position among the colonies of the Eastern Seaboard. So rapid was the growth of commerce that more waterfront construction took place in Philadelphia than in any other American port. The number of vessels clearing the port averaged 403 per year between 1749 and 1752.[30] The demand for timber reached all the way to the upper tributaries of the Delaware, and each spring logs were floated downriver from the northern timber stands.

There were four shipyards on the Delaware engaged in building seagoing ships in 1700. The shipyards in colonial Pennsylvania were very productive. Jonathan Dickenson wrote as follows in 1718: "Here is great employ for shipwork for England, it increases, and will increase our expectations." By 1720 there were at least a dozen shipyards in Philadelphia and the surrounding waterfront producing wooden sailing ships of up to 300 tons. Ten vessels were built in Philadelphia in 1722 of 458 total tonnage. Thirteen were constructed in 1723 at 507 tons. As many as twenty vessels were seen "upon the stocks at one time." Between 1684 and 1744 some 188 square-rigged, three-masted ships and 700 two-masted brigs and schooners were built in and around Philadelphia on the Delaware, averaging about 70 tons each.[31]

An east prospect of the city of Philadelphia from the Jersey Shore, 1754 (Miriam and Ira D. Wallach Division of Art, Prints and Photographs, Print Collection, New York Public Library).

Shipwrights were launching vessels from Lewes and Milton in the early 1700s. In 1720 Simon Cranston operated a small shipyard on Bread and Cheese Island near Stanton on White Clay Creek, where he built small brigs. Elizabeth Montgomery reminisced about communicants from New Jersey coming by boat to the Old Swede's Church in Wilmington.[32] There are records of shipbuilding on the Broadkill River as early as 1737.[33] From 1750 to 1850 many stout wooden vessels were built on the Christina, Brandywine, and other navigable streams downstate, including the Nanticoke, for trade with the West Indies, Ireland, and Great Britain in addition to the coasting trade. Nearly all the leading citizens of Wilmington from 1741 to 1775 owned or were interested in one or more sailing vessels, the majority of which were built locally.[34]

The first Delaware vessel launched for foreign trade went down the ways in 1740. William Shipley's brig *Wilmington* was constructed at the foot of Market Street on the Christina River. Thomas Willing, the founder of Wilmington, constructed a packet sloop for regular sailings to Philadelphia. The local administrative authority of the Port of Philadelphia was exercised by the Board of Wardens for the Port of Philadelphia, which was a colonial and city department created in 1766. The colonial era was in some ways the golden age of Philadelphia shipbuilding, with master shipbuilders and carpenters including the Penrose brothers, the Wharton family, Joshua Humphreys (1751–1838), and Manuel Eyre (1736–1805) designing and building fast coastal sailing ships and Atlantic brigantines. These naval architects would be invaluable in building vessels for the coming War of Independence.[35] Philadelphia's first significant warship was the *Hero*, constructed in April 1762. She was a 24-gun frigate built by James and Thomas Penrose and served as a model for the frigates that would follow during the War of Independence.[36]

Trade

The agriculture that had developed on the Delmarva Peninsula as well as the many mills constructed along the tributaries of the Delaware estuary drove increasing trade. The colonial period was busy with shallops carrying farm goods, grain, and milled flour from inland Pennsylvania and New Jersey farms to Philadelphia and retuning home with manufactured goods from Europe and luxuries from the Orient. This trade even extended to Baltimore via the Nanticoke River in Sussex County. Inland farmers could take their English tea in Chinese porcelain thanks to these shallopmen. These small trading vessels also carried news throughout the colonies, and the shallop owners served as bankers and commercial agents to the farmers and merchants they served.[37]

In 1774 Sam Bush of Wilmington purchased the 30-ton sloop *Ann* and began packet service between Wilmington and Philadelphia, which was an immediate success. In the years to follow he would expand his fleet with larger vessels until interrupted by the War for Independence.[38] Trade was widened when the Delaware estuary was linked to the Chesapeake via an old crooked Indian trail across the Delmarva isthmus. It was a road that linked the navigable headwaters of the Christina River with Head of Elk at the top of the Chesapeake Bay. It brought Virginia tobacco to the north in exchange for grain and manufactured goods from Philadelphia. This portage was supplemented by a cart road connecting St. Augustine just south of Port Penn and the Bohemia River. A cross-isthmus canal was envisioned from the very earliest days but was not realized until nearly two centuries later.[39]

Trade was not the only colonial maritime activity. There were numerous fishing and oystering operations reaping the bounty of the river and bay. The estuary provided local transportation as well in an age of very bad roads. Passenger packets transported people and goods up and down the river and ferries took them across to the New Jersey colony. This trade required an infrastructure that we take for granted today, but in the 18th century charts and navigational aids were primitive at best. Few people beyond a handful of local mariners knew the vagaries of shoals and currents.

River and Bay Pilots

Taken as a whole, the Delaware estuary was one of the three most important maritime systems in colonial America. It was also among the most difficult to navigate. The Delaware Bay is large but shallow, with many shoals and ledges. The tortuous natural channel is narrow, barely wide enough for two ships to pass, and subject to sharp turns. It often ices in winter, not to mention that it lies in the path of nor'easters and hurricanes in season.[40]

A mariner arriving at the mouth of the Delaware Bay would experience a broad expanse of olive-green water gradually narrowing as one voyaged north. Although the water may appear inviting, an experienced sailor would not venture farther without the aid of a local guide, a pilot who knows the shoals, flats, and channels and could safely guide the vessel upstream to safe port. This is particularly true for large ships that carry goods or arms. The first pilots were Indians who knew how to avoid the shoals at the entrance to the bay. As settlements took root onshore, the colonists who fished these waters became familiar with local conditions of wind, tide, current, and underwater topography. Before there were charts and lighthouses and buoys, these local pilots were the only reliable way to get goods upriver. For the most part, pilots became concentrated at the mouth of the Delaware Bay at Lewes and nearby Pilot Town starting as early as 1650. In 1655 the governor of New Netherlands sought those who "had a perfect knowledge of the bottom, depth and shoals of the South River."[41] The early pilots rowed out to sea upon whaling-type boats to meet the inbound oceangoing ships. A 1662 account of the water depth of the Horekill River mentions local pilots: "In 1750 the Delaware pilotboats were pinked stern boats, sharp at both ends; a usual size was 27-foot keel and an eleven-foot beam; the 'pinkie' was the lineal progeny of the 'whale boat' and when in familiar hands one of the staunchest craft that ever rode a wave."[42]

Upon approaching Cape Henlopen, masters of those ships needed to find the entrance and a safe anchorage to take on one of the pilots working out of Lewes and to wait for the rising tide to carry them up the estuary to Philadelphia. The pattern of the shoals in the river was inconsistent, as ship routes were alternatively obliterated and restored by the endless cycle of tides and currents. Navigation, either by master or pilot, was based on personal logs derived from previous experience reinforced by instinct, the latest reports from others, and faith in the sailor swinging the leadline.[43]

Navigational Aids

It was not until 1756 that a dependable chart of the entrance to the cape, its anchorages, and the bay became available. That chart, titled *Chart of Delaware Bay from the*

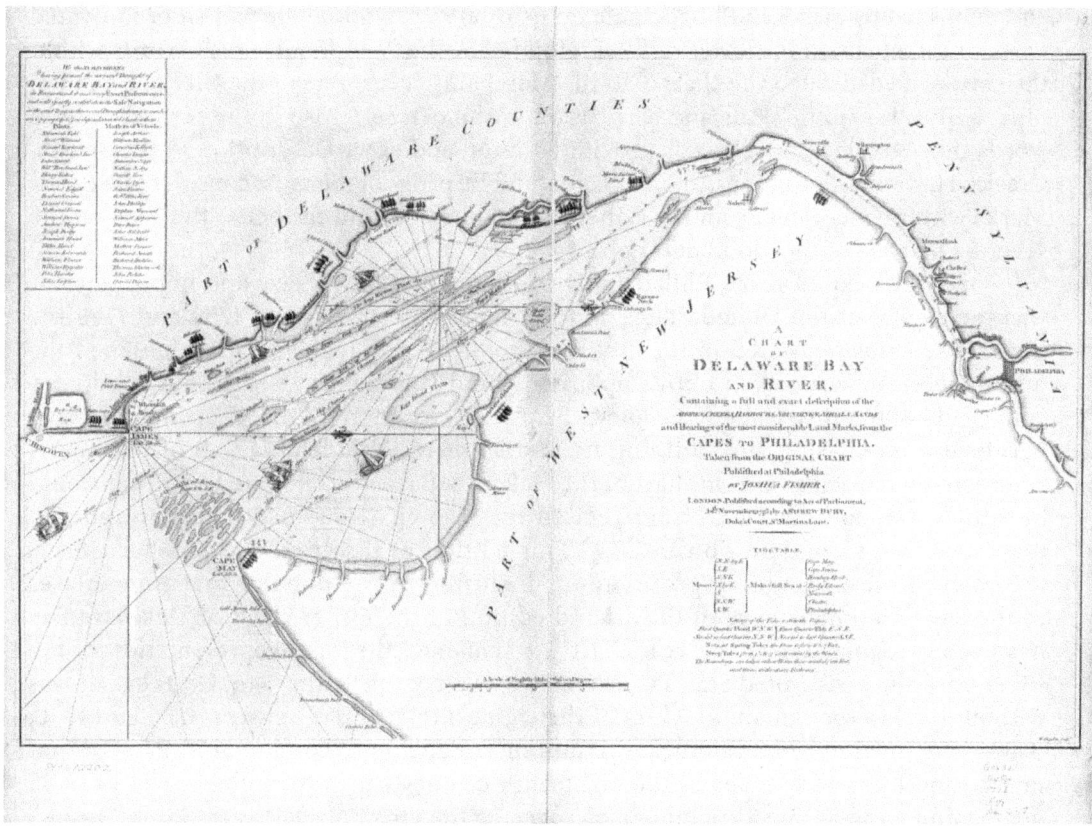

A chart of Delaware Bay and River containing "a full and exact description of the shores, creeks, harbours, soundings, shoals, sands, and bearings of the most considerable land marks, from the capes to Philadelphia" by Joshua Fisher, William Haydon, and Andrew Dury (74692202, Library of Congress, Geography and Map Division).

Sea-Coast to Reedy-Island, was published by Joshua Fisher (1707–1783), a Philadelphia entrepreneur originally from Lewes. It was based on comprehensive and accurate information gathered by Fisher and had been many years in the making. During his years as a boy in Lewes, Fisher became self-educated in mathematics and navigation and sailed the waters of the bay. Later, as a storekeeper, hatter, and exporter, as well as the brother-in-law of a pilot, he had constant contact with local shipowners and pilots. They shared their knowledge and encouraged him to produce a chart of the bay. Further encouragement came from Thomas Penn, the proprietor of Pennsylvania, who appointed him deputy surveyor general of Delaware.

Fisher moved to Philadelphia in 1746 to establish a mercantile and shipping business. There he formed acquaintances with shipowners and captains and continued his interest in the safe navigation of the bay. He took classes in mathematics, astronomy, and navigation as well as receiving assistance in determining latitudes from Thomas Godfrey, a prominent Philadelphia scientist and inventor. Fisher worked on his chart part time for years while still managing his business. When the drawing of the chart was ready, a group of Philadelphia merchants and shipowners subscribed a total of 100 pounds to defray the cost of engraving and printing. The chart was engraved by James Turner, printed by John Davis, and published by Fisher in Philadelphia on February 28, 1756. There was an ornamented label, or cartouche, at the lower right of it topped by the Penn family crest. Words within the cartouche dedicated the chart: "To the Merchants & Insurers of the City of Philadelphia ... By a Friend to Trade and Navigation. Joshua Fisher." Also in the cartouche were words that described the chart as providing "a full and exact Description of the Shores, Creeks, Harbours, Soundings, Shoals, Sands, and Bearings of the most considerable Land-Marks with a Tide-Table from the Capes to Philadelphia, and the Set of the Tide on the several Quarters of the Flood and Ebb."[44]

Over the next 20 years, Philadelphia continued to grow in size and importance. It was the capital of the United States and a principal port. Between 1750 and 1775 the tonnage of ships registered in the city rose from 7,092 to 16,809. Philadelphia led the other American seaports in both shipbuilding and volume of exports. In a good year, some 700–800 ships visited the port. Furthermore, in 1775 the Continental Navy had begun purchasing and building its first ships in Philadelphia. All of this maritime activity needed a reliable chart of the Delaware Bay and Delaware River that would be widely available. In 1775 Fisher revised his 1756 chart. He had it reengraved and published in a second edition in 1776. This edition of the chart was smaller (18$^{15}/_{16}$ × 27½ inches), making it appropriate for inclusion in the popular maritime atlases of the day. The importance of the second edition of the Fisher chart of Delaware Bay has been recognized over the years: "[It] ... remained the basic representation of the River until the first United States Coast Survey was completed in 1846. Certainly, it was without rival in the remaining years of the eighteenth century. Between 1756 and 1800, it was published in ten editions and issues of Philadelphia, London, and Paris."[45] Not many American-made maps of the eighteenth century can show influence so great in degree and so widespread in time and space as the chart of Delaware Bay by Joshua Fisher.[46]

A Lighthouse on Cape Henlopen

Their livelihood at risk from shipping losses, a group of Philadelphia merchants conducted a fund-raising lottery to build a lighthouse on 200 acres granted by the Penns as proprietors of Pennsylvania. Pilot Henry Fisher of Lewes (no relation to Joshua) "helped select the site of the lighthouse.... He also determined the proper location for the buoys in the Delaware River and Bay." It was only the second lighthouse to be erected in the New World. The seven-story octagonal structure, the Henlopen Lighthouse, was completed in 1765, with a temporary light using whale oil, and became a permanent light in 1767. There were seven windows (one at each landing), three looking east over the water, and four looking west towards "Lewestown."[47] The light was extinguished during the War of Independence so as not to aid the British[48] and was relit in 1784. In 1789 the lighthouse—together with all public beacons, buoys, piers, and their jurisdiction—was ceded to the federal government.[49] Known as the "old man of the Atlantic," it had been originally constructed a quarter mile from the sea atop a large dune. On April 13, 1926, it fell into the sea, a victim of shoreline erosion despite efforts to save it. In time, an entire system of navigation aids were erected on the Delaware estuary, including other ocean coast lights, breakwater lights, range lights, channel lights, tributary lights, lightships, and assorted buoys and markers.

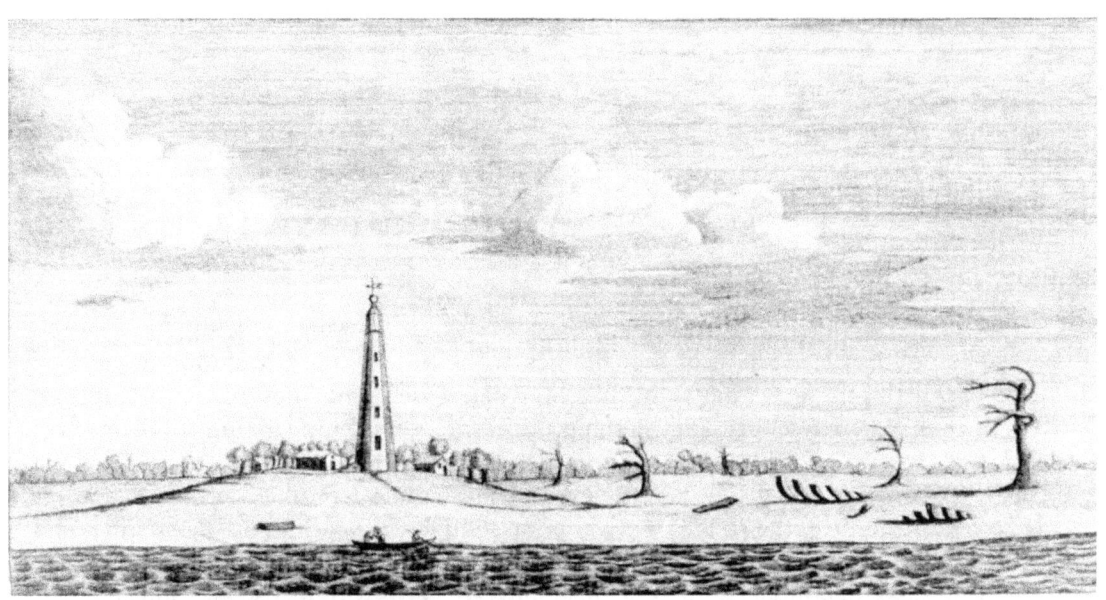

A View of the Lighthouse on Cape Henlopen, Taken at Sea, August 1780 (2004671558, Library of Congress, Rare Book and Special Collections Division).

Colonial maritime Pennsylvania, New Jersey, and Delaware were marked by the vagaries of war and piracy, weather, and the uncertainty of water and wind. But the Delaware estuary was also marked by steady forward progress in improving ships, shipbuilding skills, trade, and the safe navigation of seaborne vessels. Those trends would only be accelerated by the coming War of Independence. Throughout, the unifying thread was their common shore on the banks of the Delaware.

Two

Creating an American Navy

The political leadership of the colonies at the time of the Revolution comprised third or fourth generation native-born men, most of whom had never been to England. Although they were freeborn English subjects, they were beginning to think of themselves as Americans. In 1775 Philadelphia dominated the economic and cultural life of the Delaware Valley. It was the largest city in the colonies and its influence extended as far as Lewes, the home of the Delaware River pilots, and to the landings on the St. Jones and Appoquinimink rivers, where produce was loaded for Philadelphia markets.

So it was with political thought. Philadelphia concerns with British taxation and their fears of commercial restrictions were soon transmitted to the lower counties.[1] England's insistence upon the tea tax roused animus here as elsewhere in the colonies. Published broadsides promised tar and feathers for any pilot who should hire out to the incoming tea ship *Polly*. Captain Ayres, perhaps warned by pilots who refused to take his ship, took it to Chester. From there he was escorted to Philadelphia, where he was warned off. When she did arrive, Captain Ayres was persuaded to depart with her cargo untouched.[2] The Pennsylvania Committee of Safety resolved as follows: "That any Pilot, or other person, who shall conduct or bring any *British* Man of War, Armed Vessel, Boat, or other Craft, up the Bay of *Delaware* ... who shall refuse or neglect to lay up his Boat or Craft, or who shall put himself in the way of being forcibly taken on board the King's Ships, or who shall voluntarily serve, or offer to serve or instruct them in the navigation of the said Bay and River, shall, on proof thereof made to this Board, be deemed an enemy to *American* liberty, a traitor to his Country." With respect to American shipping the board said, "Pilots of the Bay and River *Delaware* should remain on shore, at Cape Henlopen or Cape May, until such Merchant Vessels as arrive send their Boats on shore for a Pilot, when one may repair on board, provided there is not any Man of War in sight, or in the said Bay and River; but if there is, the Captains of such Merchantmen must do the best they can for the safety of their Ships, as no Pilots must go on board in such case."[3]

Soon British ships operating without pilots began to have trouble. In May 1774, in the midst of a late-season snowstorm, the British ship *Severn* sank while seeking refuge in the Broadkill and Lewes Creek. The captain and crew were saved.[4] There were a number of significant battles. The geography of the Delaware estuary guaranteed that the coming conflict would be a maritime war equal to the struggle on land. The Royal Navy was a dominant force with almost no equal on the seas and would present a towering challenge for the colonies as they tried to import vital war materiel and munitions and to protect their coasts from the depredations of the powerful British fleet.

This was a first hint of what was to come in Delaware waters. What many people do not realize is that there were a number of significant naval battles fought off Delaware shores and scores of minor actions involving privateers, loyalists, and naval militia as well as the Royal Navy and the Continental Navy. The waters of the Delaware estuary were contested during almost the entirety of the War of Independence.

Independence

Hostilities between the Crown and the colonies broke out in the spring of 1775 when shots were fired at Lexington and Concord. The Pennsylvania colony government was initially reluctant about rebellion. The Quaker-dominated Pennsylvania Assembly opposed any form of mandatory military service. Nevertheless, Pennsylvania patriots organized some 53 battalions of volunteers. When General Washington asked for the Middle Atlantic colonies to provide additional reinforcements willing to serve six months of duty in 1776, these units were tapped as a manpower pool, though the individual units did not themselves become part of the Pennsylvania Line forces. The individuals who volunteered at this time were formed into battalions by county, known as "Flying Camps," and served on active duty until November 30, 1776. By the end of that year, Pennsylvania had adopted a new, more radical constitution that wrested control from the older conservative assembly, and in early 1777 the new assembly passed Pennsylvania's first militia law requiring compulsory military service. Ultimately, Pennsylvania contributed fourteen regiments to the Pennsylvania Line of the Continental Army.[5]

On December, 9, 1775, the Continental Congress called on the lower counties in Delaware to furnish a battalion of infantry for one year's service in the Continental Army. Colonel John Haslet's First Delaware Regiment was the original regiment formed in January 1776 of eight companies of about 800 men. Recruiting began in January, and by April 12, 1776, muster rolls recorded six companies in Dover and two companies in Lewistown (Lewes). A major portion of Sussex County remained loyal to the Crown and British ships had already arrived to blockade the bay. This placed the navigation of the Delaware estuary in peril. Some troops of the battalion of militia would remain posted in Sussex County throughout the war to guard against, and intimidate, Tory sympathizers and to secure the coastline.[6]

Delaware did not exist as a colony under British rule. As of 1704 Pennsylvania had two colonial assemblies: one for the "Upper Counties," originally Bucks, Chester, and Philadelphia, and one for the "Lower Counties on the Delaware," New Castle, Kent, and Sussex. All of the counties shared one governor. Thomas McKean and Caesar Rodney proposed the Lower Counties' simultaneous separation from Pennsylvania and Britain. When Read refused to vote for independence, McKean famously summoned an ailing Rodney, who rode overnight from Dover, Delaware, to Philadelphia in order to cast his vote in favor of independence and break the Delaware delegation's stalemate.[7] McKean and Rodney, along with George Read, represented the Lower Counties at the First Continental Congress in 1774 as well as the Second Continental Congress in 1775–76. On June 15, 1776, the Assembly of the Lower Counties of Pennsylvania declared itself independent of both British and Pennsylvania authority, thereby creating the independent state of Delaware.[8]

Some of the colonies began to form their own navies as well as raising infantry regiments. The port warden of Philadelphia took in channel markers and instructed pilots

USS *Alfred*, 1775–78, flagship of America's Navy Squadron, placed into commission by John Paul Jones. Photograph of a painting by Harry W. Carpenter, 1920 (NH 57044, Naval History and Heritage Command).

to serve only colonial shipping. The lighthouse at Henlopen was extinguished. Philadelphia built a fighting ship for itself at the same time its shipyards were fitting out the Continental Navy's first squadron including the frigates *Columbus*, *Cabot*, *Andrew Doria*, and *Alfred*.⁹

1775: The Pennsylvania State Navy

Pennsylvania's navy served during the War of Independence and afterward, until the formation of the Continental Navy. The navy's vessels functioned almost exclusively on the Delaware River and were active (in conjunction with ships of the Continental Navy) in first defending the approaches to Philadelphia during the British campaign that successfully occupied the city in 1777 and then preventing the Royal Navy from resupplying the occupying army. When the Revolutionary War broke out in early 1775, the Continental Congress resolved that "each colony, at their own expence [sic], make such provisions by armed vessels or otherwise … for the protection of their harbors and navigation on their coasts against all unlawful invasions, attacks and depredations, from cutters and ships of war."¹⁰ Pennsylvania's Committee of Safety decided that the colony's capital and seat of the Second Continental Congress, Philadelphia, would need to be protected against the incursions of British naval vessels on the Delaware River, and on July 6, 1775, it authorized the purchase and outfitting of ships for that purpose.[11] Two days later it placed its first order for an armed galley. By October, thirteen such boats had been built, at a cost of £550 each, and outfitted with a single cannon in the bow. Thomas Read was appointed as commodore of the modest fleet but was replaced on January 13, 1776, by Thomas Caldwell. Read stepped aside to command the largest ship, *Montgomery*.

The first six ships were launched by July 19, and another six had been launched by the end of August. Their names were *Bulldog, Burke, Camden, Chatham, Congress, Dickinson, Effingham, Experiment, Franklin, Hancock, Ranger, Warren,* and *Washington*.[12] Additionally, ten fire rafts were built in late 1775 and early 1776 and placed under the command of Captain John Hazelwood. The *Arnold* and the *Putnam* were built as floating batteries and were manned by Pennsylvania state marines. In April 1776 the state acquired the ship *Montgomery*, upon which Thomas Read served as captain until he received a Continental Navy commission in October 1776. In May the armed schooner *Delaware* and brig *Convention* were authorized. By the end of August 1776 the Pennsylvania State Navy consisted of 768 men manning 27 vessels, with 21 smaller vessels on order. These were armed with a four-pounder gun in the bow and were classed as guard boats.

The navy fell under the broad control of the committee of safety, which established subcommittees to manage the navy's operations and acquisitions. When the state established a new constitution, with a supreme council as its executive, the navy's administration was assigned to the council of safety. In March 1777 the council established a naval board that had full responsibility for the fleet, with the exception of the issuance of officer commissions, which authority the council retained. In September 1778 Pennsylvania established an admiralty court to adjudicate maritime cases and deal with the distribution of prizes. While no explicit legislation authorizing privateering appears to have been passed, the state did issue more than 400 letters of marque between 1776 and 1782.

The Pennsylvania State Navy saw action on May 6, 1776, when ships operating in support of the Continental Navy and its galleys engaged the British ships *Roebuck* and *Liverpool*. The British were forced to withdraw downriver to New Castle. The fleet was also active in keeping British troops away from the river's eastern shore when General George Washington retreated across New Jersey following the loss of New York City. Captain Hazelwood was instrumental in preventing German troops from quartering in Burlington, New Jersey, a town sympathetic to the Loyalist cause, by bombarding it when troops were spotted there. This forced their commander, Carl von Donop, to quarter his troops much more widely and may have contributed to Washington's successful Battle of Trenton on December 26, 1776.[13]

The Pennsylvania State Navy was responsible for defense of the river when Philadelphia was occupied by British General Sir William Howe and the Royal Navy wanted to resupply Howe's army. At first the combined Pennsylvania and Continental fleet was successful, repulsing one attempt by the British to pass the defenses of Forts Mercer and Mifflin on October 22 and 23, 1777, with the destruction of two British ships. The two forts were taken by land forces in November, and the navy was then forced to withdraw upriver. Unfavorable winds slowed their progress, and four vessels (ship *Montgomery*, schooner *Delaware*, floating batteries *Arnold* and *Putnam*) were burned to prevent their capture.[14] In April 1778 most of the fleet was destroyed in advance of expected British

HMS *Roebuck* under attack from American gunboats in the Delaware River near Fort Mifflin on October 23, 1777 (Warren, artist, NH 56439, Naval History and Heritage Command).

operations against it. However, news that the British were going to withdraw from Philadelphia led to its resurrection, and in July Captain Hazelwood reported that the brig *Convention* was ready for action. Its existence as a significant force was eclipsed by the arrival of a French fleet on the North American coast, and in August 1778 the state's assembly voted to sell off most of its remaining ships, keeping only the *Convention* and a few smaller ships.[15]

The smaller ships proved to be inadequate protection for the trade ships of Pennsylvania's merchants. In response to their petitions, the state authorized the construction of the *General Greene* in March 1779. Under her captain, James Montgomery, she cruised between New York and the Chesapeake Bay, often in conjunction with Continental Navy ships or privateers, and sent a number of prizes to Philadelphia. According to Montgomery, her crew was virtually unmanageable, and she was sold at the end of the 1779 sailing season. Her unusually low sales price aroused suspicions of collusion in the process.[16]

By 1782 the activities of the Royal Navy and Loyalist privateers again spurred Philadelphia's merchants to petition for better naval defenses. This resulted in the commissioning of the *Hyder Ally*, which was outfitted by the merchants and placed under the command of the Continental Navy's Joshua Barney. After the successful capture of HMS *Monk*, Barney took over her command, renaming her *Washington*. After a trip to the West Indies, she was sold to the Continental Navy. The *Hyder Ally* continued to patrol without significant success. By February 1783, with peace appearing near, most of the state's ships had been sold and its sailors dismissed. On April 10, 1783, the supreme executive council ordered disposal of the remaining armed vessels.[17]

Although it had limited means, and faced a world class foe, the Pennsylvania navy was successful in many of its limited tactical aims, at least for a time. The flotilla provided valuable extra time to Washington before the inevitable weight of arms forced his hand.

Read Brothers

Delaware provided three brothers who were instrumental in the ultimate victory against British rule. George Read, Thomas Read, and James Read were the sons of John and Mary Read. They were a prominent and wealthy family whose seat was Cecil County, Maryland. The Read brothers had a sister, Mary, who married another notable Delawarean, Gunning Bedford, Sr., a future state governor.[18]

George Read, the eldest, was an American lawyer and politician from New Castle. He was a signer of the Declaration of Independence, a continental congressman from Delaware, a delegate to the U.S. Constitutional Convention of 1787, president of Delaware (governor), and a member of the Federalist Party who served as U.S. senator from Delaware and as chief justice of Delaware. George Read was a member of the Naval Committee chartered by the Continental Congress. He was one of only two statesmen who signed all three of the great state papers on which the country's history is based: the original Petition to the King of the Congress of 1774, the Declaration of Independence and the Constitution of the United States.[19]

Thomas Read of New Castle was the first American to become a commodore during the Revolution. He was born in 1740 and was the brother of George Read. A veteran mariner and navigator, when the Revolution broke out he joined the fleet being assembled in Philadelphia to protect the Delaware River. He was made commodore at age 35 and commanded ships of the Pennsylvania navy. Overall naval command of the fleet was at times contentious. Thomas Read served as its first commodore, but he was replaced on January 13, 1776, by Thomas Caldwell.[20]

Read switched to the Continental Navy, where he was assigned to command the frigate *Washington*, under construction in Philadelphia at the time. Unfortunately, Thomas Read's *Washington* was not yet ready for sea and he was directed to take his ship up the Delaware River to keep it out of British hands. He took it to near his home, White Hall at Burlington New Jersey, stripped it of all useable equipment and scuttled it. Eventually, it was burned. He, his officers, and some gunners with some of their naval cannons went to Valley Forge to join General Washington. They supported the crossing of the Delaware and fought at the battle of Trenton, where Read commanded a battery made up of guns from his frigate and with it raked the stone bridge across Assunpink Creek.[21]

By the fall of 1779 Thomas Read was again back on naval orders to outfit and take command of the frigate *Bourbon*, then under construction. Difficulties delayed the launching. Eager to get back in the fight, Read accepted command of the 12-gun brigantine *Baltimore* operating off the coast and carrying dispatches to and from the American commissioners in Paris in 1778 and 1779. By the summer of 1780 he had taken a Congressional Letter of Marque for the brig *Patty* out of Philadelphia and was back in France carrying intelligence to Benjamin Franklin: "If your Excellency has Any Commands Either Publick or Private [I] Shall be happy in Executeing of them."[22] After the war Thomas Read eventually returned to the sea. He was induced by his friend Robert Morris to take command of his old frigate, *Alliance*, which had recently been bought by Morris for commercial purposes, and they made a joint adventure to the China seas. Read sailed from the Delaware on June 7, 1787, and arrived at Canton on December 22, after sailing on a track that had never before been taken by any other vessel and making the first "out-of-season" passage to China. In this voyage he discovered two islands, which he named "Morris" and "Alliance" and which formed part of the Caroline Islands. At Canton he loaded the ship with tea, which he delivered at Philadelphia on September 17, 1788, ending a record voyage without mishap. Thomas died of disease at age 49.[23] In his obituary of Thomas Read, Robert Morris said, "While integrity, benevolence, patriotism, and courage, united with the most gentle manners, are respected and admired among men, the name of this valuable citizen and soldier will be revered and beloved by all who knew him."[24]

As work began on purchasing, fitting out, and equipping the Continental Navy's first four ships, the Congress relied on the ship purchasing and contracting arrangements already established by Robert Morris and the Pennsylvania navy. To oversee that business, James Read, at 33 the youngest son of the Read family, was appointed as "Paymaster to the Fleet."[25] As the British threatened Philadelphia in September 1777, it was clear the ships building in Philadelphia would not be completed. James Read left to join General Washington's army defending the city. He rose rapidly from lieutenant to colonel for distinguished service at the battles of Brandywine, Germantown, Trenton, and Princeton. During those years James was again back in naval service. In November 1778 he had been appointed one of the three naval commissioners for the middle states. In early 1781 he was named secretary of the Congressional Marine Committee under Robert Morris. While Morris was otherwise involved with financing the Revolution, James managed the finances of the navy. For their contributions to the Revolutionary cause and the nation, both Thomas Read and James Read were elected to the Society of the Cincinnati.[26]

1775: The Continental Navy

On October 13, 1775, the Continental Congress formed the Naval Committee and established the Continental Navy for the "protection and defense of the colonies." Today, this is considered the birth of the United States Navy. In July and again in August 1775, Rhode Island had petitioned Congress to create a Continental Navy. That petition was tabled. On October 6, Congress began to debate the Rhode Island petition. Support was not unanimous. The coastal New England colonies wanted a seagoing navy. The mid–Atlantic colonies were wary. George Ross of Pennsylvania spoke against the idea of a national navy, pointing out that the Pennsylvania navy was having trouble manning the small galleys it was building. Maryland and Pennsylvania objected because "all the trade of Pennsylvania, the Lower Counties, a great Part of Maryland and N. Jersey Sails in between the Capes of Delaware Bay. And if a strong [enemy] Fleet should be posted in that Bay, Superior to our Fleet it might obstruct all the Trade of this River."[27] While the debate was occurring, on October 11, the *Pennsylvania Journal* reported news brought from London: "Eight men of war, from forty to fifty guns each are ordered for the American station ... [t]o keep cruising the American Coast [in] three squadrons, each consisting of three 74-gun ships, three armed sloops, three schooners, three bomb vessels and a battalion of Marines...."[28]

The debate resulted in a decision to arm. The Naval Committee purchased a merchant ship from financier Robert Morris, the Philadelphia-built merchant ship *Black*

Prince, which was renamed *Alfred*. It was also the most impressive, having a black hull, yellow topsides, and a black figurehead of a prince holding a sword. For the conversion of all the Philadelphia ships to warships, John Barry, former master of the *Black Prince*, was placed in charge of the rerigging. This Irish-born Philadelphia merchant sailor would become known as the Father of the United States Navy and would also compile a combat record during the War of Independence the equal of another famous contemporary, John Paul Jones.

Joshua Humphreys, who had his start designing a gunboat for the Pennsylvania navy was selected to superintend strengthening the hull, timbers, and bulwarks as well as opening the gunports on the *Black Prince*, further developing the experience that would soon make him a prominent ship designer and builder. The work on the ship was done at the shipyard of Wharton and Humphreys. Nathaniel Falconer was made responsible for ordnance and provisions. But, a young Scotsman named John Paul Jones, who had been in Philadelphia for several months seeking a naval position, was employed during the fitting-out process at the rank of lieutenant and assigned to *Alfred*. He became, in effect, the ship's acting commanding officer, procuring and training the crew in gunnery until the assigned captain, Dudley Saltonstall, arrived in late December. Thus, it was Jones who on 3 December placed the *Alfred* in commission by raising the Grand Union flag, the first time an American flag had been unfurled on a Continental warship.[29]

John Paul Jones (LC-USZ62–10884, Library of Congress, Prints and Photographs).

In December 1775 Congress created several committees to devise ways and means of furnishing the colonies with a single naval force and to oversee that force. The Naval Committee submitted a report, which was approved by Congress, calling for the construction of thirteen frigates plus eight smaller ships. These were the first American ships designed and built to be warships. Four of those—two 32-gun frigates, *Randolph* and *Washington*, and two 24-gun frigates, *Delaware*, and *Effingham*—were to be built in Philadelphia. As the conversion and construction of the Continental Navy began on the Delaware, captains of the Pennsylvania navy transferred to the Continental Navy. One of the first to go was Captain Nicholas Biddle, commissioned on December 22, 1775, to become captain of the converted *Andrew Doria* and sail with the first squadron of the navy in January 1776. Captain Charles Alexander was commissioned on April 18, 1776, and took command of the sloop *Wasp* when it returned to Philadelphia from sailing with the first squadron. Commodore Thomas Read had been moved aside from his position as commodore of the Pennsylvania Navy in January 1776 and had taken command of its flagship *Montgomery*. He was commissioned into the Continental Navy on June 6, 1776, and was to command the largest of the new ships building in Philadelphia, the 32-gun *Washington*. John Barry also was commissioned on June 6 and was to command the 28-gun *Effingham*, building in Philadelphia.[30] It is interesting to note that one of the frigates was named for Delaware before there was a state of Delaware. A possible reason was that George Read of New Castle was a prominent member of the Naval Committee. The Naval Committee recommended, and Congress approved, a list of 24 captains, including George's brother Thomas Read.[31]

In January 1776 the first four ships of the American navy sailed from Philadelphia under Commodore Esek Hopkins. The Delaware Bay was ice clogged and they did not arrive until February at the capes, where they stayed until March. During that time, they raised the first ensign of the American navy, with red and white stripes for the thirteen original states. Later, after the adoption of the stars and stripes, that ensign was replaced with one having the stars for all the states. After the arrival of two smaller ships from Baltimore, *Wasp* and *Fly*, the force sailed, not on its assigned mission to defend the southern coast but rather to the Bahamas where the Continental Marines conducted the navy's first amphibious operation to capture arms and ammunition.[32]

The Continental Navy was preparing, but the Royal Navy was ready and at the end of March 1776 they initiated a blockade of Delaware Bay. The Royal Navy had arrived to put a stopper in the bottle of the bay. On 25 March, 1776, a British squadron led by the 44-gun frigate HMS *Roebuck*—with the 22-gun *Leopard*, 20-gun *Liverpool* and *Fowey*, 16-gun *Otter* and *Kingfisher*, plus support ships—rounded Cape Henlopen. The squadron also included several smaller ships captained by Andrew Snape Hammond. These vessels arrived flying the American flag, and when the pilot boat of Henry Fisher came alongside they tried but failed to capture the pilots. The British needed a pilot, as they had no up-to-date charts of Delaware Bay. The ships operating out of Lewes were shallow-draft vessels that required no pilots. On April 1 Henry Fisher wrote from Lewes: "On Monday evening last a man-of-war and her tender came within the pitch of our cape, and anchored, as you have been informed by last express.... [I]t was Captain Hammond, of the King's ship the Roebuck, of forty-five guns ... [and] you may daily expect several large ships; therefore, I hope that you may be upon your guard, as, from what I can learn, they are to come up your river."[33]

Henry Fisher, a resident of Lewes and a Delaware Bay pilot, had been instructed to report on "every British man-of-war or armed vessel that may arrive at the Capes of Delaware."[34] Thus he had been waiting for such an event and had arranged an elaborate system of signaling to warn of the British arrival. Unfortunately, his signaling arrangements failed to give early warning, but he was able to send a written note to Philadelphia: "Gentlemen, this serves to inform you that there is a sloop-of-war coming into our road with a small tender, and as it is now night, I cannot inform you whether they are bound up the bay or not; the wind is now at south, therefore have reason to believe that they will proceed up the bay."[35]

The British, however, remained in the area of the cape. The pilot boat, stationed near the mouth of Lewes Creek, did not discover the signal at the lighthouse or see the ship that evening, as it was near dark. The British had captured the pilot boat, but the pilot and crew escaped. The British harassed and captured several small merchant vessels entering the bay. But as they were unable to capture a pilot the *Roebuck* had trouble avoiding the sandy shallows of the bay and ran aground several times. Having failed to capture a pilot, for the rest of the war British ships had difficulty avoiding the shoals of Delaware Bay and American seaman quickly learned to avoid the British blockade by running in close to shore.[36]

On April 7 a small schooner commanded by Captain Nehemiah Field of Lewes rounded the cape returning from the West Indies. As Captain Field steered his ship toward shore to avoid capture, *Roebuck* responded by dispatching several small boats to capture the schooner. In response, a company of Continental soldiers who were in Lewes began a forced march toward the schooner, which Field had run onto the sandy shore. The race to reach Field's grounded schooner turned deadly when the British boats opened fire on the troops marching across the open beach. The soldiers returned fire and continued their march, reaching the schooner first, and began unloading it. Fire was exchanged for about two hours before the British boats turned away. Throughout the war, Fisher and the pilots remained loyal to the Revolutionary cause. They continued their operations at the cape, using their intimate knowledge of the channels to assist American ships in safely navigating past the British blockade forces.[37]

1776: Action Off New Castle

On May 6 *Roebuck*, *Liverpool*, and their tender, the armed brig *Betsy*, ventured north from their usual positions off Cape Henlopen to test Philadelphia's defenses. They were sighted by Captain Alexander, in *Wasp*, returning from convoying a ship past the cape. As *Wasp*, mounting only eight two-pounders and some swivel guns, retreated north in the face of overwhelming firepower, Alexander warned some ships to alert Philadelphia. He took *Wasp* into shallow Christiana Creek for protection from the deeper-draft British ships.[38]

The next afternoon, in the waters between Wilmington and New Castle, the British were engaged by Captain Henry Dougherty in the large galley *Washington*, commanding thirteen galleys of the Pennsylvania navy. In a two-hour battle, with thirteen American guns shooting at large slow targets and 64 British guns shooting at 13 small mobile targets, *Roebuck* was forced to maneuver such that on the ebbing tide she became stuck on the soft mud bottom off the Jersey shore opposite New Castle. As the *Liverpool* came to defend *Roebuck*, the galleys ran out of ammunition and drew off. While that was happening, Alexander brought *Wasp* out to cut out the *Betsy* and have his master's mate, Joshua Barney, lead a boarding party to capture the brig (and take it to Philadelphia, where her officers were imprisoned and she was taken into the Continental Navy). The firing stopped at sundown.[39] By then the *Roebuck* was hard aground. Her boats rowed a nervous patrol around her all night. The Americans made no attack on her even when at low tide her gun ports had to be closed as she keeled over. The American row-galleys were out of shot and, by the time they received fresh powder and shot, the *Roebuck* had refloated.[40]

The following morning Alexander took the *Wasp* out again in the fog hoping to engage the grounded *Roebuck* in a hit-and-run attack. Unfortunately, the *Roebuck* had floated free and as the fog lifted *Wasp* was close in to the British ships and, while engaging and exchanging fire, was forced to run north and join the galleys positioned in a defensive line. Having discovered the tenacity of Philadelphia's defenses, the wounded British ships moved back south to their blockading area.[41] At the end of the second day the frigates had dropped down the river below New Castle. Their sails and rigging were somewhat tattered and some cannonballs were embedded in their sides. The fighting again continued at long distance with little effect. The English fired an occasional shot towards shore where hundreds of spectators had gathered to watch this battle. Finally, after stopping at Reedy Point to make repairs, the English flotilla retired to the capes on May 15. Summarizing the battle, Captain Andrew Snape Hammond of the British navy said, "[I]f the commander of the galleys had acted with as much judgment as courage, they would have destroyed [my] ship."[42]

During the spring and summer *Wasp* and *Lexington* operated in the Delaware Bay and along the nearby Atlantic coast, took prize, and recaptured American ships previously taken by *Roebuck*.[43]

Andrew Doria (misspelled *Andrea Doria* in image), 1775–1777: depicting that Continental brig receiving a salute from the Dutch fort at St. Eustatius, West Indies, November 16, 1776. The artist shows the Grand Union flag flying at *Andrew Doria's* stern and foremast peak (NH 85200-KN, Naval History and Heritage Command).

A "First Salute"

Meanwhile, on May 16, Captain Nicolas Biddle had taken *Andrew Doria* to sea for operations southward from New England toward Cape Henlopen. In four months he captured ten ships including two troop transports. *Andrew Doria* passed Cape Henlopen inbound on the morning of September 17, 1776, and anchored at Chester, Pennsylvania. There Captain Isaiah Robinson took command of the ship and took her down the Delaware on October 17 for a voyage to the West Indies to obtain a cargo of munitions and military supplies at St. Eustatius. When she reached that Dutch island on November 16, *Andrew Doria* fired a salute of 11 guns and received a reply—the first salute to an American flag onboard an American warship in a foreign port. While sailing past Puerto Rico on her homeward voyage to Philadelphia, *Andrew Doria* fought the Royal Navy's 12-gun sloop of war *Racehorse* in a two-hour battle, which ended when the British warship struck her colors. Robinson placed an American crew onboard the prize with orders to take her to Philadelphia, where both ships arrived early in January 1777.[44]

Raising the "Stars and Stripes" for the first time in home waters. Painting by F. Muller, circa 1900, depicting the raising of the Continental Ensign on board the brig *Lexington*, commanded by John Barry, 1776 (KN-457, Naval History and Heritage Command).

1776: Captain John Barry and the Lexington

The Marine Committee of the Continental Congress bought a brig, armed it, and sent it under the command of Captain John Barry to clear the Delaware Capes of privateers. This ship, the *Lexington*, had the distinction of capturing a British sloop, the first prize of the Revolution. When the English frigate *Roebuck* arrived to block the entrance to the river, the *Lexington* eluded her by keeping on the far side of the sandbars and helped colonial vessels to slip out on foggy mornings with cargos of flour and barrel staves and sometimes to return with guns and gunpowder.[45]

Lexington dropped down the river on March 26, 1776, and slipped through the British blockade on April 6. The following day she fell in with the British sloop *Edward*, a tender to the frigate *Liverpool*. After a fierce fight that lasted about an hour, *Edward* struck her colors. *Lexington* took her prize into Philadelphia and as soon as the ship was back in fighting trim Barry put to sea again.[46] On April 26 *Lexington* encountered Sir Peter Parker's fleet sailing to attack Charleston, South Carolina. Two of the British ships gave chase on May 5 off the Delaware Capes. HMS *Roebuck* and *Liverpool* chased *Lexington* for eight hours and came close enough to exchange fire with the American ship before Barry managed to elude his pursuers and reach Philadelphia safely.[47]

John Barry, "Father of the American Navy"

On March 14, 1776, John Barry was commissioned by the Continental Navy and would eventually become known as the "Father of the American Navy." He was born in Wexford, Ireland. His family was driven from Wexford by the English, and he learned a hatred of oppressing invaders when 3,000 Wexfordians were killed by an English army. Standing six feet four inches, he was a commanding figure and appeared on deck a burly, well-built, ruddy-complexioned man of dignified carriage who spoke in a commanding tone.

Commodore John Barry, "Father of the American Navy" (LC-H261-2945, Library of Congress, Prints and Photographs).

Barry began sailing as a boy with his uncle and settled in Philadelphia. He worked for several Philadelphia merchants, captaining their cargo ships to the West Indies. Just before the American Revolution broke out, he began working for the firm of Willing, Morris, and Cadwalader, who assigned him to their 200-ton ship, the *Black Prince*. Barry sailed the *Black Prince* to London and on the return voyage set a record for the longest distance sailed in one day in the entire 18th century: 237 miles in 24 hours. Upon arriving back in Philadelphia, Barry found out the war had begun. Congress apparently first employed him in October 1775, and he assisted in the efforts to outfit and supply Congress's first fleet of ships.[48]

On March 14, 1776, Barry received a captain's commission, signed by John Hancock, and was assigned the 14-gun *Lexington*. Barry sailed from Philadelphia on March 31 and engaged his first British vessel, the sloop *Edward*, on April 7, capturing the first ship by a Continental vessel in the war. *Lexington* and *Reprisal* sailed down the Delaware to Cape May on June 20, there joining *Wasp* and *Hornet*. On June 28 Pennsylvania's brig *Nancy* arrived in the area with 386 barrels of powder in her hold and ran aground while attempting to elude British blockader *Kingfisher*. Barry organized the removal of the supplies and the defense of the ship. When there were only 100 barrels of powder left, he had the main sail taken down and wrapped around the gunpowder. When they abandoned the ship, he lit the end of the sail, draped over the side of the ship, on fire. By the time a British boarding party arrived, the flames had reached the gunpowder and blew the ship sky high, killing several dozen British soldiers in a blast that was heard for miles. The Battle of Turtle Gut Inlet as it became known, brought Captain Barry to Congress's attention. He was congratulated for his bravery and ingenuity in securing the gunpowder and rescuing the crew of the *Nancy*.

On July 10 *Lexington* slipped to sea. On July 27 she captured *Lady Susan*, a ship of Lord Dunmore's Tory Fleet that operated out of the Chesapeake Bay. This privateer was commanded by William Goodrich, a member of the notorious Tory family that had plagued the shipping of Virginia and Maryland. Richard Dale, one of seven members of the *Lady Susan* crew who signed on the *Lexington* later won fame under John Paul Jones. Early in September *Lexington* took another sloop, *Betsy*. About a fortnight later lightning struck *Lexington*, forcing the brigantine home for repairs. She anchored off Philadelphia on September 26, and two days later Barry relinquished command.[49]

With repairs completed, *Lexington*, with Captain William Hallock in command, got underway for Cape Francois to obtain military cargo. On the return voyage, the British frigate *Pearl* overhauled the brigantine just short of the Delaware Capes on December 20 and captured her. The commander of the frigate removed *Lexington*'s officers but left 70 of her men on board under hatches with a prize crew. But by luring their captors with a promise of rum, the Yankee sailors recaptured the ship and took her to Baltimore.[50]

During the Revolution John Barry captured at least 20 British vessels. Captain John Barry crossed the Delaware with Washington. He fought as a soldier at the Battles of Princeton and Trenton and during the occupation of Philadelphia. By February he was back on the New Jersey coast to organize some of the remaining gunboats of the Pennsylvania navy to harass British shipping. On February 26, 1778, the Continentals captured the sloop *Alert* and four transports off Port Penn. Barry captured the armed schooner *Alert* (20 guns) and two ships loaded with supplies bound for the British Army on March 7, 1778.[51]

He next commanded the *Raleigh*, 32 guns. He sailed from Boston on September 25, 1778, and two days later was chased and attacked by three British vessels. After a nine-hour running fight, he was obliged to run the *Raleigh* ashore on an island near the mouth of Penobscot Bay but escaped to the mainland with most of his crew. Though he lost his ship, he was highly commended for his gallantry. Being without a command, in 1779 Barry accepted command of the ten-gun privateer *Delaware* and captured the British ship *Harlem*.[52] In November 1780 Barry was ordered to command the *Alliance*, 32 guns (his favorite ship), and took John Laurens, special commissioner, to France. Owing to

On May 29, 1781, USS *Alliance* (36), Captain John Barry, fell in with the ship HMS *Atalanta* (16) and the brig HMS *Trespassy* (14). *Alliance* was becalmed. The British ships used oars to maneuver athwart her stern, thus *Alliance* could use but one gun while the British ships used full broadsides. Captain Barry was wounded and forced below. *Alliance*'s colors were shot away. The British, believing she had surrendered, ceased fire. A small breeze then allowed her to bring most of her guns to bear. After several broadsides the two British ships surrendered. Note oars in use (Warren, artist, May 29, 1781, NH 56472, Naval History and Heritage Command).

the difficulty in obtaining a crew, this ship did not sail until February 11, 1781. On the passage to France, she captured the privateer *Alert* of 12 guns. On the return voyage she captured the privateers *Mars*, 26 guns, and *Minerva*, 10 guns, who were made prizes.[53]

Barry's most renowned naval encounter occurred off the coast of Newfoundland on May 28, 1781. His ship, the 36-gun frigate *Alliance*, took on two British ships, the sloop *Atalanta*, 20 guns, and the sloop *Trespassy*, 14 guns. He was severely wounded and lost consciousness, but afterward he got up and rallied his crew until they captured the two British vessels that were attacking them. He continued in command of the *Alliance*, capturing numerous prizes in 1782.[54] The last naval engagement of the Revolutionary War was fought by Barry in the *Alliance* against the British man-of-war *Sybylle* of 28 guns. Though the ship surrendered to him he was obliged to abandon it to escape from the rest of the squadron of which it was a part. At the time of the fight with the *Sybylle*, Barry was convoying the *Duc de Lauzane*, carrying money and supplies from the West Indies to the United States. His action enabled this ship to escape and reach port safely. The frigate *Alliance* was the last remaining regularly commissioned ship afloat at the close of the Revolution in 1783.[55]

After the Revolution Barry got back into mercantile shipping and made several voyages to the Orient. When George Washington reestablished the navy in 1794, Barry was made commodore of the United States Navy, receiving Commission Number One, dated

June 4, 1794. He oversaw the rebuilding of the Continental Fleet and captured several French vessels during the Quasi-War. He finally retired on March 6, 1801, after bringing the USS *United States* back to Philadelphia from the West Indies. Barry trained numerous sailors who went on to be naval leaders of the War of 1812 and is often called the "Father of the American Navy." He passed away in 1803 at his home near Philadelphia.[56]

John Barry captured numerous British prizes during the Revolution and holds the record for prize money returns in a single voyage. His commands included, in succession, the *Lexington,* 16 guns, the *Effingham,* 32 guns, the *Raleigh,* 32 guns, the privateer *Delaware,* ten guns, and the *Alliance,* 36 guns. The Delaware River span just south of Chester is named for Commodore Barry.

1777: The Battle of Philadelphia

The year before, in June 1776, a British fleet commanded by Admiral Richard Howe had arrived off New York, escorting the transports carrying the army of his brother General Sir William Howe. After the army landed on Long Island to attack New York, part of the fleet dispersed to blockade the East Coast. The frigate HMS *Roebuck* took station off Cape Henlopen. But after taking New York and as the British Army was planning their campaign to capture the American capital of Philadelphia, they chose not to take the direct approach on a narrow channel up Delaware Bay because the city was stoutly defended by a number of forts in the Delaware River and Bay along with a flotilla of Continental ships. Outflanking these strong defenses, the British entered the more lightly defended Chesapeake and landed at the head of the Elk River. The 15,000-man force, led by Admiral Howe's brother Lord Howe, skirmished with Washington at Cooch's Bridge near Newark, Delaware, then defeated Washington's forces at Brandywine before capturing Philadelphia.[57] Having taken Philadelphia, the British Army still faced Washington's forces to the north of the city, and New Jersey was still hostile territory. Lord Howe still had a logistic problem because he could not resupply and reinforce his army by sea, as the Continentals still controlled the river downstream. Thus, it was necessary to open a direct and defensible supply line from the sea to support the British forces and the many loyalist inhabitants of the city. He began to erect land batteries to attack the forts and American ships in the river.

On July 30, 1777, Henry Fisher again raised the warning that enemy ships were approaching the cape. These were warships and supply ships returning from the escort and supply fleet that had carried the British Army to the head of the Chesapeake. This armada is said to have convinced the populace of Lewes of the "seriousness of the situation." By early September a British naval force had sailed up Delaware Bay and anchored off Chester, Pennsylvania. At the fore of the assembled British fleet were the 64-gun ship-of-the-line *Augusta,* the 50-gun ship *Isis,* the 44-gun frigate *Roebuck,* the 32-gun frigate *Pearl,* the 28-gun *Liverpool,* and the 16-gun sloop *Merlin.* Other warships remained behind with the supply ships.[58]

However, the Delaware River shoreline south of Philadelphia was still in the hands of American forces, which occupied three forts. Forts Mifflin and Mercer had been constructed on the Delaware River just south of Philadelphia in order to guard against a British invasion. Fort Mifflin sat on Mudd Island on the Pennsylvania side and Fort Mercer was at Red Bank, New Jersey, across the river.[59] The only means of supplying Philadelphia

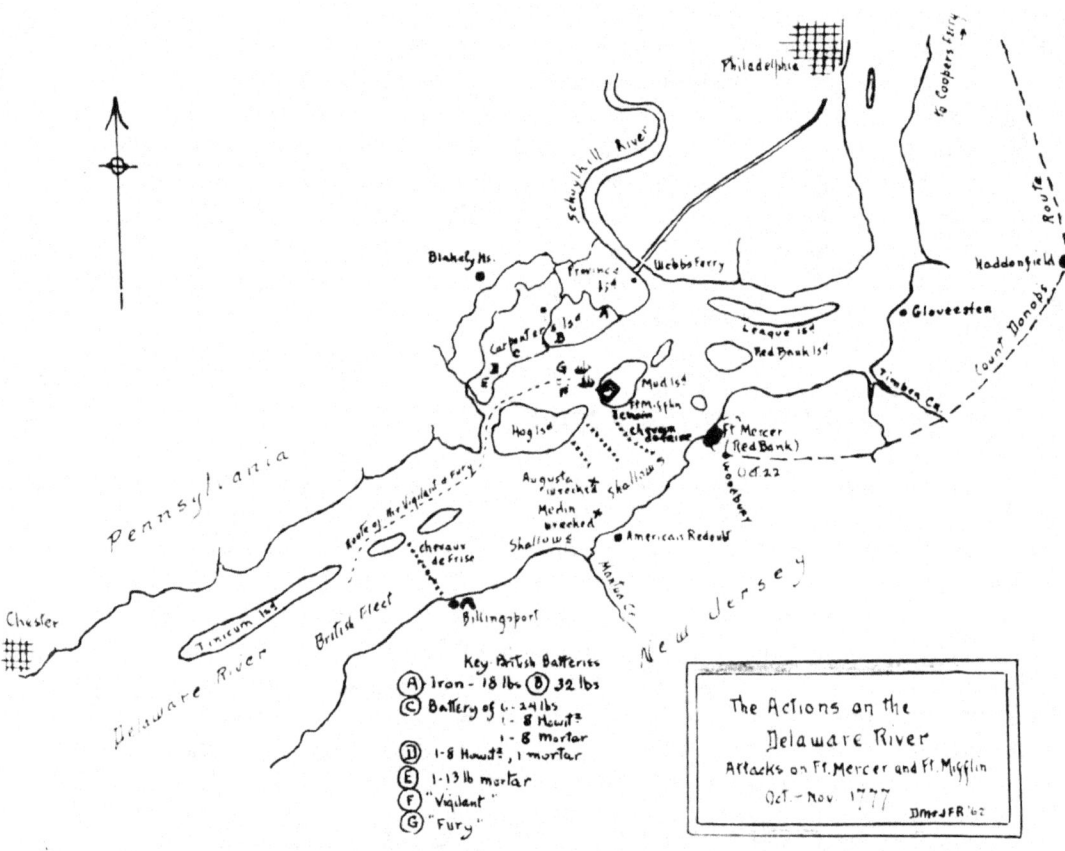

Battle at Fort Mifflin, map of actions on the Delaware near Philadelphia during the attack on Fort Mifflin and Fort Mercer, October 1777. Depicting British attacks on the Delaware River forts in 1777 the map shows the locations of the British batteries and the chevaux-de-frise placed in the river (NH 56874, Naval History and Heritage Command).

was via the Delaware River and this still lay under the control of the Americans. Any ships trying to sail up the river would be caught in the cannon fire between the two forts. General Howe knew he had to gain control of the river. George Washington knew this as well, so he hoped to maintain control of the forts in order to force Howe to abandon the city. The British needed to overcome these forts to gain access to supply their army and Philadelphia. The British Army, aided by engineer John Montresor, who had designed and initially oversaw the construction of the forts, began to besiege them from the rear. During the siege, 400 American soldiers held off over 2,000 British troops.[60]

The British navy was to support the siege by a frontal attack on the forts. But to reach the forts their ships would first have to navigate past *chevaux-de-frise*—rows of sharpened wooden spikes buried in the river bottom that could puncture the hulls of any ships inadvertently hitting them. They would also have to avoid the kegs of gunpowder that the ingenious David Bushnell—the inventor of the submarine that had unsuccessfully attacked the British fleet in New York Harbor—intended to float downstream to hit and blow up British warships. Although largely ineffective, this effort became known as "the battle of the kegs." Because of the consternation that it caused in the British

Delaware River chevaux-de-frise. Photograph of the frame timbers, showing the details of the iron-tipped, barbed points dredged from the Delaware River in 1941 used during the Revolutionary War. Two barriers were used in the river, one extending from Billings Island to Billings Fort, the second (a series) extending from Hog Island to Red Bank Island Shoal, both located midway between Chester and Philadelphia, Pennsylvania (NH 56499 Naval History and Heritage Command).

fleet, it inspired a ballad that gave a morale boost to the Revolutionary army throughout the next winter at Valley Forge.[61]

What was more important, the British ships would have to contend with the few ships of the Continental Navy that had sailed out of Philadelphia to the secure ports of Chester, Wilmington, and New Castle. Most prominent was one of the new 24-gun frigates that had been building in Philadelphia, the *Delaware,* commanded by Captain Charles Alexander. Also present were *Andrew Doria, Wasp, Fly, Reprisal,* and the prize ship *Racehorse.* In addition, there were the 48 small ships and boats of the Pennsylvania navy under Commodore J. Hazlewood.[62]

While blocking the British Navy's approach to the forts, these naval forces also assisted in the defense of the forts from land attack. While doing so, *Delaware,* in company with several smaller ships, advanced upon the British fortifications being erected and opened a destructive fire while anchored some 500 yards from shore. On September 27 *Delaware* went aground on the ebb tide and came under the concentrated fire of the British artillery. After a brave defense against overwhelming odds, Captain Alexander was compelled to surrender. As was the custom of the day, *Delaware* was taken into the British navy, where it served under the same name until 1783.[63]

U.S. vessels in conflict on the Delaware River with HMS *Augusta*, *Roebuck*, and *Merlin* near Mud Fort on October 22, 1777 (Lieutenant W. Eliot, RN, artist, 1779, NH 1074, Naval History and Heritage Command).

On October 22 a Hessian regiment of 1,200 soldiers attacked Fort Mercer. Colonel Carl von Donop led the failed attempt. The following day, October 23, a small fleet of British ships tried to navigate the chevaux-de-frise and get past the forts. The fleet was led by the 64-gun HMS *Augusta*. Cannon fire from Fort Mifflin rained down on the ships. Both the *Augusta* and the 20-gun HMS *Merlin* took direct hits and may have been damaged by the chevaux-de-frise as well. Both ships ran aground. The *Augusta* caught fire from the cannonade and the ship's magazine was breached, the explosion killing over 60 crewmen. The sailors onboard the *Merlin* set fire to the ship and abandoned her in order to prevent her being salvaged by the rebels. *Merlin* blew up. *Isis* and other ships rescued survivors and moved back downriver. The battle had started with a stunning American victory.[64]

The victories of October 22 and 23 were a great encouragement to the Americans, but General Howe became determined that he must take the river. For the British navy, time was of the essence. It was already unseasonably cold for October and ice could be seen along the shoreline. From October 26 to October 29 the area was hit by a nor'easter. Philadelphia was still essentially blockaded by the Continentals and the British Army was low on food and ammunition. Supplies were being moved ashore and upriver by rowed flatboats along the shore in the dark of night. A massive five-day artillery bombardment of Fort Mifflin commenced on November 10, aided by ships from the river. By November 10 the British shore batteries had been reinforced and rearmed. On November

Destruction of HMS *Augusta* in the Delaware River, October 23, 1777. Oil painting by an unidentified British naval officer, circa 1777. *Augusta* was destroyed by fire and powder magazine explosion off Fort Mifflin, Pennsylvania, during an engagement with American forces (NH 92863-KN, Naval History and Heritage Command).

15 the British fleet brought up a specially configured shore bombardment ship, *Vigilant*, into the shallow channel on the west side of Fort Island and bombarded the fort from 20 yards point blank. Late in the day, about 5,000 survivors of Fort Mifflin were evacuated to Fort Mercer. Some Pennsylvania navy ships, including the brig *Convention* and the sloop *Speedwell* with the Navy Board members, managed to run north past Philadelphia at night to take refuge up the Delaware River. Unfortunately, some others, including the ship *Montgomery* and the sloop *Delaware*, could not make it before the tide and winds changed. They were burned to prevent them from falling into the hands of the British. Fort Mercer was evacuated on November 20.[65] Forts Mifflin and Mercer eventually fell, but their brave actions helped delay, for more than a month, General Howe from his primary mission of decimating the main body of the Continental Army north of Philadelphia. This delay forced Howe to wait through the winter for a more opportune moment in the spring.

Other Continental ships in Philadelphia were also lost as a result of the British capture of the city. The 32-gun frigate *Washington* had been launched in August of 1776 and, along with the 24-gun frigate *Effingham*, was still uncompleted as the British approached Philadelphia. Their prospective captains, Thomas Read and John Barry respectively, were ordered to take the ships up the Delaware River to a place of safety. On October 25

General George Washington asked for the crew of *Effingham* to reinforce the crews on the ships fighting in the Delaware. On November 2 the two ships were sunk just below Bordentown, New Jersey, to deny their use to the British.[66]

Although he had lost his frigate command, Captain Barry was soon in action harassing the British navy on the Delaware River when in February he led a boat party to capture four British transports and the schooner *Alert* off Port Penn. When the British left Philadelphia the next year, he returned, hoping to get a ship, but none were ready. He took command of a ten-gun privateer named *Delaware*, owned by Thomas and Mathew Irwin of Philadelphia. While this was not a Navy ship, it was a government ship, in that it was sailing under a congressionally granted letter of marque. By 1781 Barry was back on active duty commanding the *Alliance,* in which he had an illustrious career for the rest of the war. Captain William Smith took over the privateer *Delaware*.[67]

The 32-gun *Randolph*, commanded by Captain Nicholas Biddle, was the only Philadelphia-built frigate to escape the battle of Philadelphia, having passed Cape Henlopen outbound sometime earlier. Unfortunately, in March 1778, while escorting a convoy in the West Indies, *Randolph* encountered the British 64-gun ship-of-the-line *Yarmouth*. After a sharp action of 15 minutes, *Randolph* blew up with the loss of 315 men and Captain Biddle. Only four men survived. This was the largest loss of crew by an American warship until the loss of the *Arizona* at Pearl Harbor. Of the four frigates built in Philadelphia, only the plans of *Randolph* survived. Preserved by the Wharton and Humphrey Shipyard, they came into possession of the U.S. Navy when that shipyard was taken over to become the first government navy yard.[68]

The Continental Navy Frigate Delaware

The first USS *Delaware* of the Continental Navy was a 24-gun, third-rate frigate. The United States Navy recognizes October 13, 1775, as the date of its official establishment, the date of the passage of the resolution of the Continental Congress at Philadelphia, Pennsylvania, that created the Continental Navy. On this day, Congress authorized the purchase of two vessels to be armed for a cruise against British merchant ships; these ships became *Andrew Doria* and *Cabot*.[69] By December 13, 1775, Congress had authorized the construction of thirteen new frigates rather than refitting merchantmen to increase the fleet. Five ships were to be rated 32 guns (*Hancock, Raleigh, Randolph, Warren,* and *Washington*), five were rated at 28 guns, (*Effingham, Montgomery, Providence, Trumble,* and *Virginia*), and three were rated 24 guns (*Boston, Congress,* and *Delaware*). Only eight frigates made it to sea, and their effectiveness was limited; they were completely outmatched by the mighty Royal Navy, and nearly all of them were captured or sunk by 1781.[70]

The first *Delaware* was possibly designed by Joshua Humphries and built under the December 13, 1775, order of the Continental Congress in the yard of Warwick Coates of Philadelphia. Her design is said to have been modeled closely on a Philadelphia privateer frigate called *Hero*, which fought successfully in the Seven Years War in the 1760s, and this may explain the out-of-date beakhead bulkhead that appears to have been used in so many of the Philadelphia-designed warships of the Revolution. The official designs of the 28-gun frigates and the 32-gun frigates are said to have been scaled-up versions of the *Delaware* plans. *Delaware* was supposed to have had twenty-four 9-pounders, but due to problems at the foundry she was given the larger guns intended for the frigate

The Continental Navy frigate *Delaware* (Kennard Wiggins, artist, courtesy Delaware Military Museum).

Washington. Upon the launching of *Delaware* in July 1776, Captain Charles Alexander took command. Alexander was placed under the orders of Commodore John Hazelwood of the Pennsylvania State Navy. The frigate measured 117 feet in length, with a beam of 32 feet, ten-and-a-half inches. She mounted 22 twelve-pound guns, 6 six-pound guns, and several swivel guns with a tonnage of 563.[71]

During the fall and winter of 1776 *Delaware* defended the Delaware River against British raiders. In the summer of 1777 Captain Alexander joined with Commodore John Hazelwood's Pennsylvania state ships in operations that delayed the British fleet's approach to Philadelphia and supply of the British Army.[72] *Delaware*, now under the overall command of John Barry, in company with several smaller ships, including the Pennsylvania State Navy corvette *Montgomery*, advanced upon the enemy fortifications being erected and opened a destructive fire while anchored some 500 yards from shore. On September 27 *Delaware* went aground on the ebb tide and came under the concentrated fire of the British artillery. After a brave defense against overwhelming odds, Captain Alexander was compelled to strike his colors.[73] Alexander and his officers were taken to Philadelphia and confined in the Pennsylvania State House (Independence Hall). On the night of November 30–December 1, he and four of his officers engineered a daring escape, descending from the bell tower by a rope. By December 9 they had joined with other officers and ships of the Continental and Pennsylvania navies that had escaped Philadelphia south to Chester, Wilmington, and New Castle and were re-forming.[74] The

British got *Delaware* off the mud and took her, repaired, into the Royal Navy as the HMS *Delaware*. She remained for a time with the fleet that was proceeding up the river to Philadelphia. On March 9, 1779, she took part in the capture of the Connecticut State Navy ship *Oliver Cromwell* of about 20 guns.

Sold on April 14, 1783, at the war's conclusion, *Delaware* was acquired by Mary Hayley, an English widow living in Boston. Mrs. Hayley renamed her *United States*, which she thought would annoy British authorities, and used the ship for whaling, sealing, and trading. *United States* had to visit such out-of-the way places as the Falkland Islands to do her mistress's bidding. The ship was then sold once again, to French owners who renamed her *Le Dauphin*; there is a suggestion that they used her for whaling. In 1794 she was sold at auction in Charleston, South Carolina, and was bought by a French privateer by the name of Jean Bouteille. This alarmed British authorities, and the consul combined with American officials to tried to prevent Bouteille from doing anything with his acquisition. Nevertheless, he fitted her out once more as a warship, removing her quarter galleries and "upper deck" and painting her all black. The desired result was that she should look like an innocent merchant ship so she could blend in with British convoys unnoticed. The last record of her was her departure from Charleston for Port de Paix in 1795. It is quite likely that the tired old ship foundered in a West Indies gale soon after that date. She was the last survivor of the original thirteen frigates authorized by Congress in 1775.[75]

1779: The Delaware Navy

British naval vessels were a constant menace to the people living on the shores of the Delaware Bay. The towns and farms along the estuary were subject to depredations from both loyalist privateers and the Royal Navy. The Royal Navy needed provisions and were happy to pay for them or to seize them if necessary. Tory farmers and loyalists benefited from the former, while patriotic citizens suffered from the latter. In addition, there were common thieves and outlaws preying on coastal trade. Among these was the famous Tory Jack, who raided for spoils along the river with his small gunboat. On one occasion he captured a trading merchant from Wilmington named John Harris. Tory Jack seized his vessel and disposed of Harris by placing him aboard a British frigate. Harris managed to escape and later, with a crew from Wilmington, sailed down the river and finally captured Tory Jack. They took him to the Rocks on the Wilmington waterfront and hanged him from an apple tree.[76]

The raiding by the enemy of homes and farms along the Delaware were of great concern to Delaware president Caesar Rodney. In August, Colonel Charles Pope received a commission from Rodney, for the sloop *Revenge*, thus authorizing him to become a state privateer. In November 1780 formal resolutions by both houses of the assembly authorized the president of the state to procure and fit out armed vessels, the expenses of which would be borne by the state. In effect, Delaware began creating a state navy. At the same time, Colonel Pope was authorized to take command of the state ship *Delaware*, recommend officers for commissioning, enlist sailors and marines, and make payments of accounts. He was to act under the direction of the president as commander in chief. Charles Pope became commander of the fledgling Delaware State Navy. Over the next year, he contracted to acquire and fit out more vessels, the schooners *Intrepid* and *Vigilant*.[77]

Pope did not exercise his authority to privateer in *Revenge*. A lack of funds delayed the fitting out of *Delaware* and the planned *Intrepid* remained at the shipyard in Philadelphia as Colonel Henry Neill of Lewes, who purchased the ship on behalf of the state, the shipyard owner, Thomas Salter, and the state exchanged legal documents as they wrangled over debts. Eventually Commander Pope did get *Vigilant* into action. On November 30, 1781, he sailed from Wilmington to Duck Creek to fill out his crew with reliable men from his home neighborhood. He soon received information of a privateer that had fired on a vessel transporting a unit of the Continental regiment and had forced a number of barges to shelter in creeks. He spent several days escorting these vessels safely north to Reedy Point. On December 2 he moved south hunting for the privateer ship and, on December 5 off Jones Point, he approached a vessel he expected to be the enemy. She was a topsail schooner flying the Continental flag, but when Pope approached within hailing distance the ship fired a shot, raised the British colors, and demanded *Vigilant* strike or be sunk. When Pope defied that order, the enemy fired a broadside and began constant fire. That allowed Pope to determine that the enemy had six guns to his two and decide that since he could not "return the compliment with satisfaction, chose to decline it rather than make a faint attempt."[78] He secreted his crew below and covered his guns in the hope that the enemy would send boats to board, which he could attack. When that did not occur, he withdrew to shallow water off Kitts Hummock and into Jones Creek. There he was informed that the vessel was *Fox*, mounting ten four-pound or six-pound guns and commanded by Captain Joseph Hughes Burton. On December 12 Pope learned that the *Fox* had continued to intercept and plunder passing barges and lay off Bombay Hook with the captured barges. He sailed north planning to get behind the *Fox* and allow some of the barges to flee north. En route, *Intrepid* encountered the privateer barge *Hazard* from New York, commanded by the "noted Miles Hurion." From that encounter, he learned that the *Fox* had already sailed for New York, taking a captured brig in convoy.

In expectation of winter weather, Pope returned to port in Wilmington. He let his crew go, while signing an attestation that one William Simpson had been wounded in the hand during the cruise. He remained titular commander of *Vigilant* but turned his attention to fitting out and manning *Delaware,* then in Philadelphia. The state, however, had insufficient funds. After attempting to convince the states of Pennsylvania and New Jersey to split the cost of operating the ship, Pope was directed to sell her at auction. He and the Philadelphia contractor made a last-minute offer of a loan to the state to finish the ship. A committee of the general assembly, however, declined based on lack of funds to operate her or pay back the loan. *Delaware* was sold in May 1783.[79] With that, the Delaware navy had no hope of becoming operational. Pope's career as a naval commander was over. He returned home to Duck Creek to become a rich landowner before moving to Georgia, where he died in 1803.

1779: The Second Delaware, *Privateer*

Being without a regularly commissioned ship, Captain John Barry made two cruises to Port-au-Prince in the ten-gun privateer brig *Delaware* under a letter of marque issued by Congress over the signature of John Jay. The *Delaware*, owned by Irwin and Co. of Philadelphia, carried a crew of 45 men but would be later improved to carry twelve guns and sixty men. Clerk John Kessler wrote an account of his second voyage. Kessler says the *Delaware* sailed from Philadelphia in the fall of 1779 in company with three other letters-of-marque brigs and one schooner, of which fleet Barry was made commodore and for which he arranged signals to be used. When abreast of Cape Henlopen a sail was discovered, chase was made, and on coming up found to be a British sloop of war called the *Harlem*,which was taken with about ninety men without resistance. The officers, during the chase (after heaving over all her guns), made their escape in boats. The vessel was sent to Philadelphia but the crew was landed near Chincoteague, Virginia, and delivered to a military party. Writing to Mathew and Thomas Irwin on July 18, 1779, Barry describes the capture of the *Harlem*:

> I have the pleasure to inform you that the day we left Cape May we took the sloop of war Harlem of 14 four pounders and 85 men belonging to his Britannic Majesty. The guns and other sundry things, they threw overboard without firing a shot. The Captain and about ten men went off in a whale boat but we have reason to think is overset for carrying sail as she disappeared all at once. After taking the prisoners out and putting some of our own people on board we made the best of our way for Cape Henlopen, but the next day the wind being ahead, a fresh breeze and 40 miles southward of the Cape I thought it more prudent with the advice of the other captains to land the prisoners at Sinipaxan they being too many in number to be kept on board our little fleet safely as we have all reason in the world to think we shall catch more before long.[80]

A Tense Standoff Among Allies

During the war, there was often agitation if not contest between the Continental and state naval forces. The Continental vessels impressed into service men belonging to the state navy or those bearing letters of marque of the Congress. Captain Barry's clerk, John Kessler recorded an incident that illustrates these tensions:

> At our arrival in the Delaware the pilot who came aboard informed us that the Continental frigate *Confederacy* lay at Chester and impressed the crews of the merchant vessels going up the river. This alarmed the brig's crew and many desired to be put ashore. Captain Barry addressed them thus: "My lads, if you have the spirit of freemen you will not desire to go ashore nor tamely submit your wills to be taken away, although all the force of all the frigates' boats crew were to attempt to exercise such a species of tyranny."
>
> This address satisfied them and it implied his consent to their defending themselves, they resolved to do it at all hazard and for that purpose put themselves under the command and direction of the boatswain and armed themselves with musket, pistols and boarding pikes. We arrived in hailing distance of the *Confederacy* when her commanding officer ordered the brig's main topsail to be hove to the mast. Captain Barry answered that he could not, without getting his vessel ashore. The commander of the frigate then ordered that the brig should come to anchor. Captain Barry gave no answer, but continued on his way beating up the tide and flood and wind ahead when a gun was fired from the frigate and a boat, manned, left her and came towards us.
>
> Captain Barry directed that the officers of the boat should be admitted on board, but as the men with them we might do as we pleased. The boat soon arrived and two armed officers jumped on board and on the quarter deck ordering the main topsail halyards to be cast off, which was not, however done. Captain Barry asked whether they were sent to take command of his vessel. The boat's crew were then about entering when we presented ourselves and threatened instant death to all that entered. Their officers thereon after trying to intimidate our boatswain by presenting their pistols at him, finding it, however, of no avail, they hastily sprang into their boat and left us.
>
> Another gun was fired from the frigate, when Captain Barry ordered the guns to be cleared and declared that if but a rope yard was injured by their firing he should give them the whole broadside. The third gun being fired from the frigate Captain Barry asked the name of her commander. The

answer was Lieutenant Gregory. "I advise you to desist from firing. This is the brig *Delaware*, belonging to Philadelphia and my name is John Barry."

Nothing further was said or done by Lieutenant Gregory. It was said that Mr. Gregory had once served under the command of Captain Barry and could not but know that he would not be trifled with. Thus our whole crew arrived at Philadelphia.[81]

1782: The Battle of Delaware Bay

The Battle of Delaware Bay, also known as the Battle of Cape May, was a naval engagement fought when a British squadron of three vessels attacked three American privateers escorting a fleet of merchantmen. The ensuing combat in Delaware Bay, near Cape May, ended with an American victory over a superior British force.[82]

Twenty-three-year-old Lieutenant Joshua Barney of the Continental Navy commanded the privateer sloop *Hyder Ally* during the battles. She was owned by a Pennsylvania businessman, John Wilcocks, and was issued a letter of marque. The sloop-of-war was armed with sixteen 6-pounders and had a crew of about 110 men—officers and marines—and was named *Hyder Ally* after Hyder Ali, the ruler of the Kingdom of Mysore on the Indian subcontinent and a British enemy. Also with Lieutenant Barney were the

Pennsylvania State Ship *Hyder Ally*. On April 8, 1782, the HMS *General Monk*, under Captain Rogers, in company with HMS *Quebec* and the privateer *Fair American*, entered Cape May channel in pursuit of an American merchant convoy accompanied by *Hyder Ally*, under Captain Joshua Barney. The American fleet got underway and dispersed in the bay. *Hyder Ally* engaged *General Monk* in a 10-minute battle that necessitated the English ship to strike her colors. Under a prize crew, *General Monk* was sailed to Philadelphia, Pennsylvania, where she was later purchased by the national government and taken into the Continental Navy under her original name, USS *General Washington* (Warren, artist, NH 56480, Naval History and Heritage Command).

privateer sloops *Charming Sally,* of ten guns, and the twelve-gun *General Greene.* Barney's first command was to escort a rebel fleet of five merchantmen to the Delaware Bay. During this cruise, three British ships were sighted and a battle began. British forces included the 32-gun frigate HMS *Quebec* under Captain Christopher Mason, the twenty-four-gun sloop-of-war HMS *General Monk* under Captain Josiah Rodgers, and a New York privateer brig named *Fair American* crewed by American loyalists. *Fair American* was the former American privateer *General Washington,* commanded by Silas Talbot at her capture.

At nightfall of April 7, 1782, the American convoy anchored within Cape May due to the wind, which had died down to a calm. Later that night the British in HMS *Quebec* and *General Monk* sighted the enemy fleet and anchored off the cape and made preparations to attack the *Hyder Ally,* which was considered the most formidable ship of the fleet. Unaware of the British vessels nearby, the Americans spent the night believing they were safe. The following morning three British privateers were spotted and Captain Mason signaled them to join him. Only the brig *Fair American* responded. At 10:00 A.M. the Americans sighted the British vessels approaching, so Lieutenant Barney ordered the merchantmen to flee up into Delaware Bay under the protection of *General Greene* and *Charming Sally* while *Hyder Ally* remained behind to engage.[83]

The fleet was directed to sail as close to the shoreline as possible so as to not allow a pursuit. The larger British vessels would have a hard time following in the shallow water. *General Greene* disobeyed Barney's orders and prepared for battle and *Charming Sally* grounded on a shoal and was abandoned by her crew. At about 11:00 A.M. the three British vessels were identified by the Americans. HMS *Quebec* stood off nearby Cape Henlopen to prevent the Americans from escaping Cape May into the Atlantic; but this was unnecessary, as the Americans were headed into the bay rather than into open sea. The *Fair American* led the advance with *General Monk* behind. Sometime after 12:00 P.M. the British came within range of the two American privateers. To try to lure the *General Monk* closer, Lieutenant Barney turned about as if attempting to flee. The *Fair American* opened fire with a broadside followed by another; the shots were accurate but caused little damage.

Still in a fake retreat, *Hyder Ally*'s gun ports remained closed and no shots had yet been fired by the Continentals. *General Greene* did the same as *Hyder Ally* and turned around but she grounded just outside of British gun range. The trick worked. *Fair American* broke off the effort to attack the *General Greene* as HMS *General Monk* proceeded forward to attack the *Hyder Ally.* Fortunately for Continental forces, the *Fair American* grounded in shallow water and was permanently put out of the

Captain Joshua Barney (LC-USZ62–110642, Library of Congress, Prints and Photographs).

action due to damage to her hull. Heading forward, Captain Rodgers decided to slow down and launch a boat to take the abandoned *Charming Sally*, after which he continued on until he caught up with the *Hyder Ally*. When within range of pistols, Captain Rodgers ordered her to surrender. Barney answered with a broadside of grape, canister, and round shot that raked the deck of the British sloop, killing several sailors and marines. *General Monk* replied with her bow guns, as they were the only weapons bearing down on the Americans at the time.[84]

Barney ordered his ship to port and unleashed another broadside; these shots passed through the sails and rigging of *General Monk* and damaged her main and top-gallant masts. Before the battle the British bored their 6-pounders on the *General Monk* to fire 9-pounder balls. This proved fatal when the British came within a few yards off *Hyder Ally*'s beam for a full broadside of their own. However, when they fired, the guns of the *General Monk* tore up from the deck and flipped over. Several sailors were burned as they tried to turn their guns back over. A few minutes later the two sloops had drifted close enough together to where the British and Americans could hear each other shouting commands. Barney took the opportunity to reload his cannon but he did not give his gunners the order to open fire. Instead the lieutenant shouted, "Hard a-port! Do you want him to run abroad of us?" This was another trick. Hearing this, Captain Rodgers ordered his ship to port as Lieutenant Barney ordered his vessel to starboard.

As a result, the two vessels collided and became entangled in each other's rigging. The American sailors fastened the *General Monk* to their ship to prevent her from breaking loose and then fired their broadside. The shots knocked out some of the British guns and sent the crew into confusion. The American marines sat high in the rigging of the *Hyder Ally* and poured musketry into the British. Barney's men boarded while he remained on top of the compass box to direct the attack. About this time the box was shot out from under the lieutenant but he suffered only a slight injury. Barney also ordered that his portside guns be turned around to the starboard so they could assist in the battle. After only twenty-six minutes of close-quarters combat, Captain Rodgers was wounded and all of his officers were killed except a midshipman who struck the colors. A total of twenty Britons died and thirty-three were wounded. The *General Monk* was captured and the *Fair American* was aground and stranded, so Captain Mason in HMS *Quebec* fled without actually engaging in the fight. American forces suffered the loss of four killed and eleven wounded. The *Charming Sally* was captured without a fight, the *Hyder Ally* was damaged considerably and the *General Greene* was grounded but refloated after HMS *Quebec* began her retreat. The Americans won the day and Lieutenant Joshua Barney was given command of the prize HMS *General Monk*, which had well over 300 holes shot in her sides. Later the story of the Delaware Bay action was put into print by Myron V. Brewington, author of the book *The Battle of Delaware Bay, 1782*.

Captain Joshua Barney

Barney served in the Continental Navy beginning in February 1776 as master's mate of the *Hornet* where he took part in Commodore Esek Hopkins's raid on New Providence. Later he served on the *Wasp* and was promoted to the rank of lieutenant for gallantry in the action between the *Wasp* and a British brig, the tender *Betsey*. While serving

On December 21, 1782, the United States frigate *South Carolina* (formerly *L'Indien*), under Captain Joyner, was overtaken and captured by a British squadron consisting of the frigate *Quebec*, Captain Christopher Mason, and the ship *Diomede*, Captain Matthew Squire. The *South Carolina*, originally built for the Continental Navy in Amsterdam, was sold to the king of France and later became the property of Chevalier Luxembourg, who leased the ship to American service in 1780 (Warren, artist, NH 56481, Naval History and Heritage Command).

on *Andrew Doria* he took a prominent part in the defense of the Delaware River. Barney was taken prisoner and exchanged several times. In 1779, he was again taken prisoner and imprisoned in Old Mill Prison, Plymouth, England, until his escape in 1781. He wrote an account of this in *The Memoirs of Commodore Barney*, published in Boston in 1832.

Upon returning to America, he was given command of a small fleet of privateers that were to escort several merchant ships into Delaware Bay. Barney commanded the *Hyder Ally,* the most powerful of the ships, with 16 six-pound cannons. On April 8, 1782, Lieutenant Joshua Barney won the Battle of Delaware Bay. Joshua Barney was awarded command of the *General Monk* for his bravery and sent to France with dispatches for Ben Franklin. After the war, he became a privateer for the French navy. Later, during the War of 1812, Barney was granted a letter-of-marque to operate a privateer against the British navy. When the British blockaded the Chesapeake in 1814, Barney was given command of the Chesapeake Flotilla of small boats and barges to protect Baltimore and the capital. When the fleet was overrun, Barney sank the boats and took the cannons overland to join in the defense of Washington, D.C. The poorly prepared Americans quickly fled the capital, except for Barney and his men. They inflicted heavy damage on the approaching British before their final retreat, which left the way open for the British to invade and destroy much of the city.[85]

1782: The Battle of the Delaware Capes

The Battle of the Delaware Capes, sometimes known as the 3rd Battle of Delaware Bay, was fought near the end of the Revolutionary War as the last major naval action in Delaware waters. It had an ignoble result. The marathon battle took place on December 20–21, 1782, some three weeks after the signing of the preliminary articles of peace between Great Britain and the former American colonies. In an engagement between three British Royal navy frigates—HMS *Diomede, Quebec,* and *Astrea* on the one side and the South Carolina's navy's 40-gun frigate *South Carolina,* the brigs *Hope* and *Constance,* and the schooner *Seagrove* on the other—the British were victorious. Only *Seagrove* escaped capture.[86]

The inactivity of the British, American, and French armies meant that the Royal Navy was free to concentrate on enemy trade. One group of British frigates—HMS *Diomede* under Captain Thomas Frederick and the sister 32-gun frigates HMS *Quebec* under Captain Christopher Mason and HMS *Astraea* under Captain Matthew Squires—was blockading the Delaware Bay. On December 20, 1782, they spotted a number of vessels coming out of the bay and chased after them. Frederick was told by the officer of the watch that one of the vessels was a large frigate. This was the forty-gun *South Carolina.*

South Carolina, under Captain John Joyner, had been built at Amsterdam in 1780. She originally was named *Indien* and belonged to France but the Americans hired her. The ship was the most heavily armed warship to sail under American colors during the Revolution. Joyner was attempting to dash out of Philadelphia through the British blockade on December 19 with several vessels. As well as the large *South Carolina,* the privateer brig *Hope,* commanded by John Prole, of ten guns and carrying tobacco and flour, another privateer brig *Constance,* under Commander Jesse Harding, and the six-gun schooner *Seagrove,* under Captain Benjamin Bradhurst, had joined them for protection. On December 19 *Seagrove* hailed a merchant vessel entering the river. Her master learned that three large sails had been seen patrolling off the Cape May Channel. With this information Joyner decided to proceed down the main channel and go straight out into the ocean. On December 20, in the early evening, the four vessels sailed down the channel and out into the Atlantic.[87]

In the late evening the Americans sighted three large British warships at about the same time the British sighted the Americans. Five hours out in the cruise, the *South Carolina* and the *Hope* turned south and two of the British frigates turned after them. *Seagrove* turned north, with *Diomede* in pursuit. She got close enough to fire a few shots, but the schooner sent out boats and towed into the wind. Eventually *Diomede* turned south to continue the main pursuit, letting *Seagrove* get away. While *Diomede* was chasing *Seagrove, Constance,* having never strayed from her course, had continued east and surrendered to *Quebec* and *Astrea* without pointless resistance. The British pursuit of *South Carolina* then continued through the night.

At sunrise the nearest British ship was about two and a half miles behind *South Carolina. Hope* passed *South Carolina* at least once during the pursuit, even though *Hope* was slower before the wind. Joyner suggested that Prole tow *Hope* around the British and make the pursuit into a rowing match, but Prole rejected the advice. By early afternoon the British took *Hope* under fire and she surrendered after having nearly collided with one of the British frigates. This left the *South Carolina,* which was only a mile in front of the British ships once *Hope* had surrendered.

The pursuers skillfully taking up position to limit *South Carolina*'s options in trying to get away, the British windward ship attempted to mask *South Carolina*'s wind. For eighteen hours the British chased her. When the British came in range, *South Carolina* fired her stern chasers at *Diomede*, which returned fire from her bow-guns. By midafternoon the British ships were close enough to exchange shots and could fire a broadside and return to the chase while preventing *South Carolina* from doing the same. The first of the British broadsides did major damage to *South Carolina*, leading Joyner to call his officers together to discuss whether to fight or to continue the flight. The decision was to continue the latter. By early dusk *Quebec* and *Diomede* came up alongside *South Carolina*, with *Astrea* behind in support, together with *Hope* and *Constance*. The British were soon in position to fire six broadsides, five from the *Diomede* and the other from the *Quebec*, all aimed at *South Carolina*'s masts, sails, and rigging, which within two hours were in tatters.

Joyner, now seeing the hopelessness of *South Carolina*'s situation, decided to fire her guns one last time, not wishing to surrender with his cannons loaded. He then struck, ending the battle. The British took possession of *South Carolina* and transferred their prisoners over to their ships. The British had suffered no casualties and damage to their three frigates was light, most of it being to masts and rigging. *South Carolina* had a crew of about 466 men when captured, of whom she had lost six killed and eight wounded. *Hope* had 42 crewmen. *Constance*, with another thirty men, bought the total number of American prisoners to nearly 530. Fifty German and eight British prisoners that the Americans had recruited out of captivity in Philadelphia were released, as they had once served as soldiers in General John Burgoyne's army. Because of the number of men involved, the British treated their American prisoners strictly, locking them under hatches and not allowing more than two to come up on deck at the same time.[88]

Prize crews then took *South Carolina*, *Hope*, and *Constance* to New York, where all three vessels were tried and condemned. The Royal Navy did not purchase *South Carolina*. The war was ending and with it the need for a large navy. In addition, *South Carolina*'s design had flaws. Instead, she was sold for service as a merchantman. Prize money for the captured vessels was awarded in 1784.

The United States was without a navy for nearly a decade—a state of affairs that exposed its merchant ships to a series of attacks by Barbary Pirates. The sole armed maritime presence between 1790 and the launching of the U.S. Navy's first warships in 1797 was the U.S. Revenue Cutter Service (USRCS), the primary predecessor of the U.S. Coast Guard.[89] The agrarian country envisioned by Thomas Jefferson had little consideration for defending the sea-lanes for the mercantile interests of the seaboard cities and even less inclination to spend specie on such pursuits. The nascent nation could ill afford such extravagances and saw no immediate threat that would justify the expense. Nevertheless, new threats have a way of dashing hopes for peace.

Three

Maintaining American Sovereignty and Independence

Disarmed (1785–1794)

The Revolutionary War was ended by the Treaty of Paris in 1783. By 1785 the Continental Navy had been disbanded and the remaining ships sold. The frigate *Alliance,* which had fired the last shots of the American Revolutionary War, was also the last ship in the navy. A faction within Congress wanted to keep the ship, but the new nation did not have the funds to keep her in service. National income was desperately needed and most came from tariffs on imported goods. Because of rampant smuggling, the need was immediate for strong enforcement of tariff laws. The father of the Revenue-Marine was Alexander Hamilton, the first secretary of the treasury. He asked Congress to provide a fleet of armed cutters to insure the collection of import duties from vessels entering United States waters. On August 4, 1790, the United States Congress created the Revenue-Marine, the forerunner for the United States Coast Guard, to enforce the tariff and all other maritime laws. Ten cutters were initially ordered. Two were parceled for the Massachusetts and New Hampshire coasts, one for Long Island Sound, one for the Delaware Bay, two for the Chesapeake Bay, and one each for the Carolinas and Georgia. These armed cutters were schooner rigged with lots of sail for speed, of 30–70 tons and 35–45 feet in length. They carried three to six guns each. Between 1790 and 1794, when the Navy Department was created, the Revenue-Marine was the only armed maritime service for the United States.[1]

The cutter *General Green* was launched on July 7, 1791, at Philadelphia. Her master was James Montgomery, an experienced captain who had served in the Pennsylvania State Navy as a privateer captain and captain of the Pennsylvania customs barge at Philadelphia. The *General Green* was assigned to the Pennsylvania station patrolling the Delaware Bay and River.[2] Another federal maritime organization created at the time, August 1789, was the United States Lighthouse Establishment. The Cape Henlopen Lighthouse, which had been built from subscriptions from Philadelphia merchants in 1767, was placed under the authority and care of the federal government.

America was now free from the restrictions of the British Navigation Acts; however, she was denied access to the markets of the British Empire. Furthermore, America no longer sailed under the protection of the British fleet. America found herself to be a novice small nation in a world of large predatory powers. The result was a drive by adventurous merchants to find new markets in the East Indies. The last Continental Navy frigate, *Alliance,* was sold to Philadelphian Robert Morris, who put it in the China trade.

Thomas Read presided as captain on a voyage from June 1787 to Sept 1788 and opened a new route to China through the Dutch East Indies and the Solomon Islands. On the way back with a cargo of tea he took some time out to do some exploring and discovered the Caroline Islands in the South Pacific.[3]

By 1800 there were some forty Philadelphia-based vessels engaged in the China trade, and as many more trading in South America and Europe. Philadelphia remained America's largest trading port. Grain from the Delaware Valley was the chief export. A triangular trade developed shipping flour and barrel staves to the Caribbean, sugar and rum to England, and iron and textiles back to Philadelphia. When Pennsylvania imposed a tariff in 1785, Delawareans declared Wilmington and New Castle free ports in a competitive effort to seek independent means of export. As trade revived, so did shipbuilding. Wilmington merchants built their own ship, at the foot of Market Street along the Christiana: the 250-ton brig *George Washington,* which sailed for Ireland with a cargo of flour and flax.[4]

American merchant shipping had been protected by the British Navy, and as a consequence of the Treaty of Paris and the disarmament of the Continental Navy, the United States no longer enjoyed the protection for its ships from pirates. In 1793 France declared war on Britain, which began a period of 23 years of almost continuous naval warfare between the two great powers. This created new markets and opportunities for America. Demand soared for American goods, especially in the West Indies, where the slave economy relied upon mainland imports. This brought American traders prosperity but also put them in harm's way as Barbary pirates sailed into the Atlantic. Meanwhile, France and Britain each tried to cut off the trade of the other. The neutrality of the young nation was ill respected by these combatants. American trade was whipsawed as a neutral, with no means of defense and no recourse to the tribute and bribes demanded by pirates and combatants.[5] By the end of 1793 thirteen American merchantmen had been taken by pirates. The American minister to Portugal summarized the situation: "If we mean to have a commerce, we must have a naval force to defend it."[6]

The lack of a well-organized naval department was a stumbling block, as was a pervasive political ambivalence about maintaining a standing navy. In his *American Naval History*, author Jack Sweetman summarized the political debate over establishment of the U.S. Navy: "A Congressional resolution calls for the establishment of a navy to protect American shipping from the Algerines. Supported by Alexander Hamilton's Federalist Party, which speaks for the Northeastern mercantile and maritime community, the bill is bitterly opposed by Thomas Jefferson's Republicans, who represent the agrarian South and inland areas. The latter fear that a navy will be a ruinously expensive, aristocratic institution, subversive of democratic ideals, whose glory-hungry officers will drag the country into unwanted adventures overseas."[7] By 1789 the new Constitution of the United States authorized Congress to create a navy, but during George Washington's first term (1787–1793) little was done to rearm the navy. In reaction to the seizure of the American vessels by pirates, Congress debated and approved the Naval Act of 1794, which authorized the building of six frigates.

The United States Navy Is Established, 1794

In 1794, because of threats to American maritime commerce, principally by the Barbary pirates, President Washington called for establishment of a United States Navy. Over strong objections by Thomas Jefferson and the Republicans, Congress eventually authorized construction of six frigates: three of 44 guns and three of 36 guns. John Barry was personally commissioned by Washington as the first captain in the new navy and is considered the "Father of the Navy."[8] However, after a peace treaty was signed with Algiers in March of 1796, a compromise was reached between President Adams, a Federalist, and the Republican Congress. The frigates were scaled down in size and only three were authorized to be completed: the 44-gun *Constitution*, built in Boston, the 44 gun *United States*, built by Humphreys in Philadelphia, and the 36-gun *Constellation*, built in Baltimore.

The new 44-gun vessels, which actually carried fifty or more guns, are generally called "Humphreys frigates" in homage to the Philadelphia ship designer/builder. They were more powerful than any other existing frigate and they were able to sail faster and closer to the wind than any ship of the line. They were designed to outrun anything they could not outfight.[9] Joshua Humphreys was born in Havertown, Pennsylvania, and also died there. His uncle was Charles Humphreys, a member of the Continental Congress. His son was another noted naval architect, Samuel Humphreys. As a youth, Joshua Humphreys was apprenticed to a shipbuilder in Philadelphia, Pennsylvania. During the War of Independence, he was active as a designer and played a major part in planning the *Randolph*, a 32-gun frigate.[10] When Congress passed the Naval Act of 1794 providing for the construction of six frigates, it called on Humphreys to design them. He was appointed naval constructor June, 28, 1794, and began work on these ships, the beginnings of the U.S. Navy.

Humphreys' designs called for ships that were longer and broader than usual, lower in the water, and able to equal the speed of any fighting ship. They were more stable than other ships of their time and could carry, with better maneuverability, as many guns on one deck as others did on two. Thus his frigates, which were to protect the otherwise defenseless American commerce, could compensate for the naval superiority of hostile powers and pirates. His ships were renowned for their speed and individual accomplishments, and the efficiency of his designs eventually influenced European shipbuilders.[11] The first vessel to be completed, the *United States*, was launched on May 10, 1797, and became the navy's first warship at sea; the *Constitution, Chesapeake, Constellation, President,* and *Congress* followed.[12] These vessels formed the core of the navy during the War of 1812 and scored several victories against British ships. Humphreys' skill is evident by the fact that one of these ships, the *Constitution* ("Old Ironsides"), is still afloat.

Quasi-War with France, 1798–1800

Tensions between the U.S. and France developed into the Quasi-War, which originated from the Treaty of Alliance (1778), which had brought the French into the Revolutionary War. The United States preferred to take a position of neutrality in the conflicts between France and Britain, but this put the nation at odds with both those countries. After the Jay Treaty was authorized with Britain in 1794, France began to side against the United States and by 1797 they had seized over 300 American vessels. As the war in Europe and on the high seas between Britain and France continued, the United States attempted to maintain neutrality. In 1794 John Jay had negotiated a Treaty of Amity, Commerce, and Navigation with Great Britain. In addition to resolving a number of issues remaining after the Treaty of Paris ending the Revolutionary War, it also granted the United States renewed rights to trade with British colonies in the Caribbean. As that trade increased, French warships and privateers began to inflict substantial losses on American ships and trade in the West Indies. As a result, in 1798 President John Adams attempted to negotiate a treaty with France, but his effort was aborted by the so-called "XYZ Affair" in which French officials demanded bribes before negotiations could begin. The American negotiators left.

Coupled with the United States' refusal to continue paying its debt to France on the grounds that the debt had been owed to the French crown and not Republican France, the French outrage at the U.S. led to a series of hostile responses. As a result of that diplomatic stalemate, a state of undeclared war existed between the United States and France. A wave of patriotism swept the country. A number of cities, including Philadelphia, began to build ships to give to the navy. Many former Continental naval officers and privateer captains returned to the navy from merchant service. Many young men from naval families and other patriotic men applied for appointments as midshipmen.

American privateers operated out of Philadelphia preying on French shipping, of which the most famous was the *Louisa*. Carrying a letter of marque, *Louisa* operated as a well-armed privateer in the Atlantic and Mediterranean, where its crew successfully defended against attack by French privateers and took refuge in Gibraltar.[13] The French Navy inflicted substantial losses on American shipping. Secretary of State Timothy Pickering reported to Congress on June 21, 1797, that the French had seized 316 American merchant ships in the previous eleven months. Furthermore, French marauders cruised the length of the U.S. Atlantic seaboard virtually unopposed. The administration had no warships to combat them, as the U.S. possessed only a flotilla of small revenue cutters and some neglected coastal forts.

In 1798, in response to French privateer attacks on American merchant ships, the new president, John Adams, recommended that Congress increase the strength of the navy. In April 1798 Congress created the Navy Department and authorized the completion of the remaining planned three frigates (*President, Congress, Chesapeake*) and the procurement of twelve merchant ships to be converted to warships with up to 22 guns each. Military operations during the Quasi-War involved encounters between the U.S. Navy and French privateers, first along the Atlantic coast but then mostly in the West Indies. In two major naval battles, the USS *Constellation* engaged two French ships in the Caribbean, capturing *l'Insurgente* and severely damaging *la Vengeance*. The USS *Enterprise*, USS *Eagle*, and USS *Experiment* were among the most successful U.S. ships, capturing twenty-five French privateers.[14]

The Second USS Delaware

The second U.S. naval ship *Delaware* was originally built in 1794 as the merchant ship *Hamburg Packet* in Philadelphia and purchased by the month-old navy on May 5, 1798. She was smaller than the original frigate *Delaware* and she was rated third class. Her gun deck was 84 feet, nine inches long, and she had a beam of 28 feet, with a 180-man crew. She carried sixteen, nine-pound cannon and eight, six-pound guns. Captain Stephen Decatur, Sr., was appointed to command and outfit her for sea. Decatur, a former privateer himself, was commissioned as a captain in the United States Navy on May 11, 1798. He was the father of Stephen Decatur II of War of 1812 fame.[15]

Three. Maintaining American Sovereignty and Independence 55

USS *Delaware* (formerly *Hamburg Packet*), 1798 (Kennard Wiggins, artist, courtesy Delaware Military Museum).

Decatur sailed on the first fair wind from her home port of New Castle on July 6, 1798, prepared to guard the coast from Cape Henry to Long island from French privateers. Decatur soon met the merchant ship *Alexander Hamilton*, which reported that she had been plundered by a French armed merchant ship. Sailing in company with the frigate USS *Constellation*, the *Delaware* set course for Boston in search of the enemy raider and saw her first action only one day later. Four strange sails were spotted the next evening. *Delaware* stood off as if she were alarmed that one might be an armed ship. The ruse worked. One of them gave chase, mistaking *Delaware* for a merchantman, and fell easy prey to the American cruiser. *Delaware*'s first prize, the privateer *La Croyable* of 14 guns and 54 men, was taken off Great Egg Harbor July 7, 1798. *La Croyable* was from Cape Francois, Haiti, having left that port on June 19, "being ignorant of the existence of war," as her captain stated. But as she had already captured several American vessels, she was brought into port and condemned.[16]

Decatur took the *La Croyable* to Ft. Mifflin as a war prize. She was renamed *Retaliation* and placed into service, her capture was the very first victory for the new United States Navy. She remained in United States service until the French recaptured her four months later, the only U.S. warship captured during the Quasi-War. *Retaliation* was commanded by Lieutenant William Bainbridge and her capture was only the first of many mishaps he would experience.[17]

A week later *Delaware* sailed from Cape Henlopen with the frigate *United States* under Captain John Barry. They cruised through the West Indies protecting American merchantmen and hunting down French privateers. Employing a ruse, both vessels flew the French tricolor and encountered a 50-gun ship of war also flying the French flag. They nearly came to blows before they could discover the true identity of the stranger, a British ship of war. This incident led to the adoption of a system of private signals whereby British and American vessels might recognize each other and thus avoid future mistakes. When *Delaware* returned to New Castle on September 23 she brought back as prizes the sixteen-gun French privateer *Sans Pareil* and the fourteen-gun privateer *La Jaloux*. She shared these victories with the *United States*. After some two months of fruitless patrolling in the West Indies the ships returned to New Castle. Decatur, in his instructions of December 1798, reported, "we have nothing to dread but inactivity; the French can have no force in the West Indies this winter equal to ours."[18] *Delaware* again set sail from New Castle on December 15 to convoy some ships between Cuba and the Straits of Florida. On February 6, 1799, she had a brush with the 44-gun French warship *Solebay* but escaped without damage to any of the ships in the convoy. She rendezvoused with the U.S. Revenue cutters *Governor Jay* and *General Green* convoying five smaller ships on February 8.[19]

In March *Delaware* captured the 10-gun privateer *Marsouin* off Moro Castle, Cuba. In April she convoyed her sixth merchant fleet of 142 ships into Havana, independent of those she had safely brought into that port. The merchants of that city gave a testimonial on May 6 to Captain Decatur and his crew for this signal accomplishment. It was a farewell address on the importance of his service and expressed their warm and grateful thanks for his protection of trade. Decatur returned to Fort Mifflin on May 20, 1799, and was transferred to a larger ship, the *United States*. His replacement was Captain Thomas Baker. Baker sailed *Delaware* from New Castle in July and, joining the Revenue Cutter *Eagle*, captured the French sloop *Reynard* on September 9. The *Delaware* joined the little squadron under Captain Thomas Tingey on Guadalupe Station on 18 September 1799. Command of the squadron was soon passed to Captain Richard V. Morris onboard the frigate *Adams*.[20] On October 15 *Delaware* was ordered to the Dutch Island of Curacao to protect American citizens and property from local "unprincipled men" who had given succor to the French privateers. On October 29 she chased the French brig *L'Ocean*, of ten guns

Captain Stephen Decatur, Sr., USN (1752–1808), commander of the second U.S. Navy *Delaware* (NH 50530, Naval History and Heritage Command).

USS *Delaware* (1795–1801) capturing the French Privateer *La Croyable* off Egg Harbor, New Jersey, on July 7, 1798, the first victory for the new U.S. Navy. From a punch bowl in the possession of Mr. Stephen Decatur of Kittery, Maine, in 1934 (NH 2084-A, Naval History and Heritage Command).

and seventy men, for seven hours, finally capturing her and setting free thirty American prisoners found onboard. She was taken into St. Kitts as a prize.

In November the crew was stricken with a fever that killed many men and incapacitated most of the others. She was forced to tie up in Curacao until January 23, 1800. That spring *Delaware* convoyed six ships from Curacao to New Castle, arriving on July 17. Captain Baker, still ill from the fever, was replaced by Master Commandant John A. Spotswood, who took her on more convoy duty to Havana. By March 20, 1801, the troubles with France were at an end. The *Delaware* was ordered to Norfolk, where her guns and stores were taken ashore. She was sold in Baltimore later that year for $23,799.23.[21] Of all the *Delaware* vessels this second naval ship may have had the best combat record in terms of individual ship actions with an overall record of six victories and no losses.

American naval losses may have been light, but the French had successfully seized many American merchant ships by the war's end in 1800. By the autumn of 1800 the United States Navy and the Royal Navy, combined with a more conciliatory diplomatic stance by the government of First Consul Napoleon Bonaparte, had reduced the activity of the French privateers and warships. The Convention of 1800, also known as the Treaty of Mortefontaine, signed on 30 September, ended the Franco-American Quasi-War. It ended the alliance of 1778 between the United States and France but made provisions to reestablish trade and avoid further conflict. Depredations on American shipping continued, however, until the end of the Napoleonic Wars in 1815.

Preparation for WAR to Defend Commerce, the Swedish Church Southwark, with the Building of the FRIGATE "PHILADELPHIA." **Captained by Stephen Decatur, Sr., and commissioned April 5, 1800 (2002718892, Library of Congress).**

Philadelphia Navy Yard

The original United States Navy yard and naval ship-building facility was the Philadelphia Navy Yard. It had evolved from an informal private craft organization rented by the government. Established in 1801, it was situated on seventeen acres in the Southwark District of the city along the Delaware River at the foot of present-day Federal Street.[22] Purchased by the government for $37,000, the site that Humphreys chose included his old shipyard. The tract at the foot of Federal Street, just south of Prime Street (Washington Avenue), was the first location of the Philadelphia Navy Yard, the first naval shipyard of the United States, and the foremost building and outfitting plant of the U.S. Navy Department for 75 years. An irregular rectangle in shape, it was enclosed by a high brick wall. Major buildings included barracks, a mould loft, machine shops, and two towering, gable-roofed ship houses that were the most eye-catching structures on Philadelphia's riverfront for decades. The *Philadelphia* was built at this location before the navy took over. Humphreys became the first naval constructor and was followed in that position by his son Samuel.

This location had advantages and disadvantages. It was a freshwater port nearly one hundred miles from the sea, making it more defensible. However, that same water frequently froze in winter and was subject to various shifting channels, shoals, bars, and strong currents. New York, Boston, Norfolk, and Charleston were far more accessible. Nevertheless, Philadelphia was the most important commercial center of its time. The Philadelphia Navy Yard would continue to operate until it finally closed in 1996.

As the navy grew and began commissioning more officers, many patriotic young men sought appointments as midshipman. The officers commissioned from merchant service and midshipmen appointed in 1799 and 1800 would go on to be the heroes of the War of 1812. Among the many midshipmen appointed in 1800 were two sailors of destiny from Delaware, Thomas Macdonough and Jacob Jones.

Captain Thomas Macdonough, USN (1783–1825), "The Hero of Lake Champlain." Portrait in oils, by an unknown artist (Catalog #: 80-G-K-22707, National Archives).

Thomas Macdonough

Thomas Macdonough was born on a farm near Trappe, New Castle County, to a former officer in the Continental Army as the second son of ten children who were eventually orphaned. While Thomas's sisters ran the homestead, his older brother James was appointed to the navy as a midshipman and Thomas was working as a clerk in Middletown supporting the family. James was serving with Captain Thomas Truxton on the *Constellation* patrolling the West Indies when on February 9, 1799, during the Quasi War with France, he spotted a ship flying American colors and proceeded in order to identify the vessel and perhaps escort her. After signaling and getting no answer, he moved close in and the ship took down the American colors, put up the French ensign, and fired. The ship was the French navy frigate *L'Insurgente*.[23] In the ensuing hour-and-a-half battle, *Constellation* inflicted heavy damage and casualties on *L'Insurgente* and suffered very light casualties. This was first victory of a U.S. Navy ship over a foreign naval warship. One of the few casualties was Delawarean James Macdonough, whose foot was wounded so gravely that his leg had to be amputated. James was released from the navy, and when he returned home, his brother Thomas, at 16, was about the right age to become a midshipman. Through the efforts of Delaware's Senator Thomas, the young man received an appointment as a midshipman in 1800. Thomas Macdonough first went to sea upon the *Ganges* serving in the West Indies. During his period of patrolling and escorting, the *Ganges* discovered two American ships, *Prudent* and *Phoebe*, carrying slaves from Guinea off the coast of Cuba with 134 African survivors on board.

Although the slave trade had not been totally banned in the United States, American ships were forbidden to be involved in it and American sailors were forbidden to sail on foreign slave ships. The vessels were brought back to Philadelphia for adjudication in federal court by Judge Richard Peters for violation of the 1794 Slave Trade Act. This early and little-discussed federal law, passed by Congress while in Philadelphia, prohibited American vessels from participating in the slave trade. Judge Peters, who was sympathetic to the abolitionist cause, placed the Africans under the supervision and care of the Pennsylvania Abolition Society (PAS). The Africans were given the surname Ganges and indentured throughout the Greater Philadelphia region. Later becoming free. These indentures, among the PAS Papers at the Historical Society of Pennsylvania, give us a closer look at the enslaved Africans' stories.[24]

Jacob Jones

Jacob Jones was an orphan but had a quite different life. He had been orphaned at four years of age when his father died. His father's second wife, Penelope Holt Coward, was the granddaughter of Ryves Holt, a prominent Lewes resident in the colonial period. She took Jacob to the family home in Lewes, where he lived from ages 4 to 16 during the Revolution. Clearly, a young boy would have been interested and perhaps inspired to become a navy man by all the naval activity off Lewes during that period. Later he went to Dover to be apprenticed to a prominent doctor and took medical courses at the University of Pennsylvania. He married into the doctor's family and started a practice. Soon he was well connected among the political elite and when his practice was not flourishing he was appointed clerk of the Delaware Supreme Court.[25] Unfortunately, in 1799, Jones's wife died, and he then made a hasty second marriage. However, he gave up his new wife, his infant son, his successful profession, and his political connections in Dover and at the advanced age of 31 sought an appointment as a midshipman in the navy. He had his first service under Captain John Barry on the *United States* along with the young midshipman Stephen Decatur.[26]

Captain Jacob Jones, USN, crayon portrait by Albert Rosenthal, 1918, after a painting by Rembrandt Peale. The artist presented this portrait to USS *Jacob Jones* (Destroyer #130) (NH 48739, U.S. Naval History and Heritage Command).

By 1801, to prevent a second disarmament of the navy, the outgoing Federalist administration rushed through Congress an act authorizing a peacetime navy for the first time that limited the navy to six active frigates and seven other vessels "in ordinary." These included the subscription frigates

Philadelphia and *Essex*, as well as 45 officers and 150 midshipmen, including Jacob Jones and Thomas Macdonough. The remainder of the ships in service were sold and the dismissed officers were given four months' pay. Incoming President Jefferson was lucky he hadn't abolished the navy, because he soon needed it.[27] Two Pennsylvanians of note were to also play important roles in the fledgling United States Navy.

David Porter

David Porter was born in Boston, Massachusetts, but made his adult home in Chester, Pennsylvania, when he was not on active sea service. As a youthful merchant sailor he was taken by a press crew onboard a British vessel but later managed an escape on a Danish merchantman.[28] He served in the Quasi-War with France as a midshipman aboard the USS *Constellation*, participating in the capture of *L'Insurgente* on February 9, 1799. As a lieutenant he served as second in command of the schooner USS *Experiment* during the action of January 1, 1800, in which he got shot in his arm. Porter later served in command of the armed tender USS *Amphitheatre*.[29]

David Porter, Commodore, United States Navy. Born in 1780 (died 1843), he served as commander of the gunboat *Essex*, which drove Spanish pirates from the Spanish Main (NH 117, Naval History and Heritage Command).

During the First Barbary War Porter was first lieutenant of *Enterprise*, *New York*, and *Philadelphia*. He was taken prisoner when the *Philadelphia* ran aground in Tripoli Harbor on October 31, 1803. After his release on June 3, 1805, he remained in the Mediterranean as acting captain of USS *Enterprise* and later captain of *Enterprise*. He was promoted to master commandant on April 22, 1806, and was in charge of the naval forces at New Orleans from 1808 to 1810.[30]

William Jones

William Jones was born in Philadelphia in 1760 and died in Bethlehem, Pennsylvania, on September 5, 1831. Apprenticed in a shipyard, he joined a volunteer company at the age of 16 and was present at the battles of Trenton and Princeton. Afterward he entered the Continental naval service and served gallantly as a privateer under Commodore Truxtun on the James River when that officer encountered and beat off a British ship of superior force. As a sailor, Jones was twice wounded and twice captured by the British.[31] He then entered the merchant service, but during 1790–1793 he lived in Charleston, South Carolina. He returned to Philadelphia in the latter year, and was elected to Congress as a Democrat, serving one term (1801–3). Jones played an active role in precipitating the war against England and served as secretary of the navy from January 12, 1813, to December 7, 1814. Afterward he served as president of the U.S. Bank and collector of the port of Philadelphia. He was a member of the American Philosophical Society and published "Winter Navigation on the Delaware."[32]

The Barbary War

The problems with the Barbary States had never gone away, and on May 10, 1801, the pasha of Tripoli declared war on the United States by chopping down the flag in front of the American embassy, initiating the First Barbary War. The American colonies had previously depended upon Britain, as they were subjects of the Crown, to keep the Barbary pirates in line. However, Britain was now at war with France. Britain's merchant ships were scarce and well protected, and there were plenty of warships in the Mediterranean. So the pirates focused their attentions upon United States shipping. The newly elected president, Thomas Jefferson, found that a sizable portion of the United States budget was spent on tribute and ransom to Barbary pirates in cities in what are today Libya, Tunisia, and Algeria. Jefferson refused to pay, and war was the result.[33]

President Thomas Jefferson and his Republican party opposed a strong navy, arguing that small gunboats in the major harbors were all the nation needed to defend itself. These had proved of limited value in wartime. Jefferson sent a small squadron to the Mediterranean. During the summer, the schooner *Enterprise* encountered the pasha's cruiser *Tripoli*, of about equal strength, near Malta. The *Tripoli* crew favored boarding tactics but their attempts were fended off by the *Enterprise* through superior ship handling and marksmanship, resulting in *Tripoli*'s surrender with half of her crew of 80 either dead or wounded.[34] Jefferson then sent a second, more powerful squadron with five frigates in 1802 with restrictive orders. They captured one pirate cruiser and destroyed another and mounted a naval blockade of Tripoli. However, the result was ineffective due to the shallow waters near the harbor and the deep drafts of the frigates. Two years of expensive effort had yielded very disappointing results. Delawareans Jacob Jones and Thomas Macdonough served in those initial naval squadrons.

William Jones Portrait by Gilbert Stuart (courtesy Navy Art Collection, Washington, D.C., NH 54764-KN, U.S. Naval History and Heritage Command Photograph).

A third squadron under Edward Preble was deployed in 1803 that included five shallow draft brigs and schooners backed by two frigates: *Philadelphia* and *Constitution*. *Philadelphia* was under Captain William Bainbridge, and both Jones and Macdonough were aboard. Jones was older, had served with Commodore Barry, and had been promoted and was the second lieutenant, with David Porter as first lieutenant. Macdonough was still a midshipman.[35]

The USS Philadelphia

USS *Philadelphia*, a 1240-ton, 36-gun sailing frigate, was the second vessel of the United States navy to be named for the city of Philadelphia. Originally named *City of Philadelphia*, she was built during 1798–1799 for the United States government by the citizens of that city. Funding for her construction was the result of a drive that raised $100,000 in one week, in June 1798. She was designed by Josiah Fox and built by Samuel Humphries, Nathaniel Hutton, and John Delavue. Her carved work was done by William Rush of Philadelphia. She was laid down about November 14, 1798, launched on November 28, 1799, and commissioned on April 5, 1800, with Captain Stephen Decatur, Sr., in command. Upon arriving in the Mediterranean Sea, *Philadelphia*, now led by Captain William Bainbridge, had captured a Tunisian ship *Mirboka* on August 26. Midshipman Macdonough was put aboard with a prize crew to take it into Gibraltar.[36]

Preble sent *Philadelphia* and *Vixen* ahead to begin another blockade of Tripoli. Unfortunately, while chasing a quarry in October *Philadelphia* ran aground on a reef and was captured by the Tripolitans. Captain Bainbridge and his crew including Jacob Jones were taken into harsh captivity for twenty months enduring poor living conditions and food. Despite these privations, Lieutenants Porter and Jones continued to carry out their responsibilities as leaders and educators of the ten midshipmen. They organized a school and continued the midshipmen's education in the required professional naval topics of mathematics, navigation, and tactics. Obtaining books from the Danish consul, they also conducted instruction in cultural topics and foreign languages. Meanwhile, Commodore Preble commissioned Lieutenant Stephen Decatur to put together a plan and group of men to sail into Tripoli harbor and burn the *Philadelphia*, which the Tripolitans had refloated and moved into the harbor to repair her for the use of their Navy.[37]

On February 16, 1804, Decatur took a small captured Tripolitan ketch, *Mastico*, renamed it *Intrepid* and, with 80 men including Thomas Macdonough and a Maltese Arabic-speaking pilot, sailed into Tripoli Harbor as a

Commodore Stephen Decatur (NH 52802, Naval History and Heritage Command).

damaged Maltese vessel seeking assistance. They got permission from the Tunisians on board *Philadelphia* to tie up overnight alongside.[38] In a conspicuous act of valor, the American volunteers boarded the *Philadelphia* on February 16, 1804, and were met by a group of Barbary pirates guarding their prize. A furious battle ensued, and during the bloody chaos of hand-to-hand combat a pirate made ready to end the life of Lieutenant Decatur. Reuben James, with both of his hands already wounded, in an act of selfless courage threw his hand before the cleaving blade. Willing to give his life in defense of his captain, James took the blow from the scimitar.[39] This courageous intervention allowed Decatur to retrieve his pistol and slay his assailant—and before the Tripolitan guards were aware, the Americans had boarded the *Philadelphia* and overwhelmed the guards, some 20 of whom were cut down and the rest leaping overboard. Both Decatur and Macdonough had served on her and now directed the lighting of fires strategically throughout the ship, which was soon ablaze. Decatur was the last off. The men barely made it back to their vessel before the *Philadelphia* exploded and had just cleared the harbor as shore batteries got their range. Horatio Nelson called it the most bold and daring act of the age.[40]

The following summer Preble's squadron, in league with gunboats from the king of Naples, bombarded Tripoli Harbor. Decatur led two groups of six gunboats each. They were opposed by Tripolitan gunboats and the battle became hand-to-hand combat. Macdonough was at Decatur's side throughout. The Americans took three of the nine gunboats sent out to oppose them.[41] Jonathan Meredith of Bucks County saved the life of Lieutenant John Trippe, of the USS *Vixen*, who with a party of nine men had boarded a Tripolitan ship on August 3, 1805, within the harbor of Tripoli. Heavily outnumbered,

Burning of the USS *Philadelphia* by Lieutenant Stephen Decatur, February 16, 1804. The captured Mediterranean ketch *Intrepid* entered the harbor in company with *Siren*, ably setting fire to Philadelphia and destroying the city completely (NH 56736, Naval History and Heritage Command).

the boarding party fought a fierce hand-to-hand combat in which Trippe was severely wounded; Meredith protected him from what would have been the final blow. Four days later Meredith was killed in the explosion of Gunboat No. 3 during a similar attack against the Tripolitans.[42] The war was soon over when Lieutenant Presley Neville O'Bannon and his 40 Marines reached the "shores of Tripoli" and, supported by the navy offshore, threatened to install the pasha's brother as ruler. A ransom of $60,000 was paid to release the American prisoners who had been on the *Philadelphia*.[43]

Subsequently the navy was greatly reduced once again for reasons of economy, and, instead of regular ships, many gunboats and galleys were built that were intended to enforce the various coastal embargoes of Jefferson and Madison. Of the 172 built, 20 were stationed in Philadelphia and 4 at New Castle. This strategic policy proved unsound within a decade.[44] During this period, Thomas Macdonough was sent to Middletown, Connecticut, to oversee the building of gunboats. It was here that he met his wife. About the same time, Jacob Jones returned home and was sent to Portland, Maine, to take command of a bomb ketch and escort two gunboats to New Orleans. He was given command of the brig *Argus*. He also had the honor of delivering to Commodore Preble the gold medal Congress had awarded to him for his victories leading to the resolution of the war with Tripoli.[45]

Meanwhile, the sloop *Wasp* was being converted to a sloop of war, her two masts increased to three. She was armed with eighteen guns: sixteen 32-pound carronades and two 24 long guns, crewed by 137 men. In 1810 Jones was promoted to master commandant and given command of the *Wasp*. She operated off the United States coast but was taken on a diplomatic mission to France and was in France when war broke out with Great Britain. Jones put on all sail to get back to American waters.[46]

The War of 1812

In 1812 Great Britain was at war with Napoleon's France and his conquered allies, which included most of Europe. The United States was neutral and was trying to conduct a profitable trade with both sides. To fight the war in the Baltic, Atlantic, and Mediterranean seas, the British needed a huge navy of over 500 ships. To augment their crews they were operating press gangs at home and stopping U.S. ships to impress U.S. sailors. The Royal Navy had continued to illegally press American sailors into the Royal Navy, an estimated 10,000 sailors between 1799 and 1812.[47]

On June 27, 1807, the United States was humiliated when the U.S. Navy 38-gun frigate *Chesapeake* commanded by James Barron was en route to the Mediterranean via the Virginia Capes. She was approached by the HMS *Leopard*, which ordered her to halt so she could be searched for Royal Navy deserters. When Barron refused, the *Leopard* opened fire on the unprepared *Chesapeake*, killing three Americans, wounding 18, and forcing her to strike her colors.[48] The people of Wilmington assembled on July 4 and adopted the following resolution: "Resolved that we view with the strongest sentiments of indignation and abhorrence the late unprovoked lawless and ferocious attack made by the British ship of war Leopard upon the frigate Chesapeake and the daring insult offered thereby to the flag, the government, and the people of the United States."[49] The citizens of Lewistown also held a meeting and resolved "to resort to hostile measures against Great Britain for the attainment of justice."[50] Pacifist President Jefferson tried to

Action between USS *Chesapeake* and HMS *Leopard*, June 22, 1807. Sketch by Fred S. Cozzens, copied from his 1897 book, *Our Navy: Its Growth and Achievements*. It depicts *Leopard*, at right, firing on *Chesapeake* to enforce a demand that she submit to a search of her crew for British Navy deserters (NH 74526, U.S. Naval History and Heritage Command).

stem the war tide with an embargo on exports. This brought on economic depression that especially impacted the mercantile northern states. When restrictions were loosened, impressments at sea once again resumed. When Madison assumed office in 1809 western and southern "war hawks" urged an invasion of Canada.[51]

The two belligerents in the Napoleonic wars took nearly 1,500 ships between 1803 and 1812. America was being whipsawed between the two great powers. Its economy suffered as a result, and American maritime freedom was at stake. In June 1812 President Madison declared war on Britain. In his speech to Congress he cited two principle reasons, British interference with U.S. neutral trade and the impressment of U.S. sailors.[52] The war was about defending free trade and sailors' rights. Nevertheless, the strategy was not to fight a naval war. At the outbreak of the war, the U.S. Navy had only nine frigates and eight smaller ships (four sloops and four ketches) and 170 gunboats. Madison's strategy was to invade Canada to protect the Northwest Territories from the incursions of the Indian alliance and to take territory in eastern Canada and trade land for peace. He intended to keep the navy in port to defend the coast and depend on privateers to harass British shipping and keep the British navy distracted. But the U.S. Navy wasn't playing. The navy captains either got to sea before getting orders or interpreted their orders broadly. In wartime, the Revenue Marine was placed under the command of the United States Navy. The U.S. Revenue cutter *Jefferson* made the first American capture of an enemy ship in the war, the brig *Patriot*, in June 1812.[53]

William Jones of Philadelphia was appointed as secretary of the navy in January 1813. Jones issued a stream of orders and correspondence that addressed such basic management issues as personnel and shipbuilding. His authoritative tone provoked some senior naval officers who felt that Jones's new regulations compromised their authority as captains. Jones persevered, formalizing such administrative matters as transfers, promotions, officers' complaints, and the redeployment of the ineffective gunboat fleet created by Jefferson. Jones established a correspondence system that adhered to the chain of command, enjoining, for example, junior officers from writing directly to the secretary. On the matter of ship construction he brought his management skills to bear, establishing uniformity in design, effective control of construction and maintenance costs, and oversight of the recruitment and retention of skilled shipyard workers.[54] Jones's methods might today be termed micromanagement, but they brought positive results. While he was secretary, the government-owned yards constructed the first U.S. ships of the line, several heavy frigates, and a number of sloops of war designed for commerce raiding. In addition, the government contracted local yards to build the ships on-site that later carried the day for the navy at the Battles of Lake Erie and Lake Champlain.[55]

Jones's administrative innovations were a big step toward establishing a functional department, but his most significant wartime efforts focused on America's naval strategy. "His primary energies had to be devoted to the immediate business of fighting," wrote naval historian Christopher McKee in his 1991 book, *A Gentlemanly and Honorable Profession*. The strategic naval situation facing the United States at the beginning of the War of 1812 was challenging. The Royal Navy had deployed more than 100 warships on the North American Station, including 11 ships of the line and 33 frigates. Opposing the British, the U.S. flotilla comprised 16 ships, none larger than a frigate, and many in need of repairs.[56]

That imbalance of the opposing forces made clear the need for a naval strategy of asymmetrical warfare. Fortunately for Jones, Madison and most of the navy's captains were already agreed on the essentials of a realistic strategy: Attack the British sea lines of communication with single ships while establishing and controlling the lines of communication on the Great Lakes and Lake Champlain. Commodore Stephen Decatur articulated the first element of that strategy in a letter to Jones's predecessor, Paul Hamilton: "[The] best use of the Navy would be to send single ships out with [a] large store of provisions so that they can cruise at a distance from the United States, and no more than two frigates together."[57] Jones himself spelled out the second element of the naval strategy to Commodore Isaac Chauncey, senior naval commander in the Great Lakes region: "It is impossible to attach too much importance to our naval operations on the lakes—the success of the ensuing [land] campaign will depend absolutely on our superiority on all the lakes—and every effort and resource must be directed to that object."[58]

Jones's primary achievement in the strategic area was, however, in applying the strategy dictated by the president, and doing so with consistency and clarity. That letter was part of Jones's effort to get Chauncey to take offensive action and also to support the army's offensive actions, as he was not doing so. He was building ships and would not hazard them to take on the British. In a February 1813 letter to the commanders of navy ships then refitting Jones wrote the following:

> Our great inferiority in naval strength does not permit us to meet them on this ground [in squadron action] without hazarding the germ of our national glory. We have, however, the means of creating a powerful diversion and of turning the scale of annoyance against the enemy. It is therefore intended

to dispatch all our public ships now in port as soon as possible in such positions as may be best adapted to destroy the commerce of the enemy from the Cape of Good Hope to Cape Clear and continue out as long as the means of subsistence can be procured abroad in any quarter. If anything can draw the attention of the enemy from the annoyance of our coast to the protection of his own rich and exposed commercial fleets, it will be a course of this nature.[59]

In prosecuting this element of the U.S. naval strategy, Jones's merchant marine experience was a plus, as he was able to advise his captains on the best locations at which to intercept British merchant ships. The most significant outcome of commerce raiding by U.S. Navy ships—in combination with hundreds of American privateers—was the capture of thousands of British merchantmen during the war and the ensuing pressure from those in Britain whose livelihoods were based on ocean commerce (as well as their insurers) to end the war with the United States. The result was a softening of the British bargaining position at the peace negotiations in Ghent (in present-day Belgium) that began in August 1814.

The astonishing victories of the U.S. Navy in single-ship actions—including those between the USS *Constitution* and the HMS *Guerriere* in August 1812, the USS *United States* and the HMS *Macedonian* that October, and the USS *Constitution* and the HMS *Java* in December—were a most welcome byproduct of commerce raiding. But if the American public focused on the dramatic one-on-one victories, Jones kept those unexpected combat successes in perspective. "I like these little events," he wrote to Madison at one point. "They keep alive the national feeling and produce an effect infinitely beyond their intrinsic importance."[60] It is clear Jones well understood the broader naval strategy, while recognizing the importance of civilian morale during war. These early victories raised the morale and spirits of the American public and kept New England committed to the war when the land battles in the north were not going well. These sea battles proved

USS *Constitution* and *Java*, 1812 (NH 118616, Naval History and Heritage Command).

that Britannia did not rule the waves. Hearing of these defeats, the British public and press were shocked, Parliament was dismayed, and the Admiralty was full of excuses, which were valid to a point. Four of the victories were of American frigates over British frigates. American frigates were newer, better designed, faster, and more heavily armed.[61]

Jones's policies contributed greatly to American success on the Great Lakes and to a strategy of coastal defense and commerce raiding on the high seas. In late 1814, near the end of his term, he made recommendations on the reorganization of the Navy Department. These led to the establishment of the Board of Commissioners system, which operated from 1815 until 1842.[62] Although Jones has gone largely unrecognized for his exceptional service as secretary of the navy during the War of 1812, it is clear upon examination of his record that he played a critical role. Neither a strategist nor a charismatic leader, he nonetheless forged the essential link between Madison's strategy and the naval means of executing that strategy. His management skills provided a conduit between Madison's policies and the courage and skill of the U.S. Navy's increasingly professional leaders. Thus, he was the enabler for such successful naval officers as Isaac Hull, James Lawrence, Bainbridge, Decatur, Perry, and Macdonough. Moreover, he did far more than help bring the war to a more satisfactory conclusion for the United States. By his actions in organizing the office of the secretary of the navy, he strengthened the concept of civilian control of the military that remained, for the United States, a work in progress during the conflict.[63]

The first victory to shock the English was the USS *Essex*. With the outbreak of the War of 1812, David Porter was promoted to captain on July 2, 1812, and was assigned as commander of the *Essex*. He sailed out of New York Harbor with a banner—"Free trade and sailors' rights"—flying from the foretopgallant mast, providing a catchphrase that became popular during the war. Captain Porter achieved fame by capturing the first British warship of the conflict, HMS *Alert*, on August 13, 1812, as well as several merchantmen.[64] In February 1813, on his own initiative, he sailed the *Essex* around Cape Horn and cruised the Pacific making war on British whalers. His first action in the Pacific was the capture of the Peruvian vessel *Nereyda* and the releases of the captured American whalers onboard. Over the next year, Porter would capture 12 whaleships and 360 prisoners. In June 1813 he released his prisoners on the condition that they not fight against the United States until they were formally exchanged for American prisoners of war. His usual tactic was to raise British colors to allay the British captain's suspicions, then once invited on board he would reveal his true allegiance and purpose.[65]

Porter and his fleet spent October through December 1813 resting and refitting in the Marquesas Islands. In the meantime, word of his depredations in the Pacific had gotten to London, and the Admiralty responded with immediate action, sending a squadron led by Captain James Hillyer in pursuit. Porter was serving as a commerce raider and would have reasonably been excused for evading his stronger foe, but he chose to meet his adversary instead. On March 28, 1814, Porter was forced to surrender to Captain Hillyar off Valparaiso after an engagement that became known as the Battle of Valparaiso in neutral waters with the British frigate HMS *Phoebe* and the sloop HMS *Cherub*, when his ship became too disabled to offer any resistance.[66]

Among the finest American designs was the *Constitution*. In a sharp half-hour battle on August 19 Captain Issac Hull in the frigate *Constitution* destroyed the Royal Navy frigate *Guerierre*. The *Guerriere*'s crew were most dismayed to see their cannonballs bouncing off the *Constitution*'s unusually strong live-oak hull, giving her the enduring

The Victory. Battle between the U.S. frigate *Essex* and HMS *Phoebe* and HMS *Cherub*, March 28, 1814, off Valparaiso, Chile. Drawn by Captain David Porter, USN, and engraved by W. Strickland. From the journal of a cruise made to the Pacific Ocean in the USS *Essex*, 1812–1814 (NH 2047, U.S. Naval History and Heritage Command).

nickname of "Old Ironsides." To end the battle, as was common in those days, Marine lieutenant William Sharp Bush of Wilmington (son of Captain John Bush and nephew of Major Lewis Bush, who fell at the battle of the Brandywine) led the boarding party. Unfortunately, just as he did, *Guerierre* fired its last desperate broadside. Bush was killed by a musket shot to his face, the first Marine Corps officer to be killed in combat. He was posthumously awarded a silver medal by Congress in 1835.[67]

In a battle of equals, Delawarean Jacob Jones, commanding the *Wasp* and sailing from New Castle, encountered a heavy storm, suffered damage to sail and lost a man overboard. Rather than return to port, the crew jury-rigged the sail. On October 17 Jones sighted a convoy of six ships. He closed and could tell there were six well-armed merchant ships escorted by a sloop of war, the *Frolic*. This flotilla had also been damaged in the storm. *Frolic* dropped back to hold off *Wasp* so the merchantmen could escape. Jones continued to close, and as *Frolic* approached she hauled ship to gain wind and the battle started when ships were running parallel about 60 yards apart. *Frolic* got off the first shots, doing some damage to the *Wasp*'s topmost sails.[68]

The ships continued to exchange broadsides in rough seas. The *Wasp*'s maneuvers were better executed, timed to fire when *Frolic* was on the upswell. *Wasp* hit the *Frolic* hull and deck. *Frolic* fired at the same time and hit the *Wasp* sails. *Wasp* moved ahead of *Frolic* and turned to cross the bow and rake her down her hull. *Frolic*'s bowsprit caught between *Wasp*'s forward sails and the two ships were locked together. *Wasp*'s first lieutenant, James Biddle, led a boarding party of sailors and marines to capture *Frolic*. Biddle found the captain and every officer wounded, 30 men killed and 50 injured. They had no choice but to surrender After 43 minutes, the battle was over. The *Wasp* had suffered five killed and five wounded.[69]

Three. Maintaining American Sovereignty and Independence

The capture of the sloop of war *Frolic* by the sloop of war *Wasp*, Captain Jacob Jones on October 18, 1812, "[a]fter a close Action of 43 Minutes. Soon after the Frolic Surrendered both her Masts went by the Board. She had six Merchant's Ships under her Convoy." Aquatint in colors, "Drawn & Engraved by F. Kearny, from a Sketch by Lieut. Claxton, of the Wasp" (NH 43040, U.S. Naval History and Heritage Command).

The battle over, Jones set out to repair both ships to take back to the Delaware Capes. *Wasp*'s rigging was badly damaged, with the main topmast, mizzen topgallant mast, and gaff being shot away, and almost every brace severed, making the ship unmanageable. The *Frolic* was even more heavily damaged. Both vessels were incapable of being handled. Jones received the battle flag of the *Frolic*, and it is now at the U.S. Naval Academy. Unfortunately, the 74-gun ship of line HMS *Poictiers* arrived on scene and took *Wasp* captive. *Poictiers* took *Frolic* in tow and had *Wasp* and its officers and men sail to Bermuda. *Wasp* was repaired and taken into the Royal Navy. Soon the *Wasp*'s officers were exchanged and they returned to New York as heroes. Congress presented Jones with a gold medal, promoted him to captain, and awarded him command of the *Macedonian*. Congress uncharacteristically gave *Wasp* $25,000 as prize money for *Frolic*, as if she had brought it home.[70] A commemorative written at the time was on the lips of singers at taverns ashore:

> The foe bravely fought, but his arms were all broken,
> And he fled from his death-wound aghast and affrighted;
> But the Wasp darted forward her death-doing sting,
> And full on his bosom, like lightning alighted.
> She pierced through his entrails, she maddened his brain'
> And he writhed and he groan'd as if torn with the colic;
> And long shall John Bull rue the terrible day
> He met the American Wasp on a Frolic.[71]

In February 1813 a large banquet and celebration was held in New York to honor Hull, Decatur, and Jones. New York and Philadelphia presented Jones with engraved swords. Delaware gave him an engraved silver plate. The Delaware legislature also had his portrait painted by Thomas Sully and placed it in the state house, where it remains today. Jones continued his naval career and died at the age of 82 in Philadelphia at the Naval Home. He was interred in Wilmington with great pomp and circumstance.[72]

On October 25 the *United States*, commanded by Stephen Decatur, captured HMS *Macedonian*. After the battle *Macedonian* was entered into American service, retaining its name, under Jacob Jones, commanding. [73] On December 20, off the coast of Brazil, the *Constitution* defeated HMS *Java*, which was burned after the Americans determined she could not be salvaged.[74]

Privateers

When war was declared privateers began to appear to prey upon British commerce. Soon Delaware waters swarmed with these "skimmers of the sea" based in Wilmington and Philadelphia. On July 4 three privateers lying in the Delaware were fitted out and fired salutes; they were *Atlas,* Captain David Maffett, *Spencer,* Captain Morse, and *Matilda,* Captain Noah Allen. *Matilda* sailed on July 7 under Captain Taylor, but she had barely proceeded when mutiny broke out and forty of her crew were sent to New Castle jail. Captain Allen then assumed command and proceeded on a successful voyage on which he captured the British ship *Goellet,* the privateer *Ranger,* and the schooners *Jingle, Margery,* and *Woodburn*.[75] On August 14 the British ship *Mary Ann* was brought to Cape May as the prize of the American privateer *Paul Jones*. By the end of the year American warships and privateers had taken 319 British ships worth over $12 million.[76]

In September 1812 Sir James Yeo, commander of the British frigate *Southhampton*, having heard that Captain David Porter of the Essex had maltreated a British seaman aboard his ship, sent the following challenge, published in a Philadelphia newspaper: "Sir James Yeo presents his compliments to Captain Porter, commander of the American frigate Essex and would be glad to have a tete-a-tete anywhere between the capes of Delaware and Havana where he would have the pleasure to break his own sword over his damned head, and put him forward in Irons."[77] Captain Porter replied the same day, accepting the rendezvous near the Delaware, where he would be recognized by the flag bearing the motto "Free trade and sailors' rights," which if struck, he said, "would deserve the treatment promised by Sir James." Sir James did not further respond, however.[78]

Lewes Bombarded

By 1813 the war with Napoleon was over. After the British navy's early defeats in American waters it was able to put hundreds of ships off the U.S. coast, blockading U.S. ships in port. Despite their earlier successes, by 1814 many of the U.S. Navy's best ships were blockaded in port and unable to prevent British incursions on land via the sea. Shortly thereafter the *Poictiers*, the *Belvidera*, and several smaller vessels were sent to blockade the Delaware estuary. On March 9 the *Belvidera, Poictiers, LaPaz,* and *Ulysses* took up their stations off Lewes and the Delaware Capes under the command of Commodore John de la Poer Beresford. The British squadron began to conduct raids along the coast along both sides of the Delaware Bay in an effort to disrupt maritime commerce and shipping. Many small actions resulted in numerous vessels being captured and destroyed.[79]

The sloop *Eliza and Mary* from Philadelphia bound for Lewistown was burned near Cedar Creek. A packet from Charleston was run ashore at Town Creek and also burned. The militiamen of Lewistown and Milton managed to save a schooner belonging to Colonel Payner, but the brig *Concord* was boarded by a British midshipman and seven seamen. However, the crew managed to escape up the bay in a heavy fog. The sloop *New Jersey* likewise managed to escape after its capture by *Ulysses*.[80] *Montesquieu* was not so fortunate. Unaware that war had been declared, she was returning from Canton with a cargo valued at one and a half million dollars. Her owner afterwards ransomed the vessel for $180,000.[81] In parallel actions British Admiral Cockburn was raiding in the Chesapeake Bay along the Eastern Shore attacking Havre de Grace, Frenchtown, Fredericktown, and Georgetown, threatening Wilmington trade with Baltimore and lines of communication with the south.

These blockading ships were on station for prolonged periods and needed supplies, food, and water, so they frequently sent landing parties ashore to raid the countryside. On 16 March 1813 Commodore Beresford sent the following letter to Lewes: "Sirs:—As soon as you receive this I must request you send twenty live bullocks with a proportionate quantity of vegetables and hay to the Poictiers for the use of his Britannic Majesty's squadron, now at this anchorage, which shall be immediately, paid for at the Philadelphia prices. If you refuse to comply with this request, I shall be under the necessity of destroying your town. I have the honor to be, Sir, your ob't servant J. P. Beresford, Commodore…."[82] The governor of Delaware responded: "[C]ompliance would be an immediate violation of the laws of my country, and an eternal stigma on the nation of which I am a citizen: a compliance, therefore, cannot be acceded to. I have the honor to be sir, Your most obedient servant, JOSEPH HASLET, Governor of the State of Delaware"[83] In retaliation on April 6 Commodore Beresford and his flotilla fired nearly 800 thirty-two and eighteen-pound shot into the town in addition to shells and congreve rockets. The bombardment lasted 22 hours.[84] Colonel Samuel Boyer Davis commander of the defenders at Lewes, wrote to Governor Haslet: "The attack immediately commenced, and continued till near ten o'clock. The fire from our battery silenced one of their most dangerous gunboats, against which I directed the fire from an eighteen-pounder, for which I request you immediately send me a supply of shot and powder, as it is uncertain how long the bombardment will continue. They have not succeeded with their bombs in reaching the town, and the damages from their thirty-two-pounders and canister cannot be ascertained until daylight. In this affair, you find the honor of the state has not been tarnished."[85] A spectator described the scene from above the town with an open view:

> The British ships were ranged in line of battle; the fire ceased about two o'clock, when he visited the earth works; the weather was threatening, wind easterly. Captain Byron drew off his squadron at four o'clock, a few miles, where he remained until sailing for the capes. About five hundred shots were fired. A collection was made of one hundred and fifty of small sizes and a few bombs. Houses were injured, chimneys cut almost in two, the corner posts, plates, and studs cut off in several houses. The foremast of a schooner was cut away, and another received a shot in her hull. Of two particular rockets thrown, one fell on a lot, another in a marsh. A fire was directed at the breastwork, where more than thirty men were stationed. Shot struck the battery and broke the pine logs. Two shots entered by the guns[86]

Lewes was the first use of Congreve rockets in the war, preceding Baltimore by a year. The British forces moved as far up the bay as Reedy Island, where they captured and burned some shallops and small craft then returned down the bay. Beresford's squadron withdrew to Bermuda, leaving the frigates *Statira*, *Spartan*, and the sloop of war *Martin* commanded by Commodore Stackpole.[87]

The British maintained their blockade through most of the war and continued to threaten the Delaware Coast. On June 20, 1814, the British frigate *Nieman* sent several barges with sixty men into Indian River, burning two or three coasters and shallops loaded with lumber and securing a ransom for two others.[88]

Delaware Flotilla

After his part in the *Wasp* versus *Frolic* victory James Biddle was sent to New Castle to command the four gunboats there. This was to be a temporary assignment. He soon wrote to Secretary of the Navy William Jones that if he had ten gunboats and two block ships he could take on the blockading force. He got permission to build what was commonly called the Delaware Flotilla. Wilmington merchants were writing letters to pressure the navy secretary and raising $30,000 to buy launches. He had built eight, with two more under construction when he was transferred to New York to command the *Hornet*. Biddle was relieved by Samuel Angus. In July the Delaware Flotilla sailed eight gunboats and two block sloops (*Buffalo* and *Camel*) to the south of the Bay at Crow's Shoals to attack the eighteen-gun sloop HMS *Martin*, which had run aground at Cape May.[89]

This came to be called the "Cape May Fiasco." Angus, thinking it "proper to endeavor to bring him [*Martin*] to action," ordered the flotilla, consisting of the block sloops *Buffalo* and *Camel* and eight gunboats, to weigh anchor and stand toward the enemy. Angus lined his ships up to fire on *Martin* but as they did another frigate, *Junon*, about a mile and a half away, started shelling to cover the evacuation and burning of *Martin* by its crew. The Americans, despite being plagued by poor gunpowder, delivered a brisk cannonade of the grounded sloop but did so from too great a distance. Likewise, while most of the enemy's shot missed Angus's ships, one passed through the foot of *Buffalo*'s jib and another through the under part of her bowsprit. Only one other American ship, Gunboat No. 125, suffered any damage in the inconclusive, long-range engagement, although Gunboat No. 121 was captured after straying from the formation in disobedience of Angus's orders. [90]The court of inquiry that met onboard the block sloop *Buffalo* on September 11, 1813, found Angus guilty of an error in judgment but not of any lack of personal bravery. He had shown ample courage at other times in his career, both in the Quasi-War with France and in the War of 1812. The court felt that he might have moved his command closer to the grounded *Martin*, which then might have been at the flotilla's mercy, given her condition.[91]

Three vessels were purchased in September—the sloops *Two Sisters* and *Three Sisters* and the schooner *Ruby*—and the Navy Department detailed Commodore John Rodgers for duty in Delaware Bay. Rodgers supervised the construction of fortifications at Pea Patch Island near Reedy Point. The secretary of the navy offered to appropriate $150,000 for a steam frigate to defend Delaware. It would be similar to *Fulton the First* (also known as *Demologos*), built for New York as a steam-powered floating battery. But sufficient funds could not be raised, and it was never completed.[92] Later the Americans would deploy Robert Fulton's torpedoes, known as "infernals," against British vessels off Lewes. The deployment of these floating mines was a countermeasure used by the Americans to break the stranglehold of the British blockade of the Atlantic Coast.[93]

Naval War on the Border

The Canadian frontier was the real strategic front of the war in 1813. It was Madison's aim to take territory and trade it for concessions from the British. In September 1812 Commodore Isaac Chauncey had been sent from commanding the New York shipyard to the Great Lakes with instructions to command the navy on the lakes, build a naval fleet, and gain control. He was to assist the army in invading Canada. Subordinate to him on Lake Erie was Oliver Hazard Perry, who quickly gained control of that lake. Also subordinate was Master Commandant Thomas Macdonough, who had been ordered to Lake Champlain. Macdonough began building ships but was not ready by the summer of 1813. Repeatedly harassed by British forces on the lake, he suffered setbacks but eventually got some ships built and crews trained. Unfortunately, when he sent two of his sloops, *Eagle* and *Scourge*, north on the lake to scope out the British base they were captured when the wind died. There was nothing unusual about the capture, but when it was over the British found that one of the sailors they had taken prisoner was a woman. In May 1814 Jacob Jones and the crew of *Macedonian* were ordered to Lake Ontario to take over a new ship, the *Mohawk*.[94]

Jacob Jones on Lake Ontario

Commodore Chauncey was a shipbuilder, not a fighter. He and his British counterpart Commodore Yeo got into a shipbuilding race but wouldn't risk their fleets in battle. For the British that was fine, as they were the defenders. For the United States that was not good, as they were supposed to be the attackers. If the United States did not control the lakes they could not invade. The president was so angry he wanted Stephen Decatur to take charge of Ontario but Decatur avoided the job. So Jacob Jones went instead. They arrived in May to find Chauncey ill and reluctant to sail. This gave them time to take command of the newest ship, the frigate *Mohawk*, get trained on it, and sail in July to challenge the British fleet, which retreated to its base. The U.S. controlled the lake over the summer, and the army conducted some operations until winter. It was probably clear to the British that things had changed on Ontario now that a fighting captain was on the lake.[95]

Thomas Macdonough on Lake Champlain

After a summer of limited expeditions, believing they had control of lake, the British decided to invade and attempt to cut the nation in half, separating New England from the Middle Atlantic states just as they had tried and failed to do during the Revolution. General Prevost pushed south on the west side of Lake Champlain to Plattsburg New York, where the New York and Vermont militias set up a defensive line. Stopped temporarily north of town, the British came under shelling from Macdonough's ships and halted. They waited for their stronger fleet to come down the lake and remove Macdonough's forces.[96]

Macdonough used the time well, positioning his forces anchored in Plattsburg Bay so that the southward-moving British fleet had to turn the headland, cross the current, and move north into the wind to attack, all the while in range of Macdonough's guns. He also positioned his flagship anchored so that he could turn it to use both sides for broadsides. The ships were anchored in line from north to south in the order of *Eagle*, *Saratoga*, *Ticonderoga*, and *Preble*, his van and rear protected by shoals. They all had both bow and stern anchors, with "springs" attached to the anchor cables to allow the ships to be slewed through a wide arc. Macdonough also laid out extra kedge anchors from the quarters of his flagship *Saratoga*, which would allow him to spin the ship completely around. The ten American gunboats were anchored in the intervals between the larger vessels. Because there would be no sail handling, the entire crew was available for combat. [97]Macdonough paraphrased and satirized Admiral Lord Nelson by hoisting a message to his fleet: "Impressed seamen call on every man to do his duty."[98]

Each commander enjoyed a different advantage for battle. In the 36-gun full-sized frigate *Confiance* and the 16-gun brig *Linnet* Downie had the strongest major combatants. The British also possessed the advantage of being able to throw the greatest weight of shot and had an advantage in the number of 18- and 24-pound long guns. Macdonough had a strength advantage in smaller ships and in the number of short-range 32-pound carronades plus six 42-pound carronades on the frigate *Saratoga*. Overall, Downie could dominate in a ship-on-ship running engagement whereas Macdonough could dominate in a close-in broadside battle. But Downy considered his flagship *Confiance* equal to Macdonough's entire navy. As fate would have it, of his major ships two were quickly taken out of commission: sloop HMS *Chubb* by the schooner *Ticonderoga* and brig HMS *Linnet* by the sloop *Preble*. This reduced the battle to the brig *Linnet* and *Confiance* versus *Saratoga* because the brig *Eagle* fell out of line and let *Linnet* through. Fortunately, *Ticonderoga* handled *Linnet*. *Ticonderoga* was captained by Philadelphian Stephen Cassin, who had served in the Quasi-War with France. The battle lasted two hours and a half. Macdonough was knocked out twice and lost a fifth of his crew but managed to turn the ship to fire the other guns in a broadside and *Confiance* could not continue to fight. All the British ships were lost.[99]

The surviving British officers boarded *Saratoga* to offer their swords (of surrender) to Macdonough. When he saw the officers, Macdonough replied, "Gentlemen, return your swords to your scabbards, you are worthy of them." Commander Pring and the other surviving British officers later testified that Macdonough showed every consideration to the British wounded and prisoners.[100] McDonough, Captain Henley and Lt. Stephen Cassin were awarded a Congressional Gold Medal, the resolution of which read as follows:

> Resolved, That the President of the United States be requested to cause gold medals to be struck, emblematical of the action between the two squadrons, and to present them to Captain Macdonough and Captain Robert Henley, and also to Lieutenant Stephen Cassin, in such manner as may be most honorable to them; and that the President be further requested to present a silver medal, with suitable emblems and devices, to each of the commissioned officers of the navy and army serving on board, and a sword to each of the midshipmen and sailing masters, who so nobly distinguished themselves in that memorable conflict.[101]

Battle of Lake Champlain—Macdonough's Victory. **September 11, 1814. Engraving after a painting by Chapel showing Commodore Thomas Macdonough directing his men during the action (NH 65737, U.S. Naval History and Heritage Command).**

It was Macdonough's victory on Champlain, concurrent with the successful defense of Baltimore, that convinced the Duke of Wellington not to accept his prime minister's request to go to Canada to lead the army and instead to suggest peace. Jacob Jones's presence on Lake Ontario cemented that victory. These victories denied the British negotiators leverage to demand any territorial claims against the United States. The result was the mutually acknowledged boundary between the United States and Canada that endures today, as well as newfound respect for America among foreign powers. With the end of the Napoleonic wars, impressment became a moot topic, and American pride in their naval victories furthered national unity.

Commodore Macdonough relieved Isaac Hull of command of the Portsmouth Naval Yard on July 1, 1815. In command there for three years, he returned to the Mediterranean Squadron in 1818 and was appointed commander of the 44-gun frigate *Guerriere*. In April Macdonough was stricken with tuberculosis but remained on duty.[102] After returning to America later in the year, he was given command of the USS *Ohio*, a ship of the line under construction in New York Harbor bearing 74 guns. From 1818 to 1823 Macdonough served as her captain.[103] After submitting several requests for active sea duty, he received command of the 44-gun frigate USS *Constitution* in 1824. By now a widower, he took his only son with him. However, his health continued to worsen. On October 14, 1825, Macdonough had to relieve himself of his command in order to take his son home. Intending to return to New York, Macdonough departed the Mediterranean in the merchant brig *Edwin*. On November 10, 1825, Thomas Macdonough died aboard ship while it was passing Gibraltar. In his history of the War of 1812, Theodore Roosevelt said Macdonough was the greatest figure in American naval history down to the Civil War. Four naval destroyers and one Liberty ship were named for him.[104]

Thomas Shields, 1783–1827

Thomas Shields, purser of New Orleans, was born at Bohemia Manor, Delaware, in 1783. In January 1804 he entered the navy from Middletown, Delaware, as a midshipman, eventually serving onboard the USS *Congress* (1804), USS *Constitution* (1807), and USS *Nautilus* (1809). He was appointed as a purser in 1809 and in 1811 was posted to New Orleans.[105]

During the sea battle on Lake Borgne he commanded six boats manned by approximately fifty men. On December 28, 1814, he captured a British barge containing about forty officers and men of the 14th Light Dragoons. Soon after this battle he was sent by his commander to negotiate the return of wounded prisoners. He joined a naval surgeon named Robert Morrell under a flag of truce and went into the heart of the anchored British fleet. Admiral Cochrane refused to negotiate and instead took Shields and Morrell as prisoners, as he feared the two had been sent as spies. The two negotiators were taken to the HMS *Gorgon*, which was serving as a hospital ship, where Morrell's skills were put to good use. The Americans railed at their captors for their lack of respect for the rules of war and the flag of truce but to no avail. Cochrane responded that it was not personal and that he was within the rules to prevent their immediate return. Eventually they were transferred to HMS *Ramillies* and then to a prisoner exchange at the mouth of the Mississippi River.[106]

The Second Barbary War

The European powers were preoccupied with prosecuting the Napoleonic wars, giving the Barbary pirate states an opportunity to renew their depredations among merchant sailors in the Mediterranean Sea. At the end of the War of 1812 the United States returned its attentions to this piracy problem. On March 3, 1815, Congress authorized the deployment of the navy against Algiers. Two squadrons were deployed, led by Stephen Decatur and William Bainbridge. Decatur's squadron included *Macedonian*, commanded by Jacob Jones. They visited each Barbary port and demanded a peace treaty.[107]

Shortly after departing Gibraltar en route to Algiers, Decatur's squadron encountered the Algerian flagship *Meshuda* and captured it. Not long afterward, the American squadron likewise captured the Algerian brig *Estedio*. By the final week of June the squadron had reached Algiers and initiated negotiations with the dey of Algiers. By terms of the treaty that was signed, on July 3, 1815, Decatur agreed to return the captured *Meshuda* and *Estedio*. The Algerians returned all American captives, estimated to be about 10; and a significant number of European captives were exchanged for about 500 subjects of the dey. Algeria also paid $10,000 for seized shipping. The treaty guaranteed no further tributes by the United States and granted the United States full shipping rights in the Mediterranean Sea. The U.S. Navy continued to keep a squadron in the Mediterranean and both Decatur and Bainbridge served as commanders of that squadron.[108]

In this chapter titled "Maintaining American Sovereignty and Independence," we see that the United States Navy during this period began to move past the struggle for existence as an institution and to establish itself as a strategic necessity to a young nation that had successfully resisted the privateers of France in an undeclared war at sea despite the steep cost to the treasury. The navy, after some initial difficulty, had finally turned the corner for America in freeing itself from the tribute paid to piracy and then gave a good account of itself in the face of far superior forces during the War of 1812 when it "punched far above its weight" against the Royal Navy. It had built ships, trained crews, and established fighting doctrine that made it a recognized, if minor, naval power among the world's navies. The United States was served by a navy that had helped to establish the country's place in the world as a sovereign nation.

Four

Years of Peace and Development

After decades of revolution and piracy and a second struggle with the most powerful naval fleet in the world, the nascent United States Navy became firmly established as a necessity to a growing nation. There was recognition at last that the navy could not again be abandoned at the end of hostilities. America would quintuple its commercial sea trade between 1815 and the onset of the Civil War in 1860. This surge in trade required the protection of a blue-water navy. Furthermore, the young nation was still expanding and had gained a Pacific coastline, as well as an expanded Gulf Coast, which now included Texas. There was a huge emigration to the west driven by the California gold rush as well as war with Mexico. The young navy was to play an important part in all these tides of history. These were enormous tasks for a peacetime navy that required a more rigorous structure to achieve its goals. Training, equipping, administering, and manning this navy was a formidable challenge. Technology would begin to make itself felt as well, with advances in steam-powered propulsion and ship design. The United States Navy would find itself occupied with these daunting tasks in the coming decades before the Civil War.

Three ships of the line were laid down during hostilities in the War of 1812 and completed shortly after the Treaty of Ghent ended the war. These were *Independence*, *Franklin*, and *Washington*. *Franklin* was the first ship built in what would become the Philadelphia Navy Yard at Southwark. By 1818 eight more had been laid down, but three were never completed. One of these ships was the third U.S. Navy *Delaware*, a 74-gun ship of the line, the battleship of its day. In 1822 work began on the mighty ship *Pennsylvania*, the largest sailing ship ever built for the United States Navy and the largest in the world at her launching in 1837.[1]

The navy was organized into semipermanent squadrons, foremost the Mediterranean Squadron under Bainbridge and Decatur to keep the Barbary States at bay and to enforce the treaties agreed to with the dey of Algiers. Another squadron was established in the West Indies to deal with similar piracy threats to commercial shipping as the European powers began their long withdrawal from this area of influence, preoccupied with their own European affairs. The wars of independence from the Spanish rule created power vacuums rapidly filled with buccaneers and privateers sailing under letters of marque issued by the new young southern nations. Captain James Biddle in *Macedonian* initiated action against these brigands. He was followed by Captain David Porter, who in turn was succeeded by Captain Lewis Warrington. Gradually they were able to suppress the threat and by 1829 had pacified the Caribbean Sea, ultimately taking some 65 pirate vessels.[2]

American participation in the slave trade had been outlawed by treaty in 1807 and it was labeled as an act of piracy in 1819. Nevertheless, a number of former privateers engaged in the illicit trade. The corvette *Cyane* captured nine slavers off the African coast in 1820 and continued to patrol until 1824. A small African squadron was reestablished in 1842 and continued until the time of the Civil War, but the illegal trade continued almost unabated.[3] After the War of 1812 American trade with the Orient revived and boomed. In 1831 a Salem trader, the *Friendship,* was plundered and part of her crew slaughtered in Sumatra. The navy sent the frigate *Potomac* to take punitive measures and won a guarantee of safety for the future. In 1835 it established a permanent East India Squadron, protecting American trade with China. Japan remained closed, however, until 1853, when Captain Matthew Perry, leading a flotilla of vessels, convinced the shogunate to open its ports to American trade.[4]

These decades of the early 19th century were only relatively years of peace. Struggles with Native Americans on the western frontier was an ongoing challenge for the new nation although it had no naval component. Nevertheless, the Mexican-American War of 1845 and the California gold rush fueled a demand for increased shipping and a stronger navy. The Delaware estuary would contribute in ways large and small to this maturing naval force.[5] However, the estuary itself required improvement.

Marine Infrastructure

The entrance to Delaware Bay was particularly hazardous in stormy weather, as the prevailing wind blew directly into the bay and no shelter was available except for small craft able to navigate up one of the creeks lining the estuary. The river typically iced up almost every winter. The Delaware River was long and the channel a narrow and winding obstacle course. As a result, improvements were made, including channel markers and buoys, range lights, and breakwaters. Nevertheless, the tortuous ninety-mile voyage to Philadelphia made that port less and less competitive with New York as a port of call. This was especially true of sailing ships, which, depending on winds and tides could take up to a week to make the passage. The result was an incentive to develop and improve steam-powered craft. These would prove to be utile in the confined waters of the new canals.

Chesapeake and Delaware Canal, 1824

In the mid–17th century Augustine Herman, a mapmaker and Prague native who had served as an envoy for the Dutch, observed that two great bodies of water, the Delaware River and the Chesapeake Bay, were separated only by a narrow strip of land. Herman proposed that a waterway be built to connect the two. The canal would reduce, by nearly 300 miles (500 km), the water routes between Philadelphia and Baltimore and would create, in effect, a southwest extension of the Delaware River to Baltimore and beyond.[6]

An initial survey was conducted in 1764. In 1802, following actions by the legislatures of Maryland, Delaware, and Pennsylvania, the Chesapeake and Delaware Canal Company was incorporated. In 1804 construction of the canal began under Benjamin Latrobe. The work included fourteen locks to connect the Christiana River in Delaware with the Elk

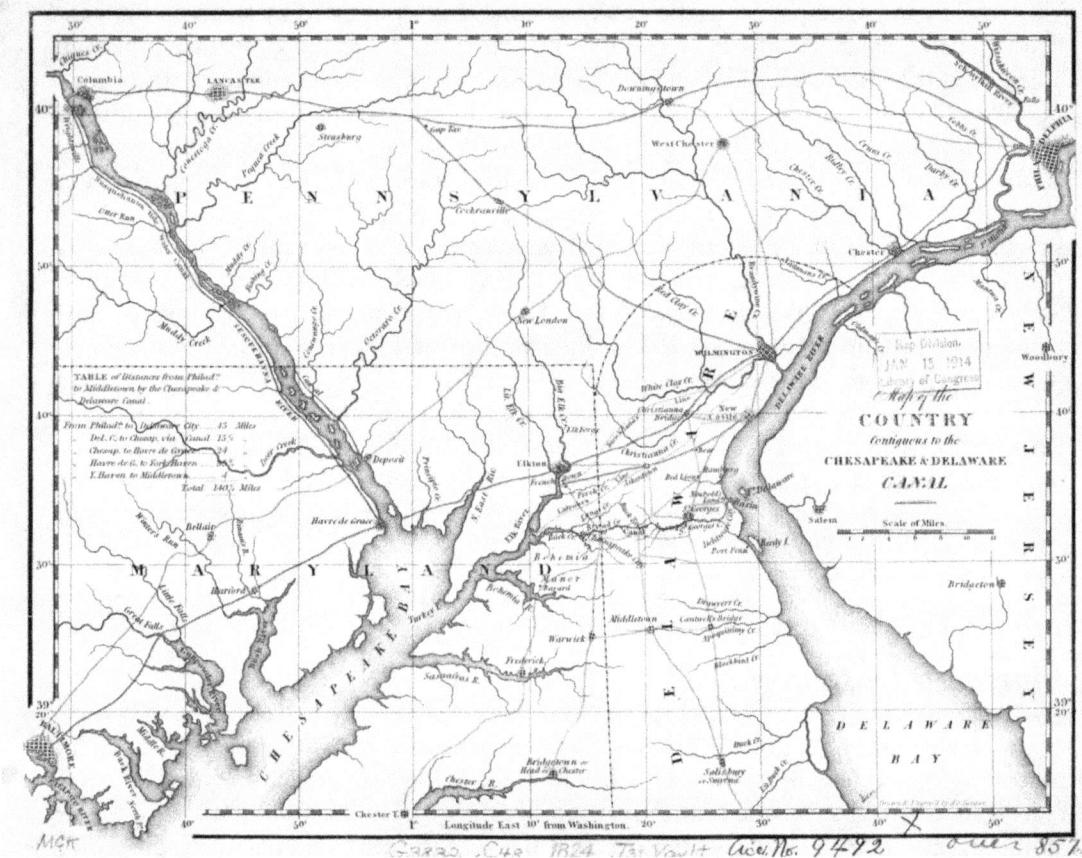

Map of the country contiguous to the Chesapeake & Delaware Canal. This chart makes clear the relationship between the two important estuaries. From the 5th general report of the Chesapeake and Delaware Canal Company, 1824 (80695657, Library of Congress).

River at Welch Point, Maryland, but the project was halted two years later for lack of funds. The canal company was once again organized in 1822, and new surveys determined that more than $2 million in capital was needed to resume construction. Eventually Pennsylvania purchased $100,000 in stock, Maryland $50,000, and Delaware $25,000. The federal government's investment was $450,000, with the remainder subscribed by the public.[7] The U.S. Army Corps of Engineers played a vital role for the canal company in 1823 and 1824, providing two senior commissioned officers to assist in determining a canal route. The engineer officers and two civilian engineers recommended a new route with four locks, extending from Delaware City westward to the Back Creek branch of the Elk River, Maryland. Given the recent events of the war with Great Britain, the strategic benefits of an interior line of supply on waterways was obvious as a military advantage.[8]

Canal construction resumed in April 1824, and in several years some 2,600 men were digging and hauling dirt from the ditch. Laborers toiled with pick and shovel at the immense construction task, working for an average daily wage of 75 cents. The swampy marshlands along the canal's planned route proved a great impediment to progress as workers continuously battled slides along the soft slopes of the "ditch" being cut. It was

1829 before the C&D Canal Company could, at last, announce the waterway "open for business." The $3.5 million construction cost made it one of the most expensive canal projects of its time.[9]

The Chesapeake Bay and the Delaware River were now connected by a navigation channel measuring nearly 14 miles long, 10 feet deep, 66 feet wide at the waterline, and 36 feet wide along the channel bottom. Teams of mules and horses towed freight and passenger barges, schooners, and sloops through the canal. Cargoes included practically every useful item of daily life: lumber, grain, farm products, fish, cotton, coal, iron, and whiskey. Packet ships were eventually established to move freight through the waterway.

Another important canal was constructed at Bordentown, New Jersey, crossing New Jersey in a northeastern direction to Staten Island. The Delaware and Raritan Canal was opened in 1838, making an inland passage possible between New York, Philadelphia, and Baltimore. It was especially useful for shipping coal from the anthracite fields in eastern Pennsylvania. Before the advent of the railroads the canal allowed shippers to cut many miles off the route along an interior waterway safe from the sometimes treacherous Atlantic seas. Its fate was tied to the coal industry as a result. The railroads ultimately displaced its usefulness and it ceased operation in 1932.[10]

While canals were connecting the upstream waters, another effort was underway at the mouth of the bay where protected waters were hard to find and at a place where water-borne trade was often congested.

Lewes Harbor Delaware Breakwater, 1826

The Lewes Harbor breakwater project began in 1826, designed by noted Philadelphia architect William Strickland and built under the supervision of the U.S. Army Corps of Engineers. The harbor was the first of its kind in the Western Hemisphere and the third in the world. Construction began in 1828 on what is now the inner breakwater, listed in its own right on the National Register of Historic Places as the Delaware Breakwater. These works consisted of a 2,100-foot main breakwater and icebreaker 1,700 feet long. Both elements were built of granite rubble from New Castle County, with earlier portions using smaller stones from the Hudson Palisades. The breakwaters are 160 feet wide at the base and 20 feet at the top. The project used 835,000 tons of stone in all.

Strickland designed a lighthouse for the harbor that was completed in 1869. This was an offshore station requiring two to three lightkeepers for weeks at a time. The harbor was a success, but it soon became apparent that it was too small. During storms as many as 200 ships would seek refuge. Shoaling within the refuge was also a problem that reduced the usefulness of this enterprise.[11]

River Dredging, 1836

In 1814 the Christina River was navigable upstream to Christina Bridge, but only as far as Wilmington for vessels drawing fourteen feet. Larger vessels such as heavily laden whaling ships could not get to their Christina wharf. They anchored at the river's mouth and their cargos were lightered. The City of Wilmington petitioned Congress to improve the harbor and deepen the channel, and in 1836 Congress appropriated $15,000 for this task. Subsequently the channel was periodically dredged and improvements were made, including the construction of a jetty at the harbor entrance. The channel was maintained at a mean depth of fifteen feet and 75 feet wide at Market Street to the jetty.[12] These improvements in marine infrastructure would facilitate the rapid advances in marine technology that began to accelerate in the decades before the Civil War.

Advances in Marine Technology

The age of steam arrived in Delaware during the War of 1812. The first steam-powered packet to ply between Wilmington and Philadelphia was the *Vestal*, which first sailed on April 24, 1812. She was later called the *Vesta* and was commanded by Captain Milner. In August a second steamboat, *Delaware*, was added to the same route. The *Wilmon Whillden* was the first iron steamboat with side wheels to run in the Delaware. She was built about 1841 for service between Wilmington and Philadelphia, where she earned a reputation for speed. A daily race was run every morning at 8:00 from the Philadelphia waterfront, where *Wilmon* left competitors *Zephyr*, *Napoleon*, and *Cohansey* in her wake.[13] Ports established on the Delaware for packet service included landings at Wilmington, New Castle, Smyrna, Dover, and Milford. The New Jersey side of the river included landings at Penn's Grove and Cape May. At the Philadelphia Navy Yard, the navy constructed a ship that was the antithesis of advanced marine technology.

Philadelphia Navy Yard: USS Pennsylvania

The Philadelphia Navy Yard had its origins in a shipyard on Philadelphia's Front Street along the Delaware River that was founded in 1776 and became an official U.S. Navy site in 1801. From 1812 until 1865 it was a big production center. The first ship launched from there was the *Franklin*, an event watched by more than 50,000 spectators. The rapid development of other shipbuilding companies pledged Philadelphia to improve production processes. It was the first shipyard in the world that used floating dry docks in the building process.[14]

Pennsylvania was one of the "nine ships to rate not less than 74 guns each" authorized by the U.S. Congress on April 29, 1816. She was designed and built by Samuel Humphreys in the Philadelphia Navy Yard. Her keel was laid in September 1821, but tight budgets slowed her construction, preventing her being launched until July 18, 1837. A long period of relative peace on the seas rendered her, if not obsolete, redundant. The largest sailing warship ever built for the United States, she had three complete gun decks and a flush spar-deck and her hull was pierced for 136 guns. However, she made only a solitary voyage.[15]

Pennsylvania shifted from her launching site to off Chester, Pennsylvania, on November 29, 1837, and was partially manned there the following day. Only 34 of her guns were noted as having been mounted on December 3, 1837. She stood downriver for New Castle, Delaware, on December 9 to receive gun carriages and other equipage before proceeding to the Norfolk Navy Yard for coppering of her hull. She departed New Castle on December 20, 1837, and discharged the Delaware pilot on the 25th. That afternoon she sailed for the Virginia Capes. She came off the Norfolk dry dock on January 2, 1838. That day her crew transferred to *Columbia*.[16] *Pennsylvania* remained in ordinary until 1842, when she became a receiving ship for the Norfolk Navy Yard, never to make for sea. She remained in the yard until April 20, 1861, when she was burned to the waterline to prevent her falling into Confederate hands. Her wreck was then salvaged and broken up.[17]

U.S. Ship of the Line "Pennsylvania," 140 Guns, N. Currier (Firm) c. 1846 (2002695929, Library of Congress).

The Philadelphia Navy Yard soldiered on, however. During the Mexican-American War the Philadelphia Navy Yard at Southwark in Philadelphia became a center for war preparations against Mexico. The yard outfitted the armed steamer *Princeton*, the brig *Delaware*, and the frigate *Brandywine* for duty on the Gulf of Mexico. It constructed the powerful side-wheel steamer *Susquehanna*, the largest vessel built at the yard to that time at 3,600 tons on a 250-foot keel.[18]

Wilmington Shipbuilding

In the 1840s two Delaware manufacturing plants that had manufactured railroad cars started building iron-hulled ships. By the time of the Civil War, Wilmington was one of the largest shipbuilding centers in the country and Harlan and Hollingsworth was the largest yard and the preeminent builder of iron ships in the country. Pusey and Jones was the fourth largest.[19]

The iron hull and the screw propulsion system came together in the late 1830s and in 1843, the leading builder of seagoing steamships in England synthesized these advances into what has been called the first modern ship: The *Great Britain*, which was a huge iron ship 289 feet long, displacing 3,270 tons. A year later Harlan and Hollingsworth launched their American counterparts, albeit on a much smaller scale.[20]

Harlan and Hollingsworth built mainly commercial ships, and many of them found their way into the navy. The first iron vessels made by Harlan were two freight steamboats to operate a line between Philadelphia and Albany via the Delaware and Raritan Canal, which connected the Delaware River with the Staten Island Sound, creating an all-water route to New York in 1838. It served primarily for transporting freight. Designed by Charles Moore, each steamboat turned twin screws with a single steam engine. They were sent to New York in July 1844 via the outside sea. The *Ocean* preceded its mate *Ashland*. Within two years both vessels were acquired by the U.S. Navy for use along the Gulf Coast during the Mexican War.

Harlan and Hollingsworth started building iron steamships at the time that marked the transition from the first to the second of the three stages in the development of the steamship internationally. The first stage, starting in the early nineteenth century, was the era of the paddle steamer, which lasted through the 1860s; the second stage, beginning in the 1830s, was that of the screw-propelled vessel driven by increasingly sophisticated "simple" engines that used the expansion of steam only once; and the third stage, starting in the 1860s, was marked by the introduction of the more fuel-efficient and more powerful marine compound engine. Although commercial wooden steamboats had been built since the early nineteenth century, the construction of iron steamships did not exist as an industry in the United States in 1840. By 1850 only three iron shipbuilding companies operated in the United States; Harlan and Hollingsworth in Wilmington, Reanie, Neafie and Company in Philadelphia and, formed in 1849, Pusey and Jones in Wilmington. By 1857 Wilmington was the leading producer of iron ships in the country. More iron tonnage was constructed in that city during the twelve-year period of 1845–57 than all the rest of the country put together.[21] The first step in this revolution in shipbuilding was the merchant ship *Bangor*.

Bangor (merchant and naval steamer, built at Wilmington, Delaware, in 1844. She served in the U.S. Navy as USS *Scourge* (1846–1848), the first iron-hulled, screw-driven seagoing ship in the United States (NH 63866, U.S. Naval History and Heritage Command).

USS *Scourge*, 1845

On May 29, 1845, Harlan launched *Bangor*, at 212 gross tons the first iron-hulled, steam-powered, propeller-driven seagoing merchant ship in the United States. She had two independent steam engines, twin screws and was the first iron ship built for deep-sea use. She had a schooner sailing rig, and her plates overlapped clinker style and were fastened with metal clamps. Out of Boston she caught fire and had to be run aground in Maine. Her hull remained sound, and she was raised and rebuilt by the navy for use as a gunboat.[22] She was renamed USS *Scourge* for use in the Mexican War, where she participated in a number of attacks. Commanded by Charles G. Hunter, she joined the forces of Commodore Matthew Perry in the Gulf of Mexico on March 29, 1847. She was part of the "Mosquito Flotilla" and was immediately assigned to take part in a concerted sea-land attack upon the port of Alvarado. On March 32, 1847, *Scourge*, acting alone, captured the port, which had been abandoned by its garrison. After this action, the vessel participated in the captures of La Peña, Palma Sola, Hospital Hill, Tuxpan, and Tabasco. Prior to the attack on Tabasco, Lieutenant Lockwood, the officer in command, became one of the first officers to protect a vessel's exposed machinery by using sandbags.[23]

Whaling, 1833–1846

In a discussion of marine technology whaling may not be the topic that springs to mind. In order to be successful it requires a specialized technology all its own. In the case of the Delaware River, whaling proved to be a false trail. Wilmington had long been eclipsed by Baltimore and Philadelphia as a commercial shipping center, but it was thought that it could be competitive in a shipping niche. Whaling fever had caught on in disparate cities like Poughkeepsie, New York, and Newark, New Jersey. Why not Wilmington? An attempt was made to establish a whaling trade when the Wilmington Whaling Company was organized on November 23, 1833. Capital was raised from many local town fathers, who then purchased the ship *Ceres*, in 1835, and later added *Lucy Ann*, *Superior*, *Jefferson*, and *North America*. This fleet made a series of sailings, some of them two years or longer. Some voyages were profitable but some were not. *Ceres* suffered bad luck, spotting many whales but landing few and returning with only half her hold containing a thousand pounds of oil for two years' work, a significant financial loss.[24] They also returned in very low morale. Her crew had endured scurvy, disappointment, and exhaustion. By 1846 the industry had declined and the firm dissolved.[25]

Not all naval advances were in the realm of technology. The navy was also interested in voyages of exploration, chart making, navigation, and finding the limits of its capabilities. A key actor was Edwin Jesse de Haven.

Edwin Jesse DeHaven

Edwin Jesse De Haven was born in Philadelphia and became a midshipman at the age of 10, serving until 1857. He participated in the United States Exploring Expedition, also known as the Wilkes Expedition after its commander, Lieutenant Charles Wilkes. It was a scientific exploring and surveying expedition of the Pacific Ocean and surrounding lands conducted by the United States from 1838 to 1842. They explored the Oregon coast, Antarctica, and numerous Pacific islands, circumnavigating the globe.

Edwin Jesse De Haven's most notable individual achievement, however, was serving as captain of the *Advance*. Along with the *Rescue* the ship participated in the Arctic search mission to discover the remains of John Franklin's earlier (1847) and ill-fated Arctic exploring expedition. Rear Admiral Sir John Franklin, an experienced British Arctic explorer, had commanded an expedition of two ships in search of the Northwest Passage across the north of Canada to the Pacific. When the ships had not returned two years later a series of search expeditions were initiated. The two American ships, *Advance* and *Rescue*, left New York on May 5, 1850. De Haven and his crew were at sea for sixteen months, spending the winter inside the Arctic Circle. He and his party found no trace of Franklin's expedition, nor did other searchers.[26] After returning from the expedition, Edwin Jesse De Haven served in the U.S. Coast Survey before spending the rest of his career at the United States Naval Observatory. He was placed on the retired list in 1862 because of impaired vision. He died in Philadelphia in May 1865.[27]

Captain Henry Benjamin Nones

On May 10, 1846, the secretary of war called for volunteers to prosecute the war against Mexico. The revenue cutter *Forward* commanded by Captain Henry Nones was in harbor in Wilmington at that time with 45 seamen aboard. She received sealed orders to proceed at once to the Gulf of Mexico, where she participated in the attack on Alvarado

USS *Delaware* (1820–1861), lithograph from *The Sailor's Magazine*, April 1831 (NH 54308, U.S. Naval History and Heritage Command).

and in the capture of Tabasco. Captain Nones' gallantry and seamanship received the commendation of Commodore Perry, who wrote, "I am gratified in bearing witness to the valuable services of the revenue Schooner *Forward* in command of Captain Nones and the skill and gallantry of his officers and men." Remaining on duty for one year Captain Nones and the *Forward* returned to Wilmington. The vessel showed many marks of hard knocks in the engagements and was refitted and repaired.

Henry Nones was the son of a Revolutionary War soldier. He also served in the Florida war in 1835. He had five sons, four of whom served in either the army or naval forces. Captain Nones also served in the Civil War.[28]

We offer the tales of two ships as an illustration of the progress of the United States Navy during this period of time. The USS *Delaware* and the USS *Brandywine* were contemporary vessels, both being launched shortly after the War of 1812 and ending their careers during the Civil War. The ship-of-the-line *Delaware* was the battleship of its day, and the *Brandywine* was a frigate, one of the most versatile and useful warships afloat. The chronicle of their activities offers a sampling of the routine duties and activities of the U.S. Navy prior to the Civil War.

USS Delaware, *Ship of the Line*

The third *Delaware* was one of "nine ships to rate not less than 74 guns each" authorized by Congress on April 29, 1816. She was built to the design of William Doughty by naval constructor Francis Grice in the Norfolk Navy Yard. Her keel was laid August 1817 and she launched October 21, 1820. Her tonnage was 2,633. *Delaware* was 196 feet and three inches in length with a beam of 53 feet. Her crew numbered 820 men. As a ship of the line she was designed to carry seventy-four 32-pound guns but sometimes carried as many as 84 guns. She was designed and built contemplating a large fleet action with a major sea power. These were relatively peaceful times, with no significant threat from a major sea power, so this large capital ship was employed somewhat sparingly, showing the flag and acting as flagship for the squadron.[29]

After construction, she was roofed over and kept at the yard "in ordinary." This term means the ship was complete but kept in floating storage. Her spars and rigging down to the lower masts, guns, and necessary stores were kept nearby for fitting out on short notice. Ships served in two basic categories: those "in ordinary" and those "in commission," which were equipped and manned for sea duty.

Mediterranean

On March 27, 1827, *Delaware* was ordered repaired and fitted for sea. She sailed February 10, 1828, under the command of Captain John Downs bound for the Mediterranean. As a large and modern capital ship, she attracted much attention. The governor and Maryland legislators visited her at Annapolis on January 18, 1828. She sailed to base at Port Mahon, Minorca, Balearic Island, arriving April 4, 1828.[30] Port Mahon, having been previously occupied by both the British and French navies, had become a typical navy town. The American squadron brought 2,000 officers and men and $150,000 into the town annually.

After transporting passengers and cargo to Leghorn, *Delaware* returned to Port Mahon to become flagship of Commodore William M. Crane. On April 22 she continued cruising with the Mediterranean Squadron until she passed Gibraltar on November 20, 1829, en route to Norfolk, arriving January 2, 1830. One of the officers sailing on *Delaware* for this cruise was passed midshipman John P. Gillis of Wilmington, Delaware. Gillis had reported to the ship in February while she was being prepared to be taken out of ordinary and had been among those getting her ready to go to sea. He had originally been appointed midshipman in 1826 and, appropriately, sailed in the new frigate *Brandywine* under Captain Jacob Jones, Delaware's hero of 1812 as commodore of the Pacific Squadron, Gillis began keeping a personal journal, or log, as expected of all midshipmen. These journals typically included notations on the ship's course, speed, latitude, and longitude at time of the entry and on weather conditions, state of the sails, operations with other U.S. Navy vessels, sightings of non–navy vessels, and personnel matters. Soon Gillis noted the following in his journal: "Commo Jones disapproving of keeping log journals—knocked off accordingly." He did, but that just gave him more time for the detailed descriptions, maps, and sketches of the ports he visited, romantic poems, short fiction, newspaper articles, and voluminous correspondence he wrote throughout his career. During this voyage on the *Delaware* he was writing a column, "Sketches of Travel," for the *Wilmington Delaware Republican*.[31]

Delaware entered the Norfolk Navy Yard 16 January and was decommissioned February 10, 1830, lying in ordinary at Norfolk until 1833. The Norfolk Navy Yard dry dock first went into operation with her docking on June 17, 1833, its pumping machinery being operated by steam. *Delaware* was the first vessel in the United States to be dry-docked. The Norfolk Dry Dock number one remains in active use.[32]

MEDITERRANEAN PATROL

Recommissioned July 15, 1833, with Captain Henry E. Ballard commanding, *Delaware* received President Jackson onboard July 29, firing a 24-gun salute at both his arrival and his departure. She departed Norfolk the next day for New York, where she was inspected by Secretary of the Navy Levi Woodbury and Vice President Martin van Buren. In New York *Delaware* received aboard Edward Livingston, a former secretary of state President Jackson had appointed minister to France in order to seek reparations for American claims against France dating back to the Napoleonic Wars. The ship also carried the wife and daughters of Commodore D.T. Patterson to join him in the Mediterranean and remove them from involvement in the so-called "Petticoat Affair." Commodore Patterson was already in the Mediterranean commanding the squadron in another effort to seek reparations. *Delaware* set sail on August 14 for the Mediterranean, where she served as flagship for Commodore Patterson and cruised on goodwill visits and for the protection of the rights and property of American citizens. She called at Cherbourg and Gibraltar en route to Port Mahon, where on November 5, 1833, Captain Ballard turned over command to Capt. John B. Nicholson. *Delaware* ranged from Port Mahon to such seaports as Toulon, Marseilles, Naples, Alexandria, Beirut, Tripoli, and Malta.

The mission of the Mediterranean Squadron in these years was primarily diplomatic—to show the flag and demonstrate American interest and goodwill and gain influence throughout the Mediterranean. Indeed, there was some lasting influence. John Lloyd Stephens, a lawyer visiting Cairo in 1835, wrote after meeting the pasha of Egypt, "He knew America, and particularly from … the visit of Commodore Patterson in the ship Delaware."[33] Heading west for a port call in Toulon before heading home, on October 11 the *Delaware* was struck by a "white squall" in the Gulf of Lyon. Sailing from Gibraltar in December 1835 she touched the Danish West Indies then, sailing northward, encountered another storm before returning to Norfolk in February 1836. She was placed once again in ordinary on March 10, 1836.

South American Cruise

In April 1841 the *Delaware* was again brought out of ordinary and placed in the dry dock at Gosport Navy Yard to be prepared for an expected cruise. David G. Farragut was already aboard as first lieutenant, a position increasingly referred to as executive officer. He had come aboard in February while *Delaware* was still in ordinary to oversee the process of fitting out and recommissioning. She was to be commanded by Captain Charles S. McCauley, who had served on the *Constellation* during the War of 1812. Within days, *Delaware* was released from the dry dock and towed down to anchor in Hampton Roads to load stores and train the crew.[34]

In mid–June Commodore Charles Morris came aboard and hoisted his flag, or broad pennant, as it was then called. As a passed midshipman during the First Barbary War, he had taken part in the daring expedition under Stephen Decatur that entered Tripoli Harbor and burned the frigate *Philadelphia*. He was later first lieutenant for Commodore Isaac Hull on the *Constitution* during the battle with the *Guerriere* and received severe wounds. In mid–July he was called to Washington and soon returned with the news that he would be taking command of the Brazil Station rather than the Mediterranean, with *Delaware* as his flagship. This was a wise choice and would be nothing new for Morris.

"Delaware" and "Cyane," Atlantic Ocean. **Artist, William H. Myers, gunner of *Cyane*. Copied from "Journal of a Cruise on the USS Cyane, 1842–1843" (NH 2022, U.S. Naval History and Heritage Command).).**

As captain commanding *Constellation* he had served as commodore of the Brazil Station in 1820.

On July 30 *Delaware* sailed for Annapolis. On August 14 more than 100 cabinet officers, members of Congress, senior army and navy officers, foreign ambassadors, and their wives visited *Delaware* to observe general quarters, sail rigging, and mock gunnery demonstrations by the crew and enjoy a cotillion with the officers. On September 7 the governor of Maryland visited. Indicating that the ship would soon be underway for the Brazil Station, on October 14 Robert Walsh, Esqr., secretary of legation to Brazil, came onboard to take passage for Rio de Janeiro. On October 22 President John Tyler, his son, and several members of Congress visited the ship. They were treated to a salute, an inspection, and general quarters with several demonstrations of the usual evolutions of a naval engagement, including firing of three rounds of blanks.

Delaware sailed November 1, 1841, for a tour of duty on the Brazil Station and anchored off Sugarloaf on December 12, 1841. There she and other ships of the American Squadron joined ships of British, French, Spanish, and Brazilian squadrons and single ships of various Italian states and a variety of other navies. Salutes, calls and return calls, and social activities among officers of arriving and departing ships became the main activity. The emperor of Brazil, Dom Pedro II, welcomed the ship with a visit on January 14, and traveling royalty from other nations visited on occasion. *Delaware* patrolled the coasts of Brazil, Uruguay, and Argentina to represent American interests during political unrest

USS *Brandywine*, 44-gun frigate built at Washington Navy Yard, commenced building in 1821, launched June 17, 1825—175 feet in length and 1,768 tons, destroyed by fire at Norfolk, Virginia, on September 3, 1864. Her first cruise was to France under command of Commodore Charles Morris, carrying General Lafayette home after his last visit to the United States (NH 56684, U.S. Naval History and Heritage Command).

in those countries. Over the next year she moved between Rio and Montevideo, spending 1–15 days at sea and remaining in each port about two months, carrying out the same routine to demonstrate the presence and commitment of the United States Navy to protecting American interests in the area. On February 19, 1843, she sailed from Rio de Janeiro for another cruise in the Mediterranean. *Delaware* returned to Hampton Roads on March 4, 1844, and was decommissioned for the last time at Norfolk Navy Yard on March 22.[35]

Burned at Her Moorings

Delaware lay at Norfolk Navy Yard until it was ordered by Admiral Hiram Paulding on April 20, 1861, that she be burned to the waterline to prevent her capture by the Confederates. At the Gosport Shipyard the commander, Captain Charles S. McCauley, had been ordered to defend the yard, especially to get the screw frigate *Merrimack* ready for sea and, if forced to evacuate, burn the ships lying in ordinary. These included the ship-of-the-line *Delaware,* of which he had been the last commanding officer. Southern sympathizers at the yard misled McCauley about the threat to the yard and he reported that he planned to evacuate.

Delaware enjoyed some 41 years of service (1820–1861) on the navy lists but was in active commission only nine of those years, the balance being spent "in ordinary" as a decommissioned vessel.[36] Another naval vessel with Delaware Valley associations representative of this era was the USS *Brandywine*. She was among the most widely traveled vessels in the navy during her long years of service.

USS Brandywine [Susquehanna]

Brandywine is notable as the final evolution of the 44-gun frigate design that began with the USS *Constitution* and her sisters a quarter-century earlier. While ships such as *Raritan* were launched in the 1840s and differed in details, their basic design was identical to *Brandywine*. *Brandywine* was also the very first warship ever built with an innovative elliptical stern that reduced the chronic vulnerability of the traditional square stern ship to enemy fire and allowed her to carry stern-mounted guns.[37]

The USS *Brandywine* was ordered from the Washington Navy Yard as the *Susquehanna*. She was laid down in 1821 and launched in 1825 as a 44-gun frigate. The sailing frigate was a fast, maneuverable warship, its principle armament (of 28 guns or more) carried typically on one deck. Unlike the 74-gun man of war, a frigate was not expected to stand in a line of battle with other battleships. Its mission was to patrol and escort and to convey messages and dignitaries. However, frigates were used as a naval "Jack of all trades" and regularly fought with their peers when circumstances dictated. *Brandywine* was destined to spend the next four decades as a versatile American vessel in almost every corner of the world's oceans.[38]

From July 1824 to September 1825 the last surviving French general of the Revolutionary War, the Marquis de Lafayette, made a famous tour of the 24 American states. At many stops on this tour he was received by the populace with a hero's welcome, and many honors and monuments were presented to commemorate and memorialize his visit. Shortly before *Susquehanna* was to be launched in the spring of 1825, President John Quincey Adams decided to have an American warship carry the Marquis de

Lafayette back to Europe in the wake of his visit to the land he had fought to free almost 50 years before. The general had expressed his intention of sailing for home sometime in the late summer or early autumn of 1825. Adams selected *Susquehanna* for this honor, and accordingly—as a gesture of the nation's affection for Lafayette—the frigate was renamed *Brandywine* to commemorate the Pennsylvania battle in which the Frenchman had shed his blood for American freedom. Launched on June 16, 1825, and christened by Sailing Master Marmaduke Dove, *Brandywine* was commissioned on August 25, 1825, Captain Charles Morris in command.[39] As an honor to the marquis, officers were selected from as many states as possible and, where practicable, from descendants of persons who had distinguished themselves in the American Revolution. One of these young men selected as officer on the *Brandywine*'s maiden voyage was 19-year-old Matthew F. Maury, who would eventually exert great influence in the science of oceanography.[40]

After fitting out at the navy yard, the frigate traveled down the Potomac River to await her passenger. Lafayette enjoyed a last state dinner to celebrate his 68th birthday on the evening of September 6 and then embarked in the steamboat *Mount Vernon* on September 7 for the trip downriver to join *Brandywine*. On September 8, the frigate stood out of the Potomac River and sailed down Chesapeake Bay toward the open ocean.[41] After a stormy three weeks at sea the warship arrived off Le Havre, France, early in October. *Brandywine*'s passenger and her captain disembarked, the former to return home and the latter to tour the country for six months to study shipyards, ship design, and other naval matters. *Brandywine* left Le Havre that same day to join the Mediterranean Squadron. En route, she stopped at the Isle of Wight in England to recaulk seams that had opened rather badly during the Atlantic crossing. Then, after being rendered more seaworthy, she resumed her voyage to Gibraltar on October 22, reaching the British bastion guarding the Mediterranean Sea's Atlantic entrance on November 2. At the end of a fortnight in port, *Brandywine* sailed for the Balearic Islands in company with the ship of the line *North Carolina* and the sloop of war *Erie*. Following an 11-day passage, the trio reached Port Mahon, Minorca, and *Brandywine* spent the next three months refitting. In February 1826 *Porpoise* arrived in Port Mahon with orders recalling *Brandywine* to the U.S., and the frigate set sail for home late in the month. She stopped at Gibraltar early in March and finally entered New York in mid–April.[42]

Pacific Ocean

After passing the rest of the spring and much of the summer in repairs and outfitting for duty in the Pacific Ocean, *Brandywine* departed New York City on September 3, 1826, as the flagship of Commodore Jacob Jones, who was sailing for the Pacific coast of South America to take over command of the American squadron in the region from Commodore Isaac Hull and his flagship, USS *United States*.[43] Fortunately, by the time the frigate joined the squadron on January 6, 1827, Spain had abandoned her efforts to reconquer her empire in the Western Hemisphere, so *Brandywine*'s tour of duty in the Pacific proved far less troubled than that of her predecessor. She directed her efforts toward protecting American citizens, especially merchant seamen who were being impressed into service by the Peruvian navy. Her own relief, the frigate *Guerriere*, arrived in the summer of 1829 and brought Commodore Charles Thompson, the squadron's new commander, along with another crew for *Dolphin*. *Brandywine* then set sail for home. She reached New York City on October 8 and was decommissioned soon thereafter.[44]

Gunboat Diplomacy

Placed back in commission on January 10, 1830, with Capt. Henry E. Ballard[45] in command, the warship set out for the Gulf of Mexico two months later to gather information concerning conditions in that area. She returned to the East Coast on July 7 and began preparations for another European deployment. *Brandywine* departed Hampton Roads, Virginia, on October 22, 1830, and headed for Gibraltar. At first, this deployment was devoted almost exclusively to sailing from one peaceful port to the next, showing the flag to maintain and enhance American prestige. However, President Andrew Jackson was determined to collect indemnities owed to the U.S. for merchant ships that had been confiscated by several European nations while under Napoleon's governments during the Napoleonic Wars. Soon *Brandywine* joined Commodore Patterson's effort to enforce that policy. He, and the commodore decided to begin with the Kingdom of Naples.[46]

While Napoleon's brother Joseph Bonaparte sat on the throne there, Naples had seized several American merchantmen and the most recent successor to the throne, King Ferdinand II, had repudiated the debts. President Jackson sent former Maryland congressman John Nelson to Naples as U.S. minister to negotiate the payment of these debts. He also dispatched Commodore Daniel Patterson to the Mediterranean with reinforcements for the squadron already there and with orders to take overall command of American forces from Commodore James Biddle. The frigate gave a physical dimension to Nelson's legal arguments.[47]

Showing the Flag

When Nelson first raised the issue of the debts, King Ferdinand refused even to consider the question. This prompted the American minister to write to Commodore Patterson asking for naval support. The commodore divided his squadron into two groups. The first contingent—headed by *Brandywine* and including *Constellation*, reached Naples on July 23, 1832, and anchored near Ferdinand's palace. This group remained in port until late in August, when it returned to Port Mahon. Beginning with *Concord*, they arrived on September 17. However, the ships of the second contingent began standing into the harbor at Naples singly. Soon the frigate *United States* arrived, followed in rapid succession by *John Adams* and *Boston*.[48]

Not a shot was fired and no explicit reference to the squadron was made during the negotiations. Nevertheless, the unspoken message of power helped the king to see the justice of the American claims and prompted him to sign a treaty promising to pay 2,100,000 ducats to the U.S. over the next nine years. *Brandywine*'s remaining months in the Mediterranean proved less dramatic. She sailed for the United States late in the spring of 1833, returning to New York on July 9 and going in ordinary out of commission two days later.[49]

Pacific Ocean

Brandywine reactivated in the spring of 1834, on April 4, Capt. David Deacon in command, and set sail on June 2 to replace *Vincennes* as flagship of the Pacific Squadron. She reached Rio de Janiero on July 22 and stayed until August 14, when she resumed her journey down the coast and around Cape Horn. *Brandywine* arrived at Valparaiso on October 3 after a stormy passage of the cape, and Commodore Alexander S. Wadsworth broke his flag in her on November 1. For the next three years, the warship plied the waters along South America's west coast protecting U.S. citizens and commerce.[50]

Finally, expiring enlistments signaled the time for *Brandywine* to sail for home, and she departed in January 1837, bringing Commodore Wadsworth back home at the conclusion of his own tour of duty. After a relatively quiet 94-day passage, she reached Norfolk, Virginia, on April 22, 1837, and was placed in ordinary on May 9, 1837. After being laid up for more than two years, the frigate was recommissioned on August 2, 1839, Capt. William C. Bolton in command. Once outfitted, she sailed for the Mediterranean on October 22. After a 19-month cruise the frigate entered New York Harbor on May 12, 1841. Later that summer *Brandywine* headed back to the Mediterranean on June 29. She completed her tour there under the command of Capt. David Greisinger and then returned to New York on July 12, 1842, to be decommissioned on July 30, 1842.[51]

China

Brandywine went back into commission on February 16, 1843, Lieutenant Charles W. Chauncey in command, and set sail for the East Indies on May 24. She reached Bombay, India, on October 24 to pick up the special envoy to China, Caleb Cushing, and took him to Macau, where he went ashore and began negotiations for a treaty. While Cushing was working to develop contacts with the Chinese government, *Brandywine* visited Manila, Hong Kong, and Whampoa. On June 16, 1844, the high commissioner appointed by the Chinese emperor to deal with Cushing, Ch'i-ying, arrived at Macau, and negotiations opened on the 21st. Following twelve days of discussions, the Treaty of Wang Hsia was signed on July 3 providing for the establishment of five American treaty ports in China. It also granted protection to American sailors shipwrecked on Chinese shores and guaranteed that both civil and criminal law cases involving Americans would be adjudicated in consular courts.

Cushing set sail in the brig *Perry* on August 29 to return to the U.S. with the new treaty. *Brandywine*, on the other hand, remained in the Orient until departing Macau carrying word of the Chinese privy council's approval of the treaty. From Hawaii, she sailed to the west coast of South America, where she made calls at several ports before setting out to double Cape Horn on her way home. At the end of a long and successful cruise, *Brandywine* stood into Norfolk, Virginia, on September 17, 1845, and was decommissioned there eight days later.[52]

Brazil

After nearly two years in ordinary, the frigate was recommissioned once more on August 30, 1847, Capt. Thomas Crabbe in command. On September 13 *Brandywine* set sail for the Brazil Station, where she cruised for more than three years protecting United States interests in the region. The warship then returned to the United States at New York City on December 4, 1850, and was decommissioned 10 days later.

Civil War

Laid up in ordinary for more than a decade, *Brandywine* finally resumed active service as a result of the Civil War. She was recommissioned at the New York Navy Yard on

October 27, 1861, Commander Benjamin J. Totten in command, and set sail immediately for Hampton Roads, Virginia, where she arrived on October 29. Housed over and converted to a storeship, the former warship supported the operations of the North Atlantic Blockading Squadron for almost three years. She spent much of that time anchored near Fort Monroe and remained so employed until a fire broke out in her paint locker on September 3, 1864, and destroyed her. She sank at her moorings at Norfolk but was later raised and sold to Maltby & Co., of Norfolk on March 26, 1867.[53]

As a bookend to the ships' histories above, we offer a more detailed biographical account of three native sons. They were rough contemporaries whose paths doubtlessly crossed in service to the United States. Camden native Henry Hayes Lockwood had a very unusual career in both the army and the navy. Samuel Francis Du Pont had a more conventional path but his star rose very far. David Dixon Porter had the longest career of all, full of accomplishments that shaped the United States Navy into the future.

Henry Hayes Lockwood (b. 1814)

Henry Hayes Lockwood is an unlikely naval hero in that he is remembered primarily as a soldier. Nevertheless, this son of Kent County, Delaware, had a lasting impact on the navy that persists to this day. Born in Camden, Delaware, in 1814, he attended the U.S. Military Academy at West Point, graduating in 1836. He then served as a lieutenant in the Seminole Indian war in Florida. After a spell as a farmer, he joined the U.S. Navy and was assigned as a mathematics professor for midshipmen aboard the frigate *United States*. The author Herman Melville was a shipmate and based the character of the professor in his naval exposé novel, *White Jacket*, on Lockwood, with whom he was well acquainted. The *United States* served in the Pacific squadron during the siege and capture of Monterey, California, in 1846.[54]

Through the efforts of Secretary of the Navy George Bancroft, the United States Naval Academy was established at an army post named Fort Severn in Annapolis, Maryland, on October 10, 1845, with a class of 50 midshipmen and seven professors. Lockwood was selected as the first head of the Department of Natural Philosophy. His brother John became the academy's first surgeon. The curriculum included mathematics and navigation, gunnery and steam, chemistry, English, natural philosophy, and French. In 1851 Lockwood was transferred to the chair of field artillery and infantry tactics, with the additional duty of professor of astronomy.

Naval histories credit much of the success of the academy to Lockwood, rating him second only to Superintendent Commodore Franklin Buchanan in organizing the establishment. He introduced the manual of arms and military drill as requirements and spent the next 16 years as an important shaping influence on the school. His academic career was interrupted by the Civil War, when he answered the call to return to Delaware to lead the 1st Delaware Infantry. He continued to serve, rising to the rank of brigadier general in the Union army.[55]

On his muster out, in August 1865, he returned to Annapolis, where he taught gunnery and other subjects of a mathematical, scientific, and tactical nature. In 1870 he was assigned to the Naval Observatory in Washington, D.C., serving there until his retirement six years later. Because of his long service at the naval academy, he was accorded the distinction of burial in its cemetery at Annapolis. His tombstone remembers his service there, citing him as one of the founders. He was the father of Arctic explorer James Booth Lockwood, who lost his life during the "Lady Franklin Bay Expedition," one of a series of searches for the Franklin expedition, while serving as second in command under Adolphus W. Greely.[56]

Samuel Francis Du Pont[57]

At the same time Jacob Jones and Thomas Macdonough continued their careers as senior officers, a representative of the next generation, Samuel Francis Du Pont, began his own naval career. Like his predecessors, he would make significant contributions to winning America's wars over a long span of years. He was born September 27, 1803, in Bayonne, New Jersey, where his father had a woolen mill. His family's close connection with President Thomas Jefferson helped secure him an appointment as a midshipman at the age of 12 by President James Madison, and he first set sail aboard the 74-gun ship of the line *Franklin* in December 1815.[58]

Du Pont's first cruise was on the *Franklin* under Master Commandant Henry E. Ballard as the flagship of Commodore Charles Stewart of the Mediterranean Squadron. *Franklin* was another product of Samuel Humphries (1815) and the Philadelphia Navy Yard.[59] As the ship was preparing to sail in the summer of 1817, she was visited by President James Monroe, who toured the ship and met with the officers. Perhaps young Midshipman Du Pont had the opportunity to thank the president for his appointment during that visit. *Franklin* sailed in the fall of 1817 for the Mediterranean to demonstrate U.S. naval presence and reinforce American diplomacy in the Mediterranean, hosting local royalty around the periphery of the sea. She was the ideal ship for the purpose, as she was "a beautiful ship both in model and efficiency. She was recently painted, inwards and out, and every bolt and stanchion on her deck was like burnished Silver, and her crew was as neat and clean in White and Blue."[60]

As there was no naval academy at the time, Du Pont learned mathematics and navigation at sea and became an accomplished navigator by the time he took his next assignment. After cruising for three years and visiting the Isle of Wight, Italy, and Algeria, Du Pont returned home. Due to the changing of ships and the absence of Captain Ballard, his training had been incomplete and he had not yet been recommended as being qualified to take the test for lieutenant. That was not unusual. At 17

Samuel Francis DuPont (1803–1865) (1227310, New York Public Library).

he was just at the average age of all serving midshipmen. Nevertheless, his father worried about his career advancement and wrote to Delaware's famous naval hero, Jacob Jones, in 1821 asking if he would take Samuel with him back to the Mediterranean on his flagship *Constitution* as he assumed command of the Mediterranean Squadron from Stewart. Jones responded in the affirmative and not only assured that young Du Pont was trained and recommended for the lieutenant's test but also arranged for him to return from the Mediterranean mid-cruise to take it.[61] Nevertheless, in those times of lingering postwar naval reductions and commensurate slow promotions, Du Pont would remain a "passed midshipman" (today's ensign) for several years.

He then served aboard the frigate *Congress* in the West Indies and off the coast of Brazil. Although he was a passed midshipman, he was promoted to sailing master during his service aboard the 74-gun *North Carolina* (sister ship to the USS *Delaware*), which sailed in 1825 on a mission to display American influence and power in the Mediterranean. Soon after his promotion to lieutenant in 1826, Du Pont was ordered aboard the 12-gun schooner *Porpoise*. He returned home for two years after his father's death in 1827 and then served aboard the 16-gun sloop *Ontario* in 1829.[62] Despite the short period in which he had been an officer by this time, Du Pont had begun to openly criticize many of his senior officers, whom he believed were incompetent and had received their commands only through political influence.

After returning from the *Ontario* in June 1833, Du Pont married Sophie Madeleine du Pont (1810–88), his first cousin as the daughter of his uncle, Eleuthère Irénée du Pont. As he never kept an officer's journal, his voluminous correspondence with Sophie serves as the main documentation of his operations and observations throughout the rest of his naval career. From 1835 until 1838 he was the executive officer of the frigate *Constellation* and the sloop *Warren,* commanding both the latter and the schooner *Grampus* in the Gulf of Mexico. In 1838 he joined the ship *Ohio* in the Mediterranean until 1841. The following year he was promoted to commander and set sail for China aboard the brig *Perry* but was forced to return home and give up his command because of severe illness.[63]

During this period at home, Du Pont also became involved with the naval reform movement that was centered at the Naval Lyceum at the Brooklyn Navy Yard. There officers debated changes that should be made to improve the professionalism of the officer corps and the quality of the enlisted sailors. Du Pont's emphasis, based on his personal experience, was on the training of midshipmen, which eventually led to his involvement with the establishment of the U.S. Naval Academy. He also supported the efforts of Captain Andrew Foote and others to end the grog ration. He did not, however, support those who wanted to end flogging.[64]

He returned to service in 1845 as commander of the 44-gun frigate *Congress,* the flagship of Commodore Robert Stockton, reaching California by way of a cruise of the Hawaiian Islands by the time the Mexican-American War had begun.

Service in the Mexican American War, 1846–1848

The United States had declared war against Mexico on May 13, 1846. Earlier, in October 1845, Commodore Sloat had received a secret order from the Navy Department that, as soon as he knew for certain Mexico had declared war against the United States, he should take possession of the port of San Francisco and blockade such ports as his force would permit. The news of the war took several months to reach the Pacific. By the time

Commodore Sloat arrived to establish U.S. control over California, Captain John C. Fremont, leading a U.S. Army topographical expedition, had moved into California. That is the situation Commodore Stockton found, when Du Pont and *Congress* took him into Monterey on July 15. On July 23 Commodore Stockton relieved Commodore Sloat as commander of the Pacific Squadron. Du Pont was given command of *Cyane*, the smallest ship in the force.[65]

Commodore Stockton set out to extend his control over Alta (Upper) California by occupying Los Angeles. He formed a force of 360 sailors and marines on the *Savannah* to carry out that operation. To support them, Du Pont and *Cyane* were to take Fremont and 160 of his volunteer force who had been mustered into military service to San Diego. Upon arrival there, on July 29, Du Pont caught the Mexican brig *Juanita*, which was about to leave with a supply of ammunition, and took it as a prize.[66]

On August 19 Commander Hull in the *Warren* and Commander Du Pont in the *Cyane* were ordered south to blockade Mazatlán and San Blas, respectively, the two biggest ports on the west coast of Mexico. Arriving at San Blas on September 2, *Cyane* captured two vessels in the harbor. Du Pont began to patrol the Gulf. On October 1 *Cyane* visited the port of Loreto, capturing two schooners, and called in the bay of Muleje, where she took two or three small craft.[67]

From Guaymas, Du Pont proceeded south to Mazatlán and resumed the blockade there when he found that Hull had gone north for supplies. While the presence of *Cyane* blocked the main harbor, small vessels were running supplies in by sailing close to the beach and surf and into an old shallow harbor that *Cyane* could not enter. After anxiously awaiting a supply ship, in early November Du Pont had to give up the blockade of Mazatlán and sail north for replenishment. In all, during his operations on the blockade, Du Pont had captured some thirty ships, burnt the most important, and taken one for the squadron. He also had learned the lesson that a blockade could not be effectively sustained unless the ships on station were frequently resupplied or replaced. This would be a lesson he would later apply during the Civil War.[68]

On December 1, arriving at San Francisco he found the *Savannah*, the *Portsmouth*, and the *Warren*. From them he learned the reasons why he had been neglected on station. The navy-marine garrisons occupying towns all up and down the coast were facing attacks by bands of local Mexican settlers. Stockton had moved his forces to San Diego to await reinforcements from General Kearney, who was bringing a few army troops from New Mexico. Du Pont received orders to join him there immediately. Filling up with water and getting what scanty supplies were available, he sailed *Cyane* for San Diego. He arrived in San Diego just in time to furnish 108 sailors from *Cyane* to their force of over 500. On January 7 and 8 that force fought two battles approaching Los Angeles and occupied the town on January 12. With the occupation of Los Angeles and the signing of the Treaty of Cahuenga on January 13, the control of Alta California by the United States was complete.[69]

Although they now had control of California, the war with Mexico continued. A second attempt to blockade the west coast of Mexico was made. Arriving at Monterey on February 8, with General Kearney and staff aboard, Du Pont unexpectedly found the frigate *Independence*, and the sloop of war *Lexington* in the harbor. *Independence* was a former ship of the line that was now a razee (cut down) frigate serving as the flagship of Commodore William B. Shubrick, who had arrived on 22 January to assume command of the Pacific Squadron. On February 17 Montgomery, in *Portsmouth*, acting on orders from Shubrick, had reimposed the blockade at Mazatlán.

Meanwhile, on March 2 Commodore James Biddle, commander of the Asiatic Squadron, had arrived at Monterey. On 27 April, under orders from Commodore Biddle, *Cyane* and *Independence* relieved *Portsmouth*, which returned to Monterey for supplies. Shubrick, now a captain, was aboard *Independence*. They assumed responsibility for the Mazatlán blockade and control of the Gulf of California. Then Shubrick in *Independence* departed for San Francisco on June 3, leaving *Cyane* as the only ship on the western coast of Mexico. In order to cover the entire area, Du Pont sailed *Cyane* back and forth between Mazatlán and Cabo San Lucas, which technically lifted the blockade. On June 20 *Portsmouth* returned from Monterey. Du Pont was short of supplies and, after discussing the situation, Montgomery and Du Pont concluded that a single-ship blockade was not effective. The second attempt to blockade the western coast of Mexico ended.[70]

On November 11 *Cyane* led *Congress* and *Independence* into the harbor of Mazatlán, and a landing party from the three ships captured Mazatlan without firing a shot. Further reinforcements were landed on November 19–20, to assist in repelling several attacks. On November 21 two American whalers, the *Magnolia* and the *Edward,* appeared offshore and the Mexicans, believing they were more naval forces, withdrew. The city remained in the hands of a 400-man naval-marine force for the rest of the war, with a few minor skirmishes with the Mexican forces nearby.

The Treaty of Guadalupe Hidalgo, ending the war, had been signed on March 10. Ironically, after all that, the treaty did not cede the Baja Peninsula to the U.S. For the time being, however, U.S. occupation continued. On April 29 Du Pont wrote to Commodore Shubrick: "The country is completely quieted, and, from what I can learn and from personal observations, I am impressed with the belief that all men of substance and respectability would decidedly prefer the American government, and will be much mortified should the territory not be included in the treaty [which had not yet been ratified by Mexico]."[71]

DuPont and *Cyane* returned to Norfolk on October 9, 1848, and received congratulations from the secretary of the navy for their significant contributions to the war.

Establishment of the Naval Academy, 1849

Du Pont served most of the next decade on shore assignment, and his efforts during this time are credited with helping to modernize the U.S. Navy. He was a member of the board that established the naval academy at Annapolis. In 1849 Secretary of the Navy George Bancroft asked him to help draw up a curriculum for the academy. Du Pont briefly served as superintendent of the new academy in 1850. An advocate for modernizing the navy, he pressed for increased emphasis on engineering and steam power and was among the leaders who organized the academy. Under his direction the curriculum included courses on engineering, mathematics, steam, and chemistry. He studied using steam to power ships and helped upgrade the Lighthouse Service's aids to navigation. He resigned as superintendent after only four months because he believed it was a post more appropriate for someone closer to retirement age. Du Pont was an advocate for a more mobile and offensive navy rather than the harbor defense function much of it was then relegated to, and he worked on revising naval rules and regulations. In 1851 he was asked to analyze the impact steam power was likely to have on America's defense and its existing system of coastal fortifications. In six months he produced the 28-page *Report on the National Defenses*, in which he articulated a strategy for modern naval warfare.[72]

Du Pont stressed the impact steam power was likely to have on naval tactics. He argued, well before Mahan, that the navy's function was to "carry the 'sword of state' on the broad ocean area" and "to contend for mastery of the seas."[73] He also emphasized the importance of the Sandwich (Hawaiian) Islands to the defense of the new West Coast of America.

After being appointed to the board of the United States Lighthouse Service, his recommendations for upgrading the antiquated system were largely adopted by Congress. Du Pont took the opportunity to become acquainted with many of the nation's influential naval and political leaders and was recognized for his intellectual ability and professional expertise.[74] In 1853 he was made general superintendent over what is typically considered the first world's fair in the United States, the Exhibition of the Industry of All Nations, held in New York City. Despite international praise, low attendance caused the venture to go into heavy debt, and Du Pont resigned.[75]

Naval Efficiency Board, 1855

For a number of years, Congress had been debating how to revitalize the officer corps of the navy. There were too many officers, including some who were incompetent or unable to perform as required. There were too many senior officers who were old and inactive. But there were also still a number of heroes of 1812, who deserved to be treated with respect and dignity by a grateful nation rather than being forced from the service as indigents. Congress could not resolve the problem by debate.

In December 1854 the secretary of the navy asked Du Pont to draft proposed legislation creating a system of retirement for the navy and a paper that could be circulated to advocate that legislation. Du Pont became an enthusiastic supporter of naval reform, writing in support of the 1855 congressional act to promote naval efficiency. Long an outspoken critic of political influence in the service, Du Pont served on the Naval Efficiency Board and worked to oust incompetent officers. In 1855 he persuaded James Dobbin, the secretary of the navy, to take action against the deadwood in that service. In February 1855 Congress passed "An Act to Promote the Efficiency of the Navy." Its object was to professionalize the service by forcing incompetent officers into retirement and promoting young, talented midshipmen.[76]

Throughout most of his career, Du Pont had been very critical of many of his superior officers, and he saw that the navy now had an opportunity to reform itself by installing a merit system of promotion. In June he was appointed to the fifteen-man Naval Efficiency Board, where he became a leading advocate for reform. In five months of deliberations, the board reviewed the careers of 712 officers and recommended that 201 be dismissed. Congress, however, backtracked and allowed officers to appeal their cases to a court of inquiry, which reinstated sixty-two of them. Du Pont himself became the subject of heavy criticism from those who were removed and their allies. A similar naval selection board process continues to this day to keep the most qualified officers advancing and moving others, less fitted, out or into retirement.[77]

Du Pont was promoted to captain in 1855. In 1857 he was given command of the steam frigate *Minnesota* and ordered to transport William Reed, the U.S. minister to China, to his post in Peking. Du Pont's *Minnesota* was one of seventeen warships parading Western force in China. After China failed to satisfy demands for greater access to its ports, on April 28, 1858, he witnessed the capture by the French and English of Chinese forts on the Peiho River. He then sailed to Japan, India, and Arabia, finally returning to Boston in May 1859. He played a major role in the receiving of the Japanese ambassador that year, accompanying him on his three-month visit to Washington, Baltimore, and Philadelphia; the trip was a breakthrough for opening Japan to American trade and investment. Du Pont was made commandant of the Philadelphia Naval Shipyard in 1860. He was responsible for overseeing all naval activities in Pennsylvania, Maryland and Delaware, as well as the security and defense of the Delaware Bay and the portions of the Chesapeake Bay providing approaches to Baltimore and Washington, D.C., as well as the coastal areas between. The states of Delaware and Maryland and the navy itself were divided between secessionists and unionists after the election of President Abraham Lincoln. Du Pont was a committed Union supporter, worried about how the political situation in Maryland would affect his responsibilities and urging his naval officer friends and those under his command to remain with the United States Navy. He expected to retire in this post, but the outbreak of the Civil War returned him to active duty.[78]

David Dixon Porter, (1813–1891) (95503132, Library of Congress).

David Dixon Porter

The star that would rise the farthest and shine the brightest was David Dixon Porter. Born in Chester, Pennsylvania, on June 8, 1813, he was one of six sons of David and Evalina Anderson Porter in a family of ten children. The family had strong naval traditions. The elder Porter's father, also named David, had been captain of a Massachusetts vessel in the Revolutionary War, as had his uncle Samuel. In the next generation, David Porter and his brother John entered the fledgling United States Navy and served with distinction during the War of 1812. David Porter was named to the rank of commodore.

In addition to rearing their own children, his parents, David and Evalina Porter, informally adopted James Glasgow Farragut. The boy's mother had died in 1808 when he was seven, and his father, George Farragut, a U.S. naval officer in the American Revolution and a friend of David Porter, Sr., was unable to care for all his children. Commodore Porter offered to adopt James, to which the boy and George agreed. In 1811 James started serving as a midshipman under Porter in the U.S. Navy and changed his first name to David. He had a distinguished career as David G. Farragut, serving as the first man to attain the new rank of admiral, instituted by the U.S. Congress after the Civil War.

After a reprimand for an 1824 incident, Commodore David Porter resigned from the navy. He accepted an offer from the government of Mexico to become their general of marine—in effect, the commander of their navy. He took with him a nephew, David Henry Porter, and his own sons David Dixon and Thomas. The two boys were made midshipmen in the Mexican navy. Thomas, age 10, died of yellow fever soon after arriving in Mexico. David Dixon, age 12, was not affected by the disease and was able to serve on the frigate *Libertad*, where he saw little action, and on the captured merchantman *Esmeralda* for a raid on Spanish shipping in Cuban waters.[79]

In 1828 David Dixon accompanied his cousin, David Henry Porter, captain of the brig *Guerrero*, in another raid. *Guerrero*, mounting twenty-two guns, was one of the finest vessels in the small Mexican Navy. Off the coast of Cuba on February 10, 1828, she encountered a flotilla of about fifty schooners, convoyed by the Spanish brigs *Marte* and *Amalia*. Captain Porter elected to attack and soon forced the flotilla to seek refuge in the harbor at Mariel, 30 miles (48 km) west of Havana. The Spanish 64-gun frigate *Lealtad* put to sea. *Guerrero* was able to break off the action and escape, but overnight Captain Porter decided to circle back and attack the vessels at Mariel. Intercepted by *Lealtad*, he could not escape. In the battle, Captain Porter was killed, together with many of his crew; the young midshipman Porter was slightly wounded. He was among the survivors who surrendered and were imprisoned in Havana until they could be exchanged. Commodore Porter chose not to risk his son again and sent him back to the United States by way of New Orleans.

David Dixon Porter obtained an official appointment as midshipman in the U.S. Navy through his grandfather U.S. Congressman William Anderson. The appointment was dated February 2, 1829, when he was sixteen years of age; this was somewhat older than many midshipmen, some of whom had been taken in as boys. Due to his relative maturity and experience—greater than that of most naval lieutenants—Porter tended to be cocky and challenge some of his superiors, which led to conflict. Except for intervention by Commodore James Biddle, who acted favorably because Porter's father was a hero, his warrant as a midshipman would not have been renewed.[80]

Porter's last duty as a midshipman was on the frigate USS *United States*, flagship of Commodore Daniel Patterson, from June 1832 until October 1834. Patterson's family accompanied him, including his daughter, George Ann ("Georgy"). The two young people renewed their acquaintance and became engaged. After Porter returned home, he completed the examination for passed midshipman and soon afterward was assigned to duty in the Coast Survey. There his pay was such that he could save enough to marry.[81] Porter and Georgy Patterson were married on March 10, 1839. Of their four sons, three had military careers, and their two surviving daughters married men who had military service or were active officers.

- Major David Essex Porter served in the army during the Civil War, but resigned after two years in the peacetime army.
- Captain Theodoric Porter made his career in the navy.
- Lieutenant Colonel Carlile Patterson Porter was an officer in the U.S. Marine Corps; his son, David Dixon Porter II, also served in the Marines, rising to the rank of major general and earning the Medal of Honor.
- One of their two surviving daughters, Elizabeth, married Leavitt Curtis Logan, who achieved the rank of rear admiral. Their other surviving daughter, Elena, married Charles H. Campbell, a former army officer who had left the service before

their marriage. Richard Bache Porter was the only child to have no relation to the military services.[82]

In March 1841, Porter was promoted in rank to lieutenant, and in April of the next year he was detached from the Coast Survey. He had a brief tour of duty in the Mediterranean, and then he was assigned to the U.S. Navy's Hydrographic Office.

Mission to Santo Domingo

In 1846 the era of peace was coming to a close. The United States had annexed the Republic of Texas, and the islands of the Caribbean seemed to be likely targets for further expansion. The Republic of Santo Domingo (the present-day Dominican Republic) had broken off from the Republic of Haiti in 1844, and the United States State Department needed to determine the new nation's social, political, and economic stability. The suitability of the Bay of Samana for U.S. Navy operations was also of interest. To find out, Secretary of State James Buchanan asked Porter to undertake a private investigation. Porter accepted the assignment, and on March 15, 1846, he left home. He arrived in Santo Domingo after some unexpected delays and spent two weeks mapping the coastline. On May 19 he began a trek through the interior that left him without communication for a month. On June 19 he emerged from the jungle, bitten by insects but with the information the State Department wanted. He then discovered that while he had been away the United States had gone to war with Mexico.[83]

Porter served as first lieutenant of the side-wheel gunboat USS *Spitfire* under Commander Josiah Tattnall. *Spitfire* was at Vera Cruz when General Winfield Scott led the amphibious assault on the city, which was shielded by a series of forts and the ancient Castle of San Juan de Ulloa. Porter had spent many hours exploring the castle when he had been a midshipman in the Mexican navy, so he was familiar with both its strengths and its weaknesses. He submitted a plan to attack it to Captain Tattnall. Taking eight oarsmen and the ship's gig, he sounded out a channel on the night of March 22–23, 1847, using the experience he had gained with the Coast Survey. The next morning *Spitfire* and other vessels taking part in the bombardment followed the channel Porter had laid out and took up positions inside the harbor, where they were able to pound the forts and castle. Doing so meant, however, that they had to run by the forts, which was contrary to the orders of Commodore Matthew C. Perry. Perry sent signals ordering the vessels to break off the bombardment and return, but Tattnall ordered his men not to look at the commodore's signals. Not until a special messenger came with explicit orders to retire did Maffitt cease firing. Perry appreciated the audacity shown by his subordinates but did not approve of the way they had disregarded his orders. After that, he kept *Spitfire* by his side.[84]

On June 13, 1847, Perry mounted an expedition to capture the interior town of Tabasco. Porter on his own led a charge of 68 sailors to capture the fort defending the city, and Perry rewarded him for his initiative by making him captain of *Spitfire*. It was his first command. It brought him no advantages, however, as the naval part of the war was essentially over.[85]

Civilian Service

In Washington again following the war, Porter saw little chance for professional improvement and none for advancement. In order to gain experience in handling steamships, he took a leave of absence from the navy to command civilian ships. He insisted that his crews submit to the methods of military discipline; his employers were noncommittal about his methods, but they were impressed by the results. They asked him to stay in Australia, but his health and the health of his eldest daughter, Georgianne, persuaded him to return. Back in the United States, he moved his family from Washington to New York in the hope that the climate would benefit his daughter, but she died shortly after the move. His second daughter, Evalina ("Nina"), also died in the interwar period.[86]

Once again returning to active duty, Porter commanded the storeship USS *Supply* in a venture to bring camels to the United States. The project was promoted by Secretary of War Jefferson Davis, who thought that the desert animals could be useful for the cavalry in the arid Southwest. *Supply* made two successful trips before Secretary Davis left office and the experiment was discontinued.[87]

In 1859 Porter received an attractive offer from the Pacific Mail Steamship Company to be captain of a ship then under construction. The offer would be effective when she was complete. He would have accepted, but he was delayed in his departure and before he could leave, war had broken out again.[88]

The relatively peaceful and prosperous time between the War of 1812 and the Civil War saw not only the secure establishment of the United States Navy but also rapid advancement in naval technology, thanks to the pioneering efforts of Delaware Valley shipbuilders. Innovations in structural shipbuilding as well as propulsion set the stage for even faster advancement due to the impetus of the Civil War. The Delaware River and Bay were improved by civil engineering efforts to better navigation, remove obstacles, deepen channels, and enhance harbor facilities fed by canals to the bountiful inland resources. Sons of the Delaware Valley would lay the foundation for leadership in the war to come.

Five

The Civil War

The American Civil War of 1861–1865 barely touched the Delaware estuary in the physical sense. But it touched nearly every soul and every community in the watershed through industry, commerce, and the effort required to sustain this existential threat to continued survival as a nation. Many sons of the Delaware Valley served in the United States Navy. Because Delaware was a divided border state and a slave state, some served in the Confederate naval forces as well. The state of Delaware was like America in miniature and split along the same geopolitical lines as the nation. When the war began there was a fear that Confederate vessels might raid along Delaware shores. On Pea Patch Island off Delaware City a strongly built and recently enlarged Fort Delaware stood as a sentinel on the river. It was capable of turning back anything the South could send against it. Fort Delaware never fired a shot in anger but later became a principal Union prison of some notoriety, eventually housing over 12,595 rebel prisoners at its peak, after the battle of Gettysburg.[1]

The Delaware River and its waterways were among the primary clandestine trade routes from New York and points north to eastern Virginia for southern sympathizers. It was an easy matter to take a train to Seaford and then proceed by water down the Nanticoke River across the lower Chesapeake Bay. Alternately one could sail along the coast and disgorge smuggled contraband at a hidden inlet or cove for transshipment overland. The inspector of customs at Seaford seized several hundred rubber overcoats and twenty compasses that were on their way to the South via Salisbury.[2]

The Chesapeake and Delaware [C&D] Canal proved its strategic value during the Civil War. In one memorable episode, at the onset of war, Virginia had seceded from the Union on April 17, 1861, and her troops marched on Washington. The capital was largely undefended by troops and fortifications. Federal troops entrained from the north were halted in Baltimore. That night all the bridges from Baltimore to the Susquehanna River were destroyed by Confederates. All rail traffic to the capital had been severed.[3]

On April 20 the government commandeered all the propeller steamers in Philadelphia capable of negotiating the locks on the C&D Canal. Troop-laden vessels steamed down the Delaware and through the canal arriving in Perryville, Maryland, at dawn the following morning. By rail to Baltimore then steamer to Annapolis then again by rail to Washington the troops arrived just as Confederate forces were amassing in Virginia at the end of the Long Bridge over the Potomac River. For the next sixty days, the canal was the vital link to provide men, supplies, and relief to Washington. This critical strategic waterway served throughout the remainder of the war in this role.[4]

Delaware River shipbuilders had pioneered iron-hulled steamships and were among the leading innovators and producers of these vessels. The foremost firm was Harlan and Hollingsworth, who built their first iron-hulled steamer in 1844. They were joined by the firm of Pusey and Jones, who had established themselves in 1849. In 1853 Pusey and Jones launched their first effort, the *Flora McDonald*, an iron-hulled side-wheel steamer.[5] In the decade before the Civil War, Wilmington shipbuilding firms led the nation in iron shipbuilding. Between 1845 and 1857 thirty-five iron-hulled vessels were constructed in the city, more than all other American yards combined. In 1857 the *Delaware State Journal* remarked on this situation: "Magnificent boat building is becoming an everyday thing in Wilmington and from all parts of the country orders are received for the building of some new vessel or steamboat. Our master mechanics have sent the name of Wilmington out over the country with a reputation stamped upon it that does credit to themselves and causes a profitable return of business."[6] Delaware River shipyards provided an almost equal number of vessels to each side during the Civil War, to the South before the war and to the North after war was declared.

The "Anaconda Plan" was the strategy for suppressing the Confederacy at the beginning of the Civil War. Proposed by General-in-Chief Winfield Scott, the plan emphasized a Union blockade of the Southern ports and called for control of the Mississippi River to cut the South in half.

Scott's Great Snake, entered according to Act of Congress in the year 1861. Cartoon map illustrating General Winfield Scott's plan to crush the Confederacy economically. It is sometimes called the "Anaconda plan" (99447020, Library of Congress).

Scott's proposed strategy for the war against the South had two prominent features: first, all ports in the seceding states were to be rigorously blockaded; second, a strong column of about 80,000 men should use the Mississippi River as a highway to thrust completely through the Confederacy. A spearhead, a relatively small amphibious force of army troops transported by boats and supported by gunboats, should advance rapidly, capturing the Confederate positions down the river in sequence. They would be followed by a more traditional army marching behind them to secure the victories. The culminating battle would be for the forts below New Orleans. When they fell, the river would be in Federal hands from its source to its mouth, and the rebellion would be cut in two.[7]

This naval strategy would isolate the South from international trade and deny markets for its cotton products as well as prevent the import of arms. It included seizing and holding Southern ports. Rear Admiral Samuel F. Du Pont gained an early victory by seizing Port Royal, between Savannah and Charleston, and making it an important Union navy base for blockading operations. Admiral David Farragut took New Orleans and Mobile. The Southern coastline was vulnerable to attacks from the U.S. Navy at many smaller ports and coastal establishments. The sounds in North Carolina and the ports of Savannah, Norfolk, Charleston, and finally Wilmington, North Carolina, would eventually fall in turn. Simultaneously, a river campaign was waged along the Mississippi and its tributaries to bisect the South.[8]

The Union blockade took the form of the North Atlantic Blockading Squadron based in Hampton Roads. Their area of responsibility was the coastlines of Virginia and North Carolina. The South Atlantic Squadron was based in Port Royal and had responsibility for the South Carolina, Georgia, and Florida coasts down to Key West. The Gulf Blockading Squadron was responsible for the Gulf Coast of the South from Key West to the Mexican border. In 1862 this squadron was split into two elements: The East Squadron headquartered in Key West and responsible for the coast from Pensacola to Cape Canaveral, and the West Squadron, responsible for an area from the mouth of the Mississippi to south of the Rio Grande.[9]

The Confederacy responded by seeking ways to penetrate the less-than-comprehensive Union maritime blockade. This porous blockade would grow more effective as the war wore on. Fast steamers were among the vessels of choice to run the blockade. They were independent of the wind and offered a lot of flexibility in maneuver, although most of them also carried sail for cruising in favorable winds. The Union found it very difficult to blockade the South with sailing vessels and did not have enough ships in any case (only ninety) during the early stages of the war. The best kind of vessel to chase a blockade-runner was a fast steamer, and the Union rushed to procure them. The South also employed commerce raiders, such as the *Florida* and the *Alabama*, which ranged all over the globe destroying Yankee shipping and diverting precious Union resources from the blockade.

Philadelphia Navy Yard

With the Confederate capture of Pensacola and the destruction of the Norfolk Navy Yard, the Philadelphia Navy Yard became even more critical to the war effort for the Union. It was the yard "nearest the seat of war," according to Captain Samuel F. Du Pont, the commander of the yard. At the onset of the war Du Pont purchased, requisitioned, and borrowed what he could for his diminutive fleet, including the merchant steamer *Phineas Sprague*, the steam packet *Union*, and the Philadelphia City *Ice Boat*. The fast side-wheel steamer *Keystone State* was purchased to chase Confederate blockade-runners. Eventually another nine private vessels were acquired.[10]

The sudden demand for steamship repair and maintenance taxed the crowded Southwark Yard. An additional 1,500 ship workers and machinists were hired. By August 24 the yard launched the wooden screw sloop *Tuscarora*. *Monongahela*, and *Juniata* would soon follow down the ways. Altogether twelve keels were laid and nine ships launched during the Civil War, averaging about one every four months.[11] The Philadelphia Navy Yard subcontracted many of its components to Delaware River shipbuilders. Nevertheless, the yard was overcrowded. A fire in 1863 exacerbated the situation. It was clear that a new yard was needed more adequate to the task. The City of Philadelphia offered League Island as an alternate site. It was not until after the war that the navy finally made a decision, in 1868. The Philadelphia Navy Yard would vacate Southwark and move to League Island at the confluence of the Delaware and Schuylkill rivers. The transition was slow. Southwark did not close until January 1876. Symbolically the last ship in the yard was the USS *Constitution*, whose repairs were still incomplete. She was moved across the river to the Wood and Dialog Shipyard in Camden.[12]

Samuel Francis Du Pont in the Civil War

At the onset of the Civil War, Captain Samuel Du Pont commanded the Philadelphia Navy Yard and was preparing to retire. The war would change his plans. When communication was cut off with Washington at the start of the Civil War, Du Pont took the initiative of sending a fleet to the Chesapeake Bay to protect the landing of Union troops at Annapolis, Maryland.

The army chief of staff, Major General Winfield Scott, proposed a strategy of strangling the Confederacy by blockades and military action that would become known as the Anaconda Plan. An army-navy federal strategy board was established to develop the implementing actions for that strategy. Du Pont was appointed to head the board as its president.[13] After the planning was complete, Du Pont was given the responsibility for leading the Atlantic portion of the blockade. He needed a base from which to operate. The Chesapeake Bay was too far for coal-fired ships to stay on station off Charleston and Savannah for long. DuPont decided Port Royal Sound at Hilton Head, halfway between Charleston and Savannah, was the ideal location.

Du Pont was promoted from captain to "flag officer" (a temporary rank). He put together a fleet of over 75 ships to attack the forts defending Port Royal, troop ships with forces to occupy them, and supply ships to create a base. His flagship was the steam frigate *Wabash*. This was the largest U.S. fleet ever created up to that time. The fleet encountered a major storm off Hatteras, North Carolina, and was scattered, but eventually they found a way to put it back together.

The sound at Port Royal was protected by two forts, Fort Walker on Hilton Head Island to the south and Fort Beauregard on Phillips Island to the north. Du Pont had his ships move towards the fort in an elliptical course. As they approached the defenses Du Pont had his ships shell the north walls of the fort, then outbound they shelled the southern walls. Finally, the ships stood off and used enfilading fire (along their length) to land

Bombardment of the Port Royal Forts, November 1861, Flag Officer Samuel F. Du Pont commanding (NH 1130, U.S. Naval History and Heritage Command).

shells within the forts. Captain John Gillis from Wilmington was commander of USS *Seminole* during this operation.[14] This battle was among the first amphibious combined operations of army-navy forces in the war. While Du Pont was shelling the forts from the sound, Fort Walker on Hilton Head was evacuated by the enemy first. A landing party from Du Pont's flagship took control until the army arrived to relieve them. Soon afterward, Fort Beauregard was evacuated and the same sequence of events occurred.[15]

Du Pont was acclaimed as the first hero of the war for the North and received commendations from the U.S. Congress for his brilliant tactical success. He was appointed rear admiral on July 16, 1862. Towards the end of 1862 he became the first U.S. naval officer to be assigned command over armored "ironclad" ships. This fleet included the monitor *Patapsco*, built in Wilmington by the Harlan and Hollingsworth yard. Though he commanded the vessels ably in engagements with other ships, they performed poorly in an attack on Fort McAllister, Georgia, due to their small number of guns and slow rate of fire. This test raised doubts with Du Pont about their capabilities against shore targets.[16]

Secretary of the Navy Gideon Welles and his assistant, Gustavus Fox, wanted to use Du Pont to demonstrate the capabilities of the "new" navy they had developed based on ironclads and monitors. The political leadership deemed a combined army-navy force unnecessary. Taking Charleston would be a high-profile demonstration as well as revenge for Fort Sumter. They wanted Du Pont to repeat his victory at Port Royal using the same tactics and naval forces as before. Du Pont, who knew the capabilities of the ships and the configuration of the harbor, was dubious of success and tried to talk both the secretary and, eventually, the president out of the operation unless he was buttressed by a larger army force in a combined operation. But Welles, who had the political aims, and Fox, who had the naval aims, had the ear of the president. DuPont was ordered to conduct the operation. Worried about being compared to the indecisive General McClellan, he agreed to try.[17]

Charleston was well defended. The geography was complex, the approach channels narrow and mined, the banks lined with gun batteries having 385 guns total, and the channel blocked with iron obstructions. Then there was Fort Sumter, itself a formidable obstacle. Du Pont's force consisted of his flagship, the ironclad *New Ironsides*, an experimental ironclad—the *Keokuk*—and seven improved monitors. The only way to approach was single file up the channel. The ships had bulky mine-clearing gear attached, which made progress slow. The operation was slow getting started, and the tide turned, making forward progress almost impossible. Du Pont's ships were caught in a blistering crossfire. Five of his nine ironclads were disabled in the failed attack, and one more subsequently sank. After two hours, *Keokuk* had hit a mine, Du Pont's flagship was stalled at a mine, two monitors were sinking, and the rest were damaged. He withdrew them before nightfall.[18]

The force withdrawn, Du Pont and his captains agreed not to try again the next day. Secretary of the Navy Welles blamed Du Pont for poor planning and for not pressing the attack and had the president remove him and appoint the president's favorite, John Dahlgren, to head the Atlantic Blockading Squadron. Du Pont himself anguished over it and, despite an engagement in which vessels under his command defeated and captured a Confederate ironclad, was relieved of command on July 5, 1863, at his own request. Though he enlisted help to get his official report of the incident published by the navy, an ultimately inconclusive congressional investigation into the failure essentially turned into a trial of whether Du Pont had misused his ships and misled his superiors. His attempt to garner the support of President Lincoln was ignored, and he returned home to Delaware then returned to Washington to serve briefly on a board reviewing naval promotions.[19]

However, subsequent events arguably vindicated Du Pont's judgment and capabilities. Later that summer Dahlgren managed to help the army land a force to take one of the outermost forts, from which they could shell Charleston. They got 35 shots off before their new gun, a very large Parrott rifle nicknamed "Swamp Angel," failed. The Union never took Charleston by sea. That city fell when Sherman's army arrived from land.

Du Pont died on June 23, 1865, while on a trip to Philadelphia and is buried in the du Pont family cemetery. In 1882 Congress authorized the creation of a statue honoring Du Pont, to be located in a newly fashionable neighborhood in the District of Columbia not far from the White House. A bronze sculpture of Du Pont by Launt Thompson was dedicated on December 20, 1884, and the traffic circle was renamed Du Pont Circle. The du Pont family, however, never liked the statue. In keeping with changing aesthetics, they hired famous sculptor Daniel French to replace the statue with a more "artistic" memorial in the form of a fountain, dedicated in 1921. The original statue was first moved to Winterthur and then to Wilmington's Rockford Park, where it now stands.[20] Fort Du Pont, at Delaware City, and three U.S. Navy vessels were named in his honor. These include the torpedo boat TB-7 and the destroyers DD-152 and DD-941.

Delaware River Shipbuilding

In order to meet the immediate need for iron-hulled vessels the government purchased all the iron-hulled ships available. The navy transformed Delaware River-built

The side-wheel steamer *Delaware*, built at Harlan and Hollingsworth Yards in Wilmington, 1861 (Kennard Wiggins, artist, courtesy Delaware Military Museum).

ships into blockade gunboats, troop transports, and supply vessels for the Union forces. Starting the war with ninety vessels, by war's end, the Union possessed 671 ships of all kinds.

Side-wheel Steamer USS Delaware

The steamboat *Delaware*, initially called the *Edenton*, was ordered in 1860 by the Albemarle Steam Packet Company. This company was made up of 24 businessmen from northeastern North Carolina who wanted to operate a steamboat in the Albemarle Sound area of North Carolina. According to the agreement, the steamboat would be built using "timbers of bar iron, attached to the hull plating via keepers." Albemarle Steam's president, Edward Wood of Edenton, grew concerned over the deteriorating situation between the North and the South. He ultimately stopped payments over fear that the steamboat, called the *Virginia Dare*, would be detained. The fourth *Delaware*, a side-wheel steamer, was built in 1861 at Wilmington, Delaware, by Harlan and Hollingsworth Company as the commercial steamship *Virginia Dare*. She was purchased by the navy on October 14, 1861, for $45,000, with Lieutenant S.P. Quackenbush in command. Renamed the *Delaware*, she was commissioned on December 7, 1861, the only naval warship named *Delaware* that was built in Delaware.[21]

She was much smaller than her ship-of-the-line predecessor, 161 feet long and with a beam of 27 feet; 8 feet 3 inches depth of hold; a draft of six feet; 357 tons; and a crew complement of up to 12 officers and 68 men. Her maximum speed was 13 knots and she was powered by a walking beam steam engine driving side-wheel paddles augmented by sail. Her sails were schooner rigged. *Delaware* was originally armed with four 32-pound cannons and one 12-pound rifle. In January 1862 this armament was changed to one 9-inch smooth bore, one 32-pounder, and one rifled 12-pounder. On October 1, 1864, a heavy 12-pounder was added but it was removed on the last day of the year.[22]

Assigned to the North Atlantic Blockading Squadron during the Civil War, *Delaware* sailed from Philadelphia on December 12, 1861. She reported off Fort Monroe for gunnery practice with her "batteries ready for action" on December 23. She then stood up the James River December 26 on patrol. On January 12, 1862, she sailed for Hatteras Inlet, North Carolina, as part of a force that convoyed General Ambrose E. Burnside and his forces in an offensive against Confederate forts. On February 7, 1862, she was underway off Roanoke Island with the North Atlantic Blockading Squadron. She took part in a five-hour shore bombardment, landing troops of the 51st Pennsylvania Regiment taken off a transport steamer.[23]

The capture of Roanoke was completed by February 8, and Delaware came to anchor with the squadron about twelve miles below Elizabeth City, North Carolina, the next day. The following day she steamed with the fleet in Albemarle Sound to engage the fortifications erected near Elizabeth City. The fort fell by early morning and *Delaware* came alongside the city wharf and made a prize of the rebel steamer *Ellis*. On February 10 she shared in the capture of five more Confederate steamers and two schooners. Other Confederate ships captured by the Federal fleet when Elizabeth City fell were the steamers *Curlew, Forrest, Fanny,* and *Seabird,* and the schooners *Black Warrior* and *Lyn Haven*.[24]

At the conclusion of those operations, Captain Stephen C. Rowan, commanding United States Naval Forces in Pamlico Sound, congratulated the men of his force for their "strict observance to the plan of attack" and their "coolness, gallantry and skill under fire" as well of their service ashore helping the citizens of the city fight the fires the retreating Confederate forces had set.[25]

On February 19 *Delaware* and seven other gunboats (*Louisiana, Morse, Hunchback, Whitehead, Barney, Perry, Lockwood*) made a reconnaissance up the Chowan River. The purpose of the voyage was to destroy two railroad bridges above the town of Winton. It was during this foray that *Delaware* was nearly ambushed at the town wharf by a force of Confederate soldiers and artillery hiding among the brush near the dock. Union commander Rush Hawkins, who was in the crosstrees of the foremast, spotted the Confederates and warned the helmsman in time to sheer off. *Delaware's* superstructure was severely shot up by rifle fire, but fortunately the artillery overshot its mark. After pulling away from the dock, *Delaware* returned fire and dispersed the Confederate militia. The next day she and the other gunboats returned to Winton. The force finding it deserted, the town was burned, partly in retaliation for the ambush. *Delaware* covered the landing of Union forces to destroy stores in the town, and when the enemy, reinforced with cavalry, counterattacked, fire from the *Delaware* held them at bay until the troops had been reembarked. *Delaware* returned to Roanoke Island on February 21 and on March 5, 1862, captured a small schooner off Brant Island. She cruised off Jones Bay the next day and capturedthe schooner *Zenith*, which was laden with corn, and a small open boat that was schooner rigged. Four prisoners and the prizes were taken to Roanoke Island.[26]

Delaware left Hatteras Inlet with the fleet and army forces on March 12 and steamed up the Neuse River to anchor within sight of New Bern by nightfall. The next morning she received onboard, from the Flag Steamer *Philadelphia,* Captain Stephen C. Rowan, commanding United States Naval Forces in Pamlico Sound. *Philadelphia* was assigned duties with the North Atlantic Blockading Squadron in October and during January and February 1862 served as squadron flagship. *Philadelphia* took part in the expedition to Hatteras Inlet in January and served as flag-steamer to Flag Officer Louis M. Goldsborough at the battle of Roanoke Island, North Carolina, on February 7–8. She also took part in the capture of New Bern and later participated in the expedition to the Dismal Swamp Canal during April 17–20. *Delaware* ran in close to the enemy's shore to cover the landing of troops by shelling the woods then ran alongside a schooner and brought off troops of the 11th Connecticut Regiment. She placed them on tenders to be carried ashore and followed the advancing troops to engage the battery on Johnson's Point.

On March 14 she returned Captain Rowan onboard flagship *Philadelphia* and after shelling the batteries on Johnson's Point ran into the wharf and sent armed boats to make prizes of the Confederate steamers *Old North State* and *Albemarle.* At 2:00 P.M. Major Generals Foster and Burnside came aboard to report the success of the army, and *Delaware* shifted to Perry Point to transport troops being withdrawn from the captured city of New Bern. She returned to Hatteras Inlet on March 16, 1862, and was off the mouth of the Pamlico River on the 21st. On that day, she took onboard from the transport steamer *Admiral* 200 soldiers of the 24th Massachusetts Regiment. These soldiers were landed at the town of Washington for two hours and then returned to the *Admiral,* which remained off Pamlico Point. On March 26 *Delaware* sent her armed boats into Pantego Creek, where she seized the schooners *Albemarle* and *Lion.* She continued operations in the rivers of North Carolina and the sounds of Albemarle, Currituck, and Pamlico until June 2, when she came off Fortress Monroe and ran up Hampton Roads to anchor in the Elizabeth River.

Delaware arrived in Hampton Roads on June 2, 1862, for service in Virginia waters until October 30. She entered the James River on June 6, 1862, and spent much of the next three months in a series of engagements with Confederate batteries at the mouth of the Appomattox River. During that summer, she served as a dispatch boat for General George B. McClellan, commander of the Army of the Potomac. She also served as a floating ambulance, transferring the army's sick and wounded. She stood out of Hampton Roads and up the Chesapeake Bay to enter the mouth of the Potomac River. She came to anchor off Aquia Creek on August 27 and on the night of August 30 heard the report of explosions in the direction of Fredericksburg, Virginia, followed by the reflection of a large fire. Her armed gig and cutter cruised the river and creeks during the nights in search of people engaged in smuggling goods across the lines. Several persons were made prisoner during this duty.[27]

S.P. Quackenbush, who had been promoted to captain, was relieved by Lt. Amos P. Foster as commanding officer on September 14, 1862. *Delaware* sent her cutter and gig into the mouth of Port Tobacco Creek the night of September 19 and passed Fort Washington on the 21st to anchor at the Washington Navy Yard. She got underway two days later and on September 24 made a prize of a scow laden with tobacco. Returning to Hampton Roads on September 25, 1862, she ran alongside *Brandywine* off Old Point on October 5 to receive 102 draftees and stores for the Federal fleet in North Carolina. She put to sea the same day and came to anchor off the town of Auburn, transferring the draftees and stores ashore. She returned to Hampton roads on October 9 to act as a picket boat in the Chesapeake Bay and captured a sloop off the mouth of the Severn River on the 26th. She arrived at Newport News on October 29, 1862, and sailed the next day to deliver canister and solid shot to the gunboats at Hatteras Inlet.[28] After operations in the Roanoke River and Albemarle Sound, *Delaware* returned to Hampton Roads. She had several encounters with enemy batteries and captured a number of small craft she sent in as prizes. During the Seven Days' Battle around Richmond, she transported wounded to Fortress Monroe at Norfolk.[29]

On November 6 Lt. Foster was ordered to proceed to New Bern with ordnance stores for the fleet, which she delivered to Hatteras Inlet on November 11. On December 5 Commander Murray of the *Hertzel* was "fortunate enough to fall in with the *Delaware*, the only vessel which will suit our purpose." So Lt. Foster took part in the naval reconnaissance of the Neuse River in cooperation with an army expedition against Goldsborough, North Carolina, from December 12 to December 16. On December 11 the *Delaware* ran aground. On the following day Commander Murray left the vessel and went aboard the *Seymour*. On December 13, according to Commander Murray's report, he "heard heavy firing in a northerly direction. At 12:30 P.M. succeeded in getting our vessel afloat, proceeded down the river, but at 1:30 ran on sunken stumps in the river and held fast until the next day when assistance came and the ship could be towed to New Bern. Here the necessary repairs were quickly effected and the vessel was again ready for service."

Similar operations delivering stores in the Roanoke River, the Neuse River, and the Pamlico River kept *Delaware* busy until January 13, 1863, when she departed Hatteras Inlet to anchor off Cape Lookout. She searched up and down the coast off Beaufort, North Carolina, and touched at Morehead City on the 21st before she entered the Roanoke River on February 2 for Plymouth, North Carolina. On February 4 she took the USS *Valley City* in tow from Plymouth and proceeded down the Roanoke River then up the coast to Hampton Roads, where on February 11, 1863, she cast the steamer off. In the following weeks, she recovered coils of rigging from the hold of the wrecked schooner *Mary E. Banks* off Cape Henry and performed picket duty in the Chesapeake Bay.[30]

Until April 5, 1863, *Delaware* cruised in the James and York rivers and Chesapeake Bay. She made frequent trips with men and stores from Hampton Roads to the North Carolina ports under Union control and patrolled the coast between those two points. She returned to Hatteras Inlet on April 6, 1863, and crossed the Albemarle Sound to enter the Neuse River for passage to New Bern, where she arrived the next day. She patrolled New Bern, Bodies' Island, and Washington, North Carolina. She continued this duty until November 27, 1863, when she was sent to Baltimore with *Henry Brinker* in tow, both vessels in need of repairs.[31]

At Baltimore, Acting Master J.H. Eldridge assumed command. On March 27, 1864, the doughty little ship returned to the waters of Virginia to patrol and perform picket duty on the James and Roanoke rivers and transport men and ordnance stores. On April 13 Eldridge was ordered to the Nansemond River on special service. Returning to Newport News, *Delaware* was stationed "on general guard of the ironclads and the *Minnesota*." On May 5 she steamed up the James River and sent out boats with grapnel hooks to clear the river of torpedoes (mines). The next day, the *Delaware* picked up 13 men from the James River when the Union armed side-wheel ferry ship *Commodore Jones*, named for Jacob Jones, a Delawarean, was blown up by a torpedo with the loss of 75 lives. *Delaware* treated the wounded and transferred the survivors to the *Mount Washington*.[32]

In April 1865 *Delaware* was operating in the northern Chesapeake Bay when President Lincoln was assassinated on April 14. As the conspirators fled, they were expected to head down the Potomac River. *Delaware*, along with other ships, was ordered to Point Lookout, Maryland, to form a line across the bay and allow no vessel to pass. All vessels were to be taken into Point Lookout to be thoroughly searched. Should any vessel try to avoid or pass the line they were to be sunk. This operation lasted until April 29, when John Wilkes Booth was captured. *Delaware* performed picket duty in the James River and transported men and ordnance stores among the other rivers of Virginia until July 13, 1865. She entered the Severn River on that date, arrived at the Washington Navy Yard on July 27, 1865, and was decommissioned on August 5, 1865.

Despite her diminutive size, *Delaware*'s Civil War record was the equal of any of her namesakes.[33] However, her career was not at an end. She continued in government service as a revenue steamer for the Treasury Department. She was sold to the Treasury Department for $40,000 (less 10 percent) on August 31, 1865. Commissioned as the USRC *Delaware*, she served as a revenue cutter. After being fitted out in Baltimore, Maryland, she was first assigned to Galveston, Texas, in 1865. She was repaired in Baltimore in 1867 at a cost of $14,100 and was then reassigned to Mobile, Alabama, in 1868. In 1872 she was ordered to replace the *Wilderness* in New Orleans, Louisiana, with orders to cruise to Mobile "occasionally."

She was extensively modified in 1873 at a cost of $11,500 and was renamed *Louis McLane* in June of that year, honoring the twelfth secretary of the treasury, Louis McLane.[34] She was then ordered to Pensacola, Florida, for duty. Here her cruising ground was from Cedar Key to Biloxi, Mississippi. She operated in the Gulf of Mexico for the rest of her career, mainly operating out of Key West. She was decommissioned on December 27, 1902, and was sold for $4,195 on October 23, 1903. She then became the merchant steamer *Louis Dolive*. The steamer was sold to the private sector in 1909 and disappeared from shipping registers in 1919, ending a 59-year career.[35]

USS Hatteras

The USS *Hatteras* was a 1,126-ton side-wheel steamer. Originally the *Saint Mary*, she was completed by Harlan and Hollingsworth in 1861 and renamed the USS *Hatteras* to assist in the blockade of Galveston. Outfitted at the Philadelphia Navy Yard as a gunboat, she was assigned to the Union blockade of the Confederacy in October 1861.[36] She sailed for Key West, Florida, on November 5, 1861, to join the South Atlantic Blockading Squadron to choke off the South's economic lifeline as part of Lincoln's Anaconda Plan. On January 16 *Hatteras* made a highly successful raid on the Cedar Keys harbor, burning several flat cars, various buildings, and seven small blockade-runners loaded with turpentine and cotton. To cap this day's work, she also captured fourteen of the 22-man garrison stationed there. Such unceasing attack from the sea on any point along the South's long coastline and inland waterways cost it dearly in losses, economic disruption, and dispersion of defense strength. After this exploit, *Hatteras* was transferred to the Gulf Blockading Squadron. On January 27 she engaged the CSS *Mobile* but failed to do any serious damage. In less than a year she captured seven blockade-runners with assorted cargos of cotton, sugar, and other goods the South was desperately striving to export for gold and much-needed trade goods. These captures netted *Hatteras*, among other things,

USS *Hatteras* (1861–1863), 19th-century print depicting the sinking of *Hatteras* by CSS *Alabama* off Galveston, Texas, January 11, 1863 (NH 53690, U.S. Naval History and Heritage Command).

some 534 bales of valuable cotton. Commander Emmons stationed four of his own men on board one prize ship, the sloop *Poody*, and rechristened her *Hatteras Jr.*, turning the erstwhile blockade-runner into a unit of the Union's Gulf Blockading Squadron.[37] Other Confederate ships taken by *Hatteras* as prizes included the steamer *Indian No. 2*, the schooner *Magnolia*, the steamer *Governor A. Mouton*, the schooner *Sarah*, the sloop *Elizabeth*, and the brig *Josephine*. The majority of these ships were captured off Vermilion Bay, Louisiana.

However, her illustrious career was cut short in early 1863, not long after she was ordered to join the blockading squadron under Rear Admiral David Farragut, who was attempting to retake the key Texas port of Galveston. *Hatteras* joined Farragut's squadron off Galveston on January 6, 1863. The Confederate Raider CSS *Alabama* had been wreaking havoc on Union merchant shipping while cruising from the Azores to the mid-Atlantic then off New England then the East Coast and then the Caribbean. In all, it had captured 20 ships. It met its first Union warship at the end of that cruise off Galveston, Texas.[38] As the blockading fleet lay to off the coast near Galveston on the afternoon of January 11, 1863, a set of sails was sighted just over the horizon and *Hatteras* was ordered to give chase. She took off in pursuit of the unknown ship and followed her as she ventured closer and closer to shore. Finally, as dusk was falling, *Hatteras* came within hailing distance of the square-rigged ship. Commander Blake demanded her identity. "Her Britannic Majesty's Ship *Petrel*," came the reply. Still suspicious, Blake ordered one of *Hatteras*'s boats to inspect this "Britisher."[39]

Scarcely had the longboat pulled away from *Hatteras* than a new reply to Blake's question rang through the night. "We are the CSS *Alabama*." With this, the famed Confederate raider began raking *Hatteras* with her heavy cannon. Through the gloom, for about 20 minutes, the two ships exchanged heavy fire at distances ranging from 25 to 200 yards. The flashes of the guns and their rumbling were heard in the Union squadron some 16 miles away, and the cruiser *Brooklyn* was dispatched to investigate and render aid if needed. But *Hatteras* had already been badly holed in two places and was on fire and beginning to sink. Captain Blake ordered the magazines flooded to prevent an explosion and reluctantly fired a single bow gun, indicating surrender and a need for assistance.

Alabama promptly sent over her boats to help remove the *Hatteras* crew and wounded. The last boatload of men had barely pulled away when the Union blockader sank, some 45 minutes after the beginning of the action. Of *Hatteras*'s crew of 126, two had been killed and five wounded. Six escaped back to the squadron in the boat originally sent out to board and investigate "HMS *Petrel*," and the remainder, including Captain Blake, were taken to Jamaica. From there they were paroled back to the United States. *Alabama* suffered only two wounded.[40] When *Brooklyn* reached the site of the battle early the following morning, she found the hulk of *Hatteras* upright in the water south of Galveston Light. Only *Hatteras*'s masts reached out of the water, and from the topmast the U.S. Navy commissioning pennant was still waving in the breeze. Even after surrendering, she had not struck her colors.

After this encounter *Alabama* moved to the South Atlantic then the Indian Ocean then the South Pacific, and then finally she returned to France. By that time she had intercepted more than 200 ships and taken or burned 65 prizes. In June 1864 it arrived in Cherbourg, France. As it left, it encountered USS *Kearsarge* off France and was sunk.[41]

A more comprehensive listing of Delaware-built Civil War vessels can be found in Appendix 2.

Confederate Naval Ships Constructed on the Delaware

Because so many Delaware Valley ships were built for southern merchants prior to the Civil War, many of them became blockade-runners. Thanks to the fortunes of war, many of these rebel vessels eventually ended up in the hands of the federal forces through surrender and capture. Over a dozen Delaware-built vessels are known to have served the Confederacy, and there were probably more, lost to history.

CSS Arizona

On January 15, 1862, Confederate forces seized the Harlan and Hollingsworth-built SS *Arizona* at New Orleans. Her U.S. enrollment was surrendered and replaced by a Confederate register on March 17, 1862. *Arizona* was converted with several other fast steamers to run the blockade to Cuba, and on her first voyage to Havana she was renamed *Caroline*. She served as a blockade-runner for the Confederacy operating from New Orleans and

Mobile to Havana.[42] On the morning of October 28, 1862, the side-wheeler was steaming from Havana to Mobile with a cargo of munitions when she was sighted by the USS *Montgomery*. The Union gunboat immediately set out in pursuit of the stranger, beginning a six-hour chase. When *Montgomery* pulled within range of *Caroline*, the latter opened fire with her 30-pounder Parrott rifle and expended 17 shells before two hits brought the quarry to heel.[43] Two boats from the blockader rowed out to *Caroline* and one returned with her master, a man named Forbes, who claimed to have been bound for the neutral port of Matamoros, Mexico, not Confederate Mobile. "I do not take you for running the blockade," the flag officer, with tongue in cheek, replied, "but for your damned poor navigation. Any man bound for Matamoros from Havana and coming within twelve miles of Mobile light has no business to have a steamer."[44]

Most of the Delaware River shipyards became idle at the end of the war. International shipping had been disrupted and American commercial hegemony had been eroded, to be replaced by foreign commerce. The government sold its large surplus of worn-out vessels at a big discount. American shipping had fallen into a permanent decline and American shipbuilding into a temporary slump. Even so, shipyards and ships are worthless without the men to sail them and to guide a successful strategy. We continue the tale here of characters previously introduced and add a few more.

David Dixon Porter

The new Confederacy laid claim to the national forts within their boundaries, but they did not make good their claim to Fort Sumter in South Carolina and Forts Pickens, Zachary Taylor, and Jefferson in Florida. They would use force if necessary to gain possession of Fort Sumter and Fort Pickens, and President Lincoln resolved not to give them up without a fight. Secretary of State William H. Seward, Captain Montgomery C. Meigs of the U.S. Army, and David Dixon Porter devised a plan for the relief of Fort Pickens. The principal element of their plan required use of the steam frigate USS *Powhatan*, which would be commanded by Porter and would carry reinforcements to the fort from New York. Because no one was above suspicion in those days the plan had to be implemented in complete secrecy.[45]

Secretary of the Navy Welles was preparing an expedition for the relief of the garrison at Fort Sumter. As he was unaware that *Powhatan* would not be available, he included it in his plans. When the other vessels assigned to the effort showed up, the South Carolina troops at Charleston began to bombard Fort Sumter and the Civil War was on. The relief expedition could only wait outside the harbor. The expedition had little chance to be successful in any case; without the support of the guns on *Powhatan* it was completely impotent. All they were able to do was carry the soldiers who had defended Fort Sumter back to the North following their surrender and parole.[46] Lincoln reasoned that the defeat had at least a redeeming feature in that Porter, whose loyalty had been suspect, was from that time on firmly attached to the Union. As Welles wrote, "In detaching the Powhatan from the Sumter expedition and giving the command to Porter, Mr. Seward extricated that officer from Secession influences, and committed him at once, and decisively, to the Union cause."[47]

The Mississippi River was the primary waterway of the Confederacy. In 1861 the Navy Department began to develop plans to open the river. The first move would be to capture New Orleans. For this Porter was given the responsibility of organizing a flotilla of some twenty mortar boats that would participate in the reduction of the forts defending the city from the south. The flotilla was a semiautonomous part of the West Gulf Blockading Squadron, which was to be commanded by Porter's adoptive brother Captain David G. Farragut, who would eventually be among the Union's most successful naval officers.[48] On April 18, 1862, the bombardment of Fort Jackson and Fort St. Philip began, but after five days of concentrated fire they seemed as strong as ever. The mortars were beginning to run low on ammunition. Farragut, who put little reliance on the mortars anyway, made the decision to bypass the forts on the night of April 24; the fleet successfully ran past the forts. The mortars were left behind, but they bombarded the forts during the passage in order to distract the enemy gunners. Once the fleet was above the forts, nothing significant stood between them and New Orleans. Farragut demanded the surrender of the city, and it fell to his fleet on April 29. The forts were still between him and Porter's mortar fleet; but when the latter again began to pummel Fort Jackson, its garrison mutinied and forced its surrender. Fort St. Philip had to follow suit. On April 28 Porter accepted the surrender of the two forts.[49]

Farragut took his fleet upstream to capture other strongpoints on the river, with the aim of complete possession of the Mississippi. At Vicksburg, Mississippi, he found that the bluffs were too high to be reached by the guns of his fleet, so he ordered Porter to bring his mortar flotilla up. The mortars suppressed the Rebel artillery well enough that Farragut's ships could pass the batteries at Vicksburg and link up with a Union flotilla coming down from the north. The city could not be taken, however, without active participation by the army, which did not happen. On July 8 the bombardment ceased when Porter was ordered to Hampton Roads to assist in Major General George B. McClellan's Peninsula Campaign. A few days later Farragut followed, and the first attempt to take Vicksburg was over. Vicksburg would continue to hold until July 1863.

Acting Rear Admiral

In 1862 the United States Navy was extensively modified. Among the features of the revised organization was a set of officer ranks from ensign to rear admiral that paralleled the ranks in the army. Among the new ranks created were those of commodore and rear admiral. According to the organization charts, the persons in command of the blockading squadrons were to be rear admirals. Another part of the reorganization transferred the Western Gunboat Flotilla from the army to the navy and retitled it the Mississippi River Squadron. The change of title implied that it was formally equivalent to the other squadrons, so its commanding officer would likewise be a rear admiral.[50] Secretary Welles decided to appoint Porter to the position, which he did despite some doubt. He wrote as follows in his diary:

> Relieved Davis and appointed D.D. Porter to the Western Flotilla, which is hereafter to be recognized as a squadron. Porter is but a Commander. He has, however, stirring and positive qualities, is fertile in resources, has great energy, excessive and sometimes not over-scrupulous ambition, is impressed with and boastful of his own powers, given to exaggeration in relation to himself,—a Porter infirmity,—is not generous to older and superior living officers, whom he is too ready to traduce, but is kind and patronizing to favorites who are juniors, and generally to official inferiors. Is given to cliquism but is brave and daring like all his family.... It is a question, with his mixture of good and bad traits, how he will succeed.[51]

Thus, Commander Porter became Acting Rear Admiral Porter without going through the intermediate ranks of captain and commodore. He was assigned to command the Mississippi Squadron and left Washington for his new command on October 9, 1862, arriving in Cairo, Illinois, on October 15.[52]

Secretary of War Edwin Stanton considered Porter "a gas bag ... blowing his own trumpet and stealing credit which belongs to others." Historian John D. Winters, in his *The Civil War in Louisiana*, describes Porter as having "possessed the qualities of abundant energy, recklessness, resourcefulness, and fighting spirit needed for the trying role ahead." Porter was assigned the task of aiding General John A. McClernand in opening the upper Mississippi. The choice of McClernand, a volunteer political general, pleased Porter because he felt that all West Point men were "too self-sufficient, pedantic, and unpractical." Winters also writes that Porter "revealed a weakness he was to display many times: he belittled a superior officer [Charles H. Poor]. He often heaped undue praise upon a subordinate, but rarely could find much to admire in a superior."[53]

The army was showing renewed interest in opening the Mississippi River at just this time, and Porter met two men who would have great influence on the campaign. First was Major General William T. Sherman, with whom he immediately formed a particularly strong friendship. The other was Major General McClernand, whom he just as quickly came to dislike. Later these two would be joined by Major General Ulysses S. Grant. Grant and Porter became friends and worked together quite well, but it was on a more strictly professional level than Porter's relation with Sherman.[54]

The success of the siege of Vicksburg required close cooperation between the army and navy. The most prominent contribution to the campaign was the passage of the batteries at Vicksburg and Grand Gulf by a major part of the Mississippi River Squadron. Grant had asked merely for a few gunboats to shield his troops, but Porter persuaded him to use more than half of his fleet. After nightfall on April 16, 1863, the fleet moved past the batteries. Only one vessel was lost in the ensuing firefight. Six nights later a similar run past the batteries gave Grant the transports he needed for crossing the river. Now south of Vicksburg, Grant at first tried to attack the Rebels through Grand Gulf and requested Porter to eliminate the batteries there before his troops would be sent across. On April 29 the gunboats spent most of the day bombarding two Confederate forts. They succeeded in silencing the lower of the two, but the upper fort remained. Grant called off the assault and moved downstream, where he was able to cross the river unopposed.[55] Although the fleet made no major offensive contributions to the campaign after Grand Gulf, it remained important in its secondary role of keeping the blockade against the city. When Vicksburg was besieged the encirclement was made complete by the navy's control of the Mississippi and Yazoo rivers. When the city finally fell on July 4, Grant was unstinting in his praise of the assistance he had received from Porter and his men. Porter's appointment as "acting" rear admiral was made permanent.[56]

The political general Nathaniel P. Banks, who was in charge of army forces in Louisiana after the opening of the Mississippi, brought pressure on the Lincoln administration to mount a campaign across Louisiana and into Texas along the line of the Red River. The ostensible purpose was to extend Union control into Texas, but Banks was influenced by numerous speculators to convert the campaign into little more than a raid to seize cotton. Admiral Porter was not in favor. He thought the next objective of his fleet should be to capture Mobile, but he received direct orders from Washington to cooperate with Banks.[57]

The Red River expedition got underway after numerous delays in early March 1864. From the start, navigation of the river presented as great a problem for Porter and his fleet as did the Confederate army that opposed them. The army under Banks and the navy under Porter did little to coordinate and instead often became rivals in a race to seize cotton. Confederate opposition under Major General Richard Taylor succeeded in keeping them apart by defeating Banks at the Battle of Mansfield, following which Banks gave up the expedition. From that time on, Porter's primary task was to extricate his fleet. The task was made difficult by falling water levels in the river, but he got most of them out, with the help of heroic efforts by some of the retreating soldiers.[58]

Fort Fisher

Wilmington, North Carolina, was the only significant Confederate port to remain open in the late summer of 1864. The Navy Department began to plan to plug this single remaining hole in its blockade. Its major defense was Fort Fisher, a massive structure at the New Inlet to the Cape Fear River. Secretary Welles believed that the head of the North Atlantic Blockading Squadron was inadequate for the task, so he at first assigned Rear Admiral Farragut to be his replacement. Farragut was too ill to serve, however, so Welles switched to Porter, who would prepare for the attack on Fort Fisher.[59]

An attack on Fort Fisher required the cooperation of the army, and the troops needed were taken from the Army of the James. Major General Benjamin F. Butler, the commander of the Army of the James, exercised one of the prerogatives of his position to

The Bombardment of Fort Fisher, January 15, 1865, engraving by T. Shussler, after a work by J.O. Davidson. It depicts ships of the North Atlantic Blockading Squadron bombarding Fort Fisher, North Carolina, prior to the ground assault that captured the fortification. Identifiable ships include USS *Monadnock* (twin-turret monitor in the right center); USS *Vanderbilt* (grey two-stack, side-wheel steamer in right foreground); and USS *New Ironsides* (at the right end of the main battle line) (NH 2051, U.S. Naval History and Heritage Command).

install himself as leader of the expedition. Butler proposed that the fort could be flattened by exploding a ship filled with gunpowder near it, and Porter accepted the idea. If successful, the scheme would avoid a protracted siege or its alternative, a frontal assault. Accordingly, the old steamer USS *Louisiana* was packed with powder and blown up in the early morning of December 24, 1864. It had, however, no discernible effect on the fort. Butler brought part of his troops ashore, but he removed his force before making an all-out assault.[60]

Enraged by Butler's timidity, Porter went to U.S. Grant and demanded that Butler be removed. Grant agreed and placed Major General Alfred H. Terry in charge of a second assault on the fort. The second assault began on January 13, 1865, with unopposed landings and bombardment of the fort by the fleet. Porter imposed new methods of bombardment this time: each ship was assigned a specific target, with the intent to destroy the enemy's guns rather than to knock down the walls. They were also to continue firing after the men ashore started their assault; the ships would shift their aim to points ahead of the advancing troops. The bombardment continued for two more days while Terry got his men into position. On the 15th frontal assaults on opposite faces—Terry's soldiers on the land side and 2,000 sailors and marines on the beach—vanquished the fort. This was the last major naval operation of the war.[61]

The Civil War was drawing to a close, and Union victory in the war was all but guaranteed. After the Confederate capital of Richmond was captured by Union forces, Porter toured the city on foot, accompanying President Abraham Lincoln with several armed bodyguards. He fondly recalled the events in his 1885 book, *Incidents and Anecdotes of the Civil War*, in which he described witnessing scores of freed slaves rushing to get a glimpse of Lincoln, whom they admired as a hero and credited for their emancipation, kissing his clothing and singing odes to him: "Twenty years have passed since that event; it is almost too new in history to make a great impression, but the time will come when it will loom up as one of the greatest of man's achievements, and the name of Abraham Lincoln—who of his own will struck the shackles from the limbs of four millions of people—will be honored thousands of years from now as man's name was never honored before."[62] Lincoln was assassinated a few weeks after his visit to Richmond. Porter, upon learning of it, was greatly upset by the news, as he admired Lincoln greatly and called him the best man he ever knew and ever would know.[63] He stated that he felt some responsibility for Lincoln's death, as had he been with him on the night of his death he might have prevented it.[64]

After the navy reduced its strength at the end of the war, Porter, like most of his contemporaries, had fewer ships to command. To make use of his undeniable talents, Secretary Welles appointed him superintendent of the naval academy in 1865. The academy at that time did little to prepare men for the duties that were expected of them. Porter resolved to change that and was determined to make the academy the rival of the military academy at West Point. An honor system was installed "to send honorable men from this institution into the Navy." The curriculum was revised to reflect the reality of naval life, organized sports were encouraged, discipline was enforced, and even social graces were taught. He brought to the faculty a group of like-minded men, mostly young officers who had distinguished themselves in the war.[65]

When Ulysses S. Grant became president in 1869 he appointed Philadelphia businessman Adolph E. Borie as secretary of the navy. Borie had no knowledge of the navy and little desire to learn, so he leaned on Porter for advice that the latter was quite willing to give. In a short time, Borie came to defer to him even on trivial routine matters. Porter used his influence with the secretary to push through several policies to shape the navy as he wanted it. In the process, he made a new set of enemies who either were harmed by his actions or merely resented his blunt methods. Borie, strongly criticized for his failure to control his subordinate, resigned after three months. The new secretary, George Robeson, promptly curtailed Porter's powers and restored civilian control of the department.[66]

The rank of admiral was created in the U.S. Navy in 1866. Naval hero David G. Farragut, Porter's adoptive brother, was named as the nation's first admiral, and Porter became vice admiral at the same time. In 1870 Farragut died, and it was expected that Porter would be promoted to fill the vacancy. Eventually he did become the second admiral but only after much controversy that was formented by his many enemies. Among them were several very powerful politicians, including some of the political generals he had contended with in the war. Porter reached the mandatory retirement age of 62 in June 1875 but was allowed to remain on active duty.

Commodore John P. Gillis, U.S. Navy 1803–1873 (2015650831, Library of Congress).

Porter's decline in influence continued, despite the prestige of his high rank. For the last twenty years of his life, he had little to do with the operations of the navy. He turned to writing, producing some histories that are of doubtful reliability but provide insights into his own beliefs and character. He also wrote some fiction that has not withstood the test of time. After twenty years of semiretirement, his health began to give way. In the summer of 1890 he suffered a heart attack, which he survived, but his health was clearly in decline. He died at the age of 77 on February 13, 1891.[67]

Commodore John Pritchett Gillis

John P. Gillis was born on September 6, 1803, in Wilmington, Delaware. He was a nearly exact contemporary of Admiral Samuel Francis Du Pont, and by comparison his career was overshadowed by him. Gillis received an appointment as a midshipman in 1825.[68] His first cruise was on the frigate USS *Brandywine* in the Pacific (1826–1829). In 1831 he was placed in command of the schooner *Albion*. Gillis was then assigned to the *Delaware*. He joined the ship in Norfolk in 1833 while it was fitting out for the Mediterranean and sailed in her under Captain Ballard. In 1834 Gillis was at sea as the master of the USS *Constellation* in the Mediterranean. He then served as executive officer aboard the receiving ship *Sea Gull* at Philadelphia (1835–1836). The following year after promotion to lieutenant, he sailed to the Pacific for his second cruise aboard the sloop of war *Falmouth*. During this cruise, he was transferred to the ship-of-the-line *Delaware*, in 1840. Two years later he served aboard the frigate *Congress* once again in the Mediterranean. He was transferred to the sloop of war *Preble* as executive officer and returned to the United States in 1843. The same year, he was attached to the frigate *Raritan* and in 1844 rejoined the frigate *Congress* on the Brazil Station. He was entrusted to bear dispatches to the commander in chief of the Pacific Squadron and returned home bearing dispatches from the U.S. minister in Brazil.[69]

When war with Mexico was declared, Gillis sailed in the sloop of war *Decatur* to join Commodore Perry in the Gulf Squadron. He distinguished himself in combat action resulting in the capture of the forts at Tuspan. Later he commanded the flotilla on the Alvarado River and became governor of the local towns. He then fell ill with yellow fever and was compelled to return home to the United States. He received letters of commendation from both Commodore Perry and the secretary of the navy for his deeds. From 1851 to 1854 Gillis was at sea again in Commodore Mathew C. Perry's Japan Expedition. In 1855 he was promoted to commander and ordered to report to the *Powhatan*.[70]

In 1861, as the Civil War began with the siege of Fort Sumter, Gillis sailed in command of the steamer *Pocahontas* for Charleston. He had received an assignment from Secretary of the Navy Gideon Welles to bring supplies to the Union troops manning the fort. When he arrived, the attack on Fort Sumter had already begun. Gillis sent a message to Washington that the flagstaff in the fort was shot away about the time the *Pocahontas* anchored there. He remained at the fort until "the little band of Union patriots had saluted their old flag by firing 50 guns and marched out with their tattered ensign to the tune of our own Yankee Doodle." The *Pocahontas* and other U.S. warships evacuated these heroic defenders.[71]

Gillis next commanded the wooden screw steamer USS *Monticello*. The *Monticello* participated in joint operations with the Union army off Newport News, Virginia. His next command was the *Seminole*. Under fellow Delawarean Samuel F. Du Pont—with the South Atlantic Blockading Squadron at the battle of Port Royal, South Carolina—the vessel came under heavy fire from Fort Walker. Gillis was the subject of mention in General Drayton's report and was promoted to post-captain in 1862, taking command of the steam sloop USS *Ossipee*. His mission was to search for the Rebel raider CSS *Alabama*, but due to defective engines on the *Ossipee* the effort had to be abandoned.[72]

By July 1863 Rear Adm. David G. Farragut had rewarded Gillis's wartime performance by placing him in command of the West Gulf Blockading Squadron. His orders were to "proceed with the vessel under your command to Galveston and take charge of the blockade of the coast of Texas." Gillis's area of operations extended from the Sabine River to the Rio Grande, with the mission to intercept Confederate shipping in and out of these ports. He would find this to be a demanding task with a limited number of ships under his command, since the Texas coastline ran for more than 400 miles. He directed his blockading squadron over this vast area from the *Ossipee*, standing just off of Galveston.[73]

The 61-year-old Gillis finally succumbed to the pressures and deprivation of some 35 years at sea. His earlier bout with disease had weakened him, and he was forced to meet a medical board. He was sent subsequently home and placed on the retired list. In 1866 he was promoted to commodore. In 1873 he was at the Philadelphia Naval Asylum when he became ill and passed away on February 25.[74] The destroyer USS *Gillis* (DD-260) was named for him.

Rear Admiral Purnell Frederick Harrington

Purnell Frederick Harrington was a career naval officer. A graduate of the U.S. Naval Academy, he was both a scholar and a blue-water sailor of uncommon ability. Born in Dover, Delaware, on June 6, 1844, he was the son of Samuel M. Harrington and Mary Lofland. Upon completion of high school he received an appointment to the U.S. Naval Academy and was mustered in as acting midshipman on September 20, 1861. On July 16, 1862, he was promoted to midshipman and, upon graduation was appointed acting ensign.[75]

Acting Ensign Harrington's first assignment was service on the USS *Ticonderoga* on duty with the North Atlantic Blockading Squadron from October 1863 through January 1864. He then was transferred to the USS *Niagara* on special service from January to June 1864, when he was transferred to the USS *Monongahela* with the Western Gulf Blockading Squadron. It was while serving on the *Monongahela* that Ensign Harrington participated in the Battle of Mobile Bay in the naval force under the command of Rear Admiral David Farragut.[76]

Dr. Robert Hill Clark, Paymaster, U.S. Navy

Commodore Robert Hill Clark was born in Frederica, Delaware, on December 5, 1818. He studied medicine at the University of New York City, graduating in 1846. He practiced medicine in Milford until 1857, when he received a navy commission as a purser. Hill's first duty was the steamship *Fulton* on an expedition to Paraguay. This was followed by a Mediterranean cruise aboard the *Iroquois*. At the outbreak of civil war hostilities, the *Iroquois* was ordered to blockade duty off Savannah, Georgia. She was instrumental in the search for the Confederate steamship *Sumter* in the West Indies but was unsuccessful.[77] *Iroquois* was next ordered to engage with Admiral Farragut's squadron in the attack on New Orleans. Clark did praiseworthy work as the ship's surgeon during this engagement. *Iroquois* then served downriver protecting Union vessels and later was sent upriver to assist in the capture of Natchez and Baton Rouge.[78]

In December 1862 Clark was ordered to Pensacola as paymaster in charge of the West Gulf Squadron and remained there until the end of the war. He was sent to Boston as paymaster and served from 1865 to 1868. Next he was ordered aboard the *Powhatan* in the Pacific. She returned to New York in September 1869 and became attached to the East Gulf Squadron. He served various peacetime tours of duty as clothing and provisions inspector and paymaster at the Philadelphia Navy Yard, the United Sates Navy Asylum, before his retirement at age 62 in 1880. He died in Milford Delaware in 1890.[79]

Colonel James Hemphill James, USMC

Born in Wilmington, Delaware, James Hemphill James was commissioned as a 2nd lieutenant in the United States Marine Corps on March 3, 1847, and served on land during the Mexican War. He then served onboard the warships USS *Raritan*, USS *Saranac*, USS *Princeton*, USS *Mississippi*, and USS *Powhatan* before being promoted to 1st lieutenant on September 1, 1853. Just after the outbreak of the Civil War he was promoted to captain (May 7, 1861), and commanded Company B of the Marine Corps battalion that fought at the 1st Battle of Bull Run on July 21, 1861, where he was praised for his "cool and steady courage" during that battle. Afterwards he was assigned to the Pacific Fleet for the duration of the war. He was promoted to lieutenant colonel on June 10, 1864, and to colonel on March 16, 1879. A year later, while in command of the Marine Barrack, Charlestown Navy Yard, Boston, Massachusetts, he died of pneumonia contracted while serving as a pallbearer in the funeral for Admiral Henry Knox Thatcher.[80]

Russell Baker Hobbs, Confederate Sailor

Russell Baker Hobbs was born in Sussex County, Delaware, in 1808. Apprenticed to a cabinetmaker, he eventually decided to become a merchant seaman. His family continued to live in Delaware while he shipped out of Philadelphia on merchant vessels. Returning to Delaware, he married Mary Paris, who died eleven years later. He then married Elizabeth Wilson, of Milton, whose family were Southern sympathizers. Early in the war Hobbs aided the Confederacy from his home in Sussex County by shipping supplies through Seaford, down the Nanticoke River, and across Chesapeake Bay to Virginia. He was arrested but released on his promise to stop aiding the enemy. A year after his parole he received a draft notice to join the Union army and instead of joining fled Delaware, going to sea once again.[81]

In August 1863 he was in Simon's Town, South Africa, located on Simon's Bay, a short distance south of Cape Town. He had arrived there aboard a merchant vessel and for unknown reasons did not leave on the same vessel. While Hobbs was waiting for another merchant vessel to join, the CSS *Alabama* anchored at Simon's Town for several days (August 9–15, 1863). His Southern sympathies rekindled, he signed on the *Alabama* as quartermaster on August 15, 1863.[82]

In his journal, George T. Fullam states that "nine stowaways from an American ship joined the *Alabama* in Simon's Bay." This is a euphemism to make what happened appear legal, since their boarding the ship with intent to join while still in port was in contravention of Great Britain's Foreign Enlistment Act (South Africa being then a British territory). The signing took place after they were in international waters. The other eight who signed aboard with Hobbs, were John Adams, F. Mahoney, Nicholas Maling, Richard Ray, John Russell, Samuel Volans, James Welsh, and P. Wharton.[83] When the *Alabama* stopped for coal in Singapore on December 22, 1863, Hobbs and other crew were given liberty, and he was one of nine who did not return. A search party was dispatched and Hobbs, along with two others, was rounded up and returned to the ship. Whether he did this intentionally or not is not known. Capt. Semmes convened a court-martial on Dec. 31, and Hobbs was disrated, or "busted," from quartermaster to ordinary seaman. Lt. Arthur Sinclair, in his book *Two Years on the "Alabama,"* lists Hobbs as a quartermaster, so it is possible that he may have regained his rank before the ship reached Cherbourg.[84] Russell B. Hobbs fought at Cherbourg and was one of about 50 men rescued by *Kearsarge* lifeboats. The men had to take the oath of allegiance as a proviso to being released, with Capt. John A. Winslow in attendance. Winslow paroled them all at Cherbourg. Hobbs then made his way to the paymaster at Southampton, where he was honorably discharged from Confederate service.[85]

On or about July 22, 1864, he arrived in New York City. With him he carried an *Alabama* service document and a paper confirming that he had taken the oath of allegiance in the presence of Capt. Winslow. The oath, in this case, was meaningless, because President Lincoln had suspended habeas corpus. Persons with questionable loyalties could be arrested and detained indefinitely without accusation or trial. Somehow Hobbs was detected but not soon enough to prevent his getting on a train headed south for Delaware. Before reaching Sussex County, Delaware, and his family, the train made its routine stop at Dover, Kent County. There, agents of the Delaware provost marshal boarded the train and arrested him. Gideon Welles, secretary of the navy under Lincoln, decided that Hobbs would be imprisoned aboard the receiving ship *Princeton*, anchored off the Philadelphia Navy Yard.[86]

Hobbs commenced his imprisonment on July 26 1864, and it took a year for the legalities to be completed, with a presidential hearing resulting in a pardon. The date of this pardon from President Andrew Johnson was July 26, 1865, and Hobbs was released from the ship the very next day, having been aboard her for a year and a day. The two documents taken from Hobbs when he was arrested are possibly filed somewhere in the U.S. National Archives. He lived out the rest of his life in Delaware, working as a house painter, and never again returned to the sea.

Russell Baker Hobbs never lived in the Confederacy nor attempted to visit there. There is in South Africa an *Alabama* ensign, probably made by crew members. It was left there after the *Alabama*'s second visit, on her way to Cherbourg.[87]

There was another Delawarean aboard the *Alabama* who was a most unusual sailor and is our next subject.

David Henry White, Freed Slave in the Confederate Navy

On the afternoon of October 9, 1862, the Confederate raiding cruiser *Alabama* had just made her latest capture, the Yankee schooner *Tonawanda*. Aboard the prize were 75 civilian passengers and among those was David H. White, a slave-servant to a Delaware businessman on his way to Europe. The *Alabama* crew was in need of men, and Captain Raphael Semmes maintained that if the Union army was treating southern negroes as "contrabands" he could well decide to take the seventeen-year-old boy along under the laws of war.[88] As the *Alabama*'s cruise continued and in the course of a few days the slave felt at home, the captain even congratulated himself of the exchange he had made. David White rendered excellent service and won the affection of everyone aboard. Captain Semmes made a decision. He proclaimed White, who was a legal slave in a Union state, to be free in the South, thus giving him the right to enlist on a Confederate warship.[89]

As a well-trained body-servant, White was not mustered as a seaman or as a gunner. Semmes appointed him a wardroom mess steward (in the muster roll he appears as "wardroom boy"). This was not because of his race or former condition but because it was the only useful job he could do. And for the very first time in his life he received the "full payment of his grade and no difference was made between him and the white waiters of the mess." He was on the *Alabama*, as a free man, from October 1862 until June 1864. He was given liberty occasionally and also assisted in the purchase of fresh food for the galley when the *Alabama* made port calls. White was cajoled by Yankee consular agents to desert while ashore in Martinique, Jamaica, South Africa, and Singapore, but "unlike others in the ship's company he never sought to leave the Confederate States Navy."

Semmes stated, full of satisfaction with his black crewman, "He seemed to have the instinct of deciding between his friends and his enemies."

During the final battle with the USS *Kearsarge* off Cherbourg, France, on June 19, 1864, White carried out his duty till the bitter end: he went down with the *Alabama* and drowned. The proud man had never told anyone that he could not swim.[90]

The success of the Union in battling the Confederate forces during the Civil War is acknowledged to be in part due to its larger population, ample resources, and industrial strength. A great deal of credit goes to the Delaware River Valley and its industrial diversity, plentiful coal, and shipbuilding facilities. The enterprise exhibited by the traders, merchants, and industrialists was evidence of the fecundity and dynamism of this area. The Union victory at sea was won by another generation of naval heroes who had roots along the banks of the Delaware. In Appendix 1 of this book you will find a listing of Delaware Valley sailors and Marines who are recipients of the Medal of Honor, which was awarded for the first time during the Civil War.

Six

Years of National Expansion, 1865–1914

The American navy shrank precipitously after the Civil War as unneeded vessels were sold at bargain prices or scrapped. At the onset of war in 1861 the American fleet consisted of 42 warships. During the war, the construction of over 200 vessels was started and an additional 418 vessels were purchased.[1] In some respects, the Union navy was the most powerful in the world in 1865. At the end of the war 51,000 officers and sailors had served the Union cause. But the American people had no appetite for continued spending on a navy. The discarded vessels were mostly shallow-draft gunboats and monitors suitable only for river and harbor work. The wartime Union navy had numbered over 700 vessels at its peak but was soon reduced to only some 175 ships. In 1880 it was the twelfth largest fleet in the world, possessing only 70 steam-powered vessels. The navy disbanded its Mississippi and Potomac flotillas as well as its Atlantic blockading squadrons and resumed its prewar organization of squadrons in Europe, the Far East, and South America.[2] Oddly, despite having pioneered ironclad construction, America did not have a global system of coaling stations upon which to rely. The navy reverted to wooden sailing ships augmented by steam. Standing orders were to use steam power only in an emergency. A captain was obliged to enter in the logbook in red ink his reasons for getting up steam.[3] These sailing ships were the kind of vessels needed for a blue-water fleet capable of covering long distances and maintaining a presence overseas. Representative of this postwar fleet was the fifth USS *Delaware*, a ship-rigged[4] wooden screw steamer.

Wooden Screw Steamer Frigate USS Delaware

The fifth USS *Delaware* was originally named *Piscataqua*, a screw-steamer frigate of the first rate *Java* class. Built in the Portsmouth Naval Yard in 1864 at a cost of $1,177,895.04,[5] she was renamed *Delaware* on May 15, 1869. The craft was launched June 11, 1866, and commissioned October 21, 1867. *Delaware* was 3,954 tons displacement, 3,177 tons burden, 336' 6" length overall, 312' 6" between perpendiculars × 46' × 21' 5". *Delaware* was powered by a single-screw, two-cylinder, horizontal, back-acting engine built by Woodruff and Beach of Hartford, Connecticut, with four main boilers and two superheating inclined boilers. Indicated horsepower was 1780, at a maximum speed of 12 knots. She had a ship's rig and two funnels.[6]

Wooden screw steamer frigate USS *Delaware* V (1866–1877) (Kennard Wiggins, artist, courtesy Delaware Military Museum).

In November 1867 *Delaware* was armed with one 60-pounder Parrott rifle, forty-two bronze twenty-pounders, two 6.4 inch 100-pound Parrotts, sixteen nine-inch smoothbore Dahlgren guns, and two twelve-pound howitzers. She had a crew complement of some 400 men including 59 Marines.[7] *Delaware* departed Portsmouth on November 7, bound for the New York Naval Yard for fitting out. She then sailed on December 16 for her assignment in the Asiatic Squadron. She left New York then touched at Rio de Janeiro, continuing via the Cape of Good Hope as *Piscataqua* under Captain Daniel Ammen, with port calls at Java, Singapore, and Manila. She arrived in Singapore on April 18, 1868, and the Philippines on May 9, 1868. She sailed once again for a brief stay in Hong Kong then arrived at Nagasaki, Japan, on June 15, 1868.[8]

She was at Shanghai on May 15, 1869, the date she was renamed *Delaware*, under the command of Captain Earl English, who had relieved Captain Ammen. She was the flagship of Rear Admiral Stephen C. Rowan, the commander in chief of the Asiatic fleet. Rowan had coincidentally served on the namesake side-wheel steamer USS *Delaware* during the Civil War. *Delaware* visited ports in China, Japan, and the Philippines. From 1868 to 1869 a civil war raged in Japan; during the course of this war, *Delaware* protected the lives of United States citizens and American interests and paid frequent calls at Kobe, Nagasaki, and Yokohama.[9]

Delaware's hull was designed by Delano and her engines by Isherwood. In the haste of war, she was built of unseasoned wood with diagonal iron bracing. This design decayed quickly, shortening her life. Hoisting her homeward-bound pennant on June 18, 1870, she returned to the New York Naval Yard by way of Singapore, Capetown, and the Cape of Good Hope. She reached quarantine station off Sandy Hook on November 18, 1870, and entered the navy yard the next day. Repairs were deemed costlier than constructing a new ship. On November 20 she hauled down the flag of Admiral Rowan.[10]

Delaware was decommissioned at sundown on December 5, 1870, after a sailing career of only four years and offered for sale at auction. The sum offered by the highest bidder was deemed inadequate, so she was maintained on the naval register "in ordinary" at the naval yard until 1877, having had brief service as a quarantine ship during this time. She foundered at her wharf in New York in February 1877 then was sold that year for $5,175 to N. McKay and broken up.[11]

The general overall lines of the fifth *Delaware* would not have been unfamiliar to the Pilgrims or of Commodore Barry of a century before. She was among the last of the wooden ship-rigged warships to be launched. Although she had a steam engine, she relied mostly on sail, a throwback in the context of the world's navies.[12]

The New Navy

In 1873 a Spanish gunboat near Jamaica captured the *Virginius*, bound for Cuba with a cargo of guns. She was a vessel of dubious status but flying the American flag. After her capture the Spanish authorities executed a number of the crew, including the American captain. The U.S. press and politicians at once called for war. The U.S. Navy was ordered to prepare for combat, only to reveal that there was virtually no navy. Matters were soon smoothed over with Spain, but a weakness had been revealed.[13]

Congress finally swung into action in the 1880s. The first ships of the "new Navy" were steel-hulled and lightly armored, or "protected," cruisers of the *Atlanta* class. The *Charleston* was the first ship to discard sail rig.[14] The revitalization of the navy began with the Naval Act of 1883 authorizing the construction of three steel cruisers and a dispatch vessel, known as the A, B, C, D ships. In 1888 Congress adopted the largest naval budget since the Civil War in order to fund construction of the armored cruiser *New York* and the protected cruiser *Olympia* and five other vessels. Later Congresses authorized additional steel warships, including the navy's first armored ship, the USS *Maine* This formed the backbone of the fleet that would later fight the Spanish-American War.[15] With a defensive war in mind the navy continued to build monitors for harbor defense and light, or unarmored, cruisers for commerce destruction. Longer-range artillery removed the need for floating batteries, and commerce raiding never won a war, so the navy began to shift towards coordinated squadrons of maneuver, with battleships described as "*sea-going* coast defense."[16]

Naval construction accelerated in the 1890s as the United States became an international economic powerhouse, fostering greater trade and the need to protect its sea-lanes and spheres of influence. A by-product of this renewed attention to naval readiness impacted the Delaware Valley through the establishment of a nautical school and a revived naval militia.

Pennsylvania Nautical School

The Pennsylvania Nautical School was established on April, 17,1889. In an effort to meet the nation's demand for trained seamen, the United States Congress passed an act on June 20, 1874, giving the secretary of the navy the authority to provide a naval vessel and instructors for a nautical school to be established at each or any of the ports of New York, Boston, Philadelphia, Baltimore, Norfolk, and San Francisco. To that end, the Pennsylvania Nautical School (PNS) was established by the General Assembly of the Commonwealth of Pennsylvania and for 58 years trained young men for careers in the maritime trades and professions.[17]

Admission to the Pennsylvania Nautical School was limited to young men between the ages of sixteen and nineteen years who were United States citizens and residents of the Commonwealth of Pennsylvania and who had a parent or guardian who also was a citizen of the Commonwealth of Pennsylvania. In 1920 the age requirement was raised to ages seventeen through twenty. As part of the admissions process, applicants had to provide letters of recommendation attesting to their sound "moral character" and possess an aptitude for a life at sea. They had to pass a physical examination by a board of medical examiners and a rigorous written academic examination in mathematics, literature, and history. Classes were admitted to the nautical school twice a year, in May and October.[18]

The course of training was approximately two years and was dependent upon the capability of the ships to complete their training cruises within the specified time. Cruises were an important element in the training of cadets and were no doubt a draw for many young men eager to go to sea. Training cruises included a crossing of the Atlantic, with visits to several ports in Europe, South America, and the West Indies. Students were instructed in "boxing the compass, knotting and splicing, the strapping of blocks, reefing and furling, heaving the lead, using the palm and needle, the handling of boats under oars and sails, swimming, etc."[19]

The Pennsylvania Nautical School's first school ship was the USS *Saratoga*, a 47-year-old, 882-ton sloop of war named after the Battle of Saratoga of the Revolutionary War. She had served in the suppression of the slave trade off the African Coast and in Perry's "opening" of isolationist Japan in the 1850s and was in the service of the school from 1890 until 1908.[20]

In 1908 the unseaworthy *Saratoga* was replaced by the USS *Adams*, a 1,397-ton combination sail and steam screw gunboat. *Adams* had served mostly in the Pacific, arriving from Samoa, where she had been a station ship. The school ships *Saratoga* and *Adams* were operated jointly by the State of Pennsylvania and the City of Philadelphia.[21] The *Adams* served for five years, until the school was discontinued on February 16, 1914, due to local disagreements and lack of funding by the state legislature. She had annually taken the cadets on summer cruises to Europe and winter cruises in the West Indies and was transferred to the New Jersey Naval Militia[22] at the outbreak of World War I.

On July 8, 1919, the Pennsylvania State Legislature reactivated the nautical school and renamed it the Pennsylvania State Nautical School. The USS *Annapolis*, a veteran gunboat of the Spanish-American War, sailed on her first cruise in June 1920 bound for the West Indies. She was designated as the nautical school's training vessel until her service ended in 1941.[23] In 1940 the administration of the school was transferred to the United States Maritime Commission and was renamed the Pennsylvania Maritime Academy. In the spring of 1942 the administration ended and the cadets were transferred to the U.S.

USS *Saratoga* (1842–1907), Le Havre France, August 1, 1900, at which time the ship was listed as the Pennsylvania Nautical School Ship (NH 108650, U.S. Naval History and Heritage Command).

Merchant Marine Academy in Kings Point, New York. The former U.S. Coast Guard cutter *Seneca*, became the nautical school's fourth school ship. In September 1942 administration of the school was returned to the State of Pennsylvania and the *Seneca* was renamed the USS *Keystone State*. In 1946 the USS *Selinur*, renamed USS *Keystone State II*, became the nautical school's fifth and final school ship. Lack of state government funding, allegations of cadet's "mutinous behavior," allegations of political corruption, and a decrease in applicants led to the closure of the Pennsylvania Maritime Academy on June 20, 1947. Approximately 2,000 cadets graduated from the nautical school before it closed in 1947.[24]

The Naval Militia of the State of Pennsylvania

In 1889 the Pennsylvania legislature passed a bill authorizing a naval militia. The militia was finally organized in January 1893 when one division of 52 men and 5 officers was mustered into service in Philadelphia. The size of the militia had grown to 217 men.[25] In early 1895 the Navy Department liaison officer issued an annual report calling for a conference of the principal representatives of the state naval militias to discuss training and their duties upon the outbreak of war. The report also identified the U.S. Navy ships that would be transferred to the state naval militias, including the USRS *St. Louis* to be the headquarters ship for the Pennsylvania Naval Militia. *St. Louis* was a sailing ship commissioned in 1828 that had a long and eventful career in naval service before being

USS *Chicago*, Protected Cruiser (1889–1935) (NH 88365, U.S. Naval History and Heritage Command).

laid up in 1866 at the Philadelphia League Island Navy Yard. There it served as the receiving ship to which naval personnel reported upon arrival. For that purpose, the main deck had been roofed over to provide for offices, classrooms, and training spaces. When she was loaned to the Pennsylvania Naval Militia, her name was changed to *Keystone State*.[26]

In 1897, upon becoming assistant secretary of the navy, Theodore Roosevelt embarked on an inspection tour and review of several state naval militias. Upon his return, he again called for the establishment of a naval reserve that would become "part of the Navy itself" and would "in no way conflict with or take the place of the present system of naval militia." The two were to exist side by side, with the reserve providing direct combat support, the militias providing a "second line of defense." The creation of a naval reserve failed to materialize before Roosevelt resigned to prepare the Rough Riders for war. It would be left to the state militias to provide the navy with the men and material to defend the coast when the U.S. went to war.[27]

Capt. Alfred T. Mahan was twice president of the Naval War College and contributed to the Spanish-American War plans. He was the author of the classic book *The Influence of Sea Power on History* (NH 64579-KN, U.S. Naval History and Heritage Command).

Ships that served with this militia until the creation of the U.S. Navy Reserve included the protected cruiser USS *Chicago* (1885), which served from April 26, 1916 to April 1917, and the ironclad USS *Wolverine* (IX-31), which served for eleven years making summer training cruises for the navy reserve.[28]

The U.S. Auxiliary Naval Force

With the declaration of war against Spain, the secretary of the navy requested, and Congress passed, emergency legislation that created the U.S. Auxiliary Naval Force. The auxiliary naval force would consist of eight old monitors that were in reserve and a "Mosquito Flotilla" of 28-gun vessels, 40 patrol boats, and numerous one-tube torpedo boats equipped and commissioned from vessels acquired by purchase or lease. This force was to be manned by volunteers and, with the governors' approval, members and entire units from state naval militias.[29]

With the establishment of the auxiliary naval force, the Fourth District was headquartered in Philadelphia and was commanded by Lieutenant J.S. Muckle, USN, who had been commissioned into the navy from the Pennsylvania naval militia. Attached to this district were his headquarters ship, again the USRS *St. Louis*, the militia-manned, heavily armed, single-turret monitors USM *Canonicus*, USM *Mahopac*, and USM *Manhattan*.

The *Manhattan* had served with Admiral David Dixon Porter in the Civil War battle of Mobile Bay, and the *Canonicus* and *Mahopac* had served in the battles for Fort Fisher and Wilmington, North Carolina. They had been decommissioned and laid up at the League Island Navy Yard.[30] In addition, the city of Philadelphia leased its Ice Boat No. 3—a side-wheel steamer built in 1873—to the navy for one dollar. The ship was armed with a single gun, commissioned as the USS *Arctic* on July 9, 1898, and assigned to the auxiliary naval force. *Arctic* was based at Philadelphia but made one trip to the Delaware Breakwater and back via New Castle and Lewes between July 28 and August 16.

Mines had been set at the approaches to the Delaware River under the purview of the U.S. Army Corps of Engineers. After the threat of war with Spain ended, the minefields in the Delaware River were dismantled by the U.S. Corps of Engineers.[31]

Intellectual Ferment

The second half of the nineteenth century witnessed an unparalleled transformation in naval thought. New technology often drives new ways of employing these new devices and weapons. It can take years for doctrine to evolve in ways that maximize the effectiveness of new technologies. The academic standard at the United States Naval Academy remained fairly low after the Civil War. Professor Henry Lockwood left the academy to join the army during the Civil War, as did many of the military faculty, leaving behind a civilian cadre of doubtful qualification. Admiral David Porter was brought to the academy to bring reform and to renew its vigor. In 1884 the Naval War College was established at Newport, Rhode Island, to improve naval doctrine and tactics. One result was the publication of Commander Alfred Thayer Mahan's seminal book, *The Influence of Sea Power on History*, a history of naval warfare, published in 1890. It details the role of sea power during the seventeenth and eighteenth centuries and discusses the various factors needed to support and achieve sea power, with emphasis on having the largest and most powerful fleet. It argued for controlling and protecting sea-lanes to protect access to maritime trade, and its precepts were quickly adopted by most major navies. Scholars consider the tome the single most influential book in naval strategy, and it remains a standard in military senior service schools to this day.[32]

This intellectual transformation drove the navy to adapt to the nascent national strategy largely influenced by Mahan's ideas to strive towards an imperialistic worldview requiring a "blue water" navy to project power around the globe on behalf of the United States. America would seek new bases and territories to coal and service its fleet as well as to construct a canal in Panama to make it possible to move its fleet expeditiously, especially given the lessons of the Spanish-American War.

Technological Advances

The second half of the nineteenth century also witnessed an unparalleled transformation in naval architecture. By the 1880s, in an era of prosperity, the United States began to retire its wooden navy. The revolutionary ironclad *Monitor* had included new technologies for combinations of steam power, armor, ironclad construction, and new armament, yet it was overall a rather poor design that would be refined over the coming

Protected Cruiser USS *Olympia* L(C-6), photographed by Hart, New York, upon her return to the United States in 1899. She is flying the four-star flag of Admiral George Dewey (NH 2894, U.S. Naval History and Heritage Command).

decades. Internationally, ship design during this period sprouted all kinds of amazing design features in the quest for the right combination by the world's navies.

Ironclads were designed for several roles, including as high-seas battleships, coastal defense ships, and long-range cruisers. The rapid evolution of warship design in the late 19th century transformed the ironclad from a wooden-hulled vessel that carried sails to supplement its steam engines into the steel-built, turreted battleships and cruisers familiar in the 20th century. This change was pushed forward by the development of heavier naval guns (the ironclads of the 1880s carried some of the heaviest guns ever mounted at sea), more sophisticated steam engines, and advances in metallurgy that made steel shipbuilding possible.

The quick pace of change meant that many ships were obsolete almost as soon as they were finished and that naval tactics and doctrine were in a state of flux. Many ironclads were built to make use of the ram or the torpedo, which a number of naval designers considered among the important weapons of naval combat. There is no clear end to the ironclad period, but toward the end of the 1890s the term *ironclad* dropped out of use. New warships were increasingly constructed to a standard pattern and designated battleships or armored cruisers. An example is the cruiser USS *Olympia*.

USS Olympia

The USS *Olympia* was a protected cruiser that saw service in the United States Navy from her commissioning in 1895 until 1922. The protected cruiser was a type of naval cruiser so known because its armored deck offered protection for vital machine spaces from fragments caused by exploding shells above. Protected cruisers were an alternative to the armored cruisers, which also had a belt of armor along the sides.[33] *Olympia* became famous as the flagship of Commodore George Dewey at the Battle of Manila Bay during the Spanish-American War in 1898. The ship was decommissioned after returning to the U.S. in 1899 but was returned to active service in 1902. She served until World War I as a training ship for naval cadets and as a floating barracks in Charleston, South Carolina. In 1917 she was mobilized again for war service, patrolling the American coast and escorting transport ships.[34]

After World War I *Olympia* participated in the 1919 Allied Intervention in the Russian Civil War and conducted cruises in the Mediterranean and Adriatic seas to promote peace in the unstable Balkan countries. In 1921 the ship carried the remains of World War I's Unknown Soldier from France to Washington, D.C, where his body was interred in Arlington National Cemetery. *Olympia* was decommissioned for the last time in December 1922 and placed in reserve.[35] In 1957, the U.S. Navy ceded title to the Cruiser *Olympia* Association, which restored the ship to her 1898 configuration. Since then, she has been a museum ship in Philadelphia, where it is now part of the Independence Seaport Museum. Designated a National Historic Landmark in 1966, *Olympia* is the oldest steel U.S. warship still afloat and the sole surviving naval ship of the Spanish-American War.[36]

Delaware Valley Shipbuilding

During the Civil War, American seagoing commerce suffered greatly, partly as a result of increased insurance costs and partly due to the uncertainties of armed conflict. Competitors of the United States filled the vacuum and America never quite recovered its former dominance of commercial sea trade. Coastal shipping remained the exception, although it too began to receive competition from the railroads. As previously mentioned, American oceanic shipping had fallen into a permanent decline and American shipbuilding was in a temporary slump.[37]

Iron-hulled vessels demonstrated their value during the Civil War, and merchant shippers began to see the advantages of this type of construction. The Delaware River yards had established their reputations as iron-hulled builders and by the 1870s the Delaware became known as the "American Clyde," for its famous British counterpart.[38]

The shipbuilding business is capital intensive, and has always been sensitive to the state of the nation's overall economy. In good times shipyards often had more work than they could handle, and in bad times they struggled to survive. A financial panic in 1873, lasting about six years, aggravated an already difficult situation. American ships were more expensive than foreign-made vessels, especially British, because of the high price of iron and labor in this country. Shipbuilders survived by making railroad cars and machinery as well as steam yachts and racers for the wealthy.[39] The build-up and modernization of the navy during the years 1885–1889 at last brought a shipbuilding boom to the Delaware. This primed the pump for orders of ferries and river steamers. Wilmington shipbuilders continued to occasionally build naval vessels. Most of these were not warships but were often support ships, especially those involved in seagoing research, fisheries, the revenue service, and lightships, among others.[40]

Two Wilmington shipyards, Harlan and Hollingsworth and Pusey and Jones, achieved international notoriety when one launched America's first all-iron, oceangoing steamer in 1844, and the other built the nation's first iron sailing ship in 1855. The two Wilmington firms exemplified the emergence of the iron shipbuilding industry. In the 1860s Harlan and Hollingsworth and Pusey and Jones led iron shipbuilding firms in the United States. Both firms developed specialties in small- to medium-sized boats (partly because of the small size of the Christina River), especially ferries, river steamboats, and luxury yachts.[41] By 1883 Harlan and Hollingsworth had a plant covering forty-three acres, a record of over two hundred iron ships built since 1836, and a dry dock capable of taking in a vessel up to 340 feet in length. Every industry from miner and workman to architect and engineer was employed—concentrating nearly fifty trades—and had developed from an area of about two acres of ground to a frontage of 2,800 feet on both banks of the Christina River.

Cramp and Sons Ship and Engine Building Company

One of the primary warship builders in the U.S. Navy was Cramp and Sons Shipbuilding. Cramp constructed nine battleships between 1893 and 1911 at its Philadelphia Yard in the Kensington section. It also produced 27 cruisers of various types from the Civil War to the end of World War I. The firm was founded by William Cramp in 1830 as a builder of standard wooden ships. During the economic "Panic of 1857" his previously prosperous little firm nearly ended when he had to sell off assets to pay his creditors.[42] Working with his sons, he managed to weather the storm. His son Charles H. Cramp managed to win eight government contracts during the Civil War. Charles led the way with advancements in steam engines, screw propellers, and iron building techniques. Their most famous contribution was the *New Ironsides*, launched in 1862, a composite of wooden hull with four inches of iron plating powered by steam driving a screw. It was, at the time, the largest wooden hull yet constructed in the United States at 232 feet long and 4,120 tons. *New Ironsides* had exaggerated "tumblehome" (the narrowing of a ship's hull with greater distance above the waterline).

She was battle-worthy due to her iron armor. At one point, she was hit some seventy times within three hours without serious damage. She was also far more seaworthy, unlike the ironclad monitors being built at that time with a low freeboard suitable only for shallow-water maneuvers.[43] The ship spent most of her career blockading the Confederate ports of Charleston, South Carolina, and Wilmington, North Carolina, during 1863–65. *New Ironsides* bombarded the fortifications defending Charleston in 1863 during the First and Second battles of Charleston Harbor. At the end of 1864 and the beginning of 1865 she bombarded the defenses of Wilmington, North Carolina in the First and Second battles of Fort Fisher.[44]

After the Civil War the company had to weather another economic crisis as orders evaporated. Many ships had been lost during the war and shippers had re-registered their remaining vessels under foreign flags. America lost about 40 percent of her merchant fleet previously engaged in foreign trade. Charles Cramp became an outspoken advocate for iron shipbuilding in his locale. Shipbuilding began to shift from the New York area to the Delaware River and from wood to iron. From 1870 to 1880 Pennsylvania led the nation in the production of iron vessels, followed by Delaware. Two-thirds of the 67 iron ships were produced in the 1870s by these two states. Cramp and Sons employed between 1,200 and 3,000 men. Downstream at the Delaware Iron Ship Building and Engine works in Chester, established by John Roach in 1871, another 1,500 shipbuilders were employed.[45]

Battleship USS *Indiana* (BB-1) built at Cramp Shipyards, Philadelphia, 1893 (NH 73974, U.S. Naval History and Heritage Command).

The ready access to plentiful Pennsylvania anthracite coal was one of the factors that made this success possible. Cramp and Sons won a contract to build a cruiser (*Zabiaka*) for the Imperial Russian Navy in the late 1870s. As a result of the naval reconstruction initiative of 1883, Congress authorized the construction of four new steel cruising vessels and four double-turreted iron monitors. These were the "A, B, C, D," cruisers (*Atlanta, Boston, Chicago,* and *Dolphin*). The cruiser contracts went to the Roach firm and the monitors to other yards including Cramp, which built the *Terror*. Cramp went on to win eleven naval contracts between 1885 and 1895 and built the USS *Indiana* (BB-1), battleship number one of the United States Navy, launched February 28, 1893. The initial phase of naval reconstruction ended with the last coastal battleships, *Mississippi* and *Idaho*, authorized in 1902 and launched in 1905.[46]

Philadelphia Navy Yard

In 1876, the Philadelphia Navy Yard outgrew its original location in the Southwark section of the riverfront and moved to League Island at the confluence of the Schuylkill and Delaware rivers. At that time, the assistant secretary of the navy, Gustavus Vasa Fox, predicted that the place would become a leading government naval facility because it could lay up the entire ironclad fleet in a safe and secure freshwater basin: "The whole of League Island, embracing an extent of land that exceeds in area the six navy yards on the Atlantic Coast will be ample for the requirements of a naval station at Philadelphia forever."[47]

The Philadelphia Navy Yard at League Island barely survived. Subject to strong flood tides and the victim of a violent storm fifteen years after its construction, it lost a floating dry dock, as the entire yard was flooded. The NavyDepartment prepared to close the yard but gave it a reprieve when permanent dry docks were built in 1891 and 1907. Further improvements included new facilities for research and testing for fuel-oil–burning engines, boilers, propellers, and wireless telegraphy. In 1911 the navy transferred the Atlantic Marine Corps Advance Base headquarters and school to League Island.[48]

Spanish-American War

The Spanish-American War (1898) was a conflict between the United States and Spain that ended Spanish colonial rule in the Americas. The war originated in the Cuban struggle for independence from Spain, which began in February 1895. Spain's repressive measures to halt the rebellion were graphically portrayed for the American public by several sensational newspapers, and American sympathy for the rebels rose. The demand for U.S. intervention became an insistent chorus after the unexplained sinking in Havana Harbor of the battleship USS *Maine,* which had been sent to protect U.S. citizens and property after anti–Spanish rioting in Havana. Spain declared war on the United States on April 24, followed by a U.S. declaration of war on the 25th that was made retroactive to April 21.

The Delaware Valley played little direct role in the Spanish-American War of 1898. She contributed her share of native sons to the cause, including Medal of Honor recipient Leonard Chadwick, apprentice first class, U.S. Navy, serving on the USS *Marblehead,* and Rear Admiral Purnell Frederick Harrington, who saw action in Cuba in command of the USS *Puritan*. A namesake ship, the USS *Wilmington*, was very active in Cuban waters during the conflict. The Delaware Valley's largest contribution to this largely naval war was its shipbuilding industry.

USS *Wilmington*

Representative of the technological advances in naval architecture after the Civil War with the "New Navy" was the gunboat USS *Wilmington* (PG-8). *Wilmington* was the lead ship in a class of two United States Navy gunboats. She was laid down on October 8, 1894, at Newport News, Virginia, and launched on October 19, 1895. Sponsored by Mrs. Anne B. Gray and commissioned on May 13, 1897, she was commanded by Chapman C. Todd.[49] After conducting sea trials and training off the East Coast, the *Wilmington* joined the North Atlantic Squadron at Key West and trained and underwent exercises in gunnery and tactics in late 1897 and early 1898 as tension between the United States and Spain was rising steadily closer to open hostilities.

On April 21, 1898, two months after the sinking of the battleship *Maine* in Havana Harbor, the U.S. declared war on Spain. Meanwhile, the navy had moved its warships into position to attack Spanish possessions in the Far East and the Caribbean. In May

Gunboat USS *Wilmington* (PG-8) (NH63584, U.S. Naval History and Heritage Command).

Wilmington participated in the Second Battle of Cardenas and was defeated, but at the Bombardment of Cardenas the next morning she sank two Spanish gunboats and two schooners without a fight. On July 15, 1898, she arrived off Cape Cruz, near Manzanillo, Cuba, and joined *Wompatuck* on station with the blockading forces.[50] The following day *Wilmington* overhauled two small charcoal-burning fishing boats off the harbor mouth and questioned their Cuban crews. From the brief interrogation the Americans learned that a submarine cable connected Santa Cruz and Jucaro. The gunboat then proceeded to the spot mentioned by the fishermen and lowered a grappling hook. Finding the cable, *Wilmington* cut it and made for Cuarto Reales to join *Helena*, *Wompatuck*, and *Hist*. On July 17 *Wilmington* led the three other ships to El Guayabal, 20 miles (32 km) north of Manzanillo. Upon their arrival at Guayabal, the warships found *Scorpion*, *Hornet*, and *Osceola*. During the afternoon hours, the four commanding officers met in conference and formulated preliminary plans for an expedition to Manzanillo to destroy Spanish shipping.[51]

Accordingly, at 3:00 A.M. on July 18, the American ships set out from Guayabal and set course for Manzanillo. At 6:45 A.M. the group split up according to plan: *Wilmington* and *Helena* made for the north channel; *Hist*, *Hornet*, and *Wompatuck* for the south; *Scorpion* and *Osceola* for the central harbor entrance. Fifteen minutes later the two largest ships entered the harbor, black smoke billowing from their tall funnels and gunners ready at their weapons. Taking particular care not to damage the city beyond the waterfront, the American gunners directed their gunfire solely at the Spanish ships and took a heavy toll of the steamers congregated there. The Spanish supply steamer *Purissima Concepcion* caught fire alongside a dock and sank at her moorings; gunboat *Maria Ponton* blew up when her magazines exploded; gunboats *Estrella* and *Delgado Perrado* also burned and sank while two transports, *Gloria* and *Jose Garcia*, went down as well. Two small gunboats, *Guantanamo* and *Guardian*, were driven ashore and shot to pieces.[52] As they were beyond the effective range of Spanish shore batteries, the Americans emerged unscathed, leaving columns of smoke to mark the pyres of the enemy's supply and patrol vessels. The 20-minute engagement ended with the attackers withdrawing to sea to resume routine patrol duties with the North Atlantic Squadron for the duration of hostilities.

Late in the summer *Wilmington* headed home and was dry-docked at Boston from September 24 until October 3. Following repairs, she left the Massachusetts coast on October 20 bound, via Charleston, South Carolina, for Norfolk. Arriving at Hampton Roads on October 31, she put into the Norfolk Naval Shipyard on the following day for further repairs, overhaul, and preparation for foreign service.[53] With the reestablishment of the South Atlantic Squadron, *Wilmington* got underway on Christmas Eve and set her course for Puerto Rico. She arrived at San Juan on December 30, 1898, but resumed her voyage south on January 2, 1899, and proceeded via Castries, Saint Lucia, to Port-of-Spain, Trinidad, where she made port on January 15.

Six days later *Wilmington* left Trinidad behind and pointed her straight stem toward Venezuela. She arrived off Barima Point and stood up the Santa Catalina River, which led to the main branch of the Orinoco. After a brief stop at the town of Las Tablas, she put into Ciudad Bolivar on January 24, where the mayor, the American consul, and a number of city officials came on board for a visit. Diplomatic affairs occupied the officers, with the commanding officer visiting the provincial governor and collector of customs. She was "full-dressed" with flags and appropriate ceremonial trappings on January 28, when she welcomed the citizens of the city on board. Two days later the gunboat departed Ciudad Bolivar to return to Port-of-Spain. She was based at Trinidad through February and into March. During this time, she visited Guanta in northern Venezuela, and Georgetown, British Guiana, then proceeded up the Surinam River to Paramaribo, Dutch Guiana.[54]

Departing Paramaribo on March 6 *Wilmington* commenced the initial leg of her cruise up the Amazon River. Navigable for nearly 2,300 miles of its 3,200-mile length during the rainy season, the Amazon and its verdant banks presented the ship's company with interesting and unusual flora and fauna as she proceeded upriver. Calling at Para and Manaus, Brazil, en route, the ship arrived at the Peruvian border at Leticia, Peru, on April 11. Heaving to, the gunboat dropped anchor off Leticia to secure permission from Peruvian authorities to proceed farther up the Amazon. With permission granted, she again got underway and arrived at Iquitos on April 13. While numerous official calls were exchanged during the visit, the gunboat also acquired a small menagerie: three monkeys and one tiger cat, presented to the ship by the Peruvians.

On April 18 *Wilmington* departed Iquitos, headed back downstream, and reached Rio de Janeiro on May 28, completing a 4,600-mile round-trip voyage on the Amazon. On June 6 she entered the Brazilian government dry-dock at Rio de Janeiro for routine bottom cleaning and remained there until July 4, when she got underway and cruised south along the coast visiting Brazilian and Uruguayan ports. She arrived at Montevideo on July 16 and spent one month operating out of that port. On August 17 she departed Montevideo. However, at 5:50 P.M. the following day, the port propeller shaft failed, resulting in a change of course back to Montevideo. Remaining in the Uruguayan port from her August 22 arrival until her departure on September 3, she steamed by her starboard engine only for Buenos Aires.[55]

Arriving on September 4, *Wilmington* broke the Argentine flag at the main and her saluting guns barked out a 21-gun salute to the Argentine nation as she entered port. After the usual boarding calls and shore visits by the American officers to the American chargé d'affaires and consul, the gunboat entered the dry-dock at Buenos Aires on September 8. Unshipping the port propeller shaft and landing the propeller and a section of the shaft on September 16, she left the dry-dock the following day with the assistance of two tugs and proceeded to basin number four at the Brazilian navy yard. *Wilmington* remained incapacitated at the basin until January 18, 1900, when she was moved to Ensenada, Argentina. Eleven days later the cruiser *Chicago* passed a towline to the gunboat, and the two ships set out for Montevideo. On February 9 steamship *Corunda* arrived with new shafts from the Brooklyn Naval Yard. Subsequently, the gunboat returned to Buenos Aires, under tow from the cruiser *Montgomery,* and entered dry-dock on March 3, 1900, nearly six months after having first been crippled by the damaged propeller shaft.[56]

Once the repairs were finally corrected after dockyard overhaul and a trial period, *Wilmington* continued cruising on the South American station through the summer and early fall of 1900. While en route to Rio de Janeiro on May 10, 1900, her inclinometer recorded 45° rolls in each direction while traversing heavy, choppy seas. On October 16 she departed Pernambuco, Brazil, bound for the Far East. Arriving at Gibraltar on November 3, she pushed on across the Mediterranean and transited the Suez Canal early in December, arriving at Port Said on the 4th. On January 21, 1901, the gunboat made port at Manila, in the Philippines, to commence her Asiatic service. Departing from Cavite on May 10, *Wilmington* headed for the China coast and called at Hong Kong on the 13th. Still nominally attached to the South Atlantic Fleet, she served in Chinese waters through 1904 on routine cruises, showing the stars and stripes along the China coast at ports such as Shantou, Xiamen, Fuzhou, Shanghai, and Hong Kong. On June 30, 1904, she was decommissioned at Cavite.[57]

On April 2, 1906, *Wilmington* was recommissioned at Cavite, with Commander William L. Rodgers in command. For the next two years, she served off the China coast, carrying out her routine cruising and "showing the flag." On December 17, 1908, the gunboat commenced her river service, on the Yangtze River as far as Hankou, with the Yangtze Patrol. Ordinary activities included the usual calls and port visits to such places as Hong Kong, Canton, and Swatow. After constructing her own target rafts and laying out a firing area, *Wilmington* conducted target practice. On one occasion, Chinese fishermen decided that the raft presented a good perch from which to fish. Repeated attempts by the gunboaters to shoo away the fishermen only ended in frustration. Finally, as she steamed slowly toward the area, she fired a few blank rounds purposely "over," and the squatters promptly abandoned their erstwhile fishing vantage point. After repairs while stationed at Hong Kong from June 30, 1912, until June 30, 1914, she resumed her routine cruises, attached to the Far Eastern Squadron, Asiatic Fleet, and continued such duty for the next five years, maintaining a presence through the Great War.[58]

Onshore Infrastructure

After the Civil War, new fortifications were constructed opposite Fort Delaware on the New Jersey and Delaware shores. Masonry forts were found vulnerable and new construction featured earthworks and parapets of sand. A ten-gun earthen battery, known at first as "Fort Opposite Fort Delaware," was established at Fort Mott with two fifteen-inch guns. A ten-gun earthen barbette battery for the new fort, which became Fort Du Pont, was built in 1864. It was named after Admiral Samuel F. Du Pont in 1899. Between 1870 and 1876, an additional twenty guns were added and emplacements for two fifteen-inch Rodman guns were built.[59]

Around 1890, breechloading guns had completely replaced the older muzzleloaders for all large guns and mortars. For seacoast fortifications, disappearing gun carriages

Delaware Breakwater, Lewes Delaware, 1891 (96506752, Library of Congress).

had proven to be a success. A combination of concrete emplacements protected by parapets of sand in front and on top became the standard of defensive design. Work began in 1897 to rebuild Fort Delaware in this new style. Three twelve-inch disappearing guns were installed at Battery Torbert. Forts DuPont and Mott were also reinforced with more powerful armament. Fort DuPont added two eight-inch mortar batteries, two twelve-inch disappearing guns, two eight-inch guns, and four five-inch guns. Fort Mott gained three twelve-inch guns, three ten-inch guns, four five-inch guns, and two three-inch guns. Minefields were also added to the nearby waters. Pea Patch Island and Fort Delaware was considered impregnable.[60]

Delaware Breakwater

The harbor at Lewes, originally built in 1828, was too small to be useful. About 25 vessels per day visited the facility, but during storms as many as 200 ships would seek refuge. In 1877 a hurricane destroyed several ships in Lewes Harbor as well as others that could not get into the harbor. Seventy sailors perished in the great blizzard of 1888. As a result, work began in order to close the opening between the icebreaker and main breakwater using the same stone as the original, the work not being completed until 1898. The Strickland lighthouse was rendered obsolete by this measure and was removed.

In 1876 Western Union Telegraph Company occupied the old lighthouse on the breakwater and the Philadelphia Maritime Exchange established a reporting station there. This facility provided advance notice of ship arrivals to Philadelphia and advised life-saving stations of shipwrecks in the bay area. The present Delaware Breakwater East End Light was built in 1885 to replace the old Strickland light.[61] An iron pier was built beginning in 1871 by the U.S. Army Corps of Engineers and completed in 1882. The 1,700-foot

(520 m) pier was designed to carry rail traffic directly out to ships in the harbor and used iron screw piles with wood decking. The pier was later adapted for use by the U.S. Lifesaving Station and the quarantine station.

National Harbor of Refuge

Deeper and longer hulls as well as an increase in seaborne trade meant that even the new improved harbor remained inadequate. In 1896 Congress authorized a new, larger program of breakwaters, the National Harbor of Refuge. Located 6,500 feet to the north of the original breakwater on a shoal known as The Shears, the new breakwater used much larger stone. The dressed and fitted masonry used individual pieces of up to 13 tons. The new breakwater was 8,040 feet long at low water and 40 feet wide. Ten icebreaker piers were built 1,250 feet to the north of dressed stone in a 1,300 feet line. The project was completed in 1901. Compared with the earlier effort, steam-powered equipment allowed the use of larger stones and sped construction. The Harbor of Refuge Light was built on this breakwater and replaced the 1767 Cape Henlopen Light, which had been abandoned in 1924 and fell into the sea in 1926.[62]

Chesapeake and Delaware [C&D] Canal

Throughout the 19th century this canal's use continued to change, with the New Castle and Frenchtown Railroad being its only major competitor. In 1872 the canal recorded its high-water mark in terms of tonnage and revenue. Thereafter it began to decline. Steam power brought larger and deeper-draft vessels that could not pass through the restricting locks. By the turn of the 20th century the decline in canal traffic and the great cost of operation and repairs brought a downward trend in canal profits. This followed a national trend. Clearly a larger, wider, and deeper waterway was needed. A disastrous flood in 1874 nearly put it out of business. The C&D Canal barely survived operating at a loss.[63] At the time, however, little thought was given to improving the existing canal. New companies were formed instead, with at least six options to consider for a new canal route. Various committees and commissions appointed to study the issue failed to agree on a plan. President Theodore Roosevelt then appointed a commission in 1906 to report on the feasibility of converting the C&D Canal to a "free and open waterway." This did not become a reality however, until after World War I.[64]

Cape Henlopen Quarantine Hospital

From 1884 until 1916 a quarantine hospital was located on the shore of the Cape Henlopen Harbor of Refuge. This hospital had its origins in the Marine Hospital Service and ended its days as part of the Naval Section Base on Cape Henlopen. In July 1884—at the recommendation of the senior senator from Delaware and by request of the authorities of Philadelphia, Wilmington, and Lewes—the Marine Hospital Service established a quarantine facility at Lewes, first utilizing the steamer *Trench Coxe*, with Dr. George W. Stoner as the Marine Hospital Service's primary acting surgeon.[65]

Under the supervision of Dr. Stoner, construction began on the Delaware Breakwater Quarantine Hospital in September and October 1884. The hospital was located about two-and-a-half miles down a one-lane dirt road from the town of Lewes and about one-half mile from the point of Cape Henlopen. The hospital complex was situated on the southwestern twenty-six acres of the one hundred forty acres of land the government had acquired in 1873 from the State of Delaware for use as the Delaware Breakwater Military Reservation. In 1889 the state ceded an additional fifteen acres. The reservation had a waterline frontage of fifteen hundred feet that began about nine hundred feet east of the Iron Pier. The first buildings included a surgeon's quarters with administrative offices, a hospital, and lazaretto with six beds, boatman's quarters, anchorage for transfer barges, boathouses, and a graveyard (inland).[66]

In May 1886 the quarantine facility was officially opened to ships carrying immigrants. The only ships required to stop for inspection at the Delaware Breakwater were those coming from an infected port or those having a person with a contagious disease aboard. Upon passing the breakwater these ships would anchor and raise the yellow quarantine flag. A small whaleboat manned by four or five hospital attendants and either the chief acting surgeon or the assisting acting surgeon proceeded to the anchored vessel. Once on board, the doctor would inspect all passengers and crew members for any signs of contagious disease. If a person was suspected of being contagious they were removed from the ship and placed in the hospital for the duration of their illness. While the sick passenger was in the hospital, the other passengers remained in the anchored ship, quarantined for two to twelve weeks, to see if anyone else developed the disease. If no disease was found, the ship passed inspection and was permitted to proceed to its next port. If that port were Philadelphia, the ship would stop at the lazaretto for Philadelphia-controlled quarantine inspection and immigration processing. The Delaware Breakwater Quarantine Hospital operated in this manner from 1886 until the fall of 1892.[67]

Then, in March 1891, legislation made the quarantine inspection of immigrants part of the Marine Hospital Service's duties and, at the same time, established a separate Office of the Superintendent of Immigration in the Treasury Department to take over the processing of immigrants from the states. All ships entering Delaware Bay were now required to stop for inspection at the breakwater and the facility was soon overwhelmed. Traffic was heavy and ships arriving late in the day or during bad weather had to wait overnight for inspection, which created a backlog for ships arriving the next day. Thus, a second government quarantine inspection and immigration station was established at Reedy Island, about 45 miles south of Philadelphia, where the Delaware River joins the Delaware Bay.[68]

Purnell F. Harrington, Captain, USN, of USS *Puritan*, during Spanish-American War, 1898.(NH 72733, U.S. Naval History and Heritage Command).

The increase in the number of ships being inspected also necessitated an expansion of the Delaware Breakwater Hospital. The Iron Pier had been transferred to control of the Marine Hospital Service in 1890. By 1895 the hospital had added a disinfecting house and a crematory and had improved the supporting infrastructure. The hospital was expanded and became the "men's hospital," while a "women's hospital" was built. Two separate detention barracks with a capacity of up to 1,000 persons and with detached dining rooms and kitchens were also built.[69]

Meanwhile, by 1910, the work of the Delaware Breakwater Quarantine Hospital had diminished to inspecting only 37 steamers and 16 sailing vessels, while at Reedy Island 1,147 steamers and 95 sailing vessels had been inspected. Thus by 1912 construction of a pier and modern hospital was underway at Gloucester, New Jersey, to support Reedy Island, with the ultimate intention of closing the old Delaware Breakwater Quarantine Hospital.[70]

During this period of national expansion two local natives came to the fore for their naval words and deeds. The first, Admiral Harrington, offers a representative story of the trajectory of naval history from the Civil War to the eve of World War I.

Rear Admiral Purnell Frederick Harrington

After shore leave at the end of the Civil War, Acting Ensign Harrington of Dover, Delaware, returned to service on the *Monongahela* and was promoted to ensign on December 21, 1865. He was a naval academy graduate and a veteran of the Western Blockading Fleet during the Civil War. After his appointment as master on May 10, 1866, Purnell Harrington was appointed lieutenant on February 21, 1867, and assigned to the U.S. Naval Academy. After a two-year tour of duty, during which he was promoted to lieutenant commander, on March 12, 1868, he was assigned to temporary torpedo duty with the USS *California* in August 1870, followed by appointment as executive officer on the USS *Pensacola*, flagship of the Pacific fleet from December 1870 through August 1873. He returned to the U.S. Naval Academy in September 1873, serving on the faculty until September 1876, when he became the executive officer of the USS *Hartford* with the South Atlantic Squadron. He returned to the faculty of the U.S. Naval Academy in January 1880 and was promoted to the rank of commander on May 28, 1881. His next sea assignment was as captain of the USS *Juanita,* on the Asiatic Station from March 1883 to January 1886, when he became commandant of cadets at the naval academy. While commanding the *Juanita* he was involved in U.S. affairs on Madagascar and the Comoro Islands, particularly the conflicted relationship between the sultan of Johanna and an American citizen, Dr. B.F. Wilson, who was a sugar cane planter.[71]

Purnell Harrington's next assignment was as inspector of the 4th Lighthouse District in Philadelphia, where he served until 1893, when he assumed command of the USS *Yorktown*, a well-armed, steel-hulled gunboat. Following his service on the *Yorktown* he went on special duty at the Navy Department in Washington, D.C., and then assumed the presidency of the steel board of the U.S. Navy. Harrington was promoted to captain, United States Navy, on March 1, 1895. After commanding the USS *Terror* with the North Atlantic Squadron from April 1896 to July 1897, Captain Harrington found himself in command of the USS *Puritan*, a monitor, at the outbreak of the Spanish-American War.[72]

Assigned to the Cuban blockade in April, *Puritan* joined *New York* and *Cincinnati* in shelling Matanzas on the 27th. After a stop at Key West in early May, the *Puritan* departed on the 20th to join the force building that would eventually move against Santiago. She linked up on the 22nd, moved to Key Frances on the Nicholas Channel in order to execute the plan to contain the Spanish Fleet at Santiago. The success of the squadron at Santiago on July 3 resulted in the almost complete destruction of the Spanish fleet. After Cuba, *Puritan* sailed for Puerto Rico, where she landed a party of U.S. Marines and shelled the Spanish positions at the Battle of Fajardo.

From November 1898 to October 1901 Captain Harrington was commandant of the navy yard at Portsmouth, New Hampshire. On March 21, 1903, he was promoted to rear admiral and became commandant of the U.S. Navy Yard at Norfolk, Virginia. On June 6, 1906, after an illustrious career of service in the United States Navy and to the republic, Rear Admiral Harrington was placed on the retired list. His final military duty was in connection with the Jamestown Exposition from July 1906 to January 1908.[73]

A scholar in the area of nautical engineering, he wrote a number of articles bearing such titles as "The Coefficient of Safety in Navigation" and "Notes of Navigation and the Determination of Meridian Distances for the Use of Naval Cadets at the U.S. Naval Academy." He is listed among the "founding fathers" of the U.S. Naval Institute.[74]

On August 5, 1868, Purnell Frederick Harrington married Mia N. Ruan of St. Croix, Danish West Indies, and they had four children including Colonel Samuel Milby Harrington, USMC. Rear Admiral Harrington died at his home in Yonkers, New York, on October 20, 1937.[75]

Another Delawarean, Leonard Chadwick of Middletown, had a naval career that was worthy of an adventure novel or movie. He exhibited great personal courage on repeated occasions in the service of the U.S. Navy as well as halfway around the world in Africa.

Leonard Chadwick, Apprentice First Class, U.S. Navy, USS Marblehead

On board the USS Marblehead during the operation of cutting the cable leading from Cientuegos, Cuba, 11 May 1898. Facing the heavy fire of the enemy, Chadwick set an example of extraordinary bravery and coolness throughout this period [Medal of Honor Citation].[76]

Leonard Chadwick was born on November 24, 1878, in Middletown, Delaware. He enlisted in the U.S. Navy in Philadelphia on October 26, 1895. He was described as being 5' 7" tall, with blue eyes and light brown hair. During his enlistment, he served aboard the USS *Richmond, Vermont, Constellation, Alliance, Puritan, Brooklyn, Texas,* and *Marblehead*.[77]

When the war with Spain broke out in 1898, a naval blockade of the Spanish colony island of Cuba was established by the United States. The gunboat USS *Nashville* and the cruiser USS *Marblehead* were given a very specific task in May of 1898. They were to steam to the area of the port at Cienfuegos, locate two separate underground cables, haul them up onto workboats, and chop a large piece out of each one. If this could be accomplished the island would not be able to make any contact with the outside world, especially Spain. The navy had already blockaded all around the island and had control of the seas, and all that remained was to destroy these cables. The Spanish governor in Havana, General

Blanco, still maintained communication with other Caribbean bases as well as the home government in Madrid through the oceanic cables.[78]

Both warships were to provide two vessels each: two steam launches and two sailing launches. Lieutenant Cameron Winslow was placed in charge. The steam launches would be required to tow the sailing launches in close enough that the men onboard could row close to the shore to find and haul up the cable and chop a piece out of each. Each launch consisted of twelve men, half of them armed with pistols, the others with rifles. The steamers would then back off and take a position where the Marine sharpshooters could provide the cover necessary for the men to do their jobs. The operation had to be performed in daylight in order to see the cables. The night before the operation started volunteers were called for, and more than could be used stepped forward. Chadwick was one of thirty men to be assigned the duty of locating and cutting the cables. Many spent their time loading up on supplies for the next day, ensuring their cartridge belts were fully loaded, and even sat down to write wills and letters to their parents back home.[79] The mission was dangerous for several reasons. The water was very choppy, tides were strong, and the coastline was rocky. Scraping a boat on the outcroppings of rocks would instantly sink it. The waters were also shark infested and had been mined. The boats would be operating very close to the shore.[80]

Approaching shore there was a cable house serving as a terminus for the underwater cables. When the first cable was located, about twenty feet below the surface, several attempts at grabbing it finally succeeded and after quite an effort it was hauled to the surface and draped across the bow of the two sailing launches. The men had to then decide how to cut it. After several tries with various tools it was decided to hacksaw through the cable. This would take about one-half hour—per end—as the cable was as thick as a man's wrist. It was so tiring that they had to constantly relieve the fellow doing the sawing with another sailor.[81]

As all this was going on, the enemy in rifle pits and through outcroppings of rock all along the shore, were sniping at the boats, barely a hundred yards offshore. The enemy used smokeless powder in their Mausers and machine guns, making detection of their positions difficult. The *Nashville* and the *Marblehead* had bombarded the area before the attack began, but with enemy reinforcements brought in after the bombardment the ships had to start firing their shells again, only this time it was right over the heads of their own men in the smaller craft. More than one would have comments about this after the event. Still, the enemy shots were poking so many holes in the workboats that some reported having to take bullets out of their cartridge belts and stick them into the holes just to keep afloat.[82] After the first cable was cut and some 150 feet coiled of it up in the boat, the two vessels moved even closer to shore to get at the second cable line. They were successful and about 100 feet of that one was chopped out also.

After action reports suggest that as many as 200 enemy were killed. But the U.S. losses were limited to one killed, one mortally wounded, and six severely wounded. The operation lasted three hours but was a success. It had been one of the biggest operations in this short war. Leonard Chadwick was one of 52 men to receive the Medal of Honor for this dangerous assignment. He received his medal on July 7, 1899.[83]

Leonard Chadwick's military adventures were far from an end. His bravery at Cienfuegos was no fluke. Within two months of leaving the navy in mid–1898 Chadwick became involved in the shipping of mules to South Africa, prior to the Boer War. Hundreds of thousands of mules had already been "expended" during the war, and orders were sent for replacements all across Canada, the United States, and elsewhere. All in all, there may have been as many as 300 Americans in the Boer forces during the war, while some estimates of American participants on the British side run into several thousand. Winston Churchill covered the war as a correspondent and noted that many Americans and other foreigners were in the ranks of the Imperial Light Horse, a cavalry unit raised in Johannesburg in September 1899 to serve with the British army during the war that broke out the following month.[84]

Arthur Conan Doyle was also in South Africa at the time and subsequently wrote a definitive history of the war. He reported that an entire squadron of Roberts' Horse was composed of "Texas cowboys," many of whom came to South Africa tending the thousands of horses and mules shipped from America for the British army and stayed on to soldier in colonial regiments. Roberts' Horse was formed in January 1900 as one of many colonial volunteer units raised particularly for the war.[85]

Within very short order Chadwick joined an army cavalry unit, the Lord Roberts' Horse. Over the next year he would so impress his superiors that Lord Roberts himself would write not one but three letters to his superiors about this man. Each letter amounted to what is called a Mention in Dispatches, and each was actually a medal of bravery in itself. Trooper Leonard Chadwick was elected by his comrades as the most distinguished soldier in a South African colonial unit and was accordingly awarded one of the commemorative scarves knitted by Queen Victoria. It must have come as some surprise that the most outstanding South African soldier was an American. Chadwick received the Distinguished Conduct Medal for his bravery at Paardeberg and received a Mention in Dispatches by Lord Roberts on April 2, 1901.[86] Within a year Chadwick had fought in battles at Paardberg, Sannah's Post, Diamond Hill, Prinsloo, Heidelberg, and the Relief of Kimberley. He'd become a prisoner of war for a very short time and even got promoted to corporal for his bravery. At the end of his service he would come away from South Africa with six campaign bars to his service medals. He was probably entitled to a seventh. He was nominated for the Victoria Cross probably three different times and was awarded the Distinguished Conduct Medal (one down from the VC) for bravery.[87]

During the Boer War HRH Queen Victoria took a very deep interest in her men fighting in South Africa from her many colonies. She treasured the constant letters from her favorite grandson, Christian, who was serving in the war with the rank of major and was a member of General Hillyard's staff. He would often write about the bitterly cold nights. It is felt that due to these letters the Queen thought she would like to send a token of her concerns, but to just a highly select few. She crocheted eight scarves that ultimately were worn like a sergeant's sash by their lucky recipients.[88] These were sent in two batches, one going to Christian with instructions that the first four were to go to four privates, each representing one of the queen's colonies, those being Cape Colony, New Zealand, Australia, and Canada. Each of these four were to be selected by the men—not those with ranks and certainly not the officers. Each regiment was to hold a vote, select the bravest soldier in the unit, and pass those names along. Privates would narrow down the vote and ultimately end up with four men, these being the bravest of the bravest of the bravest.[89]

Leonard Chadwick, the American Medal of Honor recipient, was selected to represent the thousands who fought on behalf of Cape Colony. When the name was presented to the queen it came with the concern that this fellow was an American and ought not to be selected. The queen overruled those objecting and Chadwick became one of the bravest, and one of only four in the world as a private to get the "Queen's Scarf" (he later made corporal).⁹⁰ Of the four privates awarded the scarf, he was the only one with a Distinguished Conduct Medal as well and had more campaign bars than any of the other privates or even the sergeants who got the scarf. Some would say that he thus became one of the most decorated soldiers in all of North America. The records are not clear, but it would appear that the scarf may have been awarded for Chadwick's bravery when he rode out to help save wounded under very heavy fire at the battle of Koorn Spruit or because of his helping to save the heavy field guns from capture by the enemy at Sannah's Post.⁹¹

Chadwick came back to the U.S. in 1901 and worked as a union representative. His activities at one point were thought to be anti–American and even the FBI had him under their eyes for a while until they realized that he was truly a hero and rumors about him were false. He also worked as an insurance agent and as a laborer in the iron industry until 1923, when a dislocated elbow took him out of that profession. In 1937 he was declared totally disabled. Chadwick never married and died alone at his home in a rooming house of asphyxiation and alcoholism on May 18, 1940. He was interred in Mount Hope Cemetery, Mattapan, Massachusetts. He was given a full military funeral and it was said that he was buried in Massachusetts with his Medal of Honor sitting on his chest. His marker notes that he was a Medal of Honor recipient and indicates that his rank was that of a GM 3, that being a gunners mate third class. There is no indication on the stone that he had been awarded the Queens Scarf and was one of only eight people in the world to be so honored.⁹²

There was also another kind of hero bred on the Delaware's shores. Using mostly local men, a new organization dedicated to saving lives was formed.

U.S. Life-Saving Service

Combining increasing trade and ship-borne traffic with treacherous shoals, bad weather, and difficult currents, it became clear that something needed to be done about shipping losses along the Delaware coast. A volunteer life-saving service was established as early as 1854 but was inadequate to the task. In 1871 Congress created the new Life-Saving Service and appointed Sumner Increase Kimball to lead it. Historically there had been terrible loss of life and property off the Delaware Capes, including the *Three Brothers* in 1775 (200 lives lost), and the *Faithful Steward* in 1785 (180 lives lost).⁹³

Five stations would be constructed in Delaware—at Lewes (1884), Cape Henlopen (1876), Rehoboth Beach (1878), Indian River Inlet (1876), and Bethany Beach (1907). A station was also established in Ocean City, Maryland (1880).⁹⁴ The stretch of coastline between Dewey Beach and Bethany Beach, Delaware, was especially treacherous. The Indian River Life-Saving Station was the second built in Delaware in 1876 for use by the United States Life-Saving Service, a government organization created to respond to the alarming number of shipwrecks along the coastlines of the United States. This building was originally located 400 feet closer to the shore, but a sand dune began to form around it almost as soon as it was finished, and it was moved to its present location in 1877.⁹⁵ Each year from September through April six surf men and a keeper lived at the station. Their duty was to patrol the beach to warn ships in danger. If a shipwreck did occur these men were responsible for rescuing the ship's crew and passengers as well as saving and salvaging the ship's cargo. The men worked night and day in all kinds of weather without fail. Two-man patrols at four-hour intervals would walk the beach in both direc-

Six. Years of National Expansion, 1865–1914   155

Lifesaving Station, Cape May, New Jersey, 1901 (det1994016778/PP, Library of Congress).

tions until reaching their counterparts at the other stations searching for signs of vessels in distress.[96] If they sighted a vessel in distress they would signal by firing a Coston flare and initiate a rescue response. In most cases their watchfulness prevented further damage and reduced casualties. There is an example in a report from the log on June 17, 1890: "At 6 o'clock in the morning the keeper of the Indian River Inlet Station twice warned off a strange sloop that was trying to enter the inlet and was in danger of stranding on the shoals, and finally directed her, by signals, how to steer in crossing the bar."[97] Another example that typifies the mission was recorded on October 28, 1884:

> At 9 o'clock in the morning the schooner *Dan*, of New Castle Delaware carrying a crew of four men bound from Frankford Delaware to Philadelphia with a cargo of pine wood, while attempting to pass out of Indian River Inlet on her way to sea was becalmed and swept by a strong ebb tide on the beach at the north side of the inlet, about a mile south of the Indian River Station. The life-saving crew started at once to her relief, but as the tide was falling rapidly she was soon left high and dry. They carried out an anchor however, and made all necessary preparations, so that at high water in the evening when they boarded her she was floated off, without much difficulty, and enabled to proceed on her voyage, apparently uninjured.[98]

The fourth station to be established (1884) on the Delaware coast, the Lewes Station proved its usefulness almost immediately when the brave surf men responded to one of the most ferocious storms of the 19th century—the Great Blizzard of 1888. A quiet March quickly turned deadly as gale-force winds, freezing seas, and blinding snow descended upon the area. Ships that had sought refuge behind the Delaware Breakwater were wrecked on the wall and hundreds of sailors clung to frozen lines and icy masts throughout the night waiting for assistance from the men of the Lewes Station. The next morning the Lewes station men were joined by the crews of Cape Henlopen and Indian River and began the life-threatening job of saving as many as they could. Beginning with the wreck of the *Allie H. Belden,* the men saved scores of sailors and brought them to rest at the Marine Hospital at Cape Henlopen under the care of Dr. David Hall. It was easily the most well-known rescue of the Lewes Station. The Lewes crew also served admirably during the gales of April and September 1889.[99]

As sail gave way to steam, however, fewer and fewer wrecks occurred along Delaware's shore. In 1915 the U.S. Life-Saving Service merged with the Revenue Cutter Service and the modern United States Coast Guard was formed.[100] The Indian River Inlet station today remains in its original location and has been restored and serves as a museum. The Lewes station was relocated to Cape Henlopen, where it served as a men's club and, from October 1940 until June 1943, as the first building used by the Harbor Entrance Control Post (HECP) on Fort Miles. Later still, it was part of the Fort Miles Surf Club—an officer's club—before being moved to Rehoboth Beach, where it still stands today as the Rehoboth Beach VFW. The boathouse stands on the banks of the Lewes & Rehoboth Canal at the foot of Shipcarpenter Street as part of the outdoor museum associated with the *Overfalls* Lightship, a Historic National Landmark, moored there. The Rehoboth station still exists as a private residence in Shipcarpenter Square in Lewes, Delaware. The Ocean City Station has also been preserved and still stands.[101]

Profile of a Surf Man: Washington A. Vickers

Washington A. Vickers was born in Dorchester County, Maryland, on November 28, 1842. He was the grandson of Nathan Vickers and Elizabeth Hooper Vickers, whose father, John Hooper, owned the land that is now Seaford, Delaware. Little is known of Washington Vickers' early life except that his father died when he was four years old. As a young man, he enlisted in the Confederate States of America, at Richmond on October 31, 1862. He was a private in Company G, 2nd Maryland Infantry. Mr. Vickers was wounded at Gettysburg and spent most of his service as a hospital attendant at Chimborozo Hospital in Richmond. He signed the amnesty oath on June 30, 1865.[102]

Vickers enlisted in the United States Life-Saving Service as a surf man at Hog Island, Virginia, and was transferred to the Assateague (Virginia) Life-Saving Station in 1878. Eight years later, in 1886, he was appointed the keeper of the Indian River station. During 1907 he became the keeper of the Bethany Beach, Delaware, station, then retired from there. During his almost fifty years of service Vickers was on the scene of many of the notable shipwrecks that occurred on the Delaware coast: *Red Wing, J.W. Somers, Anna Murray, Addie, Wm. H. Davidson,* and *Ira D. Sturgis.*[103] He went to his heavenly station on February 28, 1930, at age 88.

The following letter by Vickers offers a peek at the routine of a surf-man keeper. It is an excerpt from a letter written while he was stationed at Assateague Beach, Virginia.

Life-Saving Station
Chincoteague Island
March 3, 1881

Dear Uncle, Joseph Neal in Seaford, Delaware

I never experienced such a cold winter before. We have had a rough winter on the beach.

A great many disasters have occurred all along on the coast. There is a Bark (*the Syringa*) ashore now about sixteen miles above here loaded with sugar, probably will go to pieces tonight. She went ashore this morning at five o'clock. The Life-Saving crew at Green Run, Maryland took off the crew. We took a crew off a vessel about a month ago about five miles off shore. The vessel (a schooner, the D. *Ellis* at Turner Shoal) struck an outer shoal and sunk. We were the first in time to rescue them. We have had to board several vessels this season.

This is a very important branch of service. There have been a great many lives saved this season by the Life-Saving Service.

Respectfully, Washington A. Vickers[104]

War with Spain

After exercising with the North Atlantic Squadron on January 25, 1898, the battleship USS *Maine* began a port visit to Havana, Cuba, to demonstrate a commitment to the protection of U.S. commercial interests during the ongoing insurgency. The ship anchored in the center of the port, remained on vigilant watch, allowed no liberty, and took extra precautions against sabotage. On the evening of February 15, 1898, the battleship was torn apart by a tremendous explosion that shattered the entire forward part of the ship. Out of 350 officers and men onboard that night, 252 were dead or missing. Eight more were to die in Havana hospitals during the next few days. As a result of the reports attributing the disaster to Spanish sabotage, public opinion in the U.S. was so inflamed that there were calls for a declaration of war on Spain.[105]

As war drew near, much of the Atlantic Fleet was in Key West for exercises and would become the squadron assigned to blockade Cuba and support army operations. There were few auxiliaries to maintain the navy at sea or to support army operations ashore. On March 9 Congress passed a $50 million emergency defense appropriation bill and the navy began acquiring vessels. Among the vessels purchased was the new Lewes steam pilot boat *Philadelphia No. 1*, which had been built by the Philadelphia shipyard of Neafie and Levy and just been placed into service at the cape. The boat was bought by the navy for $100,000, converted to a gunboat and commissioned as the USS *Peoria*. The *Peoria* was sent to Key West and from there she escorted transports to Cuba for a landing and supported that landing. The Pilots' Association for the Bay and River Delaware made do with several older boats but immediately ordered another steam pilot boat, *Philadelphia No. 2*, from the same shipyard for about $70,000—a nice profit on the deal.[106]

Another force of major combatants was formed into a "Flying Squadron" to intercept the Spanish Home Fleet forming in the Cape Verde Islands. But the force was positioned at Hampton Roads to block the Spanish fleet from approaching Cuba. There was widespread fear among the American populace that if the Spanish fleet approached the U.S. the coast would be undefended. To allay that concern, several ships had been recalled from Europe to form a Northern Patrol Force to operate from the Delaware Capes northward in defense of the coast or coastal trade. Plans were already in place for the defense of 15 harbors and strategic points on the Atlantic and Gulf coasts, including the approaches to Delaware Bay and using minefields.[107]

Coast Signal Service

In April, Captain C.F. Goodrich, USN, was directed to organize the Coast Signal Service in accordance with the recommendations of a board the secretary had approved earlier. After the declaration of war with Spain on April 19, Captain Goodrich was directed to establish the signal stations, and within two weeks the entire system was placed in operation.[108] The organization of the Coast Signal Service divided the Atlantic and Gulf coasts into seven districts corresponding to the districts of the Lighthouse Service and the Life-Saving Service of the Treasury Department. Each district had a commanding officer, most likely originally the naval officers assigned as inspectors of the lighthouse districts. They reported directly to Captain Goodrich at his headquarters aboard the ex-USS *New Hampshire*, then serving as the armory of the First Naval Battalion of New York.[109]

The system comprised 230 stations, consisting of the existing lighthouses, life-saving stations, and coastal weather stations plus 36 primary stations, to be manned by naval militiamen. All stations were connected to the telegraph or telephone systems of the Lighthouse and Life-Saving Services. The Lighthouse, Life-Saving and Weather Service personnel served as coast watchers to alert the primary stations and headquarters of ships approaching or transiting along the coast. The primary stations had the additional function of communicating with the ships to ascertain their identity, port of origin, destination, and intent.[110]

Cape Henlopen was home to one of the primary stations of the Coast Signal Service, established in the abandoned Philadelphia Maritime Exchange building adjacent to the Cape Henlopen Lighthouse. That location was selected because it retained a telegraph line to Lewes from which warning could be sent to Philadelphia.

Coast Signal Service Station on Cape Henlopen

Like all the primary stations, the one on Henlopen was manned by a chief quartermaster in charge, three quartermasters second class and a cook. Two of the quartermasters were qualified signalmen, often ex-merchant seamen; the other two were expert telegraphers, often civilians who had enlisted into the navy. The five navy men serving at the Cape Henlopen Coast Signal Service Station were all members of the Pennsylvania naval militia and were all enlisted into the U.S. Navy on April 21, 1898, and discharged on August 12, 1898:

- Walter H. Spence, enlisted as seaman and appointed as chief quartermaster;
- Richard Carter, enlisted as seaman and appointed as quartermaster second class;
- Austin H. Long, enlisted as seaman and appointed as quartermaster second class;
- Louis P. Maier, enlisted as seaman and appointed as quartermaster second class;
- J.F. Beatty, enlisted as landsman and probably served as cook.[111]

As a primary station, the mission of the Cape Henlopen station was to receive warnings of approaching ships from cooperating lighthouse or lifesaving stations by telephone, semaphore wigwag signals, or flares at night and then to alert Second District headquarters by telegraph. The primary stations would interrogate and communicate with approaching ships. In addition, the stations were responsible for coastal navigation services by providing a landmark against which ships could fix their position. They did so by flying the national ensign atop the mast and flying the blue with white square "PUP" flag on one yardarm in daytime and maintaining red and white lights in a vertical line at night.

During the short period of the war the station did not sight an enemy, as there was none along the coast to sight, but served to keep the Navy Department advised of the movements of its own ships and afforded the various navy yards, such as League Island in Philadelphia, with advance information of the arrival of ships as they passed Cape Henlopen en route for stores, overhauls, or repairs. Its major contribution was in allaying the fears that Lewes and other cities and industries of the Delaware Bay would be threatened by a surprise attack from the Spanish Home Fleet, which was rumored to have sailed from Spain upon the outbreak of war.[112]

Following the war this system was put into reserve, ready for reestablishment should it be needed. Although it was never used again, it became the predecessor that set the stage for the development of a U.S. naval communications system.[113]

Lessons Learned from the War

This sudden but short-lived need for ships, officers and men to respond to a naval threat demonstrated to Captain Bartlett that "the necessity of establishing a United States Naval Reserve, which the Department has for many years pointed out, has been most thoroughly proved. The time is appropriate to ask for legislation on the subject, and the Department can no doubt rely on the sagacity and energy of the present Committees on Naval Affairs in the Senate and House of Representatives to procure the authority of law."[114] However, no action was taken and the creation of a naval reserve would be a continuing goal of the navy in the years to come. Of more immediate concern, the war marked the first steps toward world power status for the United States. To demonstrate and maintain that status, a large, modern navy would be built. And, to support that navy during far-flung operations, improved naval communications would be required.

As shown by the presence of the Navy Signal Station on Cape Henlopen during the Spanish-American War, the navy communicated between ships and from ship to shore by signal flags and flashing lights. In 1896 Guglielmo Marconi, drawing on the work of many predecessors, patented his apparatus for transmitting electrical impulses and signals by the use of radio waves. He demonstrated that it was possible to send and receive telegraphic signals by radio waves over practical distances. Almost immediately the U.S. Navy became an interested and active investigator of the utility of the technology at sea, and it soon had a large number of coastal wireless telegraphy stations, including one on Cape Henlopen. With the advances of technology, these became the naval radio stations required to support the operations of the navy, including its visits to the cape.[115]

When approving the proposals for additional stations, the Navy General Board headed by Admiral Dewey commented that "radio telegraph" stations would also be of use to the new Naval Patrol Force being developed for coastal defense and, therefore, the commandants of the naval districts should be asked to designate locations in their districts where stations were desirable. By 1904 some 30 coastal stations had been proposed and approved, extending along the Gulf and East coasts, including one at Cape Henlopen. In 1904 the navy acquired additional land for a wireless station.

The Facilities and Equipment of the Cape Henlopen Wireless Telegraphy Station

In October 1905 the navy chief of the Bureau of Equipment reported that 23 shore stations already had been equipped and 13 more were being built, including the station at Cape Henlopen, which was "nearing completion." The layouts of the original naval wireless stations were all similar. They covered about three acres and consisted of a main building for living quarters, an operations building, a power building, and a storage building. The vertical transmission antenna masts were built like the masts of sailing ships, constructed of several long wooden poles lashed together by steel wire rope and held upright by a number of guy wires. They were 120–150 feet tall depending on the height of their placement above sea level. The mast at Cape Henlopen was 150 feet. This mast height would theoretically give a maximum line of sight transmission distance of 137 miles, but initial ranges were more like 30–50 miles, increasing with technology to about 100 miles by 1909. The horizontal receiving antenna consisted of two poles about 150 feet apart with multiple wires strung between them.

The official 1905 report of the navy chief of equipment indicated that Cape Henlopen was to receive a three-kilowatt transmitter made by Massie Telephone and Telegraph.[116]

The Operations of the Wireless Telegraphy Station

The number of government wireless telegraphy stations was mushrooming. The navy proposed to expand the number of its shore stations to 60, the Army and Weather Bureau had begun to establish systems, and 75 commercial stations were proposed or being built. Transmissions by wireless telegraphy stations were completely unrestricted and increasingly interfering with each other. To bring order to that competitive environment, President Roosevelt established the Interdepartmental Board of Wireless Telegraphy. In July 1904 that board unanimously recommended that the navy assume responsibility for all U.S. government radio. In that role, coastal naval wireless telegraphy stations such as Cape Henlopen received meteorological information from the Weather Bureau and provided weather reports and storm warnings to ships at sea and forwarded reports from ships at sea to the bureau. Information concerning wrecks, derelicts, ice, and other dangerous obstructions to navigation was received from ships and provided to the Hydrographic Office.

The navy set out to create a high-powered, long-range, worldwide communications network. The first high-power station was the Naval Radio Station, Arlington, Virginia. On February 13, 1913, this station was placed in commission and shortly thereafter the battleship USS *Delaware*, operating in the vicinity of the Azores, established radio contact.[117]

The Expanding Navy Visits the Cape

From 1900 to 1914 the total naval force level grew from 180 to 224 ships. Within that total the number of battleships increased from eight to thirty-four. In 1907 sixteen of those battleships participated in the world cruise of the Great White Fleet, the nickname for the United States Navy battle fleet that completed a voyage around the globe from December 1907 to February 1909 to "show the flag" on behalf of the nation. The newest addition to the fleet, the submarine, grew in number from zero to thirty-six and rapidly advanced in technology. These types of ships were frequently at the Cape Henlopen breakwater.[118]

The USS *Holland* (SS-1) was the first submarine commissioned into the U.S. Navy, at Newport, Rhode Island, in October 1900. The boat was immediately towed to Annapolis, Maryland, where it served as a training submarine preparing officers and crews for the new classes of subs being built. On its first major voyage, it stopped at the Delaware Breakwater on December 10, 1901. On another trip, on April 29, 1902, an explosion occurred as the submarine was approaching the breakwater. Lieutenant Arthur MacArthur, the brother of Douglas MacArthur, and a number of crewmen were injured. They were taken to the Breakwater Quarantine Hospital for treatment. The sub was towed to the Brooklyn Navy Yard but eventually returned to the Philadelphia League Island Navy Yard for repairs, again passing the cape.

In October 1909 the submarine USS *Plunger* (A-1) commanded by Ensign Chester W. Nimitz and accompanied by the USS *Tarantula* (B-3) and the USS *Viper* (B-1) were being escorted by the USS *Castine* (Gunboat #6) to their new home port in Charleston, South Carolina. While secured at the cape, *Viper* dragged anchor and was blown ashore. The crew of the Lewes Life-Saving Station assisted in refloating the sub. When commissioned in November 1911, USS *Skipjack* (E-1) had been equipped with the new technologies of gyrocompass and radio. She began testing that equipment under her first commanding officer, Lieutenant Chester W. Nimitz, who was also commander, Submarine Division Three. On February 23, 1912, while moving from Boston to Norfolk, the submarine stopped at the Delaware Breakwater and was undoubtedly in contact with Naval Radio Station, Lewes.

In September 1909 Lewes took part in the 300th anniversary celebrations of Henry Hudson's explorations along the American coast. At Lewes the Hudson-DeVries Celebration recognized that Hudson's 1609 visit to Delaware Bay was the impetus for David DeVries founding a Dutch colony near Cape Henlopen. During the celebration, the armored cruiser USS *Montana* (ACR-13) visited Lewes. Governor Simeon Pennewill and other dignitaries were hosted at a reception aboard and the people of Lewes were invited on a tour. The old destroyer tender USS *Dixie* and eight old torpedo boat destroyers also were present.

After 1910 a wide variety of surface ships operated at the cape as a result of the initiative of a Lewes pilot, Charles Clampitt. On his recommendation the navy selected the area off the cape as the official course over which the Norfolk and Philadelphia navy yards would conduct sea trials for newly built or overhauled ships. The first ship to undergo trials was the USS *Roe* (DD-24) after commissioning in September 1910. After an overhaul at Philadelphia and upon completion of a yard period in November and December of 1911, USS *Idaho* (Battleship #24) steamed on the measured-mile course off Lewes for standardization runs and rolling experiments. After anchoring overnight inside the breakwater at Lewes on December 17–18, the battleship conducted rolling experiments off Brown Shoal and anchored off Bombay Hook on December 19. Those operations at the cape displayed the preparations the navy was already making for what appeared to be a coming war.[119]

Organizing to Defend the Coast

In March 1915, at the urging of the under secretary of the navy, Franklin Roosevelt, Congress finally authorized the creation of the U.S. Naval Reserve Force (USNRF), which Roosevelt's cousin Theodore had been requesting since before the Spanish-American War. In May 1915 Congress authorized establishment of the post of chief of naval operations

(CNO), with a staff for coordinating naval training, supply, and planning. In December 1915 the Fourth Naval District was formally established, with headquarters at the League Island Navy Yard in Philadelphia and responsibility for the area of Pennsylvania, Southern New Jersey (south of Barnegat Light), and Delaware. In April 1916 new regulations for naval districts were issued, placing them under the control of the CNO. District commandants were directed to establish the Inshore Patrol Force comprising "sections" of different kinds of forces. Their operations would be conducted and supported from a "section base."[120]

A war had begun in 1914, and it was on its way to the shores of the Delaware.

Seven

The Great War, 1914–1918, and through 1925

The United States Navy leadership was initially complacent to the hostilities that had broken out in Europe in 1914. They studied the conflict for military lessons but saw none that immediately applied to the American fleet. A two-battleship per year construction plan initiated by Theodore Roosevelt in 1908 and continued by his successors in the Taft and Wilson administrations had seemed sufficient to the country's needs. The opening of the Panama Canal in 1914 further strengthened the navy, with its ability to easily move from one ocean to the other. The fleet, they felt, was adequate to the immediate task, and they focused on personnel and training reform.

The combatants had initiated policies that impacted neutral shipping. Several large sea battles in the North Sea—at Dogger Bank and Jutland in 1916—resulted in a less than sterling victory for the highly regarded British Grand Fleet. A shocked American political leadership pressed for a more ambitious construction program. Feeling that his hands had been tied, President Wilson said, "Let us build the biggest navy in the world and then we can do as we please!"[1] Within sixty days Congress had passed the Naval Act of 1916 authorizing ten battleships within three years, along with six battle cruisers, ten scout cruisers, fifty destroyers, and sixty-seven submarines.

The loss of the *Lusitania* with 128 American lives in 1915 was a shocking war crime to most Americans, turning public opinion against Germany. Germany amended its rules of engagement as a result of a strong protest by President Wilson that bought time and limited its undersea warfare regarding neutrals. But by 1917 Germany revoked its policy and returned to unrestricted submarine warfare, betting it could bring Britain to its knees by starving it out before America would enter the war and make a significant difference. The interception of the German secret "Zimmerman telegram" promising spoils to Mexico if she would enter the war against America was the last straw and forced the hand of President Wilson, who took it as an act of war.[2]

America entered the war in April 1917, and its role in the naval war would be shaped by several important factors.

Submarines

Submarines were a new naval technology, useful as a scouting platform but thought of as a marginal player, like commerce raiders. It took time for a cohesive doctrine to evolve for offensive undersea operations and even longer for anti-submarine operations.

Initially, no one thought they might make a strategic difference. In a navy dominated by surface warriors and battleship admirals, realization was slow to dawn at the overall impact of the U-boat threat. Precious warships should be reserved for defending the sea-lanes and American coasts, it was thought. The Panama Canal and American ports were of more strategic value than chasing submarines. Nevertheless, as a result of U-boat depredations Britain was hemorrhaging shipping at an unsustainable rate. She was losing up to 20 percent of her ships at sea. In April 1917 the allies suffered the loss of 835,000 tons. In June another half million tons of unconvoyed shipping was lost. This loss was repeated again in July and August. It turns out that this was *the* strategic threat. The allies would be in a long game of "catch-up." Several remedies were tried.[3]

The convoy system had been used initially during the Napoleonic Wars. Convoying was a way to counter the threat, but some thought of it as simply a way to make a bigger target group. Furthermore, the ships could proceed only as fast as the slowest vessel and then only after a lengthy assembly. Convoying was first tried on passages to nearby Norway. Eventually it proved to be a large part of the solution, especially when escort was by capable warships.[4]

America began to focus its industrial resources on both building mass-produced merchant ships to fill the losses already sustained and aggressively building anti-submarine vessels. It suspended the ambitious naval construction program passed only the year before, which was of little use in an emergency. Instead, industry concentrated on anti-submarine vessels. A program to construct 258 destroyers was initiated,[5] and the Delaware estuary would play a major role in this industrial expansion.

Because there was a shortage of destroyers, they were augmented by 200-foot "Eagle" boats manufactured by Ford Motor Company. The real workhorses, however, were the wooden 100-foot submarine chasers, also called "mosquito boats" or the "splinter fleet." These employed newly developed "hydrophones" to determine the direction of a sub. Working in threes they could triangulate a position. Over 440 of these tiny craft were constructed for the Allied fleets. Many of them were products of Delaware River shipbuilders. Allied submarines were also to prove a deadly threat to U-boats in proportion to the numbers involved.[6]

The navy established some fifteen anti-submarine bases in Europe including Queenstown, Ireland; Brest, France; and Gibraltar. When Commander Taussig arrived in Queenstown with the first batch of American destroyers on May 4, the British commander, Vice Admiral Lewis Bayly, asked, "When would Taussigs's squadron be ready to start patrol?" Taussig replied, "We are ready now—as soon as fueled."[7]

Another solution to the U-boat menace was to mine the approaches to the U-boat bases in the North Sea—a massive project requiring over 100,000 mines in three sections, each 35 by 230 miles. A new mass-manufactured antenna mine with an increased range helped to make this possible. A great mine barrier had been laid across almost the whole of the North Sea by the time of the armistice. The psychological damage to the U-boat crews was nearly equal to the actual damage caused, as the crews had to navigate through this lethal maze.[8]

Ferrying Troops

A significant naval mission would be to transport American troops to France. This would prove to be the biggest troop movement by sea ever undertaken up to that time.

Photograph shows the SM UC-5, a German Type UC-I minelayer submarine (U-boat), which was captured by the Allies, brought to New York City, and renamed *U-Buy-a-Bond*. The submarine, shown in Central Park, took part in the Liberty Loan Parade in New York City on October 25, 1917 (ggb2006000981, Library of Congress).

The navy commandeered over twenty American ocean liners as well as impounded German and Dutch liners such as the *Mt. Vernon* and the *Leviathan*, some forty ships in all. Over two million American soldiers including thirty thousand Marines were taken to the fight. They were escorted by a force of some 24 cruisers under the Cruiser and Transport Force commanded by Rear Admiral Albert Gleaves. American vessels carried 46 percent of American soldiers. The rest were carried primarily by British vessels. No troop ship was ever sunk at sea by German U-boats. The ships used a route to the south of the regular shipping lanes and were aggressively escorted by warships. The Germans largely ignored them as they focused on cutting off British shipping lanes hoping to starve that country into submission.[9]

The High Seas Fleet

The German High Seas Fleet remained a threat from its protected lair in the Baltic Sea. It never sallied forth after Jutland except for minor raids, but nevertheless posed a potential threat during the whole of the war. Five coal-burning American battleships (*Delaware*, *New York*, *Texas*, *Wyoming*, and *Florida*) were sent to Scapa Flow to augment the British Grand Fleet and free up some of their warships for other duties. This battleship squadron was commanded by Rear Admiral Hugh Rodman. A second squadron of

Naval Aircraft Factory, Philadelphia, Pennsylvania. Hull of an experimental F6L flying boat under construction at the Naval Aircraft Factory, October 19 1918. Note influenza precaution sign in the left background. The Spanish influenza epidemic was then extremely active in Philadelphia (NH 41731, U.S. Naval History and Heritage Command Photograph).

battleships was sent to Ireland late in the war to counter the threat of the High Seas Fleet. The squadron included *Nevada*, *Oklahoma*, and *Utah*, commanded by Rear Admiral Thomas S. Rodgers.[10] Altogether the American contribution to the Allied naval effort amounted to 354 U.S. Naval vessels at the time of the armistice, or about a third.[11]

Naval Aviation

The nascent naval air arm went into high gear as the war commenced. Training quickly ramped up for aviators and support personnel. Air bases for anti-submarine patrols were established in Britain, France, and Ireland. Navy bombers struck shore targets in Belgium and the submarine pens along the English Channel. Although they saw only a few months of active operations, over 1,600 naval air pilots carried out over 22,000 sorties, flying over 2,000 aircraft, dropping 99,000 pounds of bombs, supported by 20,000 men.[12] The air operations were mostly subordinate to British command employing seaplanes.

New quarters and blimp hangar, U.S. Naval Air Station, Cape May, New Jersey, February 5, 1919 (NH 113030, U.S. Naval History and Heritage Command).

In 1917 the navy established a "section base" in Cape May to provide training, vessel support, and communication facilities for coastal defense. Initially, the navy converted an abandoned amusement center, built along the oceanfront, for military use. The old skating rink became the mess hall and sleeping quarters, the stage was made into a galley, and the "human roulette wheel" and the "barrel of fun" became a brig. A U.S. Navy seaplane and LTA (lighter-than-air—airship, or blimp) patrol base was constructed on the eastern-most part of Cape May. Established on October 6, 1917, it was commissioned as a naval air station on December 4, 1917. During the First World War, Cape May operated twelve seaplanes and one dirigible. When the old wooden structure burned down in 1918 the navy built standard military facilities along the harbor front. Among them was a hanger, 700 feet long and 100 feet high, for dirigibles.[13]

At the Philadelphia Naval Yard facilities, a naval aircraft factory was built in the late summer of 1917 to manufacture aircraft for the navy. Its first order was for fifty Curtis H-16 flying boats. By mid-1918 it employed 3,640 workers at its 47-acre site on League Island.[14]

Onshore

The navy built railway mounts for some of its big fourteen-inch guns for action on the Western Front. With a thirty-mile range they fired 782 rounds and did serious damage to rail junctions and ammunition dumps behind enemy lines. The Marine Corps fought with valor at Chateau-Thierry, Belleau Wood, and St. Mihiel. Over 8,000 Marines were engaged,[15] 1,600 being killed and 2,500 wounded. These casualties amounted to over half the total force.[16]

The Coast Guard

The United States Coast Guard at war's beginning had fifteen cruising cutters, 200 officers, and 5,000 men. In wartime it became a naval asset and was dedicated almost exclusively to the anti-submarine mission of escorting and screening convoys. The coast guard took a significant loss when the cutter *Tampa*, bound for England, disappeared in a loud explosion with the loss of 111 crew along with four naval personnel. The service suffered greater losses in proportion to its strength than any of the other United States armed forces in World War I.[17]

Approaches from the Sea

The 1914 annual report of the Waterfront Development Foundation, titled *Boosting Port of Philadelphia,* offers the following description of the state of the port of Philadelphia on the eve of World War I:

> The approach to the city is by way of Delaware River and Bay, the two together forming a commodious tidal estuary with natural broad deep water extending for 35 miles from the ocean to the entrance of the improved ship channel from which point a distance of 53 miles to Market Street, Philadelphia, the channel is from 600 to 1000 feet wide and is at present 30 feet deep at low tide. It is maintained at this depth by dredges of the U.S. government which are continually at work upon it and contract work is now underway for deepening it to 35 feet and widening it from 800 to 1200 feet.
>
> Between Cape May on the New Jersey side of the Bay, and Cape Henlopen on the Delaware side, which two capes flank the entrance to the lower Bay, the width of the estuary is 10 miles. It widens to nearly 23 miles at Maurice River Cove a few miles above the Capes, and then gradually contracts to four miles in width at Bombay Hook, opposite the entrance to the improved channel, and narrowing continually, by the time Philadelphia is reached is about one-half mile wide along the city riverfront.
>
> The river is excellently lighted from the capes to the mouth of the improved channel by powerful lighthouses built in the bay along the limits of deep water, and from the entrance of the artificial channel to the city by gas buoys and sets of shore range-lights located on the center lines of various reaches of the channel and forming a continuous guide from one end of it to the other. More than fifty navigation lights are passed between the capes and the city, or an average of about one to each two miles. The buoying for day use is equally good in character.
>
> Fluctuation of tidal level is felt as high up as the city of Trenton—33 miles above Philadelphia—but is not excessive at any time, and tidal current never exceeds three miles per hour. The variation between high and low tide is 4.5 feet at the capes, and six feet at Reedy Island about half way between the capes and the city, 5.5 feet at Philadelphia, and about three feet just below the falls at Trenton, the head of navigation.
>
> From New Castle, a distance of 29 miles below Philadelphia and extending up to its headwaters the river is fresh water and this is a vast benefit to vessels tying up in port. Philadelphia is the only Atlantic Coast port situated on fresh water.[18]

On the eve of World War I, Philadelphia was the greatest manufacturing city in the country in heavy machinery and steel and iron products, with easy access to Pennsylvania coal. It had a population of nearly two million people, in a state of eight million, producing 5 percent of the nation's manufactures, ranking second only to New York as a port. The port had nearly 200 piers with 160,000 lineal feet of berthing. They were capable of accommodating large, deep-draft, oceangoing vessels, affording dockage for about one hundred ships at a time. A belt-line railroad served the entire waterfront, allowing goods from any part of the country to be delivered to any wharf without rehandling.[19]

Philadelphia Quartermaster Terminal

During World War I a huge military port terminal was erected in Philadelphia to serve as part of a vast system designed to move men and materiel quickly and efficiently to France. The terminal occupied a tract of land 3,800 feet in length along a ship canal that had a depth of 25 feet and length of 1,600 feet. Special tracks were constructed measuring 1,100 by 160 feet, with nine large storehouses together with living quarters for stevedore troops. A series of warehouses were also constructed. Another port terminal had a pier extending 1,100 feet with over 400,000 square feet of shed storage.[20]

Philadelphia Navy Yard

During World War I the Navy Department established shipbuilding ways, a naval aircraft factory, and a submarine base, as well as started to construct a third dry-dock that promised to make League Island a first-class naval base and shipbuilding yard. It served as a home station for the reserve fleet as well. However, it constructed only a handful of ships during the war and scrapped two battle cruisers on the ways after the war.[21] A harbor patrol of the river from Marcus Hook to Bristol was maintained by the Board of Commissioners of Navigation using the vessel MS *Quay* to guard the approaches to the Port of Philadelphia and the navy yard.

In January 1917 a "suspicious outbreak" of twenty-one cases of influenza struck sailors aboard the USS *Minneapolis* anchored at the Philadelphia Navy Yard.[22] A month later, four other ships had been stricken. This would be the initial wave of the infamous "Spanish Influenza" pandemic. By October, Philadelphia would be among the hardest hit cities in the country, with 11,000 deaths in one month. The casualties from this outbreak would equal the combat casualties during World War I for the United States. Worldwide an estimated fifty million people were afflicted. The City of Philadelphia recorded 4,857 deaths from the disease during just one week in October 1918. This naturally had an impact on productivity for the war effort.[23]

Hog Island

Shipbuilding during World War I in Philadelphia was dominated by the massive enterprise at Hog Island. In 1917, as part of the World War I effort, the U.S. government contracted American International Shipbuilding to build ships and a shipyard at Hog Island. It was built from scratch in less than ten months on 846 acres of fields and marsh. At the time, Hog Island was the largest shipyard in the world.[24] Hog Island was the first shipyard ever built for mass production of ships from fabricated parts and subassemblies, produced at dozens of subcontractors. Upwards of 300 freight cars per day arrived bearing

Hog Island Shipyard, Chester, Pennsylvania. On Decoration Day, May 31, 1919, during launch ceremonies for five cargo ships. Note the long row of building ways, ramps, and cranes, and the prefabricated parts lying at the heads of the ways (NH 43184, U.S. Naval History and Heritage Command).

prefabricated materials from as far away as Kansas. It had 50 slipways, 7 wet docks and a detention basin. Hog Island employed 35,000 daily workers. Only two basic designs, EFC 1022 and EFC 1024, were to be fabricated at the yard, and these became collectively known as "Hog Islanders." They were 7,500 deadweight tons each. The Type A design (1022) was a cargo carrier and the Type B (1024) was designed to transport troops. Both were very modern simple designs geared toward mass production, and aesthetic considerations were ignored. The vessels were fueled by oil rather than coal, with modern geared turbines of 2,500 shaft horsepower (1,900 kW) capable of producing up to 15 knots (28 km/h, or 17 mph).[25]

There was a minimum of frills with no sheer (upward curve at the bow or stern), resulting in a squat, angular silhouette. The hulls were symmetrical from the sides, and this combination produced an unconventional look and profile. These ships were considered ugly but well-built and had good performance in terms of capacity and speed. The profile created a form of camouflage because the lack of sheer in the bow, high stern, and the evenly balanced superstructure made it difficult for submarines to tell which direction the ships were going. The Hog Island contract was for 180 ships, but only 122 were completed and none were completed in time to be used before the war ended.

The first ship (named the SS *Quistconck* for the Lenape Indian name for the site) was christened August 5, 1918, by Edith Bolling Wilson, wife of President Woodrow Wilson. On May 30, 1919, the Hog Island shipyard launched five vessels in forty-eight minutes and ten seconds. The shipbuilding continued until January1921, after which the facility was rapidly demolished. Fifty-eight, or nearly half, of the Hog Islanders were sunk during World War II. The Liberty ships built during World War II used a similar concept of production but a completely different design.[26]

The site is today the home of Philadelphia International Airport.[27] Hog Island lives on today as a Philadelphia delicacy. The "hoagie" or "hoggy," known elsewhere as the submarine sandwich, was the World War I version of fast food consumed by shipyard workers. A second, smaller yard was constructed at Bristol by the Merchant Shipbuilding Corporation.

Cramp and Sons Shipbuilders

In 1906 the British launched the first all big-gun battleship, the HMS *Dreadnought*. It immediately made every other capital ship on the seas obsolete such was its technological advance. The initial American response was to build its own dreadnought, the USS *South Carolina* (BB-26), launched at Cramp in 1908, followed by *Wyoming* (BB-32) in 1911. During World War I Cramp and Sons built 46 torpedo boat destroyers and nine merchant ships for the navy, and one estimate claimed they had built one-fourth of the American naval tonnage used in the First World War. Cramp employed around 5,000 workers just before the war, that number doubling during the war years of 1917 and 1918.[28]

Wilmington Port

Despite a confluence of three rivers, the Brandywine, the Christina, and the Delaware, Wilmington did not have a port worthy of the name and was dependent on Philadelphia imports. The citizens of Wilmington voted in 1913 to build harbor facilities in their city. It was a timely decision. With war in 1917 the United States found that it lacked sufficient facilities to handle oceangoing ships. A feasibility study was done by John Meigs, former director of wharves, docks, and ferries for the City of Philadelphia. The study recommended the establishment of a deepwater facility near Pigeon Point.

In 1919 the state legislature approved construction of a port facility on 105 acres of the East Christina River. Construction began in 1921, including three connecting rail spurs, dredging the river, and new roadways. Meigs was named as design engineer and was assisted by DuPont Company engineers. A 1,210-foot quay was constructed capable of handling multiple ships, with a berth depth of 23 feet. Warehouse storage of 120,000 square feet and open storage of ten acres were provided. The Port of Wilmington opened in 1923 then three large cranes were added. Typical cargos of that time included lumber, wood pulp, cork, jute, burlap, lead, ore, fertilizer, and petroleum products.[29]

Wilmington Shipyards

The First World War brought Wilmington to prosperity as munitions works, shipbuilders, and foundries went into action. Harlan and Hollingsworth built seventy ships during the war and continued to manufacture ships until 1926. At its peak, Harlan and Hollingsworth employed about 7,500 people in three shifts.[30] More than 2,000 employees worked for Pusey and Jones during the Great War building ships. A second shipyard was added in Gloucester City, New Jersey, but after producing nineteen ships the yard was changed to the New Jersey Shipbuilding Company. A third major shipyard, the Jackson and Sharp firm, built grain barges, car floats, lighters, tugs, ferry boats, tow boats, schooners, and dump scows. While the shipyard kept busy, iron and steel shipbuilding quickly eclipsed wood shipbuilding. Jackson and Sharp produced 15,617 tons of shipping in 1906, compared to 48,671 tons for Pusey and Jones and 43,016 tons for Harlan and Hollingsworth.[31]

The Jackson and Sharp plant "launched the largest tonnage of wooden boats put out by any American shipyard" between 1914 and 1915. It was contracted in 1917 to build eight wooden submarine chasers, and about one hundred men did the job within six months. Boat repair at the shipyard took on added importance during the war. Jackson and Sharp produced a variety of rail cars, acid buckets, and powder trays for the DuPont Powder Company's munitions work. The plant also manufactured tables, benches and pontoons.[32]

Downstate Shipyards

Small shipyards in downstate Delaware also enjoyed the bounty of government contracts during the war, building predominately small wooden ships. William G. Abbott of Milford, the state's primary builder of wooden schooners during this period, registered twelve vessels at the Port of Wilmington between 1900 and 1920. These vessels ranged in size from a sloop of fourteen tons to a four-masted schooner of over seven hundred tons. John Moore and the Smith and Terry Company, both of Bethel along the Nanticoke River, continued to build ships into the second quarter of the century. A few manufacturers, such as the Vinyard Shipbuilding Company of Milford, maintained a steady business with the construction of pleasure craft, some of which were repurposed as patrol craft. Vinyard built the submarine chasers SC-144, 145, and 146. The SC-144 was one of the first to join the patrol group at Cape May. The SC-145 operated with the patrol group out of Lewes, and the SC-146 was sent to France.[33]

Delaware River Shipbuilding Baseball League

The war wasn't all toil and effort. Recreation played an important role in maintaining morale. This was as important in the civilian community as it was among those in uniform. Among the most popular activities were the shipyard baseball leagues. Baseball leagues flourished in American shipyards during World War I as legions of workers built warships and troop transports to safeguard the Atlantic sea-lanes and carry men and materiel to Europe. According to Jim Leeke in an article published in the 2013 *National Pastime*, among the best of these circuits was the Delaware River Shipbuilding League of 1918. Centered in Philadelphia, it represented eight shipyards operating along the river in Delaware, New Jersey, and Pennsylvania. When the First World War ended with the armistice, many shipyards downsized or closed by the following spring. The Delaware River Shipbuilding League briefly fielded six amateur teams before folding in 1919.[34]

Ferry Lines

World War I triggered significant industrial expansion on the Lower Delaware. The DuPont Powder Works received enormous war orders and had to open new facilities at several sites in New Jersey to meet increased product demand. Thousands of powder workers from the tri-state region were recruited for the new plants located in the vicinity of Penn's Grove, New Jersey. The majority of the Pennsylvania and Delaware workers took Wilson Line ferries across the Delaware River to Penn's Grove to get to work. By 1916 the Penn's Grove ferries alone were making sixteen sailings daily. Two separate ferry entities, Christina Ferry Company and the Wilmington and Penn's Grove Transportation Company were established to accommodate this new traffic. New ferry piers had to be built at Deepwater Point and Carneys Point, New Jersey. Overwhelmed by this new traffic, the Wilson Line purchased several steamers to handle the new ferry service load. During peak years, steamboats and ferries made more than thirty Wilson Line sailings from Wilmington every day.[35]

Naval Section Base at Cape Henlopen

Few realize the scope of the large naval facility that made its home in Delaware during the Great War. In 1914 the war in Europe was raging, and it was possible that the United States would be drawn into it. Precautions were being taken to defend shipping in the approaches to Delaware Bay. Naval section bases were established on Cape Henlopen and Cape May. Almost all traces of the Henlopen naval facility have long since disappeared.

William H.J. Manthorpe, Jr., in a comprehensive history of the U.S. Navy at Cape Henlopen, describes the naval response to the threat of war at the Delaware Capes in his book, *A Century of Service: The U.S. Navy on Cape Henlopen, Lewes, Delaware, 1898–1996*: "A 'Naval Section Base' is a shore base under the overall command of a Naval District Commandant, as distinguished from a 'Naval Base' or 'Naval Operating Base' which are under the command of a Fleet Commander."[36]

At Cape Henlopen, the planned closing of the existing Public Health Service Delaware Breakwater Quarantine Hospital was deferred and the hospital continued at a reduced level of operations. The suitability of that facility and its piers as a naval base had been demonstrated in August 1914 when two destroyers on neutrality patrol stopped there and again when, over the Christmas–New Year's period of 1914–1915, the battleship USS *Ohio* was quarantined there. As the U.S. entered the war, in April 1917, the cape was defined by presidential executive order as a "defensive sea area." A navy delegation met with the mayor of Lewes to make arrangements for the navy to occupy the former quarantine hospital facilities and piers as a naval section base, under the command of the commandant of the Fourth Naval District.[37]

By the spring of 1918 the headquarters and administrative offices had been moved to the Lewes Coast Guard Station. The principal part of the base occupied the piers and administrative buildings of the former quarantine hospital, while the hospital barracks became the base enlisted living quarters (BEQ). There were about 800 men stationed at the base, and the accommodations were quite primitive. Nevertheless, life was not all hard for the sailors assigned. The bay provided recreation close at hand, the band provided lively entertainment, and there was a YMCA on base. The sailors who did get into Lewes were treated well. The rector of St. Peter's Church made his rectory a home for the men and had a dozen to fifty lodgers a night.[38]

Naval Section Base Lewes was established primarily to serve as home to the varied organizations and personnel responsible for the routing, control, and support of the vast numbers of naval combatants and transports that would soon be en route from Philadelphia to Europe. Among the first convoys to form up at the cape in June 1917 was one of cruisers and transports, including the navy transport USS *Hancock* (AP-4), carrying the Fifth Marine Regiment to join the American Expeditionary Force in France.

The first naval force based at the Section Base Lewes was the minesweeping section. The section was composed of steam-powered, wooden-hulled vessels from the menhaden fishing fleets that operated in waters adjacent to the Delaware Breakwater. The largest of these was the *Delaware*, acquired from the Delaware Fish Oil Company of Lewes. The *Delaware* was taken by the navy in May 1917, converted to a minesweeper, and placed in commission as the USS *Delaware* (SP-467). At least nine other Delaware Bay menhaden fishing vessels were purchased outright, rapidly converted for minesweeping service at the Philadelphia Navy Yard, commissioned into the navy, and assigned to Lewes.[39]

While the minesweeping section was being formed at Lewes, the patrol section was being formed at Cape May. The patrol section consisted mainly of private yachts acquired by donation or purchased from individual owners. They were converted for navy use, equipped with weapons—generally a main battery of a single pedestal-mounted gun and a secondary battery of a machine gun as well as depth charges—and commissioned. Most patrol craft were based at Cape May, but at least two were based at Lewes: the USS *Drusilla* (SP-372), which had been acquired from the Philadelphia millionaire Anthony J. Drexel, and the USS *Juniata* (SP-603). Patrol craft patrolled the shipping lanes approaching the cape and at the harbor entrance. The Lewes units served as guard ships in the harbor and on neutrality duty.

With the signing of the armistice, all war activities ceased. Convoys and patrols were suspended, and district vessels were decommissioned and returned to their respective owners. The base at Lewes was abandoned, and demobilization was begun and carried out promptly.[40]

War Comes to Delaware Shores

Submarines were sighted in local waters on May 20, 1918. At the end of that month the U-151 *Deutschland* laid a cluster of mines off Cape Henlopen and continued north to cut a transatlantic cable off New York. Then, on June 2, what came to be known as "Black Sunday," the sub sank three schooners and three steamships and damaged two other ships off the coast of New Jersey, about fifty miles southeast of Barnegat Light. The largest was the *Carolina*, which was torpedoed off New Jersey; thirteen out of the three hundred passengers and crew were killed. The British steamer *Appleby* brought nineteen numb survivors into Lewes, where the local residents were shocked by their woeful conditions.[41]

The following day the tanker *Herbert L. Pratt* broadcast that it had been torpedoed three miles off Cape Henlopen, literally within sight of shore. It had been en route to Philadelphia. The Lewes pilot boat *Philadelphia* soon arrived to evacuate crewmen. Some

SS *Herbert L. Pratt* (American tanker, 1918) under salvage after hitting a mine, June 1918. By the time this view was taken, buoyancy had been restored to the ship's forward section and she had raised steam in preparation for going to Philadelphia, Pennsylvania, for repairs. Note the diagonal line on her hull, sloping down and aft from the quarterdeck break, representing the degree to which her bow had been submerged (NH 83121, U.S. Naval History and Heritage Command Photograph).

remained aboard and, with a salvage crew, righted the ship. Two warships and a flotilla of smaller boats rushed to its assistance. On closer inspection, it was found to have struck a mine in its forward section. It was towed to the Delaware Breakwater by this armada of rescuers. In the resulting confusion, a lookout reported the wake of a submarine, and a wild goose chase ensued. Every vessel that had a weapon blasted away at the phantom submarine, and the roar of gunfire rattled windowpanes on Second Street in Lewes. Not since the War of 1812 had war been this close and menacing to the townspeople. At the breakwater the *Pratt* was quickly refloated by attaching pontoons and towed by the salvage tug USS *Tasco* to the pier at the section base, where the ship was righted, the hole patched, and power restored. *Pratt* was able to sail to Philadelphia under its own power. William H.J. Manthorpe Jr., said, "In the belief that a submarine was in the area, search operations were begun. Soon section base minesweepers located and destroyed three mines. With the mine threat identified, the Commanding Officer of the Section Base was directed to stop all outgoing vessels and the port of Philadelphia was closed temporarily until such time as the Commandant was assured that the channels to sea were safe and free from mines. Several Fleet minesweepers—USS *Widgeon* (AM-22), USS *Teal* (AM-23) and USS *Kingfisher* (AM-25)—moved from Philadelphia to Lewes."[42]

In July and August three other Deutschland-type subs operated in the cape area. U-156 sank one ship off northern New Jersey before moving north. U-140 sank one ship farther at sea before moving south. Next U-117, nearing the middle of what had already been a very successful cruise, entered cape area waters, sinking one tanker and then another off Barnegat Light and then laying mines in the area. On the way south past the cape, the sub was attacked by a navy plane and subchaser. After escaping to sink a small coastal schooner, U-117 laid more mines in the area of Fenwick Light and then moved south to create more havoc. On 18 September, a month after U-117 had left the area, the USS *Minnesota* (BB-22), an older battleship serving as a training ship, hit one of the mines laid by U-117 off of the Fenwick lightship. The ship was able to contain the damage and proceed to the cape and Philadelphia under her own power. But even long after U-117 had departed, the effects of her visit remained. Two merchant ships were sunk in October off Barnegat Inlet by the mines U-117 had laid earlier. Then, just as the war was ending, on 9 November, USS *Saetia* (ID No. 2317), a navy support cargo ship, encountered another of U-117's mines and sank 10 miles southeast of Fenwick Island Shoal. All eighty-five hands survived to come ashore at Ocean City and Cape May. Some of the mines laid by U-151 and U-117 were still being found in early 1919.[43]

Submarines and mines were not the only hazards to shipping during the war. The naval tug *Cherokee* was caught at sea in a gale on February 27, 1918. Its crew of forty men gallantly fought a 50-mile per hour wind; the aging hulk had never been designed for blue-water cruising. It was headed south from Philadelphia. Off Fenwick Island its steering gear broke, and it floundered in the seas. The wireless operator kept in touch until the seas closed over him. Ten men scrambled onto one life raft and four onto another. Two were washed off the second raft, and two more later died. The ten survivors were semiconscious when the British tanker *Admiral* rescued them. In all, thirty crewmen were lost.[44]

The *City of Athens* was a passenger liner going from New York to Savannah along the Delaware coast early on the foggy morning of May 1, 1918. It carried sixty-eight passengers and sixty-six crew members, most of them asleep in their cabins. The French destroyer *La Gloire* loomed out of the mist on a collision course, its bow smashing into

USS *Delaware* (BB-28) anchored in Guantanamo Bay, Cuba, January 1, 1920 (61253, U.S. Naval History and Heritage Command).

the bow of the *City of Athens*. Everyone in the fore part of the *Athens* was killed. Fire erupted, only to be smothered by the incoming rush of water. An SOS was sent from the radio shack, but the *Athens* sank within four minutes. *La Gloire* launched lifeboats to pick up survivors still dressed in their nightclothes. The passenger list included twenty-four U.S. Marines, of whom seven perished. The death toll was sixty-nine, with sixty-five surviving.[45]

We end this chapter on the First World War with the tale of the USS *Delaware*, a story that partially captures some of the background on naval development just prior to the war as well as how the U.S. Navy deployed and operated during the war. The story of the *Delaware* encapsulates the progress of the navy during the first two decades of the new century.

USS Delaware, *America's Dreadnought*

In 1888 Kaiser Wilhelm II was crowned as the regent of the German Empire. He was the 29-year-old grandson of England's Queen Victoria and within two years had deposed Emperor Otto von Bismarck, who had assembled the rising Teutonic continental empire. Kaiser Wilhelm's great ambition was to build a navy that would rival Britain's Royal Navy, making Germany a world power. Britain had ruled the seas almost unchallenged since the days of Nelson during the Napoleonic wars. Thus began a rivalry that initiated an arms race between the two nations some have pointed to as a cause of the Great War in 1914. The escalating sums of treasure and manpower exacted a toll on the national treasuries as each nation tried to outdo the other. The rivalry also inspired other participants to join the contest, such as Japan and the United States.

Nineteenth-century naval architecture was in technological transition from wooden hulls to ironclads, from sail to steam, from smoothbore to rifled cannon, with a corresponding evolution of tactics. The simplest definition of a warship is simply a waterborne platform with the purpose of defeating other enemy warships. This requires an armament scheme to bring fire on other ships, which can include cannons or missiles or torpedoes. As warships evolved over the centuries there were always trade-offs and compromises between offensive and defensive capabilities, between speed and range, and between weight and maneuverability, as well as armor versus armament. A vessel had to be seaworthy in all types of conditions, able to engage an enemy at sea as well as on land. The evolution of the capital ship in the second half of the 19th century had still not settled on a final design despite many experimental paths. Warships at the turn of the century had a bewildering array of different armaments including torpedoes and guns of various caliber and size and were still constructed to ram an enemy. They were generally ironclad and had forgone sails and were powered by steam engines fueled by coal.

Admiral John A. "Jacky" Fisher

Admiral John A. "Jacky" Fisher, the new first sea lord of the Royal Navy, proposed radical reforms to the construction of battleships in 1904. He envisioned a ship that would carry the largest caliber guns possible in the greatest number. All things being equal, the ship with the biggest gun has the longest range and the heaviest firepower.

This is the ship that would prevail. Lesser calibers were worthless until in range. Fisher wrote, "In designing this ship, the most powerfully arranged armament has been made the first consideration. Absolutely nothing has been allowed to stand in the way of the most nearly perfect power and scope of the guns…. Being a battleship, she will have to fight other battleships. Having speed, she can choose the range at which she will fight."[46] Furthermore, speed provides the flexibility to determine the place of action. The faster boat establishes the range that is most desirable. The faster vessel can maneuver to the place where her guns outrange her foes, rendering their fires useless. Fisher summed it up by writing, "The fast ship with the heavier guns and deliberate fire should absolutely knock out a vessel of equal speed with many lighter guns, the number of which militates against accurate spotting and deliberate hitting."[47]

Tearing a page from the experience of Admiral Togo in the Japanese victory over Russia at the Battle of Tsushima Straits, in May1905 the British naval attaché warned the Admiralty of the shortcomings of the Russian fleet, providing an impetus to build the ships of Fisher's design.[48]

HMS Dreadnought

Fisher had such a craft built that embodied speed and heavy armament at the expense of other factors. This ship mounted ten 12-inch guns at a time when most other capital ships had only four. Using radically new turbine steam engines, the craft was capable of 21 knots when most other ships could manage only 16–18 knots. The ship was christened the HMS *Dreadnought*. She was launched after only one year of construction and went to sea in October 1906. It was a quantum leap and headline news all over the world. The new ship offered a capability equal to two or three ships for only a modest increase in size and cost (about 10 percent).

Dreadnought immediately rendered all other such ships on the seas obsolete (including Britain's own fleet) and became the synonym for battleship. She was the template for all that would follow. Fisher's basic design philosophy would reign until the very end of the battleship line, another half century, when the capital ship was superseded by the aircraft carrier. Every navy in the world came to the realization that the *Dreadnought* could be matched only by one like it, which none of them possessed. This awareness served to accelerate the shipbuilding arms race between England and Germany as well as among the other seagoing powers.

The United States

During the twilight of President Theodore Roosevelt's administration, he dispatched sixteen U.S. Navy battleships of the Atlantic Fleet on a voyage of circumnavigation of the globe, from December 16, 1907, to February 22, 1909. The hulls were painted white, the navy's peacetime color scheme, decorated with gilded scrollwork, and with a red, white, and blue banner on their bows. These ships would later come to be known as the Great White Fleet.

The purpose of the fleet deployment was multifaceted. It served as a showpiece of American goodwill as the fleet visited numerous countries and harbors. Additionally, the voyage of the Great White Fleet demonstrated both at home and on the world stage that the U.S. had become a major sea power in the years after its triumph in the Spanish-American War. The voyage also provided an opportunity to improve the sea- and battle-worthiness of the fleet.

The fourteen-month–long voyage was a grand pageant of American sea power. Manned by 14,000 sailors, the fleet covered some 43,000 nautical miles (80,000 km) and made twenty port calls on six continents. The fleet was impressive, especially as a demonstration of American industrial prowess (all eighteen ships had been constructed after the Spanish-American War), but already the battleships represented the suddenly outdated "pre-dreadnought" type of capital ship, as the first battleships of the revolutionary *Dreadnought* class had just entered service. But the voyage of the Great White Fleet was also an advertisement for America's naval deficiencies.[49]

President Theodore Roosevelt, who had at one time been assistant secretary of the navy and had written a history of the naval War of 1812, was an enthusiastic supporter of the navy. At the urging of Admiral Dewey, the two men convinced Navy Secretary Charles Bonaparte of the necessity of an all big-gun battleship. In due course, they convinced Congress to pass the necessary authorization. The United States commissioned its own Dreadnoughts in 1905, the USS *South Carolina* and USS *Michigan*. These were steps in the right direction, but due to a 16,000-ton weight limitation imposed by Congress, they were a compromised half step. The *South Carolina* class was inferior in speed and armament to the *Dreadnought*. However, they had one design feature that was superior: they were able to bring all their guns to bear for a broadside, so they could match the firepower of the *Dreadnought* with two fewer guns. Because their development and construction was more protracted and more care had been given to planning, they were judged to be better protected and armored as well.[50]

The navy's Bureau of Construction and Repair (C&R) was able to convince Congress that the unrealistic weight limitation constraints should be removed. The C&R labored to provide the best new design possible under the congressional restrictions and limitations. In addition to speed and firepower, an important consideration for American capital ships was range. America had naval responsibilities in the vast Pacific Ocean that would require them to operate far from refueling bases. Britain had plentiful coaling stations strategically located around the globe, an advantage America did not enjoy. The congressional language of the authorizing act of June 26, 1906, was for a battleship "carrying as heavy armor and as powerful an armament as any known vessel of its class, to have the highest practicable speed and the greatest practicable radius of action." The 1906 legislation called for two ships of the new design. These would later be known as the USS *Delaware* (BB-28) and the USS *North Dakota* (BB-29).[51]

USS Delaware *(BB-28)*

The Bureau of Construction and Repair proposed plans for a ten-gun, 20,500-ton battleship that had been developed earlier but rejected due to the tonnage limit. She was provisionally to be named the USS *New Constitution*. Her original naval appropriation funded $100,000 for the restoration of the original *Constitution* (Old Ironsides) and $10 million for the construction of the *New Constitution*. What would that new ship be called? The people of Delaware thought it should be named for their state. Theodore Roosevelt's secretary of the navy, Charles Bonaparte, was lobbied by the Delaware Congressional Delegation and deluged with letters by Delawareans urging that the ship be named in honor of their state. Senator James Allee and Representative Hiram Burton cited to the secretary the fact that their state was "the only one of the older states of the union that has not been given the distinction of a battleship."[52]

The Delaware Historical Society supported the effort to sell Congress and the secretary of the navy on the idea. At that time, Delaware was the only one of the original thirteen states and one of only three states in the nation (Montana and Utah were the other two) not to have a U.S. naval ship bearing its name (although there had been previous naval vessels bearing the state's name). The time was right, and the cause was just. The society passed a resolution of support invoking Delaware's bravery in the Revolutionary War, the War of 1812, and the Civil War, as well as Delawareans who had served in the U.S. cabinet, as reasons why the new ship should bear the state's name.[53]

The campaign succeeded, and the USS *Delaware* (BB-28) was laid down at Newport News Shipbuilding on November 11, 1907, the sixth ship of the fleet to bear that name. On February 6, 1909, the new ship slid down the ways, pushing stern foremost into the briny and making the "World's Largest Naval Splash," according to a headline in the *San Francisco Call*. The newspaper added the following on September 1907:

> The *Delaware* is the very largest battleship ever launched. When Great Britain launched her Dreadnaught less than two years ago, the last word in magnitude of battleships was thought to have been uttered.
>
> The "Dreadnaught fever" then seized the other powers. Germany, France, Japan and the United States all accepted it as a challenge. With the least ado over the matter, the United States has now come forward with a vessel that will be 2100 tons heavier than the Dreadnaught, and nearly that much heavier than any other warship building or projected abroad. The Delaware will have 20,000 tons displacement when completed. This great splash may be only the beginning; after all. Such naval enthusiasts as Rear Admiral Richmond Pearson Hobson predict—nay, demand—battleships of 30,000 tons!

Anne P. Cahall, sponsor of USS *Delaware*, launched February 6, 1909, at Newport News, Virginia (ggb2004003508, Library of Congress).

Miss Anne P. Cahall, of Bridgeville, Delaware, on behalf of Governor Lea accepted appointment as sponsor for the launching. Governor Lea asked Miss Cahall to christen the new American dreadnought as a courtesy to his successor, Governor-elect Simeon S. Pennewill, who became chief executive of the state before the battleship was launched. Miss Cahall was a niece of the governor-elect and of Judge James Pennewill. Her father, Dr. Lawrence M. Cahall, was a prominent physician at Bridgeville.[54] With the announcement of the launching of the battleship bearing the state's name, the Women's Christian Temperance Union of Delaware renewed its fight to have the giant vessel christened with water (she was christened with champagne). She was commissioned for sea duty on April 4, 1910, with Captain C.A. Grove in command. She was trim and beautiful and the pride of Delaware and the U.S. Navy. USS *Delaware* was the most powerful battleship in the world at the time of her construction. According to the *Los Angeles Herald* (October 1909):

> UNCLE SAM'S first two Dreadnoughts, the battleships *North Dakota* (BB-29) and *Delaware* (BB-28), are practically completed and soon will be in commission. The *Delaware* is now having her powerful guns installed at Newport News and the *North Dakota* is getting ready for her trial at Quincy, Massachusetts. These two leviathans differ from the other battleships of our navy in many respects aside from their tremendous size. The most striking difference is noted in the long, rakish hulls, the absence of the high superstructures so predominant in the older ships and the five immense turrets which protect the ten twelve-inch rifles that each of the ships will carry. It is estimated that either the *Delaware* or the *North Dakota* with their high speed will be more than a match for any other three ships now in the navy. The *North Dakota* is to have her speed trials November 2, and if she comes up to expectations she will be a vessel to be feared by anything that floats the seas. These great fighting machines each cost $10,000,000.

The *San Francisco Chronicle* dubbed the ship "Uncle Sam's New Constitution" describing it as "the Most Powerful Battleship Afloat, More Destructive and Terrible than the new Floating Giant, the English 'Dreadnaught.'" The *Amador Ledger* added, "These ships will be far more powerful than any others in the navy and will rival their monster prototype, which is the boast of the British navy."

The *Delaware* class was significantly more powerful than its predecessors, the *South Carolina* class. The *Delaware* class matched the standard of the Dreadnought, and exceeded it in some respects. The only restriction Congress placed on their design was that the hull and machinery could not exceed $6 million. *Delaware* was constructed in only 27 months, a record at the time for a capital ship.

Ship Characteristics

Delaware was 519 feet (158 m) long overall and had a beam of 85 feet 4 inches (26.01 m) and a draft of 27 feet 3 inches (8.31 m). She displaced 20,380 long tons (20,710 t) as designed and up to 22,060 long tons (22,410 t) at full combat load. She had a crew of 55 officers and 878 men. She was among the first battleships painted in a gray war paint, giving her a somber look compared to the sparkling white of the peacetime navy. *Delaware* had a very broad and high bow, giving her lots of freeboard, especially forward, and offering the ability to weather heavy seas and still fire her guns forward—an important advantage in a fight.

She bore only two smokestacks. She had two fighting "skeleton" towers, each mounted forward of one of the smokestacks, of a lattice-like design of iron tubing and cable, nearly impossible to shoot away in tests. These towers were each about 120 feet high and 30–40 feet in diameter at the base. The British used tripod masts for the same purpose, though not as high as American towers, which were a large and tempting target for enemy gunners. A fire control station was at the top of each tower linked by telephone to the plotting room and guns to give fire direction.[55]

Amenities

Delaware had an electrical plant that powered her lighting, hoists, boat cranes, gun turrets, and six searchlights. She had a complete machine shop for fabricating parts and

USS *Delaware* (BB-28) firing her main battery guns during battle practice, June 26, 1920. Photographed by A.E. Wells (60569, U.S. Naval History and Heritage Command).

making repairs while at sea. Forward was a generously sized full hospital. The crew quarters and dining areas were protected by armor plate.

Armament

The ten 12-inch (30 cm), 45-caliber main guns would be in five turrets, two forward in a superfiring arrangement (one firing over the other) and three aft. These were an additional two guns compared to the preceding *South Carolina* class. The after turrets were arranged with one in a superfiring position over the sternmost two, which were centered back-to-back on the aft deck.

The gun housings were the Mark 8 type, and they allowed for depression to minus 5 degrees and elevation to 15 degrees. The guns had a rate of fire of 2 to 3 rounds per minute and fired 870-pound (394.6 kg) shells, of either armor-piercing (AP) or common types. The guns were expected to fire 175 rounds before the barrels required replacement. The two ships carried 100 shells per gun, or 1,000 rounds in total. At 15 degrees elevation, the guns could hit targets out to approximately 20,000 yards (18,290 m). They were fed from electrical hoists from the ten ammunition magazines onboard.[56]

Secondary Armament

The USS *Delaware*'s main armament was supplemented with fourteen five-inch guns for anti-destroyer defense. These were arrayed five on each side with two forward on the main deck and two aft on the main deck abeam number five turret. They had a rate of fire of six to eight rounds per minute. While these guns were considered an improvement by the navy over that of the *South Carolina* class, their placement remained problematic, as even in calm water they were extremely wet and thus difficult to man. The forward guns were moved into the superstructure after sea trials. The casemate-mounted secondary armament was one deck below the main deck and provided the majority of the complaints from shipping water from the forward positions and breaking the flow of the bow wave, imparting extra drag on the design. The *Delaware* was also fitted with two 3"/50 caliber Mark 11 antiaircraft (AA) guns in 1917. The Mark 11 was the first 3" AA mounting issued by the U.S. Navy.[57]

As was standard for capital ships of the period, she carried a pair of 21-inch (530 mm) torpedo tubes, submerged in her hull on the broadside. Most dreadnought and pre-dreadnought battleships were armed with torpedo tubes as well as guns. The *Delaware* mounted a side-loading torpedo tube. Torpedoes were transported along a monorail above the tube and then lowered into it. Orders to the crew to fire were delivered through the speaking tube. It was generally conceded that torpedoes were an extremely effective weapon but their underwater tubes were a hazard because they constituted weak points in systems of bulkheads protecting against underwater hits. For a time, therefore, U.S. designers and planners expected to move the tubes topside, where they presented a fire and explosion hazard. They were therefore omitted from the ships reconstructed during the interwar period.[58]

Armor

The main armored belt was eleven inches (279 mm) thick, while the armored deck was two inches (51 mm) thick. The gun turrets had twelve-inch (305 mm)–thick faces and the conning tower had 11.5-inch (292 mm)–thick sides. These ships were expected to do most of their firing at ranges less than 10,000 yards (9,100 m). At such distances, deck strikes would be a rare event.[59]

Propulsion

Power for the USS *Delaware* came from two vertical triple expansion steam engines turning two propellers. These were reciprocating engines, unlike her sister ship *North Dakota*, which utilized a new turbine engine design. She had a coal capacity of 2,340 tons. The ship generated a top speed of 21 knots (39 km/h, 24 mph). The ship had a cruising range of 6,000 nautical miles (11,000 km, 6,900 mi) at a speed of 10 knots (19 km/h, 12 mph). A real innovation was her ability to burn either coal or fuel oil or both. This was the first American battleship to do so. Burning oil gave the ship the ability to rapidly build steam for a quick departure. A quick boost of fuel oil on a coal burning cruising ship can offer an accelerant in an emergency as well.[60]

Delaware was the first American battleship capable of steaming for 24 hours straight without suffering a breakdown or needing repairs. According to the *New York Tribune* in October 1909:

THE *DELAWARE* (BB-28), THE FIRST AMERICAN DREADNOUGHT.
Exceeded the contract speed of 21 knots on the standardization runs yesterday over the Rockland (Me.) course making 21.98 knots and breaking the speed record for American battleships.

Early Service

After a brief trial voyage, *Delaware* returned to Newport News on October 26, 1909, in preparation for her commissioning. As she entered the Virginia Capes she flew three brooms from her masthead signifying a "clean sweep" at sea for her preliminary trials. Having completed initial sea trials and training off Newport, Boston, and Provincetown, she joined the U.S. Atlantic Fleet at Hampton Roads on September 1, 1910. Participating in the annual summer maneuvers at the southern drill grounds she and *North Dakota* bested the other sixteen battleships in gunnery, *Delaware* taking the top trophy only months after her commissioning.[61]

Following further training off the Virginia Capes and Thomkinsville, New York, with the First Division, First Battleship Squadron Delaware, steamed to Wilmington, Delaware, on October 3, 1910, to receive a set of silver from the state. The 22-piece set includes gravy boats, coffee urns, and serving utensils, and some less common items such as an electrolier, or electric candelabra. The standout piece is a 45-pound punchbowl with an eagle on the pedestal. Housed in a plate glass and cherry wood case, it was used for ceremonies when dignitaries visited in foreign ports. The set cost about $10,000, a princely sum at the time, raised through charitable contributions small and large and aided by a $1,000-grant from the state. Raising money for the silver set was part of the people's patriotic duty at the time. The ship was also presented portraits of Commodore Jacob Jones, Commodore Thomas Macdonough, and Rear Admiral Samuel Francis DuPont, all legendary naval heroes of Delaware.[62]

The people of Delaware took enormous patriotic pride in *Delaware*'s handsome lines. The sailors were entertained and regaled with the town's hospitality, the officers and crew of the ship enjoying a port visit for most of a week, departing on October 9. The October 5, 1910, *Evening Journal* reported, "To be sure the social pleasures are for the officers of the battleship, but 'Jack' ashore, with plenty of money right after pay day is having his own good time in Wilmington. Even if he didn't have any money he would have a good time this week, for street cars carry him free, theaters admit him free and there will be dances for him, and there are other pleasures that will link Wilmington and enjoyment synonymously for time to come."

Proceeding south, *Delaware* briefly paused at Hampton Roads for alterations before joining the Atlantic Fleet's First Division. Later that fall, *Delaware* and her consorts departed on November 1, 1910, crossing the Atlantic with the First Division Atlantic Fleet, and made visits to Britain (Weymouth) and France (Cherbourg). Returning in January 1911, she participated in winter maneuvers off Guantanamo Bay, Cuba.[63] She made passage for Norfolk on January 14, 1911. While steaming north to Hampton Roads, the battleship suffered a boiler explosion on January 17, which killed eight. It was reported in the *New York Times* on January 18:

WARSHIP EXPLOSION KILLS EIGHT SEAMEN.
THEIR BODIES ARE DRAGGED FROM THE *DELAWARE*'S STEAM-FILLED BOILER ROOM ANOTHER DYING. STORY TOLD BY WIRELESS.
BATTLESHIP WAS SAILING TO HAMPTON ROADS FROM CUBA TO CONVEY THE CHILEAN MINISTER'S BODY HOME.

Washington, Jan. 17.—Eight men met instant death and one man was so badly burned that he probably will die as a result of a boiler explosion aboard the battleship *Delaware* at 9:20 o'clock this morning, the cause of which is as yet unexplained, according to a wireless message tonight to the Navy Department from Capt. GOVE. The Delaware was on her way to Hampton Roads from Guantanamo,

Cuba, and had been designated to transport the body of Senor Cruz, late Chilean Minister to the United States, back to Chile, instead of the South Carolina, whose propeller met with a mishap. The nine victims were on duty in the boiler room when the accident occurred. A terrific shock sent the crew scurrying below and nine bodies were dragged from the cloud of hot steam that hissed through the hold. Capt. GOVE'S message to the Navy Department reads: "At 9:20 A.M., Jan. 17, three backheaders, Nos. 8, 9, and 10 of Boiler "0" in Fireroom 4 blew out explosively, killing eight and injuring one, who will probably die, these being all the men on duty in the fireroom. Board of officers appointed immediately to investigate and report. Not yet reported.

Making repairs in Norfolk, *Delaware* departed on the 31st to carry the remains of Anibal Cruz, the Chilean ambassador to the United States, back to Valparaiso, Chile, and transferred the ambassador's remains, arriving on March 11.[64] She put to sea again on the 21st, touching at Rio de Janeiro, and arrived at Punta Arenas then called at Boston before steaming to New York Navy Yard on May 5, 1911. Repairs were made in the yard. Rear Admiral Charles E. Vreeland embarked to represent the navy during the forthcoming coronation ceremonies in England for George V. On June 4 she stood out of New York Harbor and reached Portsmouth, England, on June 5 to participate in a coronation naval review for King George V and Prince Albert on June 24. She was the largest ship present at this naval review.[65] She sailed for Boston on June 28 and debarked Rear Admiral Vreeland on July 9. *Delaware* completed this round-trip without taking any coal on board during the voyage, leaving some 600 tons of coal in her bunkers at the conclusion of her journey and proving she had very long sea legs.

She conducted a busy schedule of battle exercises with the fleet off Cape Cod Bay and the Virginia Capes areas. She then steamed from the New York Navy Yard on December 31, 1911, for winter base at Guantanamo Bay, Cuba. In the early spring she returned to Hampton Roads before entering New York Navy Yard for repairs. *Delaware* participated in tactical exercises off Newport before returning to Hampton Roads on June 3, 1912. Here she passed in review before President Taft, who was on board the *Mayflower*.[66]

Two days later she set sail to Annapolis to embark midshipmen on a training cruise off New England, landing her squadron for the Bunker Hill Day celebration in Boston on Flag Day, June 14, and returning to Annapolis on August 30, 1912. This would be a recurring mission for her throughout her history. It is a safe bet that many of the future U.S. naval commanders who won World War II first went to sea upon the decks of the *Delaware*.

Delaware was in the Presidential Fleet Review in New York on October 14 and conducted fleet exercises and battle tactics in waters extending from New England to Charleston, South Carolina, until December 10, 1912. She then departed Hampton Roads in company with the battleship *Arkansas*, which embarked the president of the United States, William H. Taft, at Key West, Florida.[67]

Delaware took on board other members of the presidential party and the two battleships got underway from Key West on December 21 for the Panama Canal Zone. All passengers debarked upon arrival at Colon three days later, and Captain Hugh Rodman left the *Delaware* for two days at the invitation of President Taft. (In 1914 Rodman was appointed for duty as Marine superintendent of the Panama Canal, which officially opened on August 15, 1914.) The distinguished passengers were returned to Key West on December 29 and *Delaware* celebrated the New Year in New York for an overhaul that lasted until March 31, 1913. She once again resumed her routine of maneuvers off Black Island Sound and the Virginia Capes. She sailed from New York on May 31 to embark midshipmen from Annapolis. *Delaware* spent the summer training these men in waters off New York and Newport. The middies were debarked at Annapolis on August 24, and *Delaware* exercised in the Chesapeake Bay before she put to sea from New York on October 2 in the company of battleships *Wyoming* (BB-32) and *Utah* (BB-31) bound for Villefranche France. They paid a goodwill visit to the French port from November 8 to November 30, 1913.[68] She returned to Norfolk for voyage repairs and then practiced maneuvers in fleet battle practice off Guantanamo Bay. She then proceeded to Vera Cruz, Mexico, and there—from February 16 to March 5, 1914— she "flew the flag" as a diplomatic signal to that city during the crisis of the Mexican Revolution.

The *Badger Madison Journal* reported on the Atlantic Fleet in February 1914 and offers a snapshot of the fleet and the contemporaries of the *Delaware* at that time:

OUR POWERFUL NORTH ATLANTIC FLEET

This is to be considered be the most powerful battle fleet in the world. Recently it returned from the Mediterranean and left Hampton Roads for the south. During the last battle practice each of the vessels made a record for herself while the flagship Wyoming (BB-32) broke the world's record at target practice. The photograph shows the nine ships in the order in which they usually sail. The Wyoming is in the lead at the right, and is followed by the Florida (BB-30), Utah (BB-31), Delaware (BB-28), North Dakota (BB-29), South Carolina (BB-26), Rhode Island (BB-17), Georgia (BB-15), and New Jersey (BB-16).

The following battleships that were dispatched to Mexican waters included the:
Ohio (BB-12), Virginia (BB-13), Nebraska (BB-14), Connecticut (BB-18), Louisiana (BB-19), Vermont (BB-20), Kansas (BB-21), Minnesota (BB-22), Mississippi (BB-23), Idaho (BB-24), New Hampshire (BB-25), Michigan (BB-27), Arkansas (BB-33), New York (BB-34) & Texas (BB-35).

Basing her operations from Norfolk during the next two years, *Delaware* once more cruised off Vera Cruz and Tuxpan, Mexico, protecting American interests during the periods July 8–October 9, 1914, and again January 3–April 3, 1915.[69] *Delaware* anchored in the North River of New York with the entire Atlantic Fleet on May 17, 1915, for review by President Woodrow Wilson and was again reviewed the next day as she passed out to sea with the fleet. She engaged in operations off the Virginia Capes and an extensive overhaul at the Norfolk Navy Yard from June 7, 1915 until January 6, 1916. She regained her sea legs with maneuvers off Cuba and fleet tactics off the New England coast. But her dominance of the seas was to be short lived. By 1914 the *Delaware* class had already been bypassed as the "most powerful class afloat." In relatively short order, succeeding improvements were made to the *Florida* class, (1909–1910) the *Wyoming* class (1910–1912), and the *New York* class (1908–1914) ships, each more heavily armed and armored than its predecessor.

Nevertheless, there were critics. In November 1914, after the outbreak of the Great War, at hearings conducted by Representative A.P. Gardner in the Senate Naval Affairs Committee, military engineer Willard S. Isham was cited. He said, "The United States Ship *Delaware* (BB-28) class, the most formidable type of Dreadnought and pride of the American Navy are nevertheless inefficient for their lack of ability to scout an enemy position at sea. This type, as well as those now building, is so far outclassed by ships of foreign nations that they are obsolete, and from a strategic standpoint 'no better than floating fortresses,' in which speed and armament have been sacrificed for armor plate. We possess no ships capable of operating at such a distance from our battle fleet as to screen its formation and strength from the scout ships of an enemy."[70] Mr. Isham added, "Our battleships are defenseless in a fog or at night. Thirty-two of our older battleships, carrying guns of equal or lesser power than those in the Idaho, are inefficient for the purposes for which they were designed because they are out-ranged by foreign ships having guns of superior range and possessing superior speed." A *New York Tribune* article in February 1916 article reported, "Only 19 First Class capital ships available for war, all based in the Atlantic Fleet."[71]

World War I

In 1917 Germany elected to resume full unrestricted submarine warfare. They anticipated this would bring America into the war, but the Germans gambled that they could defeat Britain by this means before the U.S. could mobilize. As the result of careful calculations, the German high command firmly believed that their submarines could not only prevent the large-scale transportation of American troops across the Atlantic but furthermore could cut the sea communications of her European enemies to such an extent as to force them to an early surrender through lack of supplies from overseas. German planners estimated that if the sunken tonnage exceeded 600,000 tons per month, Britain would be forced to sue for peace after 5 to 6 months. The Germans hoped their submarines would be the decisive weapon to win the war.

U.S. Naval Priorities

In response, the U.S. Navy set out to meet the following wartime challenges:

- Provide armed escort vessels for merchant convoys, minimizing the submarine threat;
- Provide the sea bridge to move the American army to the theater of operations;
- Reinforce the Grand Fleet with American battleships;
- Defeat the submarine through technology advancements (sonar, mines);
- Create a naval aviation arm to assist escort and scouting;
- Augment the army with Marines and artillery.[72]

The main theater of World War I was the Western Front. In order to relieve the British and European allies already on the front line, the United States Navy was tasked with transporting millions of American soldiers and supplies across the Atlantic to France as soon as possible. The U.S. Navy was ill prepared for war though; the only solution was to begin deploying whatever was available on convoy duty and arming merchantmen with small naval guns and armed guard detachments. Overseas American troop movements in U.S. transports began with the sailing of the *Tenadores*, *Saratoga*, and *Havana* from New York, escorted by the USS *Seattle*, the USS *DeKalb* (troop transport), and the destroyers *Wilkes*, *Terry*, and *Roe*—on June 14, 1917. The movement grew at an astonishing pace, as the following aggregate troop numbers transported before the armistice demonstrates: United States Navy–911,000; other United States ships–41,500; British ships–1,007,000; other foreign ships (French, Italian, etc.)–121,000. Only the fastest vessels, such as the *Leviathan*, the *Northern Pacific*, and the *Great Northern*, were allowed to go unescorted, their high speed being considered sufficient protection.[73]

Battleship Employment

Within a few weeks after the United States entered World War I its battleship force, which had been cruising in Cuban waters, was sent to the Chesapeake Bay. With the American entry into the Great War on April 6, 1917, the *Delaware* was assigned to the Chesapeake Bay to train five-inch gunnery crews before their assignments to other naval craft as well as armed merchant ships. Thirteen armed guard crews of five men each were trained simultaneously, as well as a great number of apprentice firemen, seamen, and mechanics.

Some idea of the scope of the problem of training men may be gained from the fact that at war's start there were 70,000 men and officers in the navy, whereas at the time of the armistice the number had been increased to 538,000. In addition to keeping itself ready for service by extensive maneuvers during most of the war, the battleship force was largely engaged in this work of training. Recruits would be sent to the greatly expanded training stations onshore for a short preliminary period of training and then to the battleships in Chesapeake Bay for a finishing course of several weeks, including the actual firing of guns for target practice. Finally, the men were transferred to ships in active service at sea. *Delaware*'s sister ship *North Dakota* spent virtually the entire war in service as a training ship based stateside on the Eastern Seaboard.

The British first sea lord sent an urgent request to Washington for four coal-burning battleships to reinforce the Grand Fleet in July 1917.[74] The Royal Navy was short of manpower to face the growing submarine threat and required experienced crews for its new cruisers and destroyers. It planned to take five of its pre–*Dreadnaught* battleships out of commission and use their crews elsewhere. The American battleships were to fill the gap left behind.[75] The Americans had their own naval personnel problems. Many of the experienced and trained gunnery crews from the battle fleet were lent to armed merchantmen to defend against the submarine menace. The readiness of the battle fleet was lowered by their inexperienced replacements. The Royal Navy request was initially rejected. The U.S. Navy doctrine based on Alfred Thayer Mahan's theories was to keep the battle fleet concentrated. America had 14 modern dreadnaught battleships at the outbreak of war in April 1917 but only 74 destroyers. These were too few to screen the dreadnaughts and the other 23 pre-dreadnaught class battleships, ten armored cruisers, and 25 light cruisers of the fleet. The cost of the aggressive dreadnaught building campaign came at the expense of lesser ships in the years before the war.

America was wary of splitting its fleet in light of the possible threat of a two-ocean war and an unpredictable Japanese presence in the Pacific. The U.S. had already given up a number of destroyers for convoy duty that were needed to screen the battleships. Destroyers and other similar warships of the escort type were thought to be the most effective means of sinking German submarines and protecting merchantmen so destroyer squadrons were based in the British Isles. Battleships without the scouting and screening of destroyers were vulnerable, and the destroyers were in short supply.

A visit to Britain by the two senior American admirals resulted in grudging acknowledgment of the notion of sending an advance force interposed between America and her enemy. They also recognized that the nation wouldn't tolerate a fleet that simply stayed home in a postwar budget battle. On November 7 the British request was approved.[76]

Arrival of the American Fleet at Scapa Flow, December 7, 1917. Oil on canvas by Bernard F. Gribble depicting the U.S. Navy's Battleship Division Nine being greeted by British Admiral David Beatty and the crew of HMS *Queen Elizabeth*. Ships of the American column are (from front) USS *New York* (BB-34), USS *Wyoming* (BB-32), USS *Florida* (BB-30) and USS *Delaware* (BB-28) (NH 58841-KN, courtesy U.S. Navy Art Collection, Washington, D.C., U.S. Naval History and Heritage Command).

The Grand Fleet

Delaware entered the Boston Navy Yard for voyage repairs on November 15, 1917, and joined Battleship Division Nine at Lynhaven Roads on the 24th. She put to sea the following day in company with battleships *New York* (BB-34), *Wyoming* (BB-32), and *Florida* (BB-30). Off the Grand Banks the flotilla encountered 90-mile per hour gales and enormous seas. Ships boats were crushed and hatches sprung. They reached Scapa Flow in the Orkney Islands on December 17 for duty with the Sixth Battle Squadron, British Grand Fleet. *Delaware* and her consorts were greeted by Admiral Sir David Beatty and the crew of the HMS *Queen Elizabeth*. The American fleet was placed under the operation control of the Admiralty. British flag signals, radio codes, tactical maneuvering orders, and fire control methods were adopted and Royal Navy signalmen were lent to the ship to teach British methods. *Delaware* anchored in the Forth River at Rosyth, Scotland, the next day and spent much of the next six months protecting allied shipping in ocean lanes and approaches between that port and the Orkney Islands. Target practice in Pentland Firth revealed shortcomings in gunnery that fell short of British wartime standards. American rate of fire and accuracy needed much improvement.

Admiral Hugh Rodman was the American battleship force commander and had previously been the captain of the *Delaware* (1912–1913). He had an amicable relationship with his British colleagues, and he and his American captains were frequent dinner guests with Admiral Beatty at Aberdour House in the Firth of Forth. The Americans were welcomed with a baseball diamond and a couple of days off for the Fourth of July. Up to 200 of the crew were given liberty onshore in relays. The Americans as guests on British ships complained that the ships "were too cold for men brought up in American homes. They were likewise poorly ventilated by our standards."

In their first sortie on their own, *Delaware* sailed with the squadron from the Orkney Islands on February 6, 1918, as part of a supporting force of British cruisers under Rodman's command for a convoy bound for the coast of Norway with an escort of eight British destroyers. While waiting for the appearance of the returning convoy off Stavanger on February 8, battleship *Florida* maneuvered to clear a torpedo wake, destroyers dropped depth charges into the sea, and another torpedo crossed ahead of *Delaware* by several hundred yards. Three minutes later her lookout aloft reported the wake of a torpedo dead ahead of *Delaware*, which put her rudder hard left and passed just inside its wake. The destroyers drove off the raiding U-Boat and *Delaware* returned to Scapa Flow on February 10. However, after the war, German naval records revealed that no U-boats had attacked battleships that day off Norway.

The American squadron added USS *Texas*, a fifth battleship, so the division could maintain four ships on alert, allowing one to refit and repair as needed. *Delaware* was a part of the escort for another convoy off the coast of Norway (March 8–12) and then sailed with the Grand Fleet on April 24 to reinforce the 2d Battle Cruiser Squadron, which was on convoy duty and expected contact with the enemy. Only the vessels of the advance screen made any contact, and the chance for sea action faded.[77]

Delaware stood out of Scapa Flow with the Sixth Battle Squadron on June 30, 1918, joined by a submarine screen of British destroyers. This force was escorting the Mining Squadron into the North Sea that afternoon when *Delaware* spotted the wake of a submarine periscope at 500 yards and let go with six rounds of 3-inch shells to discourage the enemy. The destroyers moved in to drop depth charges and Delaware parted company with the Mining Squadron on July 1, for return to Scapa Flow. After six months of service the gunnery had been much improved. Rodman reported it as being "extremely fine, much better than we have ever done previously." Admiral Beattie did not agree. He regarded the Americans as "second string" and used them sparingly in operations. They were assigned last in line, "where they were least likely to interfere with the movements of the fleet."

Photograph shows Admiral Hugh Rodman (1859–1940), who served as an officer in the United States Navy during the Spanish-American War and World War I. He was captain of the USS *Delaware* and later commander of the American Battleship Force with the Sixth Battle Squadron, British Grand Fleet (2014695930, Library of Congress).

Delaware put to sea from Scapa Flow on July 6, 1918, with the Sixth Battle Squadron and arrived at the Forth River anchorage of Rosyth on the 8th. King George V inspected the ships of the squadron on July 22. *Delaware* cleared Rosyth after being relieved by *Arkansas* (BB-33) on July 30, 1918, for her return to the United States after eight and half months on station. She was escorted out to sea by the British destroyers *Restless* and *Rowena* and reached Hampton Roads on August 12.[78]

During the early stages of the war the commerce of the Allies was plagued by German cruiser raiders. By 1917 these had all been accounted for, but there was always a possibility of others escaping from Germany and raiding the important transatlantic lines of communication. After the adoption of the convoy system, this danger was deemed to be even greater because of the concentrated form in which raiders were likely to find their prey. It was for this reason that convoys were escorted by cruisers during most of the transatlantic passage. Toward the latter part of the war, when it became more and more apparent that the German High Sea Fleet did not intend to risk another fleet action, it was feared that the Germans might detach one or more of their fast and very powerful battle cruisers for the purpose of raiding in the North Atlantic. Against such a raider the ordinary cruiser escort would have been powerless, and plans were therefore formulated to protect convoys with battleships should the occasion arise. Accordingly, a division of American battleships under Rear Admiral T.S. Rodgers, comprising the *Nevada, Oklahoma,* and *Utah,* was dispatched to Berehaven, Ireland, and held in readiness for this duty as soon as any reports were received of the escape of German battle cruisers. The Germans failed to send out any battle-cruiser raiders and therefore this force had no opportunity of engaging the enemy.

During the war, nine American battleships served in European waters, under the command of Admiral Rodman, six with the grand fleet and three at Berehaven, Ireland. Not one ever met the German High Seas fleet.[79]

Postwar Service

Delaware remained at York River until November 12, 1918, at war's end. After overhaul in the Boston Navy Yard and refresher training in the waters of Cuba she came off Annapolis on June 4, 1919, to embark midshipmen for their summer training along the New England coast until she put them ashore on August 28. She conducted exercises off Fort Pond Bay and Newport and was in Hampton Roads on October 31 when she manned the rail for King Albert of Belgium. She sailed from New York on December 6, 1919, to pick up Marines at Philadelphia for transportation to Santo Domingo and Port au Prince, Haiti. She was visited by the president of the Republic of Haiti while in port on December 15 and after debarking passengers at Philadelphia spent the Christmas holidays in Boston.[80]

Delaware cleared port on January 6, 1920, to base her winter operations from Guantanamo Bay and returned to New York on May 1 to prepare for another summer of training midshipmen in waters off the New England coast. She then sailed to Boston for an overhaul (October 18–January 3, 1921). She returned to the Caribbean for Division Five Atlantic Fleet maneuvers and transited the Panama Canal on January 20, 1921, for battle practice with the combined Atlantic and Pacific Battle Fleet bound for Callao, Peru.[81]

Delaware returned to Hampton Roads for the Presidential Fleet Review of April 28, 1921, and spent the next two years in operations from Boston to Norfolk, which included summer training for midshipmen along the Northeast coast, winter operations off Cuba, and spring maneuvers with the combined fleets off Panama Bay. She made two midshipmen practice cruises, one to Colon, Martinique, and other ports in the Caribbean, and another to Halifax, Nova Scotia, between June 5 and August 31, 1922.[82]

In March 1923 *Delaware* visited the Panama Canal, a platform for a fact-finding junket, evidently. In a letter dated March 15, to his wife Catherine, Delaware senator L. Heisler Ball wrote as follows:

> I am here on the Battleship Delaware about 100 miles out from Panama, on the Pacific Ocean. Came out last evening, and we are to return tomorrow evening. Am having a wonderful time, enjoying every minute of the time, eat three meals a day, and sleep all night. Tomorrow evening after returning on the Delaware I rent a fishing boat with a half-dozen others and we go out for a two days fishing trip which am looking forward to with a great deal of pleasure. The weather is fine, just like a summer day, but plenty cool enough to sleep at nights. The Canal is a wonderful engineering structure which can only be appreciated when seen. Capt. McNeely is the Commander of the Delaware, and we are invited out to a late dinner tonight with the other officers. The Captain gave his quarters to me so I have a fine room with bath, just like asea in a first-class hotel.

A week later Ball added this:

> Tomorrow morning at six thirty we sail from here for Kingston [and] from there we go to Port Antonia, I understand we drive across Jamaica from Kingston to Port Antonia to give us a good view of the interior of the island. Then we go from there to Santiago Cuba then around Guantanamo, from there to Port Au Prince, Santos Domingo—San Juan–St. Thomas and thence to Washington arriving April 14th. It has certainly been a wonderful trip. Last night we attended a grand reception hosted by the president of Panama in our honor and had a wonderful time. Yesterday afternoon saw the inter-Battleship sports and saw some fine mates—our boys from the Battleship Delaware winning the most of the contests, which was a very gratifying time.[83]

Delaware's last hurrah was a midshipmen cruise the summer of 1923 to Europe in company with battleships *Arkansas, Florida,* and *North Dakota*. Departing Hampton Roads on June 9, she paid port calls at Copenhagen, Denmark; Greenock, Scotland; Cadiz, Spain; and Gibraltar. She debarked her middies at Annapolis on August 28.

With the signing of the Washington Naval Treaty earlier that year, the U.S. Navy agreed to tonnage limits for the fleet. As part of the treaty, the United States agreed to scrap *Delaware* and *North Dakota* upon the completion of USS *Colorado* (BB-45) and USS *West Virginia* (BB-48). *Delaware* entered Norfolk Navy Yard August 30, 1923, and her crew was transferred to *Colorado* (BB-45), a newly commissioned battleship assigned to replace *Delaware* in the Fleet. *Delaware* was visited by the American Legion delegates at Marble Head, Massachusetts (September 3–10). Moving to Boston Navy Yard in September, she was stripped of warlike equipment. She entered Boston Navy Yard on September 10 to prepare for inactivation and was decommissioned on November 10, 1923. Her name was stricken from the active navy list on November 27. Sold for scrap on February 5, 1924, to the Boston Iron and Metal Company for $231,862.50, she was scrapped in accordance with the Washington Treaty on the limitation of armaments.[84]

The USS *Delaware* had a short service life of only fifteen years. Born as a "state of the art" weapon, she was quickly obsolete in a period of rapid technological progress stressed by the fact of war. In her combat career she barely fired a shot in anger—and then only defensive fire from her secondary guns. The battleship was trumped by the submarine as the enemy's decisive sea weapon. Indeed, the resumption of unrestricted submarine warfare was the very cause of the entry of the United States into the war.

Delaware had been designed as a speedy heavyweight to trade blows with the enemy, but the enemy rarely appeared and *Delaware* never met her designated foe. She was never given the chance to show her stuff in a grand battle of opposing fleets. Nevertheless, she served a useful purpose, primarily as a ship "in being." Her presence alone as a powerful warship aided the conflict in Mexico. Under her mighty guns, other allied ships could do their job of moving men and materiel without fear along the coast of Mexico. Joining the British Grand Fleet in Scapa Flow, her very presence added to the weight of allied sea power, bottling up the Germans in their home waters. Her place in the battle fleet made a contribution to the successful blockade of goods to the Central Powers. Had there been no *Delaware* and no superior Allied fleet, German surface raiders would have cut the sea-lanes that provided the materiel of war for the Allies. The German submarine force very nearly managed to do this all by themselves. One can conclude that *Delaware* made a positive contribution to the war effort and was a useful deterrent during peacetime.

The USS *Delaware* performed the tasks of a capital warship, showing the flag, training young officers, engaging in soft-power diplomacy as the "big stick." Because she was born in a time of rapid technological nautical advancement, her time was abbreviated. She served only fifteen years, but her time with the fleet filled every Delawarean with patriotic pride.

Eight

World War II

During World War I most allied navies had reprioritized, scrapping their capital ship-building programs in order to construct antisubmarine craft. After the war, most were financially exhausted, and only Japan and the United States contemplated strengthening their navies. The United States revived its ambitious original 1916 naval building program. But in the economic recession of 1921 she had second thoughts and participated in arms limitation talks. A ten-year "holiday" on capital ship construction was negotiated along with scrapping existing ships to achieve a 5:5:3 ratio for the United States, Britain, and Japan respectively. Altogether, some 66 ships were to be scrapped by the participants.[1]

Eighteen battleships were retained by the United States as well as two aircraft carriers. When the treaty limitations expired in 1936 the U.S. Navy was at last building up to strength. This bust-boom cycle had an impact on Delaware Valley shipyards. President Roosevelt and Congress had authorized new construction as much to relieve unemployment as to advance national security. The Second Vincent Act of 1938 authorized an eight-year replacement program amounting to 102 ships and a tonnage increase of 20 percent over treaty limits. At the time of the Pearl Harbor attack in 1941 the U.S. Navy's combat ship strength was as shown in the table below:

Type of Vessel	In Commission	Under Construction
Battleships	17	15
Carriers	7	11
Cruisers	37	54
Destroyers	171	191
Submarines	111	73[2]

Although the attack on Pearl Harbor was perceived as a sneaky surprise, the conflict with Japan had long been foreseen by navy planners. The navy was already in the process of doubling the fleet and was building the doctrine and plans to respond to the Japanese threat in the Pacific with increased carrier and aviation resources and amphibious operations. Meanwhile, a naval replay of the First World War was shaping up in Europe as a belligerent Hitler began rearming Germany, allied with Fascist Italy. The island nation of

Britain, with a far-flung empire, was threatened by commerce raiders and the U-boat menace against its lines of supply. When hostilities arose in 1939 American neutrality was threatened at once. An undeclared war between the United States and Germany opened on September 4, 1941 when the destroyer *Greer* was attacked by the submarine U-652. *Greer* counterattacked with depth charges. Neither combatant yielded to any visible effect. The United States began convoy escort missions that same month to the Atlantic midpoint south of Iceland, where Royal Navy escorts would assume responsibility. First blood was drawn in October when USS *Kearney* was struck and eleven Americans were killed. Two weeks later the destroyer *Reuben James* was sunk with the loss of over 100 lives.[3]

The Second World War was fought by the United States on a vastly larger scale than was the First World War in naval terms. Large-scale amphibious operations in North Africa, Sicily, Italy, and France in the Mediterranean, the anti-submarine campaign in the Atlantic, ferrying and convoy operations to the Allied Soviet Union, a build-up in Britain for a cross-channel invasion, and an island-hopping amphibious campaign in the Pacific over vast distances enumerate only the major operations undertaken. There were countless minor campaigns in the Aleutian Islands, Iceland, the China/Burma/India Theater and more. These struggles were under the sea, upon the sea, in the air, and ashore courtesy of a much-enlarged U.S. Marine Corps.

Our task here is not to describe the multitude of naval actions during the Second World War but to assess their impact on our topic—the Delaware River and Delaware Bay. As in every previous conflict, facilities were constructed, ships were launched, bases were built, and men were trained and deployed as they had been for centuries. As in many other conflicts, the threat came to America's very front door once again. This time it was in the form of U-boats off the Delaware Capes.

Submarine Warfare

The war with the Axis first manifested itself off the Delaware Capes as part of the Battle of the Atlantic. The "Second Happy Time," also known among German submarine commanders as the "American shooting season," was the informal name for a phase in the Battle of the Atlantic during which German submarines attacked merchant shipping and Allied naval vessels along the East Coast of North America. The first "Happy Time" was in 1940–41 in the North Atlantic and the North Sea. Adolf Hitler and Benito Mussolini declared war on the United States on December 11, 1941, and their navies could begin the second "Happy Time."[4]

The Second Happy Time lasted from January 1942 to about August of that year and involved several German naval operations including Operation Paukenschlag (Operation Drumbeat) and Operation Neuland. German submariners called it the happy time or the golden time as defense measures were weak and disorganized and the U-boats were able to inflict massive damage with little risk. During this period, Axis submarines sank 609 ships totaling 3.1 million tons, with the loss of thousands of lives, mainly those of merchant mariners, against a loss of only 22 U-boats. Although less than losses during the 1917 campaign of the First World War, this was roughly one-quarter of all shipping sunk by U-boats during the entire Second World War.[5] From January to May in 1942 the German U–Boat wolf packs worked the East Coast. During the war as many as 108 merchant ships were sunk or damaged from torpedoes, mines, and shelling in American waters off that coast. Another 43 were lost to hostile enemy action in the Gulf of Mexico during the war.[6] The entrance to Delaware Bay was one of the prime hunting areas for these U-boats, as Philadelphia built 35 percent of all ships constructed in World War II.

While the U-boats operated in their assigned positions they were tended by the U-boat tanker ships loaded with fuel and supplies for them farther out in the Atlantic. In 1942 the coastal defenses had not been worked out for submarine detection. The U.S. government did not order a blackout of seacoast cities until June 1942 and ships were not organized into convoys with armed escorts. For part of 1942 the Chesapeake and Delaware Canal was still closed from the SS *Waukegan* collision with the St George's Bridge, which had sent the bridge crashing into the canal and closed it. Ships had to run out into the Atlantic to go from Norfolk or Baltimore to Philadelphia. The U-boats would watch the entrances to Delaware Bay and Chesapeake Bay as they constricted the ship traffic into a narrow area.[7]

The campaign was an unmitigated disaster for the Allies. In sending the U-Boats to the East Coast, German Admiral Karl Doenitz said, "There were admittedly, anti-submarine patrols, but they were wholly lacking in experience. Single destroyers, for example, sailed up and down the traffic lanes with such regularity that the U-boats were quickly able to work out the timetable being followed." Some called it "America's Second Pearl Harbor" and placed the blame for the nation's failure to respond quickly to the attacks on the inaction of Admiral Ernest J. King, commander-in-chief of the U.S. fleet. Others pointed out that the belated institution of a convoy system was at least in substantial part due to a severe shortage of suitable escort vessels, without which convoys were seen as being actually more vulnerable than lone ships. Some of the attacks were visible from shore as explosions and fire. The beaches were littered with the flotsam of torpedoed ships and occasional corpses.[8] The submarine attacks continued intermittently throughout the war. Their impact was finally lessened due to improvements in Allied anti-submarine detection and defense.

USS *Jacob Jones* (DD-130) photographed circa 1930s. Built by New York Shipbuilding in Camden, New Jersey, in 1918 (NH 67838, U.S. Naval History and Heritage Command).

A local example that brought home the lessons of anti-submarine vigilance to the Delaware Valley was the loss of the USS *Jacob Jones*[9] off the Delaware Capes. On the morning of February 27, 1942, *Jacob Jones* departed New York Harbor and steamed southward along the New Jersey coast to patrol and search the area between Barnegat Light and Five Fathom Bank. Shortly after her departure she received orders to concentrate her patrol activity in waters off Cape May and the Delaware Capes. At 3:30 P.M. she spotted the burning wreckage of tanker *R.P. Resor*, torpedoed the previous day east of Barnegat Light. *Jones* circled the ship for two hours searching for survivors before resuming her southward course. Cruising at a steady 15 knots through calm seas, she last reported her position at 8:00 P.M. and then commenced radio silence. A full moon lit the night sky and visibility was good; throughout the night the ship, completely darkened without running or navigation lights showing, kept her southward course.

At first light on February 28, 1942, an undetected German submarine, U-578, fired a spread of torpedoes at the unsuspecting destroyer. The torpedoes were not detected and two or three struck the destroyer's port side in rapid succession. According to *Jones* survivors, the first torpedo struck just aft of the bridge and caused major damage. Apparently, it exploded the ship's magazine. The resulting blast sheared off everything forward of the point of impact, destroying completely the bridge, the chart room, and the officers' and petty officers' quarters. As *Jones* stopped dead in the water, unable to signal a distress message, a second torpedo struck about 40 feet forward of the fantail and carried away the after part of the ship above the keel plates and shafts and destroyed the after-crew's quarters. Only the mid-ships section was left intact.[10]

All but 25 or 30 officers and men, including Lieutenant Commander Black, were killed by the explosions. The survivors, including a badly wounded, "practically incoherent" signal officer, went for the lifeboats. Oily decks, fouled lines and rigging, and the clutter of the ship's strewn and twisted wreckage hampered their efforts to launch the boats. *Jones* remained afloat for about 45 minutes, allowing her survivors to clear the stricken ship in four or five rafts. Within an hour of the initial explosion she plunged bow first into the cold Atlantic. As her shattered stern disappeared, her depth charges exploded, killing several survivors on a nearby raft (as had happened to the *Jacob Jones*— DD-61—in 1917). It was the first sinking of a U.S. warship following the Japanese attacks in the Pacific.[11] At 8:10 A.M. an army observation plane sighted the life rafts and reported their position to *Eagle 56* of the Inshore Patrol. By 11:00 A.M., when strong winds and rising seas forced her to abandon the search, she had rescued twelve survivors, one of whom died en route to Cape May. The search for the other survivors of *Jones* continued by plane and ship for the next two days but none were ever found.[12]

Some other well-known ships were sunk due to war activity in the winter months of 1942. On January 27, 1942, the *Francis E. Powell*, a 7,800-ton Atlantic Refining Company Tanker, was torpedoed by U-130. Seventeen of the survivors were bought into Lewes, Delaware. Ten more were taken into Chincoteague. Four were missing and assumed dead.[13] On February 4, 1942, the Panamanian United Fruit Company ship *San Gil* was hit by a torpedo, killing two engine room workers. The 38 survivors took to the lifeboats and the U-boat surfaced and fired fifteen shots into the ship to sink it. Unable to sink it by shell fire, the U-boat fired a second torpedo into it, finally sinking it fifteen miles south of Fenwick Island. About six hours later the freezing men were picked up by the USCG cutter *Nike* and transported to Lewes, Delaware.[14] On February 4 and 5 the twin ships SS *India Arrow* and SS *China Arrow* were carrying oil. On February 4 the *India*

Arrow took a torpedo and broke into flames, sinking. The ship lost 26 men, and about a dozen survivors made it to Atlantic City. On February 5 the *China Arrow* was hit by two torpedoes, then the U–Boat surfaced and finished off the tanker. Thirty men made it into three lifeboats they had lashed together and spent the next three days adrift until a navy patrol plane spotted them. The coast guard cutter *Nike* was called to their rescue and they were taken in to Lewes.[15]

The 3,915-ton British freighter *Gypsum Prince* was sunk just 1.1 miles off of the Cape Henlopen point on March 4, 1942. She was headed toward the port of Philadelphia with a full load of gypsum (a substitute for fertilizer) when at 6:40 A.M., while visibility was still bad, her lights out and radio silent, she collided with the British tanker *Voco* sailing out of Philadelphia on an outward-bound course. She is considered a "war casualty" because she was trying to avoid detection at night by running with her lights and radio off. As we know, a ship at night stands out like a Christmas tree on the water and provides an easy target for submarines. Six crew members from the *Gypsum Prince* died, but twenty were saved and carried into Lewes.[16] The *SS Hvoslep*, a 1650-ton Norwegian freighter, was torpedoed March 10, 1942, two miles east of the Fenwick Island Shoal buoy. Sixteen survivors were picked up out of a crew of 20.[17]

Defending the River and Bay

Another threat that never materialized was the possibility of aerial or surface seaborne attacks on the shipyards, refineries, and other industry in the Delaware Valley. The Philadelphia, Chester, and Wilmington shipyards, DuPont Powder Works, Bellanca Aircraft Company in New Castle, Baldwin Locomotive Works, Remington Arms, Pedricktown Ordnance, Frankford Arsenal, industry in Trenton—arms, ammunition, clothing, and chemical factories—were all vulnerable to attack from Axis forces. The Delaware River and Bay was a well-fortified estuary. Its defenses included submarine nets, mines, and coastal artillery augmented by regular patrols offshore by naval craft and airborne patrol by military aircraft and blimps.[18]

The Civil Air Patrol was initiated in 1941 to support the regular patrols by military aircraft. Delaware is home to one of the original "Coastal Patrol" units, based in Rehoboth Beach. Using private aircraft, the "Flying Minute Men" patrolled the Atlantic Ocean for German submarines and operated off small unpaved airports.[19] The Pearl Harbor attack also brought a push for passive defensive measures such as camouflage, blackouts, and better fire and blast protection in the event of an enemy air attack.

In July 1940 the navy created Navy Basic War Plan, Rainbow No. 1 (WPL-42), and President Roosevelt mobilized the plan in April 1941. The Harbor Entrance Control Post (HECP) was established to coordinate with the Army Artillery Commands as well as the captain of the port (COTP) to monitor ship entry into the bay.[20]

On February 18, 1942, the Harbor Entrance Control Post (HECP) at Cape Henlopen was assigned control of the fleet tug USS *Allegheny* (AT-19) as a station ship at the entrance to the channel leading into the harbor with the 75-foot coast guard cutter "653" assigned as relief. That area was maintained as a mine-swept anchorage by a group of coastal minesweepers (AMC) known as the "little sisters," based at Cape May and commanded by Commander William B. McDonald, USNR.[21]

The three forts at mid-river—Fort Delaware, Fort Du Pont, and Fort Mott in New Jersey—had stood sentinel for a century and were obsolete by modern standards. The defenses were moved south to Fort Saulsbury near Slaughter's Beach just after World War I. However, by 1941 the primary coastal artillery defense of the Delaware Bay was installed at Fort Miles near Cape Henlopen. The twelve-inch battery at Fort Saulsbury was transferred to "Camp Henlopen," designated "Construction number 519," which would become Fort Miles.

Strategically located next to the Delaware Bay, Cape May was one of the points of defense against a German attack on the Philadelphia Naval Yard, where U.S. warships were assembled and surrounding oil refineries abounded. A gun battery was established on a rise at the point on Cape May. This battery was coordinated with other batteries on the opposite cape under the command of Fort Miles. It would be a German priority to interrupt the war effort at this strategic estuary. The sinking of the *Jacob Jones* led to the construction of the Cape May Canal. U.S. Navy and U.S. Coast Guard ships could access the Delaware Bay without sailing into the ocean off Cape May Point, where German subs lurked throughout the war. Merchant ships also used the canal. Germans sank 10 ships within a mile of the New Jersey coast.[22]

A 1939 study revealed that the Kreigsmarine might be able to stand offshore and shell U.S. positions outside the range of defenders. As a consequence, 16-inch long-range guns were installed at Fort Miles. Fort Miles represented the zenith of coastal artillery development, as well as the swansong of this particular form of defense, which was rapidly replaced by the advancement of missiles and aircraft after the war. The Delaware National Guard's federalized 261st Coast Artillery (Harbor Defense) moved to Cape Henlopen in the Spring of 1941, bringing 155mm guns to cover the entrance to the bay. They established a headquarters that would eventually encompass outposts at the Delaware forts as well as Fort Mott and the 155mm battery at Cape May Point in New Jersey.[23]

The development of permanent gun batteries on Fort Miles began in earnest. There would be one battery of 16-inch guns (Battery Smith), a battery of 12-inch guns (Battery 519), and two batteries of 6-inch guns (Battery Hunter and Battery Herring). Soon the 21st Coast Artillery Regiment arrived to deploy mines at the harbor entrance and provide antiaircraft defenses. In addition to the mines, the underwater harbor defenses would include navy magnetic loops and hydrophones for the detection of submarines. Radar and searchlights provided additional detection resources. It was this combination of coast and harbor defenses that the Harbor Entrance Control Post (HECP) was to coordinate.[24] Lingering reminders of the war in the area are the observation or fire control towers that were constructed, two in New Jersey and eleven along the Delaware coast, which still stand. These reinforced concrete structures were designed to give an unobstructed and extended view enabling the crews to spot enemy targets and in cooperation with other posts to triangulate their position for the gun crews at Fort Miles.[25]

As part of its responsibility for harbor defense, the army had planned the establishment of Harbor Defense Command Posts (HDCP). In the spring of 1941 the chief of naval operations and chief of staff of the army approved a memorandum setting forth the "Mission, General Operation and Desirable Location of the Harbor Entrance Control Post" (HECP)[26] During the first months of 1942, duty must have been frustrating for the officers and men of the post. The anti-submarine warfare operations, as well as search and rescue operations in Fourth Naval District waters, were being run by the Eastern

Sea Frontier Joint Operations Office, Delaware Group, at Cape May. As a subordinate command of that organization with good communications facilities, the HECP was well aware of the ongoing war off the cape. The communications section would receive the SOS signals from ships and could follow the rescue operations. At night the watch personnel could see the bright flashes from exploding tankers and by day observe the great columns of black smoke from burning oil. Then the ships bringing the survivors from those attacks would arrive to be identified by the HECP watch and brought into port. The beach was fouled with tar balls and pieces of sunken ships, a lingering reminder to all hands of the havoc they were witnessing.[27]

U.S. Coast Guard Beach Patrols

The coast guard had an 83-foot cutter and three patrol boats based in Lewes under the Fourth Naval District. Their task was to patrol the waters and perform search and rescue missions for downed aircraft and ships in distress. They also had responsibility for patrolling the beaches, which were mostly restricted areas during wartime. Spurred by the three landings of enemy agents on Long Island, at Ponta Vedra, Florida, and Machias, Maine, in June 1942, the FBI recommended that the coast guard establish beach patrols. Originally, two-man patrols were envisioned. A central headquarters was established on the beach front in south Rehoboth Beach at the DuPont home with a barracks in the H. Rodney Sharpe home next door and a hospital in the adjacent R.R.M. Carpenter home.

Being short of manpower, the coast guard recognized that dogs could be trained and used to enhance a one-man patrol. Dog patrols began in August 1942. Horse patrols eventually became the principal means of guarding the beaches at night. The horses were stabled on property at the southwest end of the bridge over the Lewes-Rehoboth Canal and from there they pranced right down Rehoboth Avenue to get to the beach.[28]

The War Comes to the Delaware Capes

On June 10, 1942, a submarine was detected off the cape and a search was conducted, but no contact was made. On the 13th the first part of the largest convoy yet created at the cape—47 ships—sailed before fog set in. While that weather created excellent conditions for a submarine attack there had been none. Thus, it was presumed that the sub had been a minelayer and had left the area. The cape had been closed and sweeping operations conducted across the entrance in the area from Overfalls and McCrie Shoals to Hen and Chicken Shoal. Four mines were located and found to have been TMB magnetic mines timed for 80 days. Throughout that period the Moran Towing and Transportation Company tug *John R. Williams* had been engaged in towing ships that had scattered from the convoy and run aground while avoiding the reported mines and the minesweeping operations.[29]

Then about dusk, around 8:00 on Wednesday, June 24, just as cape-area residents and vacationers were leaving the restaurants in Lewes or strolling on the Rehoboth boardwalk, an enormous explosion and huge flash occurred just off the entrance to the harbor. *Williams*, returning to Cape May after a trip to Fenwick to help a French ship, for some reason had cut across the suspected mined area and struck one of 15 mines that had been laid by the German U-boat U-373 on June 11. The small size of the tug, 396 tons, did little to contain the impact of the explosive power of the 2,000-pound TMB mine. Parts of the tug were strewn over a wide area. Only a lucky four of the 18-man crew survived. They were picked up by USS YP-334, which had been escorting *Williams* on its trip south.[30]

The Allied navies gradually but successfully overcame the U-boat threat with improved anti-submarine techniques and tools. They gained experience and strength as the arsenal of democracy out-produced the foes. The U-boat fleet faced diminishing returns and it became a very dangerous task for the submarines to go to sea against the formidable Allied force. The Battle of the Atlantic was largely won by the end of 1943. Nevertheless, the Germans persevered with their efforts until the very end of the war, despite the danger and their lack of success. The cadre and armament at Fort Miles was correspondingly gradually reduced as the war progressed to its conclusion.

A few months before the war ended on May 8, 1945, the German navy sent six boats from bases in Norway to attack the East Coast and, the Germans hoped, to repeat the successes of Operation Drumbeat. U-853 and U-858 were part of that attack. While U-853 sank one of the last ships destroyed in World War II, the collier *Black Point*, near the entrance to Long Island Sound, the U-boat was attacked May 5–6, 1945, by four American hunter-killers and became the last one destroyed in U.S. waters. Its sister ship managed to survive and offer a satisfactory coda to the war at the Delaware Capes.[31]

On 4 March 1945, U-858, a Type IXC U-boat, departed Kiel, Germany, and after a brief stop in Horton, Norway, it set out on its second war patrol as part of wolf-pack *Seewolfe*. After reporting its position south of Iceland on April 4 and 5, it patrolled without success and without detection. After the German surrender on May 8 both the U.S. and German navies broadcast messages for all German submarines to surface and fly the flag of surrender. USS *Muir* (DE-770) and USS *Carter* (DE-112), a Wilmington-built ship, were operating as part of Task Force 63, which had effectively stymied *Seewolfe*'s operations.[32]

On May 10, off the New Jersey coast, *Muir* and *Carter* approached a shape through a dense fog. The shape was U-858, her flag of surrender (actually a shower curtain) barely visible even at close range. Two other ships, USS *Pillsbury* (DE-133) and USS *Pope* (DE-134), were standing by and were detailed to put a prize crew aboard, accept the surrender, and escort U-858 to the U.S. Naval Base at Cape May, New Jersey. This was the first German submarine to surrender to U.S. naval forces in WWII and, most appropriately, the surrender took place in the general location where the USS *Jacob Jones* (DD- 131) had been the first U.S. naval ship sunk by a German submarine in WWII. Since the U-858 was ultimately to go to Philadelphia for technical exploitation, with some of the personnel going to Washington for intelligence interrogation and others to the army as POWs, the decision was made to take the sub past the HECP into the Harbor of Refuge for docking at the Fort Miles pier. Commander F.P. Norfleet, the officer in charge of the Joint Operations Office, Eastern Sea Frontier, Delaware Group, came over from Cape May to formally complete the paperwork associated with the surrender. Lieutenant Robert Brown did the translating. On July 12, 1945, the HECP was disestablished.[33]

U-858, German submarine, Type 1xC, is brought to anchor at Cape Henlopen, Delaware, in May 1945 after being surrendered at sea. On her conning tower (with megaphone) is Lieutenant Commander Willard D. Michael, officer in charge. Note Sikorski HNS-I helicopter and blimp overhead (80-G-K-3319-A, U.S. Naval History and Heritage Command).

Shipbuilding

During the Great Depression in the 1930s Delaware Valley shipbuilding suffered from a lack of orders. But business took an upturn as America began to rearm itself in preparation for the war gathering momentum in Europe. When war was declared, the navy required more and more ships. Hog Island was gone, replaced by a WPA project municipal airport. However, ships could now be built faster on fewer ways thanks to mass production techniques like prefabrication and the use of large cranes to assemble whole ship sections and components. The Dravo Yard was among the newest. Together with Jackson and Sharp, Pusey and Jones, Sun Ship, New York Ship, and a revived Cramp's, they brought vitality to the "American Clyde" once again for the duration of the war.[34]

Philadelphia Naval Shipyard

During World War II the Philadelphia Naval Shipyard at League Island built fifty-three ships, and converted or overhauled 1,218 more on behalf of the U.S. Navy and eight other Allied powers.[35] Employment at the Philadelphia shipyard rose from 30,000 to 60,000 workers at its peak in 1944. When war had erupted in 1939 the Navy Yard began to mobilize. The keel was laid for the battleship *New Jersey* on September 16, 1940. President Roosevelt visited the yard four days later, inspecting the battleships *New Jersey* and *Washington*, the naval aircraft factory, and top-secret PT boats. The neutral Navy Yard performed top secret and possibly illegal repairs on combatant Britain's vessels *Furious*, *Resolution*, and *Manchester*.[36]

Finding skilled labor was the greatest challenge of all. The Philadelphia Naval Shipyard had to compete for workers from other Delaware Valley contractors and private yards. Labor issues were to be a difficulty throughout the war. Women, minorities, and even some German POWs were employed to fill the gaps. Over 20 percent of the workforce left within a few months of hire, some to enlist, more dismissed for absenteeism, and even some who simply left for no reason, without notice. There were complaints about unfair promotion policies, abuse by uniformed military personnel, and favoritism towards white male employees, issues shared by all the shipbuilding yards during the war.[37]

The Pearl Harbor attack brought a push for passive defensive measures in the industrial littoral area such as camouflage, blackouts, and better fire and blast protection in the event of an enemy air attack. The navy had developed war plans for coastal defense based on naval district organization, and President Roosevelt mobilized the plan in April 1941. The Delaware and New Jersey coasts became part of the North Atlantic Coastal Eastern Sea Frontier. The commandant of the Fourth Naval District and the Philadelphia Navy Yard served as commander. Rear Admiral Adolphus E. Watson was responsible for coastal defense from Staten Island to Cape Henlopen. His assets were blimps at Lakehurst Naval Air Station and aircraft and boats at Cape May Section Base and the Henlopen Naval Section Base.[38]

The Pearl Harbor attack brought the realization that the destroyers *Cassin* and *Shaw* were lost. Both had been built at League Island in 1935. Furthermore, the battleships *Oklahoma*, *Utah*, and *Pennsylvania*, all modernized at the navy yard, had been sunk or crippled as well. "We are determined not only to replace the ships which we made and were lost," navy yard officials announced, "but to send many more in their place to take up the fight and our fight where the *Cassin* and *Shaw* had to leave off."[39]

Naval Base Philadelphia—Philadelphia Naval Shipyard, 350-ton hammerhead crane, League Island, Philadelphia (pa3398, Library of Congress, Prints and Photographs).

From Pearl Harbor to VJ Day the Philadelphia Naval Shipyard built forty-eight new warships, converted forty-one, repaired and overhauled 574, completed and dry-docked 650, outfitted over 600, and degaussed 700 vessels. The naval aircraft factory built over 500 aircraft, and the propeller shop made 5,500 ship propellers. The navy receiving station processed over 70,000 recruits. On the first anniversary of Pearl Harbor the navy yard launched the USS *New Jersey*, but the engineers had underestimated the drag resistance necessary to safely launch the ship. *New Jersey* raced down the shipways and traveled 1,000 feet beyond the engineering estimate and made for her namesake New Jersey shore-

USS *New Jersey* (BB-62) at anchor, probably in the Delaware River (NH 92634, U.S. Naval History and Heritage Command).

line, where she struck the muddy riverfront. The later battleships *Wisconsin* and *Iowa* were launched successfully without incident. The yard built 24 destroyer escorts, 14 LSTs, and three aircraft carriers during the war. Even before the war ended orders began to be cancelled, and some ships already underway were scrapped.[40]

USS *New Jersey* (BB-62)

After its unorthodox launching in 1942 the *New Jersey* went on to compile a remarkable combat record. USS *New Jersey* ("Big J" or "Black Dragon") earned more battle stars for combat actions than the other three completed *Iowa*-class battleships in her class and was the only U.S. battleship providing gunfire support during the Vietnam War. During World War II *New Jersey* shelled targets on Guam and Okinawa and screened aircraft carriers conducting raids in the Marshall Islands. During the Korean War she was involved in raids up and down the North Korean coast, after which she was decommissioned into the U.S. Navy reserve fleet, better known as the "mothball fleet." She was briefly reactivated in 1968 and sent to Vietnam to support U.S. troops before returning to the mothball fleet in 1969. Reactivated once more in the 1980s, *New Jersey* was modernized to carry missiles and recommissioned for service. In 1983 she participated in U.S. operations during the Lebanese civil war.[41]

New Jersey was decommissioned for the last time in 1991 (after serving a total of 21 years in the active fleet), having earned a Navy Unit Commendation for service in Vietnam and 19 battle and campaign stars for combat operations during World War II, the Korean War, the Vietnam War, the Lebanese civil war, and service in the Persian Gulf. After a brief retention in the mothball fleet, she was donated to the Home Port Alliance in Camden, New Jersey, and began her career as a museum ship on October 15, 2001.[42]

Cramp Shipbuilding Company

Cramp and Sons shipyard was shut down in 1927 and remained dormant for a dozen years. In the late 1930s the secretary of the navy launched an attempt to reopen the yard. Settling old financial claims and back taxes, the new yard opened under the name of Cramp Shipbuilding Company. By May 1941 there were 700 ship workers on the payroll. By August 1942 the payroll had mushroomed to 10,000 including about 1,000 workers who had been employed there during World War I. Cramp built six light cruisers, 22 submarines, and nearly a score of auxiliary craft during the war.[43]

New York Shipbuilding Corporation

New York Shipbuilding was an American-operated firm from 1899 to 1968, ultimately completing more than 500 vessels for the U.S. Navy, the United States Merchant Marine, the United States Coast Guard, and other maritime concerns. Its best-known vessels include the destroyer USS *Reuben James* (DD-245) and the cruiser USS *Indianapolis* (CA-35). *Reuben James* was lost to German U-boats even before war was declared. *Indianapolis* was lost late in the war after delivering vital components for the atomic bomb dropped on Hiroshima. Her surviving crew was in the water for several days, ravaged by sharks.[44]

New York Ship's World War II production included all nine *Independence*-class light carriers (CVL)), built on *Cleveland*-class light cruiser hulls; the 35,000-ton battleship USS *South Dakota* (BB-57); and 98 LCTs (Landing Craft Tank), many of which took part in the D-Day landings at Normandy.[45]

Sun Shipbuilding

A subsidiary of the Sun Oil Company owned by the Pew family from Pittsburgh, Sun Shipbuilding had launched its first ship from its Chester, Pennsylvania, yard in 1917. In the decades that followed, Sun built oil tankers, primarily for the Standard Oil Company. On the eve of World War II, it had eight shipways, each large enough to build a single ship, and two large dry-docks for repairing damaged ships. By the start of World War II it was among the country's five largest shipyards. Twenty slipways were added during the war, making it the country's largest shipyard. In May 1941 the United States Maritime Commission asked Sun to expand its facilities in order to construct the vital oil tankers necessary for a two-ocean navy. Sun quickly received a contract for ninety-two tankers. Powered by 7,240-horsepower turbo electric engines, the 523-foot T-2 tanker had a cruising range of more than 12,000 miles.

Sun launched its first T-2, the *Esso Gettysburg*, in February 1942. To fulfill its government orders, Sun quickly expanded and streamlined production until it could complete a ship, from the laying of the keel to launch, in just seventy days. By late 1943 it was operating four major shipyards containing twenty-eight ways together with associated shops, cranes, railroad facilities, and dry-docks. At its peak, Sun employed between 35,000 and 40,000 workers. By war's end Sun had launched 318 vessels, including 35 cargo ships, 35 barges, and 8 military vessels. Sun Shipbuilding built two hundred eighty-one T2 tankers during World War II, about 40 percent of the U.S. wartime total. It also built hospital ships, cargo ships, and escort carriers for the United States Maritime Commission.[46]

Merchant marine and navy demand forced Pennsylvania's shipyards to employ large numbers of African-American and women workers. In the Philadelphia Naval Shipyard, African-American men were most numerous among the riggers, while women were concentrated in the aircraft factory, where they represented almost 25 percent of the workforce. Plagued by racial tensions, the Sun Ship Company in 1943, on the suggestion of the publisher of the state's most influential African-American newspaper, the *Pittsburgh Courier*, undertook a unique experiment. In Number 4 Yard, African Americans filled every position from janitors and welders up to supervisors. At peak production Yard 4 employed about 6,200 blacks, with 2,800 more working in Sun Ship's integrated yards. In May 1943 Yard 4 launched the *Marine Eagle*, the first ship built entirely by black workers. By March 1945 Yard 4 had launched fifteen ships and thirty-five car floats.[47]

Dravo Corporation Shipbuilders

Dravo Corporation, located in Wilmington on the Christina River where the old Bethlehem Steel yards had been, constructed 16 destroyer escorts, 65 landing ships medium (LSM), five landing ships tank (LST), five patrol craft, and scores of lighters, tenders, and barges. The LSM vessels were described as "ugly ships for ugly jobs." Over 200 feet long, each could accommodate a crew of five officers and forty-eight men. These versatile craft were armed with two 40mm antiaircraft guns and four 20mm guns. They could hold up to 54 troops, five medium tanks, or three heavy tanks.[48]

Several of the destroyer escorts were built for the Free French and South American countries. One, the *Senegalais*, launched in a snowstorm on Armistice Day, 1943, sank a U-boat within months after being commissioned. LST Number 21, known to her coast guard crew as the *Blackjack Maru*, fought in four theaters and traveled 25,000 miles from Burma to North Africa to Italy and France. She was the first to touch shore during the Normandy invasion in the Gold Beach assault area. She ferried men and supplies to France and returned with wounded soldiers and German prisoners. Equipped with rails, she carried freight cars across the English Channel. A sister ship, LST 16, was converted into a mini–aircraft-carrier for Piper Cub spotter planes.[49] Many of these were built utilizing a mass-construction technique where components were shipped in pieces by rail and then assembled in Wilmington. Dravo pioneered upside-down construction, assembly-line methods, welding, and other techniques and became the largest shipbuilding yard on the riverfront. Altogether, it manufactured some 187 vessels during the war and employed over 11,000 shipbuilders.[50]

Wilmington became a magnet for women who also wanted to work, like the "Rosie the Riveter" character. Housing was so tight that people had to subdivide their apartments or houses to make room for skilled workers and women who came to work in the area.

Pusey and Jones

Pusey and Jones employed more than 3,500 people during WWII to build tankers and freighters for the U.S. Maritime Commission. They delivered 21 seagoing ships to the war effort. The largest ships built in Wilmington, they were over 420 feet long with beams of over 60 feet. They couldn't be launched headlong into the Christina River but had to be launched sideways because they were too big to fit. Pusey and Jones also built some 22,000 aluminum gun turrets for Flying Fortresses as well as thrust bearings, pistons, and cylinder heads for Liberty ships.[51]

American Car and Foundry Company

American Car and Foundry notably built 412 plywood Higgins boats along the Wilmington waterfront during the war, officially called Landing Craft Vehicle Personnel (LCVP). These ubiquitous craft were the backbone of allied amphibious landings some 20,000 built in all. American Car and Foundry also made ten minesweepers, assorted barges, lighters, and pontoon vessels.[52]

Vinyard Shipbuilding Company

Vinyard Shipbuilding, in Milford, Delaware, employing 120 shipworkers, built ten subchasers and six motor launches during the war.[53]

Wilmington Marine Terminal

After its initial construction, improvements continued to be made to the Wilmington Marine Terminal. The wharf was extended and rail tracks were added along with an additional 25 acres of open storage. Another 35 acres of land was purchased and water depth was increased to 30 feet. Despite the great depression in the 1930s, business at the port continued to grow. When World War II began, the growing needs of the port were subsumed by higher priorities. It became difficult to find labor to unload the ships arriving, so the port turned to the local high schools to find a part-time work force able to handle the wartime task of maintaining the port productively. Nevertheless, early in the war (March 1942) the port served as a ready assembly yard for jeeps, trucks, and tank repair vehicles totaling 1,400 freight carloads, materiel that was desperately needed. Some went to the British Eighth Army, some to Stalingrad, and others to the Chinese battling Japan. The port shipped 600,000 cases of canned goods, petroleum products, and general cargo for the war effort. Further expansion would have to await the end of the war.[54]

Notable Delaware Valley Sailors of World War II

In many ways, the war remains fresh in the collective memory of residents of the Delaware Valley. A few veterans remain, as well as many more family members with a first-hand memory of the sailors who defended the United States. We will offer a few stories representative of the valor typical of our homegrown sailors but cannot hope to give them full credit for all their deeds, as they are too numerous to capture in their entirety.

Two Delaware sailors were killed on December 7, 1941, during the Pearl Harbor attack. Both served on the USS *Shaw*, whose magazine exploded during the attack. They were George A. Penuel Jr., of Millsboro and Paul G. Gosnell of Wilmington, the first of many Delaware sailors and Marines to give their lives for their country during World War II.[55]

Space does not permit us to give anything like a full account of the valor of the men of the Delaware Valley who served, but the following are some of the most noteworthy examples.

Ensign Edgar Rees Bassett

Edgar Rees Bassett of Philadelphia served at the Battle of Midway as a naval aviator. He was awarded the Navy Cross posthumously for his deeds while assigned to the USS *Yorktown* during that critical turning point in the war in the Pacific. He joined Fighting Squadron 42 aboard the USS *Yorktown* on June 9, 1941, as the squadron was preparing for its first Neutrality Patrol cruise in the Atlantic Ocean. Bassett was considered one of the more colorful characters among the fighter pilots of Fighting Squadron 42 and remained associated with *Yorktown* for the rest of his brief life. He was noted more than once for his aggressive performance of duty in the first few months of World War II, especially for his strafing of Japanese gun emplacements and barges during the aircraft carrier raid on Lae and Salamaua, New Guinea, on March 10, 1942.[56]

During the Battle of the Coral Sea, which took place between May 4 and 8, 1942, Bassett shot down a Mitsubishi F1M2 "Pete" floatplane over Tulagi in the Solomon Islands. During the *Yorktown* air group attack on Japanese shipping there on May 4 he strafed

Grumman F4F-4 Wildcat fighter, Fighting Squadron 41 (VF-41), in flight, circa early 1942. A similar aircraft was flown by Edgar Bassett and Edward Bayers at the Battle of Midway (80-G-7026, U.S. Naval History and Heritage Command).

the Japanese destroyer *Yuzuki* as she fled Tulagi Harbor. On the morning of May 7 he flew one of the fighters that protected Torpedo Squadron 5 in its attack on the Japanese aircraft carrier *Shoho*. That same evening he helped to disperse a group of Japanese dive bombers and torpedo planes in the vicinity of the *Yorktown* task force. On the morning of May 8 he flew combat air patrol over Task Force 17 and assisted in the downing of one Japanese plane during the Japanese attack on *Yorktown*.

Assigned to Fighting Squadron 3 aboard *Yorktown* along with several other Fighting Squadron 42 pilots just before the Battle of Midway, Bassett flew one of the six Grumman F4F Wildcat fighters covering Torpedo Squadron 3 in the attack on the aircraft carriers of the Japanese Mobile Force on the morning of June 4, 1942. When the Japanese combat air patrol swarmed over the torpedo planes and their escorting fighters, Ensign Bassett was shot down in flames at the outset and killed.[57]

Captain Edward H. Bayers, USN

Edward H. Bayers was born in 1910. His home of record was Bethany Beach, Delaware. Enlisting in the navy in 1928, he became a naval aviator and flew everything from biplanes to jets. During World War II he served aboard the USS *Enterprise* during the Battle of Midway in June 1942 as a fighter pilot and section leader in Fighter Squadron Six (VF-6), which flew Grumman F4F-4 *Wildcats*. He was awarded the Navy Cross for his deeds during that battle. His citation read as follows:

> Sighting two Zero Fighters on 4 June, Lieutenant, Junior Grade, Bayers, with bold aggressiveness and great personal risk, pressed home a persistent attack against these enemy aircraft until he had shot the leader down in flames. While diving to escape the surviving wingman, who had out-maneuvered him and gained the offensive, he sighted a Japanese Torpedo Plane approaching the USS YORK-TOWN. Too intent upon protecting our aircraft carrier to be deterred by the threatening proximity of the enemy fighter, he intercepted the Torpedo Plane and destroyed it. Again, on 6 June, as member of an attack group assigned to repel a Japanese naval force, he defied a fierce barrage of concentrated anti-aircraft fire to strafe and seriously damage an enemy destroyer.[58]

Later in the war he was presented the Distinguished Flying Cross (DFC). At this time he was flying F6F-5 *Hellcats*. The citation for this medal follows:

> Lieutenant Commander Edward Howard Bayers ... for heroism and extraordinary achievement while participating in aerial flight as the pilot of a carrier-based fighter plane in Fighting Squadron ELEVEN (VF-11), embarked in USS HORNET (CV-12), in action on 9 January 1945, in the vicinity of Formosa. While attacking an enemy convoy, he dove through intense and accurate anti-aircraft fire to secure direct rocket hits upon an enemy destroyer, inflicting such damage that the vessel exploded and sank.[59]

Bayers was awarded a second DFC for actions just three days later:

> For heroism and extraordinary achievement while participating in aerial flight as pilot of a carrier-based Fighter Plane in Fighting Squadron ELEVEN (VF-11), embarked in USS HORNET (CV-12), in action on 12 January 1945, in the vicinity of French Indo-China, while attacking an enemy destroyer escort, causing such serious damage that the vessel probably sank.[60]

Edward Bayers became the first former enlisted man and former VF-2 fighting chief to command a fighter squadron during World War II when he took command of VF-3, the "Crazy Cat" squadron, aboard the new *Yorktown* (CV-10) in January 1945. He took part in possibly the longest dogfight in World War II, which lasted some 35 minutes.

Eighteen Japanese fought against four VF-3 Hellcats. All four VF-3 aviators survived. When the war was over Bayers continued as commanding officer of VF-3 at NAS Oceana, his squadron being one of the first to fly the new F8F-1 "Bearcat." Commander Edward H. Bayers served as NAS Port Lyautey Base operations commander from 1955 to 1958. He then retired as a full captain.

Dr. J. Douglas Blackwood

J. Douglas Blackwood of Philadelphia served in both world wars. He enrolled in the Naval Coast Defense Reserve as an assistant surgeon April 14, 1917. Dr. Blackwood served on transports in the Atlantic during World War I, earning the Navy Cross for attending the sick and wounded when the troop transport *President Lincoln* was torpedoed May 31, 1918. He entered the Regular Navy in 1919 and served in various ships and at naval hospitals in the United States and abroad in the years that followed.[61]

Blackwood served the people of Haiti from 1927 to 1930 when assigned to a public health unit on that island. Appointed medical inspector with the rank of commander in 1938, he reported to the cruiser *Vincennes* (CA-44) on September 30, 1940, and was on board during the critical early months of America's participation in World War II. During the Battle of Savo Island on August 9, 1942, one of the many sea fights during the Solomon Islands campaign, a cruiser/destroyer force was surprised at night by Japanese cruisers and dealt a crushing blow. Blackwood was killed when the *Vincennes* was sunk along with two other cruisers and a destroyer. In 1943 the destroyer escort USS *J. Douglas Blackwood* (DE-219) was named in his honor.[62]

Howard Franklin Clark

Howard Franklin Clark was born in Wilmington, Delaware, on September 15, 1914. Graduating from the U.S. Naval Academy on June 2, 1938, he served at sea until 1940, when he underwent flight training. Reporting to aircraft carrier *Lexington* (CV-2) on April 1, 1941, as a member of Fighter Squadron 3, he won a Distinguished Flying Cross on February 20, 1942, when he brought down an enemy bomber attempting to attack the carrier.

During the Battle of the Coral Sea, Clark again and again engaged enemy aircraft in utter disregard of his own safety until his plane was shot down. Lieutenant (JG) Clark was posthumously awarded a second Distinguished Flying Cross for his heroism during the battle (May 7–8, 1942). USS *Howard F. Clark* (DE-533) was a *John C. Butler*-class destroyer escort acquired by the U.S. Navy during World War II.[63]

Lieutenant Commander Arthur Dowling

Arthur Dowling of Greenville, Delaware, was commissioned in September 1940 and served his country during World War II and the Korean War and remained in the naval reserves, retiring as a commander. In 1945 Lieutenant Commander Dowling was awarded the Navy Cross by the president of the United States for:

> extraordinary heroism as Commanding Officer of the rescue vessel USS PCE(R) 855 in action against enemy forces during the amphibious assault and capture of Okinawa, Ryuku Islands, from April to June, 1945. Operating at an isolated and exposed station for a prolonged period of intensive combat,

Lieutenant Commander (then Lieutenant) Dowling repeatedly brought his ship alongside burning and sinking ships and, although frequently forced to fight off enemy air attacks during these rescue operations, valiantly directed the rescue of numerous survivors of these stricken ships. His inspiring leadership, intrepid spirit and courageous devotion to duty reflect the highest credit upon Lieutenant Commander Dowling and the United States Naval Service.[64]

Rear Admiral Wilmer Earl Gallaher

Wilmer E. Gallaher was born in Wilmington, Delaware, in 1907 and graduated from the U.S. Naval Academy in 1931. During World War II he was commanding officer of Scouting Squadron Six (VS-6) attached to the USS *Enterprise* (CV-6) during the Battle of Midway in June 1942. This battle marked the turning point in the war in the Pacific, when the navy shattered the Japanese fleet and sank six of its carriers.

Leading a squadron of eighteen Douglas Dauntless SBD-3 dive-bombers of Scouting Squadron Six, Lieutenant Gallaher was cited for the following:

[E]xtraordinary heroism in operations against the enemy while serving as Pilot and Squadron Leader of a carrier-based Navy Scouting Plane and Squadron Commander ... during the "Air Battle of Mid-

Battle of Midway, June 1942. A Douglas SBD-3 Dauntless scout bomber (Bureau # 4542), of USS *Enterprise*'s Bombing Squadron Six (VB-6), is parked onboard USS *Yorktown* (CV-5) after landing at about 1140 hrs on June 4, 1942. This plane, damaged during the attack on the Japanese aircraft carrier *Kaga* that morning, landed on *Yorktown*, as it was low on fuel. It was later lost with the carrier. Note damage to the horizontal tail and dual stripes painted on the fin (95557, U.S. Naval History and Heritage Command).

way," against enemy Japanese forces on 4–6 June 1942. Participating in a devastating assault against a Japanese invasion fleet, Lieutenant Gallaher, with fortitude and resolute devotion to duty, pressed home his attacks in the face of a formidable barrage of anti-aircraft fire and fierce fighter opposition. His courageous aggressiveness and inspiring leadership were contributing factors to the success of our forces and were in keeping with the highest traditions of the United States Naval Service.[65]

Sometime after 10:20 A.M., Lt. Gallaher, 35, dove on the Japanese carrier *Kaga*. Gallaher's bomb was the first of five 500-pound bombs that hit *Kaga* that day, ultimately sinking one of Japan's largest carriers. Lieutenant Wilmer Earl Gallaher had seen the USS *Arizona* at Pearl Harbor. He watched as the bomb from his Dauntless tumbled onto the carrier and exploded on the flight deck. Gallaher recalled thinking at that moment, *Arizona, I remember you!*

During the Korean War Captain Gallaher was awarded the Legion of Merit for exceptionally meritorious conduct in the performance of outstanding services to the government of the United States as commander, Naval Forces Far East, from July 16, 1951 to July 9, 1953. Gallaher retired from the navy in 1959 and died in 1983.[66]

Rear Admiral Frank Lesher Johnson

Frank Lesher Johnson of Delaware City, Delaware, graduated with the U.S. Naval Academy class of 1930. During World War II he was commanding officer of the destroyer USS *Fletcher* (DD-445) during a successful attack on a Japanese submarine in South Pacific waters on February 11, 1943. Establishing sound contact after a patrol plane had located the hostile vessel, Lieutenant Commander Johnson, by skillful direction, dropped a nine-charge pattern on a deliberate approach. Within a period of eleven minutes following the rapid detonations, three violent explosions erupted, sending large quantities of debris to the surface and leaving an immense oil slick as positive evidence of the destruction of the enemy submarine. He was awarded the Silver Star for these actions. In addition, he received the Legion of Merit for his performance as commanding officer of the *Fletcher* in the Solomon Islands:

> Lieutenant Commander Johnson helped disrupt numerous air attacks and attacked and sank a submarine. In two-night bombardment operations against Munda, his ship led the task group into position. He brought his vessel through a series of fierce engagements without damage.[67]

Commander Johnson served as commanding officer of the destroyer USS *Purdy* (DD-734) in the vicinity of Okinawa on April 6, 1945. When the USS *Mullany* was abandoned after being severely damaged during an enemy suicide attack, Captain Johnson made the final decision to place his ship alongside her, despite the presence of enemy planes, in an attempt to put out the serious fires raging close to the stricken ship's aftermagazines. Undaunted by the imminent danger of the magazines exploding, he carried out successful measures to extinguish the flames, thereby making possible the salvage of a valuable combatant unit of the U.S. fleet. He was awarded the Navy Cross for these valorous deeds.

Only a week later Johnson continued to exhibit valor. In action against Japanese forces off Okinawa, on April 12, 1945, the USS *Purdy* was maintaining Radar Picket Station Number One approximately 50 miles north of an important Japanese transport area. He was awarded a second Navy Cross. The citation read:

USS *Purdy* (DD-734) en route to the United States with Destroyer Division 122 (80-G-440450, U.S. Naval History and Heritage Command).

Captain Johnson aggressively met the sudden challenge of seven vicious suicide planes, and struck furiously at each plunging craft, shooting down four planes, assisting in the destruction of two more and damaging another. Stoutly determined to save his ship despite the severe damage inflicted during the final phase of the action, he gallantly directed his crew in restoring the PURDY to maximum combat efficiency. A daring and forceful leader in the face of overwhelming opposition, Captain Johnson, by his expert seamanship and professional skill, heroically brought the PURDY to port under her own power.[68]

Johnson retired as a U.S. Navy rear admiral. He died in 1984.

Stanley Fly Kline

Stanley Fly Kline of Graterford, Pennsylvania, enlisted in the United States Naval Reserve on February 2, 1927, and served on active duty in World War II. During Operation Torch, the amphibious landings in North Africa, on November 8, 1942, Kline was assigned to the British Royal Navy warship HMS *Hartland* as a member of a naval anti-sabotage party. As *Hartland* entered the harbor at Oran, Algeria, she came under heavy fire from Vichy French ships and shore batteries. When a shell exploded in a compartment occupied by the boarding party, the survivors found themselves trapped by fire and fumes. Kline crawled through a small overhead hatch, wormed his way along the deck under a hail of shells and machine gun fire, opened a large hatch, and assisted 42 men to safety. He then turned to loading ammunition clips for an automatic rifle and continued his heroic conduct with complete disregard for his own safety until he was killed by a shell explosion. Kline was awarded the Silver Star posthumously for his conspicuous gallantry at Oran. The U.S. Navy destroyer escort USS *Kline* (DE-687) was named for him.[69]

Rear Admiral John "Jack" Elwood Lee

John Elwood Lee was born September 20, 1908, in Wilmington, Delaware, and graduated from the U.S. Naval Academy in 1930. At the war's onset, he made four war patrols in the Atlantic as commanding officer of the submarine S-12.[70]

On October 19, 1942, LCDR John E. Lee took command of the submarine USS *Grayling* (SS-209). He was commanding officer of the *Grayling* on the fourth, fifth, and sixth war patrols of that submarine during the period October 19, 1942 to April 25, 1943, in enemy controlled waters of the Southwest Pacific. According to his citation, "During this period of intense activity, Lieutenant Commander Lee distinguished himself by his brilliant tactical knowledge and sound judgment in maneuvering his vessel into advantageous striking positions so skillfully and aggressively as to destroy seven enemy ships, totaling 34,957 tons, and damaged an additional 27,500 tons, despite persistent and violent hostile counter measures."[71] He was awarded the Navy Cross for these exploits. Following the war, the television series *The Silent Service* featured the war efforts of the U.S. submarine service. The exploits of LCDR Lee and the USS *Grayling* were featured in one of its episodes.

Lee was Commanding Officer of the USS *Croaker* (SS-246) on her first war patrol during the period July 19, 1944 to August 31, 1944, in enemy-controlled waters of the East China Sea. Lee's citation read, "Penetrating enemy air and surface escort screens, Captain

USS *Grayling* (SS-209). Fleet Admiral Chester W. Nimitz, USN, has signed this photograph, "At Pearl Harbor on 31 December 1941 hoisted 4-star Admiral's flag on USS Grayling and took command of U.S. Pacific Fleet" (NH 58089, U.S. Naval History and Heritage Command).

Lee maneuvered his ship into a favorable position to strike and launched bold torpedo attacks to sink an enemy light cruiser of 5,100 tons. Continuing his aggressive actions, he directed further torpedo attacks to sink three hostile ships, including a 10,000-ton tanker, for a total of 12,500 tons."[72] He received his second Navy Cross for these actions. Lee was commanding officer of the USS *Croaker* (SS-246) on her second war patrol during the period September 23, 1944 to November 10, 1944, in enemy-controlled waters of the East China Sea and was awarded his third Navy Cross for these deeds: "Skillfully penetrating strong enemy escort screens, Commander Lee launched seven vigorous night surface torpedo and gun attacks to sink four enemy ships totaling over 16,000 tons and damage four additional vessels totaling over 11,000 tons."[73]

Lee totaled some 15 confirmed ships sunk of approximately 63,457 tons. He was credited with another 28,500 tons in damaged enemy shipping during his command of the *Grayling* and the *Croaker* during seven successful wartime patrols. By the end of the war Commander Lee had received three Navy Crosses, a Silver Star, and a Bronze Star, the defining decorations of a naval career that saw him rise to rear admiral. Only about thirty people have ever won three Navy Crosses. USS *Croaker* (SS-246) is now a museum ship in Groton, Connecticut.

From 1953 to 1956 Captain Lee was the commanding officer of the submarine base in New London, Connecticut, where he officially accepted the world's first nuclear powered vessel, the USS *Nautilus* (SSN-571). Captain Lee finished his naval career in 1957 as commander in San Diego of Submarine Flotilla 1, which consisted at the time of 30 diesel-powered submarines, two submarine tenders, and two rescue vessels.[74]

Rear Admiral Lewis Smith Parks

On December 7, 1941, the day the Japanese attacked Pearl Harbor, Admiral Parks, of Wilmington Delaware, then a commander, was the skipper of the submarine *Pompano*. She was strafed by Japanese planes as she was cruising about 100 miles off the coast of Oahu.

In 1942, Parks won his first Navy Cross—the highest decoration for heroism in the navy after the Medal of Honor—for a war patrol as commanding officer of the USS *Pompano* (SS-181), in which he was credited with sinking about 17,000 tons of enemy shipping near Wake Island. The citation said this was accomplished "despite intensive enemy air and surface antisubmarine patrols and the fact that his ship was partially disabled as a result of bombing and depth charge attacks."[75] On a subsequent patrol, aboard the *Pompano*, he was awarded a second Navy Cross for sinking 16,485 tons of shipping in the East China Sea by "pressing home every favorable attack opportunity with courageous skill and efficiency ... despite vigorous antisubmarine measures on the part of the enemy."[76]

From late 1942 to 1943, Parks served on the staff of the commander of submarines in the Atlantic Fleet. On November 9, 1943, he returned to the Pacific as a captain in command of Submarine Division 202 aboard the USS *Parche* (SS-384). As commander of a submarine "wolf pack" he won his third Navy Cross for actions in the Luzon Straits and the South China Sea in which "seven enemy ships and two patrol craft totaling 57,000 tons were sunk and five additional enemy ships totaling 33,930 tons were damaged ... in the face of severe enemy countermeasures."[77] The *Parche* also received a Presidential Unit Citation for its service under Parks:

USS *Pompano* (SS-181) afloat immediately after her launching, at the Mare Island Navy Yard, California, March 11, 1937 (NH 44005, U.S. Naval History and Heritage Command).

[The ship] exposed by the light of bursting flares ... defied the terrific shell fire passing close overhead to strike again and sink a transport by two forward reloads, braving the mounting fury of fire from the damaged and sinking tanker to fight it out with a completely disorganized and confused enemy. Maneuvering swiftly to avoid destruction as a fast transport closed in to ram, the *Parche* ... as a climax to forty-six minutes of violent action retired unscathed with a record seven enemy ships and two patrol craft totaling 57,000 tons sunk, and five additional enemy ships totaling 33,930 tons damaged in the face of severe enemy countermeasures.[78]

In the Korean conflict Parks commanded the cruiser *Manchester* at the Inchon landing and in other operations. He was chief of information in the Navy Department from 1952 to 1954. In 1957 he commanded the battleship-cruiser force of the Atlantic Fleet just before the battleships were put in mothballs. He retired from the navy in 1960. In addition to the three Navy Crosses, his decorations included three Legions of Merit. Admiral Parks died at the age of 80 in 1982.[79]

Lieutenant Commander William Ellison Pennewill

William Ellison Pennewill, born in Dover, Delaware, on February 20, 1907, was an aviator of the United States Navy killed on June 23, 1942, as a result of a crash. Pennewill was appointed midshipman on June 18, 1925. Commissioned ensign on June 6, 1931, he reported for duty under instruction in flying at the Naval Air Station Pensacola, Florida.

His next duty was in Salt Lake City, then with Scouting Squadron 10–S aboard *Chicago* (CA-29). On March 7, 1932, he reported for duty with the Aircraft Scouting Force until June 2, 1934, when he was transferred to Bombing Squadron 3–B, aboard *Ranger* (CV-4). He returned to the Naval Air Station, Pensacola and on August 2, 1941, joined the 16th Bombardment Wing. After serving at the Savannah Air Base, Geoegia, until March 6, 1942, he was assigned duty involving flying in connection with the fitting out of Escort Scouting Squadron Twelve.[80]

On May 29, 1942, as lieutenant commander, he was in command of the squadron and while serving in this capacity was killed, on June 23, 1942, as a result of an airplane crash while on duty at the Naval Air Station Kodiak, Alaska. He was posthumously awarded the Distinguished Flying Cross for outstanding achievement in aerial flight in contact with the enemy, for leading his inexperienced squadron in a series of remarkable flights over strange terrain and through most severe weather conditions, and for gallantly giving his life in the service of his country.

The USS *Pennewill* (DE-175) was a *Cannon*-class destroyer escort built for the United States Navy during World War II and was named for Lieutenant Commander William E. Pennewill.[81]

Louis William Prost

Louis William Prost of Wilmington piloted a navy airship in World War II. Performing ocean surveillance, he and his crew kept Nazi submarines at bay from U.S. shores and Atlantic convoys. Commander Prost enlisted in the navy in 1942. He took preflight training at the University of Georgia and practical training at Evansville University in Indiana. After winning his pilot wings, he was selected for lighter-than-air training at Moffett Field in California and Lakehurst Naval Air Station, New Jersey.[82]

Prost flew anti-submarine patrols out of South Weymouth, Massachusetts, until the war's end. Though a small group, the 1,500 pilots and 3,000 men of America's fleet of about 125 Goodyear blimps escorted 89,000 Allied ships safely to Europe. They lost only one airship. Prost was awarded the Air Medal for flying from Bermuda to the Azores— the longest wartime flight of an airship. He was copilot on a navy airship that broke the Russian record of 123 hours aloft; the U.S. ship flew for 170 hours. After the war Prost instructed lighter-than-air pilots at Lakehurst, until his discharge in 1947. He remained in the naval reserve until retirement in 1980.[83]

Lieutenant Commander John Keane Reybold

John Keane Reybold, born at Delaware City, Delaware, on January 11, 1903, was appointed midshipman July 13, 1922, and commissioned ensign on June 3,1926. Having served in various ships, including *Idaho*, *Utah*, *Simpson* (on the Asiatic Station), and *Omaha*, he assumed command of *Cowell* on June 17, 1940. Detached on September 23, he briefly commanded *Claxton* and on October 31 assumed command of *Dickerson* (DD-157). Commissioned lieutenant commander on January 1, 1941, he commanded *Dickerson* on Neutrality Patrol and, after December 1941, on coastal patrol and Icelandic convoy escort duty until March 19, 1942. On that date, *Dickerson,* en route to Norfolk, was fired upon by a nervous merchantman, SS *Liberator. Liberator*'s shells hit the destroyer's charthouse, killing Lieutenant Commander Reybold and three others.[84]

U.S. Navy blimp K-23 being walked out onto the field for a test flight December 12, 1942 (80-G-26360, U.S. Naval History and Heritage Command).

USS *Reybold* (DE-177) was laid down on May 3, 1943, by the Federal Shipbuilding and Dry Dock Company, Port Newark, New Jersey, launched as *Reybold* (DE-177) on August 22, 1943—sponsored by Mrs. John K. Reybold, the widow of Lt. Comdr. Reybold—and commissioned on September 29, 1943.[85]

Rear Admiral LeRoy Coard Simpler

LeRoy Coard Simpler was born in Lewes, Delaware, and raised in Milton. He attended the U.S. Naval Academy in 1929 and chose a career in naval aviation. In 1935, as a lieutenant junior grade, he had been on the airship USS *Macon* when it crashed and burned off San Francisco, ending the navy's flirtation with airships

In the late summer and autumn of 1943 Lieutenant Commander Simpler commanded Fighting Squadron Five (VF-5) attached to the aircraft carrier USS *Saratoga* (CV-3), flying F4F-4 Wildcats. While on patrol in the Solomon Islands in the vicinity of Guadalcanal, Simpler's squadron saw repeated combat action, and Simpler was awarded the Distinguished Flying Cross for deeds at this time as recorded in his citation:

> Leading his squadron in a vigorous and determined attack against an enemy air group headed toward our surface forces, Lieutenant Commander Simpler, with utter disregard for his own personal safety, in the face of tremendous anti-aircraft fire, contributed greatly to the aggressive fighting spirit and

high combat efficiency that enabled his squadron to destroy nineteen Japanese aircraft and damage three more.[86]

Simpler was also presented a second award of the Distinguished Flying Cross for actions "during operations against the Japanese-occupied Solomon Islands on 7 August 1942. Boldly leading twelve planes of his squadron in determined and repeated machine gun strafing attacks against enemy land troops and sea installations, Lieutenant Commander Simpler assisted effectively in silencing Japanese opposition and assuring the consummation of our landing operations without undue casualties. His inspiring leadership and loyal devotion to the accomplishment of this important mission were instrumental in the successful invasion of our forces in that area."[87]

During the period of September 11, 1942 through October 6, 1942, Lieutenant Commander Simpler led his fighter squadron "against overwhelming formations of enemy Japanese aircraft in the Solomon Islands area, contributing to the destruction of 17 Japanese planes, and personally shooting down one Zero-type fighter. His squadron accounted for a total of 35 enemy planes during service in the area from 11 September to 6 October 1942." He was awarded the Navy Cross for this series of combat actions.[88] Later in his career, Captain Simpler was awarded the Legion of Merit with Combat "V" "for exceptionally meritorious conduct in the performance of outstanding services to the Government of the United States as Naval Liaison Officer in the Joint Operation Center from 29 June to 27 July 1953."[89] Rear Admiral LeRoy Coard Simpler died in 1988.

Strickland Trewelow

Signalman Third Class Strickland Trewelow of Rehoboth Beach, Delaware, was awarded the Bronze Star by his commanding officer aboard the USS *Haynsworth* for heroic and meritorious achievement on April 6, 1945. When his vessel was hit by an enemy suicide bomber, an intense gasoline fire broke out by his station. He manned a fire hose for cooling a 40mm magazine and maintained his station in spite of the fact that machine gun ammunition from the crashed plane was exploding in all directions about 20 feet away from him.

The Future

During the two world wars the Delaware Valley shipbuilding reached its apogee and was truly the arsenal of democracy in terms of manufacturing and industrial strength. The industrial infrastructure that provides this source of pride began to fade after the war. The old shipyards are mostly gone, and the military facilities and forts that once lined the river and bay are public parks and ruins.

The Delaware estuary remains an important strategic maritime resource, a significant waterway supporting trade and commerce. As a shipbuilding center it is but a pale shadow of its former role as "America's Clyde." Reaching its industrial apex during World War II, it is unlikely we will ever see so many men going to sea in uniform from the Delaware Valley. Nor will we see again the shipyards and fleets of warships of that time. The navy yard is closed, and the shipbuilders have shuttered their facilities, which have been redeveloped. World War II was the last time the United States had an enemy threat approach her shores. Short of an existential threat to the nation, we will not see this level of effort again. The Delaware River has survived pirates, ambitious European powers, the mighty British fleet, and the U-boat menace. Will it someday be tested again? It seems likely the next test will be an ecological or economic threat rather than a military one as sea levels rise with global warming. The strategic importance of the Delaware River and Delaware Bay will remain and will offer an enticing target for a future foe in ways we cannot foresee today.

Appendix 1: Delaware Valley Sailor and Marine Medal of Honor Recipients

This is a list of Delaware Valley sailors and Marine Medal of Honor recipients, broadly interpreted by the author to include natives of the Delaware Valley and those who chose to make their home near the Delaware River and Delaware Bay. These lists are often never quite ideal, depending upon the interpretation of their home of record or origin.[1]

Charles Baldwin

Rank and organization: Coal Heaver, U.S. Navy. Born: 30 June 1839, Smyrna, Delaware. Accredited to: Pennsylvania. G.O. No.: 45, 31 December 1864.

Citation:

U.S. Navy Medal of Honor, Obverse of a Medal of Honor (NH 95030-KN, U.S. Naval History and Heritage Command).

Serving on board the USS *Wyalusing* and participating in a plan to destroy the rebel ram Albermarle in Roanoke River, May 25, 1864. Volunteering for the hazardous mission, C.H. Baldwin participated in the transfer of two torpedoes across an island swamp. Weighted by a line which was used to transfer the torpedoes, he swam the river and, when challenged by a sentry, was forced to abandon the plan after erasing its detection and before it could be carried to completion. Escaping the fire of the muskets, C.H. Baldwin spent two days and nights of hazardous travel without food, and finally arrived, fatigued, at the mother ship.

A navy destroyer was named for him, the USS *Baldwin* (DD-624), launched in 1942.

Edward Barrett

Rank and organization: Second Class Fireman, U.S. Navy. Born: 1855, Philadelphia, Pennsylvania. Accredited to: Pennsylvania. G.O. No.: 326, 18 October 1884.
Citation:

On board the USS *Alaska* at Callao Bay, Peru, 14 September 1881. Following the rupture of the stop-valve chamber, Barrett courageously hauled the fires from under the boiler of that vessel.

Edward C. Benfold

Rank and organization: Hospital Corpsman Third Class, U.S. Navy, attached to a company in the 1st Marine Division. Place and date: Korea, 5 September 1952. Entered service at: Philadelphia, Pennsylvania. Born: 15 January 1931, Staten Island, New York.
Citation:

For gallantry and intrepidity at the risk of his life above and beyond the call of duty while serving in operations against enemy aggressor forces. When his company was subjected to heavy artillery and mortar barrages, followed by a determined assault during the hours of darkness by an enemy force estimated at battalion strength. Benfold resolutely moved from position to position in the face of intense hostile fire, treating the wounded and lending words of encouragement. Leaving the protection of his sheltered position to treat the wounded when the platoon area in which he was working was attacked from both the front and rear, he moved forward to an exposed ridge line where he observed two marines in a large crater. As he approached the two men to determine their condition, an enemy soldier threw two grenades into the crater while two other enemy charged the position. Picking up a grenade in each hand, Benfold leaped out of the crater and hurled himself against the on-rushing hostile soldiers, pushing the grenades against their chests and killing both the attackers. Mortally wounded while carrying out this heroic act, Benfold, by his great personal valor and resolute spirit of self-sacrifice in the face of almost certain death, was directly responsible for saving the lives of his two comrades. His exceptional courage reflects the highest credit upon himself and enhances the finest traditions of the U.S. Naval Service. He gallantly gave his life for others.

Joel Thompson Boone

Rank and organization: Lieutenant (Medical Corps), U.S. Navy. Place and date: Vicinity of Vierzy, France, 19 July 1918. Entered service at: St. Clair, Pennsylvania. Born: August 2, 1889, St. Clair, Pensylvania.
Citation:

For extraordinary heroism, conspicuous gallantry, and intrepidity while serving with the 6th Regiment, U.S. Marines, in actual conflict with the enemy. With absolute disregard for personal safety, ever conscious and mindful of the suffering fallen, Surg. Boone, leaving the shelter of a ravine, went forward onto the open field where there was no protection and despite the extreme enemy fire of all calibers, through a heavy mist of gas, applied dressings and first aid to wounded marines. This occurred southeast of Vierzy, near the cemetery, and on the road south from that town. When the dressings and supplies had been exhausted, he went through a heavy barrage of large-caliber shells, both high explosive and gas, to replenish these supplies, returning quickly with a sidecar load, and administered them in saving the lives of the wounded. A second trip, under the same conditions and for the same purpose, was made by Surgeon Boone later that day.

John Brazell

Rank and organization: Quartermaster, U.S. Navy. Born: 1837, Philadelphia, Pennsylvania. Accredited to: Pennsylvania. G.O. No.: 45, 31 December 1864.

Citation:

Served on board the USS *Richmond* in the action at Mobile Bay, 5 August 1864, where he was recommended for coolness and good conduct as a gun captain during that engagement which resulted in the capture of the rebel ram Tennessee and in the destruction of Fort Morgan. Brazell served gallantly throughout the actions with Forts Jackson and St. Philip, the Chalmettes, batteries below Vicksburg, and was present at the surrender of New Orleans while on board the USS Brooklyn.

Henry Brutsche

Rank and organization: Landsman, U.S. Navy. Born: 1846, Philadelphia, Pennsylvania. Accredited to: Pennsylvania. G.O. No.: 45, 31 December 1864.

Citation:

Served on board the USS *Tacony* during the taking of Plymouth, N.C., 31 October 1864. Carrying out his duties faithfully during the capture of Plymouth, Brutsche distinguished himself by a display of coolness when he participated in landing and spiking a 9-inch gun while under a devastating fire from enemy musketry.

David M. Buchanan

Rank and organization: Apprentice, U.S. Navy. Born: 1862, Philadelphia, Pennsylvania. Accredited to: Pennsylvania. G.O. No.: 246, 22 July 1879.

Citation:

On board the USS *Saratoga* off Battery, New York Harbor, 15 July 1879. On the morning of this date, Robert Lee Robey, apprentice, fell overboard from the after part of the ship into the tide which was running strong ebb at the time and, not being an expert swimmer, was in danger of drowning. Instantly springing over the rail after him, Buchanan never hesitated for an instant to remove even a portion of his clothing. Both men were picked up by the ship's boat following this act of heroism.

Smedley Darlington Butler

Rank and organization: Major, U.S. Marine Corps. Born July 30, 1881, West Chester Pennsylvania. Appointed from Pennsylvania. G.O. No. 177, 4 December 1915. Other Navy awards: Second Medal of Honor, Distinguished Service Medal

Citation:

For distinguished conduct in battle, engagement of Vera Cruz, 22 April 1914. Maj. Butler was eminent and conspicuous in command of his battalion. He exhibited courage and skill in leading his men through the action of the 22d and in the final occupation of the city.

Second Citation:

As Commanding Officer of detachments from the 5th, 13th, 23d Companies and the marine and sailor detachment from the USS Connecticut, Maj. Butler led the attack on Fort Riviere, Haiti, 17 November 1915. Following a concentrated drive, several different detachments of marines gradually closed in on the old French bastion fort in an effort to cut off all avenues of retreat for the Caco bandits. Reaching the fort on the southern side where there was a small opening in the wall, Maj. Butler gave the signal to attack and marines from the 15th Company poured through the breach, engaged the Cacos in hand-to-hand combat, took the bastion and crushed the Caco resistance. Throughout this perilous action, Maj. Butler was conspicuous for his bravery and forceful leadership.

Leonard Chadwick

Apprentice First Class U.S. Navy, USS *Marblehead*

Citation:

"On board the USS *Marblehead* during the operation of cutting the cable leading from Cientuegos, Cuba, 11 May 1898. Facing the heavy fire of the enemy, Chadwick set an example of extraordinary bravery and coolness throughout this period."

George Robert Cholister

Rank and organization: Boatswain's Mate First Class, U.S. Navy. Born: 18 December 1898, Camden, New Jersey. Accredited to: New Jersey. (Awarded by Special Act of Congress 3 February 1933.)
Citation:

For extraordinary heroism in the line of his profession on the occasion of a fire on board the U.S.S. *Trenton*. At 3:35 on the afternoon of 20 October 1924, while the Trenton was preparing to fire trial installation shots from the two 6-inch guns in the forward twin mount of that vessel, 2 charges of powder ignited. Twenty men were trapped in the twin mount. Four died almost immediately and 10 later from burns and inhalation of flames and gases. The 6 others were severely injured. Cholister, without thought of his own safety, on seeing that the charge of powder from the left gun was ignited, jumped for the right charge and endeavored to put it in the immersion tank. The left charge burst into flame and ignited the right charge before Cholister could accomplish his purpose. He fell unconscious while making a supreme effort to save his shipmates and died the following day.

Robert T. Clifford

Rank and organization: Master-at-Arms, U.S. Navy. Born: 1835, Pennsylvania. Accredited to: Pennsylvania. G.O. No.: 45, 31 December 1864.
Citation:

Served on board the USS *Shokokon* at New Topsail Inlet off Wilmington, N.C., 22 August 1863. Participating in a strategic plan to destroy an enemy schooner, Clifford aided in the portage of a dinghy across the narrow neck of land separating the sea from the sound. Launching the boat in the sound, the crew approached the enemy from the rear and Clifford gallantly crept into the rebel camp and counted the men who outnumbered his party 3 to 1. Returning to his men, he ordered a charge in which the enemy was routed, leaving behind a schooner and a quantity of supplies.

Frank William Crilley

Rank and organization: Chief Gunner's Mate, U.S. Navy. Born: 13 September 1883, Trenton, New Jersey. Accredited to: Pennsylvania. (19 November 1928).
Citation:

For display of extraordinary heroism in the line of his profession above and beyond the call of duty during the diving operations in connection with the sinking in a depth of water 304 feet, of the USS *F-4* with all on board, as a result of loss of depth control, which occurred off Honolulu, T.H., on 25 March 1915. On 17 April 1915, William F. Loughman, chief gunner's mate, U.S. Navy, who had descended to the wreck and had examined one of the wire hawsers attached to it, upon starting his ascent, and when at a depth of 250 feet beneath the surface of the water, had his lifeline and air hose so badly fouled by this hawser that he was unable to free himself; he could neither ascend nor descend. On account of the length of time that Loughman had already been subjected to the great pressure due to the depth of water, and of the uncertainty of the additional time he would have to be subjected to this pressure before he could be brought to the surface, it was imperative that steps be taken at once to clear him. Instantly, realizing the desperate case of his comrade, Crilley volunteered to go to his aid, immediately donned a diving suit and descended. After a lapse of time of 2 hours and 11 minutes, Crilley was brought to the surface, having by a superb exhibition of skill, coolness, endurance and fortitude, untangled the snarl of lines and cleared his imperiled comrade, so that he was brought, still alive, to the surface.

Thomas Cripps

Rank and organization: Quartermaster, U.S. Navy. Born: 1837 Philadelphia, Pennsylvania. Accredited to: Pennsylvania. G.O. No.: 45, 31 December 1864.
Citation:

As captain of a gun on board the USS *Richmond* during action against rebel forts and gunboats and with the ram Tennessee in Mobile Bay, 5 August 1864. Despite damage to his ship and the loss of several men on board as enemy fire raked her decks, Cripps fought his gun with skill and courage throughout a furious 2-hour battle which resulted in the surrender of the rebel ram Tennessee and in the damaging and destruction of batteries at Fort Morgan.

George W. Cutter

Rank and organization: Landsman, U.S. Navy. Born: 1849, Philadelphia, Pennsylvania. Accredited to: Pennsylvania. G.O. No.: 176, 9 July 1872.
Citation:

On board the USS *Powhatan*, Norfolk, Va., 27 May 1872. Jumping overboard on this date, Cutter aided in saving one of the crew of that vessel from drowning.

Charles Deakin

Rank and organization: Boatswain's Mate, U.S. Navy. Born: 1837, New York, New York. Accredited to: Pennsylvania. G.O. No.: 45, 31 December 1864.
Citation:

As captain of a gun on board the USS *Richmond* during action against rebel forts and gunboats and with the ram Tennessee in Mobile Bay, 5 August 1864. Despite damage to his ship and the loss of several men on board as enemy fire raked her decks, Deakin fought his gun with skill and courage throughout a furious 2-hour battle which resulted in the surrender of the rebel ram Tennessee and in the damaging and destruction of batteries at Fort Morgan. He also participated in the actions at Forts Jackson and St. Philip.

John Dempster

Rank and organization: Coxswain, U.S. Navy. Born: 1839, Scotland. Accredited to: Pennsylvania. G.O. No.: 59, 22 June 1865.
Citation:

Dempster served on board the USS *New Ironsides* during action in several attacks on Fort Fisher, 24 and 25 December 1864; and 13, 14, and 15 January 1865. The ship steamed in and took the lead in the ironclad division close inshore and immediately opened its starboard battery in a barrage of well-directed fire to cause several fires and explosions and dismount several guns during the first 2 days of fighting. Taken under fire as she steamed into position on 13 January, the New Ironsides fought all day and took on ammunition at night despite severe weather conditions. When the enemy came out of his bombproofs to defend the fort against the storming party, the ship's battery disabled nearly every gun on the fort facing the shore before the cease-fire orders were given by the flagship.

Ralph E. Dias

Rank and organization: Private First Class, U.S. Marine Corps, 3d Platoon, Company D, 1st Battalion, 7th Marines, 1st Marine Division (Rein) FMF. Place and date: Que Son Mountains, Republic of Vietnam, 12 November 1969. Entered service at: Pittsburgh, Pennsylvania. Born: 15 July 1950, Shelocta, Indiana County, Pennsylvania.
Citation:

As a member of a reaction force which was pinned down by enemy fire while assisting a platoon in the same circumstance, Pfc. Dias, observing that both units were sustaining casualties, initiated an aggressive assault against an enemy machinegun bunker which was the principal source of hostile fire. Severely wounded by enemy snipers while charging across the open area, he pulled himself to the shelter of a nearby rock. Braving enemy fire for a second time, Pfc. Dias was again wounded. Unable to walk, he crawled 15 meters to the protection of a rock located near his objective and, repeatedly exposing himself to intense hostile fire, unsuccessfully threw several hand grenades at the machinegun emplacement. Still determined to destroy the emplacement, Pfc. Dias again moved into the open and was wounded a third time by sniper fire. As he threw a last grenade which destroyed the enemy position, he was mortally wounded by another enemy round. Pfc. Dias' indomitable courage, dynamic initiative, and selfless devotion to duty upheld the highest traditions of the Marine Corps and the U.S. Naval Service. He gallantly gave his life in the service to his country.

William Doolen

Rank and organization: Coal Heaver, U.S. Navy. Born: 1841, Ireland. Accredited to: Pennsylvania. G.O. No.: 45, 31 December 1864.
Citation:

On board the USS *Richmond* during action against rebel forts and gunboats and with the ram Tennessee in Mobile Bay, 5 August 1864. Although knocked down and seriously wounded in the head, Doolen refused to leave his station as shot and shell passed. Calm and courageous, he rendered gallant service throughout the prolonged battle which resulted in the surrender of the rebel ram Tennessee and in the successful attacks carried out on Fort Morgan despite the enemy's heavy return fire.

Frank Du Moulin

Rank and organization: Apprentice, U.S. Navy. Born: 1850, Philadelphia, Pennsylvania. Accredited to: Pennsylvania. G.O. No.: 84, October 1867.
Citation:

On the 5th of September 1867, Du Moulin jumped overboard and saved from drowning Apprentice D'Orsay, who had fallen from the mizzen topmast rigging of the Sabine, in New London Harbor, and was rendered helpless by striking the mizzen rigging and boat davit in the fall.

Austin J. Durney

Rank and organization: Blacksmith, U.S. Navy. Born: 26 November 1867, Philadelphia, Pennsylvania. Entered service at: Woodland, Mo. G.O. No.: 521, 7 July 1899.
Citation:

On board the USS *Nashville* during the operation of cutting the cable leading from Cienfuegos, Cuba, 11 May 1898. Facing the heavy fire of the enemy, Durney set an example of extraordinary bravery and coolness throughout this action.

Walter Atlee Edwards

Rank and organization: Lieutenant Commander, U.S. Navy. Place and date: Sea of Marmora, Turkey, 16 December 1922. Born: 8 November 1886, Philadelphia, Pennsylvania. Accredited to: Pennsylvania. G.O. No.: 123, 4 February 1924 (Medal presented by President Coolidge at the White House on 2 February 1924). Other Navy award: Navy Cross.
Citation:

For heroism in rescuing 482 men, women and children from the French military transport Vinh-Long, destroyed by fire in the Sea of Marmora, Turkey, on 16 December 1922. Lt. Comdr. Edwards, commanding the USS *Bainbridge,* placed his vessel alongside the bow of the transport and, in spite of several violent explosions which occurred on the burning vessel, maintained his ship in that position until all who were alive were taken on board. Of a total of 495 on board, 482 were rescued by his coolness, judgment and professional skill, which were combined with a degree of heroism that must reflect new glory on the U.S. Navy.

Charles Robert Francis

Rank and organization: Private, U.S. Marine Corps. Born: 19 May 1875, Doylestown, Pennsylvania. Accredited to: Pennsylvania. G. O. No.: 55, 19 July 1901.
Citation:

In the presence of the enemy during the battle near Tientsin, China, 21 June 1900, Francis distinguished himself by meritorious conduct.

Isaac N. Fry

Rank and organization: Orderly Sergeant, U.S. Marine Corps. Accredited to: Pennsylvania. G.O. No.: 59, 22 June 1865.
Citation:

On board the USS *Ticonderoga* during attacks on Fort Fisher, 13 to 15 January 1865. As orderly sergeant of marine guard, and captain of a gun, Orderly Sgt. Fry performed his duties with skill and courage as the Ticonderoga maintained a well-placed fire upon the batteries to the left of the palisades during the initial phases of the 3-day battle, and thereafter, as she considerably lessened the firing power of guns on the mount which had been turned upon our assaulting columns. During this action the flag was planted on one of the strongest fortifications possessed by the rebels.

Samuel Gross

(Real name **Samuel Marguiles**)
Rank and organization: Private, U.S. Marine Corps, 23d Co. Born: 9 May 1891, Philadelphia, Pennsylvania. Accredited to: Pennsylvania.
Citation:

In company with members of the 5th, 13th, 23d Companies and the marine and sailor detachment from the USS Connecticut, Gross participated in the attack on Fort Riviere, Haiti, 17 November 1915. Following a concentrated drive, several different detachments of marines gradually closed in on the old French bastion fort in an effort to cut off all avenues of retreat for the Caco bandits. Approaching a breach in the wall which was the only entrance to the fort, Gross was the second man to pass through the breach in the face of constant fire from the Cacos and, thereafter, for a 10-minute period, engaged the enemy in desperate hand-to-hand combat until the bastion was captured and Caco resistance neutralized.

Edmund Haffee

Rank and organization: Quarter Gunner, U.S. Navy. Born: 1832, Philadelphia, Pennsylvania. Accredited to: Pennsylvania. G.O. No.: 59, 22 June 1865.
Citation:

Haffee served on board the USS *New Ironsides* during action in several attacks on Fort Fisher, 24 and 25 December 1864; and 13, 14, and 15 January 1865. The ship steamed in and took the lead in the ironclad division close inshore, and immediately opened its starboard battery in a barrage of well-directed fire to cause several fires and explosions and dismount several guns during the first 2 days of fighting. Taken under fire, as she steamed into position on 13 January, the New Ironsides fought all day and took on ammunition at night despite severe weather conditions. When the enemy came out of his bombproof to defend the fort against the storming party, the ship's battery disabled nearly every gun on the fort facing the shore before the cease-fire orders were given by the flagship.

Richard Hamilton

Rank and organization: Coal Heaver, U.S. Navy. Born: 1836, Philadelphia, Pennsylvania. Accredited to: Pennsylvania G.O. No.: 45, 31 December 1864.
Citation:

Hamilton served on board the U.S. *Picket Boat No. 1*, in action, 27 October 1864, against the Confederate ram Albemarle which had resisted repeated attacks by our steamers and had kept a large force of vessels employed in watching her. The picket boat, equipped with a spar torpedo, succeeded in passing the enemy pickets within 20 yards without being discovered and then made for the Albemarle under a full head of steam. Immediately taken under fire by the ram, the small boat plunged on, jumped the log boom which encircled the target and exploded its torpedo under the port bow of the ram. The picket boat was destroyed by enemy fire and almost the entire crew taken prisoner or lost.

Alexander Hand

Rank and organization: Quartermaster, U.S. Navy, USS *Ceres*. Born in Delaware in 1836, Alexander Hand enlisted in the U.S. Navy in May 1861 for three years. He was noted as being 5 foot 9 inches tall, dark complexioned with blue eyes. Alexander was assigned briefly to the USS *Allegheny*, USS *Brandywine*, and the Washington (D.C.) Navy Yard before being assigned to the USS *Ceres* on September 1, 1861. The USS *Ceres* was a 4th rate side-wheel steamer of 144 tons with a 40-man crew. It was armed with one rifled 30-Pounder and one 32-Pounder gun.[2] The USS *Ceres* was assigned to Major General Ambrose Burnside during his expedition to the Hatteras Inlets in North Carolina. The expedition was assigned to land 15,000 soldiers in the rear of the main Confederate Army and disrupt their supply lines.

On the morning of February 8, 1862, the USS *Ceres* opened fire on Fort Barlow at Pork Point, North Carolina, with its 32-Pounder and on rebel steamers with its rifled 30-pounder. While loading the 32-pounder, Alexander Hand was slightly wounded by the premature discharge of the gun. Overwhelmed by the landing of Union troops and outgunned, the Confederates gave up 40 pieces of artillery and 3,000 prisoners. After this initial assault, a mopping-up expedition continued throughout the summer months. On July 9 a show of force was deemed necessary in front of the town of Hamilton, and the USS *Ceres* along with other ships steamed toward that destination. Leaving their base in Plymouth, North Carolina, the ships chugged on past the towns of Williamson and

Jamesville on their 40-mile journey to Hamilton. They had not gone far when they were fired on by thick lines of rebel sharpshooters on both sides of the banks of the river. The ships returned the fire for two hours while moving onward toward their appointed destination. During this fire two men were killed and ten were wounded. When they finally reached Hamilton it was deserted.

For his part, Quartermaster Hand had courageously returned the fire of the sharpshooters during the attacks and was commended by his commander for his brave conduct. This commander recommended Hand and 2nd class Fireman John Kelley for the Medal of Honor. On April 3, 1863, General Order #11 came down bestowing the Medal of Honor on Alexander Hand, making him one of the first honorees of the medal. Two months later he was discharged. After his discharge Hand entered the 1st Delaware Infantry as a substitute. It appears that he spent his entire army service in the hospital from the injuries received in the navy. By 1879 he was living on the farm of Halbert Hoffman of Baltimore County, Maryland. By 1880, in the last trace of him, he was reported as receiving a pension of $6.00 a month.[3]

Citation:

> Fired on by the enemy with small arms, Quartermaster Hand, U.S. Navy, while serving on the USS *Ceres* in the Roanoke River near Hamilton, North Carolina, courageously returned the raking fire and was spoken of for "good conduct and cool bravery under enemy fire," by his commanding officer in the erection of barricades.

Joseph Edwin Hill

Rank and organization: Chief Boatswain, U.S. Navy. Born: 4 October 1894, Philadelphia, Pennsylvania. Accredited to: Pennsylvania.

Citation:

> For distinguished conduct in the line of his profession, extraordinary courage, and disregard of his own safety during the attack on the Fleet in Pearl Harbor, by Japanese forces on 7 December 1941. During the height of the strafing and bombing, Chief Boatswain Hill led his men of the line handling details of the USS *Nevada* to the quays, cast off the lines and swam back to his ship. Later, while on the forecastle, attempting to let go the anchors, he was blown overboard and killed by the explosion of several bombs.

William Charlie Horton

Rank and organization: Private, U.S. Marine Corps. Place and date: Peking, China, 21 July to 17 August 1900. Entered service at: Pennsylvania. Born: 21 July 1876, Chicago, Ill. G. O. No.: 55, 19 July 1901.

Citation:

> In action against the enemy at Peking, China, 21 July to 17 August 1900. Although under heavy fire from the enemy, Horton assisted

John Johnson

Rank and organization: Seaman, U.S. Navy. Born: 1839, Philadelphia, Pennsylvania. Accredited to: Pennsylvania. G.O. No.: 176, 9 July 1872.

Citation:

> Serving on board the USS *Kansas* near Greytown, Nicaragua 12 April 1872, Johnson displayed great

coolness and self-possession at the time Comdr. A.F. Crosman and others were drowned and, by extraordinary heroism and personal exertion, prevented greater loss of life.

William Jones

Rank and organization: Captain of the Top, U.S. Navy. Born: 1831, Philadelphia, Pennsylvania. Accredited to: Pennsylvania. G.O. No.: 45, 31 December 1864.

Citation:

As captain of a gun on board the USS *Richmond* during action against rebel forts and gunboats and with the ram Tennessee in Mobile Bay, 5 August 1864. Despite damage to his ship and the loss of several men on board as enemy fire raked her decks, Jones fought his gun with skill and courage throughout the prolonged battle which resulted in the surrender of the rebel ram Tennessee and in the damaging and destruction of batteries at Fort Morgan.

John D. Kelley

Rank and organization: Private First Class, U.S. Marine Corps, Company C, 1st Battalion, 7th Marines, 1st Marine Division (Rein.). Place and date: Korea, 28 May 1952. Entered service at: Homestead, Pennsylvania. Born: 8 July 1928, Youngstown, Ohio.

Citation:

For conspicuous gallantry and intrepidity at the risk of his life above and beyond the call of duty while serving as a radio operator of Company C, in action against enemy aggressor forces. With his platoon pinned down by a numerically superior enemy force employing intense mortar, artillery, small-arms and grenade fire, Pfc. Kelley requested permission to leave his radio in the care of another man and to participate in an assault on enemy key positions. Fearlessly charging forward in the face of a murderous hail of machine gun fire and hand grenades, he initiated a daring attack against a hostile strongpoint and personally neutralized the position, killing 2 of the enemy. Unyielding in the fact of heavy odds, he continued forward and single-handedly assaulted a machine gun bunker. Although painfully wounded, he bravely charged the bunker and destroyed it, killing 3 of the enemy. Courageously continuing his 1-man assault, he again stormed forward in a valiant attempt to wipe out a third bunker and boldly delivered pointblank fire into the aperture of the hostile emplacement. Mortally wounded by enemy fire while carrying out this heroic action, Pfc. Kelley, by his great personal valor and aggressive fighting spirit, inspired his comrades to sweep on, overrun and secure the objective. His extraordinary heroism in the face of almost certain death reflects the highest credit upon himself and enhances the finest traditions of the U.S. Naval Service. He gallantly gave his life for his country.

John Lawson

Rank and organization: Landsman, U.S. Navy. Born: 1837, Pennsylvania. Accredited to: Pennsylvania. G.O. No.: 45, 31 December 1864.

Citation:

On board the flagship USS *Hartford* during successful attacks against Fort Morgan, rebel gunboats and the ram Tennessee in Mobile Bay on 5 August 1864. Wounded in the leg and thrown violently against the side of the ship when an enemy shell killed or wounded the 6-man crew as the shell whipped on the berth deck, Lawson, upon regaining his composure, promptly returned to his station and, although urged to go below for treatment, steadfastly continued his duties throughout the remainder of the action.

Nicholas Lear

Rank and organization: Quartermaster, U.S. Navy. Born: 1826, Rhode Island. Accredited to: Pennsylvania. G.O. No.: 59, 22 June 1865.

Citation:

Lear served on board the USS *New Ironsides* during action in several attacks on Fort Fisher, 24 and 25 December 1864; and 13, 14, and 15 January 1865. The ship steamed in and took the lead in the ironclad division close inshore and immediately opened its starboard battery in a barrage of well-directed fire to cause several fires and explosions and dismount several guns during the first 2 days of fighting. Taken under fire as she steamed into position on 13 January, the New Ironsides fought all day and took on ammunition at night despite severe weather conditions. When the enemy came out of his bombproofs to defend the fort against the storming party, the ship's battery disabled nearly every gun on the fort facing the shore before the cease-fire order was given by the flagship.

Pierre Leon

Rank and organization: Captain of the Forecastle, U.S. Navy. Born: 1837, New Orleans, Louisiana. Accredited to: Pennsylvania. G.O. No.: 11, 3 April 1863.
Citation:

Serving on board the USS *Baron De Kalb*, Yazoo River Expedition, 23 to 27 December 1862. Proceeding under orders up the Yazoo River, the USS Baron De Kalb, with the object of capturing or destroying the enemy's transports, came upon the steamers John Walsh, R. J. Locklan, Golden Age and the Scotland sunk on a bar where they were ordered fired. Continuing up the river, she was fired on, but upon returning the fire, caused the enemy's retreat. Returning down the Yazoo, she destroyed and captured larger quantities of enemy equipment and several prisoners. Serving bravely throughout this action, Leon, as captain of the forecastle, "distinguished himself in the various actions."

William Levery

Rank and organization: Apprentice First Class, U.S. Navy. Born: 3 June 1879, Pennsylvania. Accredited to: Pennsylvania. G.O. No.: 521, 7 July 1899.
Citation:

On board the USS *Marblehead* during the operation of cutting the cable leading from Cienfuegos, Cuba, 11 May 1898. Facing the heavy fire of the enemy, Levery displayed extraordinary bravery and coolness throughout this action.

Benjamin Lloyd

Rank and organization: Coal Heaver, U.S. Navy. Born: 1839. England. Accredited to: Pennsylvania. G.O. No.: 45, 31 December 1864.
Citation:

Serving on board the *USS Wyalusing* and participating in a plan to destroy the rebel ram Albemarle in Roanoke River, 25 May 1864. Volunteering for the hazardous mission, Lloyd participated in the transfer of two torpedoes across an island swamp. Serving as boatkeeper, he aided in rescuing others of the party who had been detected before the plan could be completed, but who escaped, leaving detection of the plan impossible. By his skill and courage, Lloyd succeeded in returning to the mother ship after spending 24 hours of discomfort in the rain and swamp.

Harry Lewis MacNeal

Rank and organization: Private, U.S. Marine Corps. Born: 22 March 1875, Philadelphia, Pennsylvania. Accredited to: Pennsylvania. G.O. No.: 526, 9 August 1899.
Citation:

On board the USS *Brooklyn* during action at the Battle of Santiago de Cuba, 3 July 1898. Braving the fire of the enemy, MacNeal displayed gallantry throughout this action.

Edward S. Martin

Rank and organization: Quartermaster, U.S. Navy. Born: 1840, Ireland. Accredited to: Pennsylvania. G.O. No.: 59, 22 June 1865.

Citation:

On board the USS *Calena* during the attack on enemy forts at Mobile Bay, 5 August 1864. Securely lashed to the side of the Oneida which had suffered the loss of her steering apparatus and an explosion of her boiler from enemy fire, the Calena aided the stricken vessel past the enemy forts to safety. Despite heavy damage to his ship from raking enemy fire, Martin performed his duties with skill and courage throughout the action.

Frederick W. Mausert III

Rank and organization: Sergeant, U.S. Marine Corps, Company B, 1st Battalion, 7th Marines, 1st Marine Division (Rein.) Place and date: Songnap-yong, Korea, 12 September 1951. Entered service at: Dresher, Pennsylvania. Born: 2 May 1930, Cambridge, N.Y.

Citation:

For conspicuous gallantry and intrepidity at the risk of his life above and beyond the call of duty while serving as a squad leader in Company B, in action against enemy aggressor forces. With his company pinned down and suffering heavy casualties under murderous machine gun, rifle, artillery, and mortar fire laid down from heavily fortified, deeply entrenched hostile strongholds on Hill 673, Sgt. Mausert unhesitatingly left his covered position and ran through a heavily mined and fire-swept area to bring back 2 critically wounded men to the comparative safety of the lines. Staunchly refusing evacuation despite a painful head wound sustained during his voluntary act, he insisted on remaining with his squad and, with his platoon ordered into the assault moments later, took the point position and led his men in a furious bayonet charge against the first of a literally impregnable series of bunkers. Stunned and knocked to the ground when another bullet struck his helmet, he regained his feet and resumed his drive, personally silencing the machine gun and leading his men in eliminating several other emplacements in the area. Promptly reorganizing his unit for a renewed fight to the final objective on top of the ridge, Sgt. Mausert boldly left his position when the enemy's fire gained momentum and, making a target of himself, boldly advanced alone into the face of the machine gun, drawing the fire away from his men and enabling them to move into position to assault. Again, severely wounded when the enemy's fire found its mark, he still refused aid and continued spearheading the assault to the topmost machine gun nest and bunkers, the last bulwark of the fanatic aggressors. Leaping into the wall of fire, he destroyed another machine gun with grenades before he was mortally wounded by bursting grenades and machine gun fire. Stouthearted and indomitable, Sgt. Mausert, by his fortitude, great personal valor, and extraordinary heroism in the face of almost certain death, had inspired his men to sweep on, overrun and finally secure the objective. His unyielding courage throughout reflects the highest credit upon himself and the U.S. Naval Service. He gallantly gave his life for his country.

Hugh Miller

Rank and organization: Boatswain's Mate, U.S. Navy. Born: 1859 Philadelphia, Pennsylvania. Accredited to: Pennsylvania. (Letter Capt. N. Judlow U.S. Navy, No. 8326/B; 21 November 1885.)

Citation:

For jumping overboard from the USS *Quinnebaug,* at Alexandria, Egypt, on the morning of 21 November 1885 and assisting in saving a shipmate from drowning.

Joseph Mitchell

Rank and organization: Gunner's Mate First Class, U.S. Navy. Born: 27 November 1876, Philadelphia, Pennsylvania. Accredited to: Pennsylvania. G.O. No.: 55, 19 July 1901.
Citation:

In the presence of the enemy during the battle of Peking, China, 12 July 1900, Mitchell distinguished himself by meritorious conduct.

Louis Fred Pfeifer

Rank and organization: Private, U.S. Marine Corps (served as **Theis, Louis F.**, during first enlistment). Born: 19 June 1876, Philadelphia, Pennsylvania. Accredited to: New Jersey. G.O. No.: 85, 22 March 1902.
Citation:

Serving on board the USS *Petrel*; for heroism and gallantry, fearlessly exposing his own life to danger for the saving of the others on the occasion of the fire on board that vessel, 31 March 1901.

Hugh Purvis

Rank and organization: Private, U.S. Marine Corps. Born: 5 March 1846, Philadelphia, Pennsylvania. Accredited to: Pennsylvania. G.O. No.: 169, 8 February 1872.
Citation:

On board the USS *Alaska* during the attack on and capture of the Korean forts, 11 June 1871. Braving the enemy fire, Purvis was the first to scale the walls of the fort and capture the flag of the Korean forces.

William Rees Rush

Rank and organization: Captain, U.S. Navy. Born: 19 September 1857, Philadelphia, Pennsylvania. Accredited to: Pennsylvania. G.O. No.: 177, 4 December 1915. Other Navy award: Distinguished Service Medal.
Citation:

For distinguished conduct in battle, engagements of Vera Cruz, 21 and 22 April 1914. In command of the naval brigade, Capt. Rush was in both days' fighting and almost continually under fire from soon after landing, about noon on the 21st, until we were in possession of the city, about noon of the 22d. His duties required him to be at points of great danger in directing his officers and men, and he exhibited conspicuous courage, coolness and skill in his conduct of the fighting. Upon his courage and skill depended in great measure success or failure. His responsibilities were great, and he met them in a manner worthy of commendation.

Aaron Sanderson

Rank and organization: Landsman, U.S. Navy. Entered service at: Philadelphia, Pennsylvania. Birth: North Carolina. G.O. No.: 59, 22 June 1865.
Citation:

The President of the United States of America, in the name of Congress, takes pleasure in presenting the Medal of Honor to Landsman Aaron Sanderson, United States Navy, for extraordinary heroism in action while serving on board the USS *Wyandank* during a boat expedition up Mattox Creek, Virginia, 17 March 1865. Participating with a boat crew in the clearing of Mattox Creek, Landsman Anderson carried out his duties courageously in the face of a devastating fire which cut away half the oars, pierced the launch in many places and cut the barrel off a musket being fired at the enemy.

General Orders: War Department, General Orders No. 59 (June 22, 1865)
Action Date: March 17, 1865.

Isaac Sapp

Rank and organization: Seaman, Engineer's Force, U.S. Navy. Born: 1844, Philadelphia, Pennsylvania. Accredited to: Pennsylvania. G.O. No.: 169, 8 February 1872.
Citation:

On board the USS *Shenandoah* during the rescue of a shipmate at Villefranche, 15 December 1871. Jumping overboard, Sapp gallantly assisted in saving Charles Prince, seaman, from drowning.

Oscar Schmidt, Jr.

Rank and organization: Chief Gunner's Mate, U.S. Navy. Place and date: At sea, 9 October 1918. Entered service at: Pennsylvania. Born: 25 March 1896, Philadelphia, Pennsylvania. G. O. No.: 450, 1919.
Citation:

For gallant conduct and extraordinary heroism while attached to the USS *Chestnut Hill*, on the occasion of the explosion and subsequent fire on board the U.S. submarine chaser 219. Schmidt, seeing a man, whose legs were partly blown off, hanging on a line from the bow of the 219, jumped overboard, swam to the sub chaser and carried him from the bow to the stern where a member of the 219's crew helped him land the man on the afterdeck of the submarine. Schmidt then endeavored to pass through the flames amidships to get another man who was seriously burned. This he was unable to do, but when the injured man fell overboard and drifted to the stern of the chaser Schmidt helped him aboard.

James A. Stewart

Rank and organization: Corporal, U.S. Marine Corps. Born: 1839, Philadelphia, Pennsylvania. Accredited to: Pennsylvania. G.O. No.: 180, 10 October 1872.
Citation:

Serving on board the USS *Plymouth*, Stewart jumped overboard in the harbor of Villefranche, France, 1 February 1872 and saved Midshipman Osterhaus from drowning.

William G. Taylor

Rank and organization: Captain of the Forecastle, U.S. Navy. Born: 1831, Philadelphia, Pennsylvania. Accredited to: Pennsylvania. G.O. No.: 59, 22 June 1865.
Citation:

On board the USS *Ticonderoga* during attacks on Fort Fisher, 24 and 25 December 1864. As captain of a gun, Taylor performed his duties with coolness and skill as his ship took position in the line of battle and delivered its fire on the batteries on shore. Despite the depressing effect caused when an explosion of the 100-pounder Parrott rifle killed 8 men and wounded 12 more, and the enemy's heavy return fire, he calmly remained at his station during the 2 days' operations.

William Thompson

Rank and organization: Signal Quartermaster, U.S. Navy. Entered service at: Boston, Massachusetts. Birth: Cape May County, N.J. G.O. No.: 17, 10 July 1863.

Citation:

During action of the main squadron of ships against heavily defended Forts Beauregard and Walker on Hilton Head, 7 November 1861. Serving as signal quartermaster on board the USS *Mohican*, Thompson steadfastly steered the ship with a steady and bold heart under the batteries; was wounded by a piece of shell but remained at his station until he fell from loss of blood. Legs since amputated.

James M. Trout

Rank and organization: Second Class Fireman, U.S. Navy. Born: 1850, Philadelphia, Pennsylvania. Accredited to: Pennsylvania.
Citation:

Serving on board the USS *Frolic*, Trout displayed gallant conduct in endeavoring to save the life of one of the crew of that vessel who had fallen overboard at Montevideo, 20 April 1877.

First-Class Fireman Joseph E. Vantine, USN, (1835–1904)

Joseph E. Vantine was born in Philadelphia, Pennsylvania, in March 1835. He served in the U.S. Navy during the Civil War as a crewmember of USS *Richmond*. Vantine took part in the attack on Port Hudson on March 14, 1863, when Rear Admiral Farragut tried to move the Union navy up the Mississippi River to stop Confederate use of the river. After Richmond's fireroom was filled with steam by an enemy shot, Vantine entered the steam-filled room and hauled hot fires from the furnaces until the room was safe. He was awarded the Medal of Honor for his performance. Joseph E. Vantine died on May 5, 1904, and is buried at New Castle, Delaware.
Citation:

The President of the United States of America, in the name of Congress, takes pleasure in presenting the Medal of Honor to First Class Fireman Joseph E. Vantine, United States Navy, for extraordinary heroism in action while serving on board the USS *Richmond* in the attack on Port Hudson, Louisiana, 14 March 1863. Damaged by a 6-inch solid rifle shot which shattered the starboard safety-valve chamber and also damaged the port safety valve, the fireroom of the Richmond immediately filled with steam to place it in an extremely critical condition. Acting courageously in this crisis, First Class Fireman Vantine persisted in penetrating the steam-filled room in order to haul the hot fires of the furnaces and continued this action until the gravity of the situation had been lessened.

Joseph White

Rank and organization: Captain of the Gun, U.S. Navy. Born: 1840, Washington, D.C. Accredited to: Pennsylvania. G.O. No.: 59, 22 June 1865.
Citation:

White served on board the USS *New Ironsides* during action in several attacks on Fort Fisher, 24 and 25 December 1864; and 13,14, and 15 January 1865. The ship steamed in and took the lead in the ironclad division close inshore and immediately opened its starboard battery in a barrage of well-directed fire to cause several fires and explosions and dismount several guns during the first 2 days of fighting. Taken under fire as she steamed into position on 13 January, the New Ironsides fought all day and took on ammunition at night despite severe weather conditions. When the enemy came out of his bombproofs to defend the fort against the storming party, the ships battery disabled nearly every gun on the fort facing the shore before the ceasefire order was given by the flagship.

Richard Willis

Rank and organization: Coxswain, U.S. Navy. Born: 1826, England. Accredited to: Pennsylvania. G.O. No.: 59, 22 June 1865.

Citation:

Willis served on board the USS *New Ironsides* during action in several attacks on Fort Fisher, 24 and 25 December 1864; and 13, 14 and 15 January 1865. The ship steamed in and took the lead in the ironclad division close inshore and immediately opened its starboard battery in a barrage of well-directed fire to cause several fires and explosions and dismount several guns during the first 2 days of fighting. Taken under fire as she steamed into position on 13 January, the New Ironsides fought all day and took on ammunition at night, despite severe weather conditions. When the enemy troops came out of their bombproofs to defend the fort against the storming party, the ship's battery disabled nearly every gun on the fort facing the shore before the ceasefire order was given by the flagship.

Appendix 2:
Delaware-Built Civil War Vessels

Delaware-Built Union Ships[1]

USS *Amaranthus* was a wooden screw tug built in Wilmington in 1864. She served as a tug and storeship with the South Atlantic Squadron until decommission in August 1865. She became a merchantman and was renamed *Christiana*.

USS *Aster* was a wooden screw steamer tug built in Wilmington and was originally named *Alice*. She was wrecked at Carolina Shoals on October 8, 1864.

USS *Clinton* was a Wilmington-built tugboat launched in 1863. Her primary task was to guide ships in harbors, but she was also tasked with patrol duties. The first ship to be named *Clinton* by the navy, this screw tug was purchased June 14, 1864, under the name *Lena Clinton*. She was assigned to duty with the North Atlantic Blockading Squadron for picket and tug service in the James River and at Norfolk Navy Yard until the end of the war.

USS *Hatteras* was a 1,126-ton side-wheel steamer. A second *Saint Mary* was completed by Harlan and Hollingsworth in 1862 and renamed the USS *Hatteras* to assist in the blockade of Galveston. She was outfitted at the Philadelphia Navy Yard as a gunboat and assigned to the Union blockade of the Confederacy in October 1861

Hatteras sailed for Key West, Florida, on November 5, 1861, to join the South Atlantic Blockading Squadron to choke off the South's economic lifeline as part of Lincoln's Anaconda Plan. On January 16 *Hatteras* made a highly successful raid on the Cedar Keys harbor, burning seven small blockade-runners loaded with turpentine and cotton, several flat cars, and various buildings. To cap this day's work, *Hatteras* also captured 14 of the 22-man garrison stationed there. Such unceasing attack from the sea on any point along her long coastline and inland waterways cost the South dearly in losses, economic disruption, and dispersion of defense strength. After this exploit, *Hatteras* was transferred to the Gulf Blockading Squadron. On January 27 she engaged CSS *Mobile* but failed to do any serious damage.

In less than a year *Hatteras* captured seven blockade runners with assorted cargos of cotton, sugar, and other goods the South was desperately striving to export for gold or much-needed trade goods. These captures netted *Hatteras*, among other things, some 534 bales of valuable cotton. Commander Emmons stationed four of his own men onboard one prize ship, the sloop *Poody*, and rechristened her *Hatteras Jr.*, turning the erstwhile blockade-runner into a unit of the Union's Gulf Blockading Squadron.

Other Confederate ships taken by *Hatteras* as prizes included steamer *Indian No. 2*, schooner *Magnolia*, steamer *Governor A. Mouton*, schooner *Sarah*, sloop *Elizabeth*, and brig *Josephine*. The majority of these ships were captured off Vermilion Bay, Louisiana. However, her illustrious career was cut short in early 1863, not long after she was ordered to join the blockading squadron under Rear Admiral David Farragut, who was attempting to retake the key Texas port of Galveston. *Hatteras* joined Farragut's squadron off Galveston on January 6, 1863.

The Confederate Raider CSS *Alabama* had been wreaking havoc on Union merchant shipping while cruising from the Azores to the mid–Atlantic then off New England then the East Coast and then the Caribbean. In all, she had captured 20 ships. She met her first Union warship at the end of that cruise off Galveston Texas.

As the blockading fleet lay to off the coast near Galveston on the afternoon of January 11, 1863, a set of sails was sighted just over the horizon and *Hatteras* was ordered to give chase. She took off in pursuit of the unknown ship and followed her as she ventured closer and closer to shore. Finally, as dusk was falling, *Hatteras* came within hailing distance of the square-rigged ship. Commander Blake demanded her identity. "Her Britannic Majesty's Ship *Petrel*," came the reply. Still suspicious, Blake ordered one of *Hatteras*'s boats to inspect this "Britisher. Scarcely had the longboat pulled away from *Hatteras* than a new reply to Blake's question rang through the night: "We are the CSS *Alabama*." With this, the famed Confederate raider began raking *Hatteras* with her heavy cannon. Through the gloom, for about 20 minutes, the two ships exchanged heavy fire at distances ranging from 25 to 200 yards (23–183 m). The flashes of the guns and their rumbling were heard in the Union squadron some 16 mi (26 km) away, and the cruiser *Brooklyn* was dispatched to investigate and render aid if needed.

But *Hatteras* had already been badly holed in two places and was on fire and beginning to sink. Captain Blake ordered the magazines flooded to prevent explosion and reluctantly fired a single bow gun, indicating surrender and a need for assistance. *Alabama* promptly sent over her boats to help remove *Hatteras*'s crew and wounded. The last boatload of men had barely pulled away when the Union blockader sank, some 45 minutes after the beginning of the action. Of *Hatteras*'s crew of 126, two had been killed and five wounded. Six escaped back to the squadron in the boat originally sent out to board and investigate "HMS *Petrel*," and the remainder, including Captain Blake, were taken to Jamaica and from there paroled back to the United States. *Alabama* suffered only 2 wounded.

When *Brooklyn* reached the site of the battle early the following morning, she found the hulk of *Hatteras* upright in the water south of Galveston Light. Only *Hatteras*'s masts reached out of the water, and from the topmast the U.S. Navy commissioning pennant was still waving in the breeze. Even after surrendering, she had not struck her colors.

After this encounter *Alabama* moved to the South Atlantic then the Indian Ocean and the South Pacific then finally returned to France. By then it had intercepted more than 200 ships and taken or burned 65 prizes. In June 1864 it arrived in Cherbourg France. As it left it encountered USS *Kearsarge* off France and was sunk.

USS *Jonquil* was a wooden-hulled screw steamer tug originally named *J.K. Kirkman*, built in Wilmington and acquired in 1863. She was decommissioned on October 21, 1865.

USS *Larkspur* (1863) was a steamer-tug built in Wilmington in 1863 as *Pontiac*. She was used by the navy as a tugboat. The new tug was assigned to the South Atlantic Blockading Squadron based at Port Royal, South Carolina. She served there during most of the remainder of the Civil War towing and repairing the ships of the blockade, steaming along the Confederate coast gathering information about activity ashore, carrying messages between ships of the squadron, and providing countless other services that helped the Union navy strangle the South.

On December 8 she was ordered to St. Simons Sound, Georgia, to seek word of General Sherman's army, which was expected to end his famous march to the sea. Four days later she was sent to Savannah to assist the Union army after it reached the sea. During the remainder of the war the tug operated at Charleston and Port Royal. She decommissioned in Philadelphia on July 8, 1865.

USS *Louisiana* was built in 1860 by the Harlan and Hollingsworth Iron Shipbuilding Company. She was an iron-hulled screw steamer with two funnels rigged as a schooner with three masts. *Louisiana* was purchased by the Navy at Philadelphia July 10, 1861.

Assigned to the North Atlantic Blockading Squadron, *Louisiana* operated along the Virginia coast, blocking the passage of blockade-runners and attacking them at their bases. She participated in the battle for Roanoke Island, which denied the use of coastal inlets and seaboard towns to the blockade runners and tied down Confederate troops. On September 13, 1861, with the *Savannah*, *Louisiana* engaged CSS *Patrick Henry*, but shot from both sides fell short. Two of her boats destroyed a schooner fitting out as a Confederate privateer near Chincoteague Inlet and two days later she captured the schooner *S.T. Carrison* with a cargo of wood near Wallops Island. *Louisiana*'s boats surprised and burned three Confederate vessels at Chincoteague Inlet on October 28 and 29.

On January 2, 1862, *Louisiana* was ordered to Hatteras Inlet to prepare for the invasion of the Carolina sounds. For the next three years she patrolled, supported army troops, and made raids along the intricate water system whose eventual capture would be a mortal blow to the Confederacy. She captured the schooner *Alice L. Webb* on November 5, 1862, then joined in the army–navy expedition that captured Greenville, four days later. On May 20, 1863, one of her boat crews captured a still-unrigged schooner in the Tar River.

Fort Fisher, guarding Wilmington, North Carolina, was the key to the base Northern commanders foresaw the South employing after the fall of Charleston. Commodore David Porter and Maj. Gen. Benjamin Butler, knowing that an assault on so powerful a defense would be long and costly, hoped to reduce it by blowing up an explosive-laden ship under its walls. *Louisiana* was designated for this assignment, and early in December she proceeded to be partially stripped and laden with explosives. She left Hampton Roads December 13 in tow of *Sassacus* and five days later arrived off Fort Fisher. Here *Wilderness* took up the tow. The final attempt was made on December 23, when *Wilderness* brought *Louisiana* into position under Fort Fisher late in the evening. Commander Rhind and his crew lit the fuses and kindled a fire aft, then escaped in small boats to *Wilderness*, waiting anxiously for the fuses to explode. They failed, but the fire set aft worked its way from the stern to the powder and blew *Louisiana* up as planned but with little effect.

USS *Para* was a wooden schooner built in Wilmington in 1860. She was used by the navy to patrol navigable waterways of the Confederate states to prevent the South from trading with other countries. She was assigned first to the Gulf Squadron and participated in the bombardment of Forts Jackson and St. Philip April 18–24, 1862. Transferred to the South Atlantic Blockading Squadron, she operated along the southeastern coasts for the remainder of the war. *Para* captured the blockade-runner *Emma* in June 1863. In New Smyrna, Florida, she captured a sloop and an unladen schooner, burnt several vessels, and destroyed all buildings that had been occupied by troops. She escorted troops up the St. Mary's River to obtain lumber and engaged Confederate forces along the riverbanks to cover the transports as they took on the lumber. She captured the steamer *Hard Times* then covered the retirement of the transports February 16–23, 1864. *Para* was decommissioned on August 5, 1865.

USS *Pilgrim* was an iron-hulled screw steamer built by Pusey and Jones as a *Maria*-class tugboat in 1864. Pusey and Jones served as a subcontractor for the Philadelphia Naval Yard building engines and boilers for the federal side-wheelers *Juniata* (1862), *Mingo*, and *Wyalusing* (1863). They built for the army the screw steamers *Stanton*, *Wells*, *Foote*, and *Porter* in 1864 providing engines and boilers.[2] After the war, Pusey and Jones built the revenue cutters *U.S. Grant*, (1871) and *Walter Forward* (1882).[3]

USS *Rescue* was a small (111-ton) iron-hulled steamer built by Harlan and Hollingsworth in 1861. She served the navy during the blockade as a gunship and dispatch boat. After the war's end, *Rescue* continued to serve the navy as a tugboat and fireboat.

Rescue joined the Potomac Flotilla prior to mid-September and took up station near Alexandria, Virginia. On September 18, she seized the schooner *Harford* and her cargo of wheat and tobacco. On October 11 the *Rescue*, with *Resolute* and *Union*, captured and burned the schooner *Martha Washington*, which had been awaiting Confederate troops in Quantico Creek. On October 28, *Rescue* was detached from the Potomac Flotilla and ordered to the Rappahannock River for duty in the North Atlantic Blockading Squadron. On November 6 she captured and burned the schooner *Ada* and on the 8th seized the ammunition storage ship *Urbana*. She was then ordered to Port Royal and duty in Samuel F. Du Pont's squadron, then blockading Charleston.

On September 2, 1863, she resumed duty with the Potomac Flotilla. Stationed in the St. Mary's area, she remained in the Potomac Flotilla through the end of the Civil War. After the war, she proceeded to Washington, D.C., where for the next 24 years she served as a district craft, first as a tug then as a fireboat.

***Willmon Whillden*,** an iron-hulled paddlewheel steamer built by Harlan and Hollingsworth in 1845 (only the fourth iron-hulled vessel built by them), was present at the famous confrontation at Hampton Roads between the *Virginia* (*Merrimac*) and the USS *Cumberland*. As *Cumberland* sank, the *Whillden* raced to the rescue of those sailors. Because she was an early design, the *Whillden*'s boilers were exposed above deck. When she came under fire the *Virginia*'s shells went clean through her boiler, although she survived the encounter.[4]

Union Monitors Built by Harlan and Hollingsworth

Monitors were the first ironclad warship built without rigging or sails, based on a design by John Ericsson. The *Monitor*-class of warship was characterized by spindle-type cylindrical turret bearing twin guns on an iron hull with overhanging armored deck. The iron hull was a box structure with pointed ends.

Monitor USS *Patapsco* (1863–1865). Pencil sketch by an unidentified artist depicting the ship engaging Confederate batteries on Sullivan's Island, Charleston, South Carolina, during the Civil War. A note on the artwork states that *Patapsco* had a red top to her smokestack (NH 95087, Collections of the Library of Congress, U.S. Naval History and Heritage Command).

USS *Napa* was a *Casco*-class twin-screw, light-draft monitor built for operation in shallow inland waters. These warships sacrificed armor for a shallow draft and were fitted with a ballast compartment designed to lower them in the water during battle.

The single-turret *Napa* was built by Harlan and Hollingsworth and launched November 26, 1864. Though the original designs for the *Casco*-class monitors were drawn by John Ericsson, the final revision was created by Chief Engineer Alban B. Stimers following Rear Admiral's Samuel F. Du Pont's failed bombardment of Fort Sumter in 1863. By the time the plans were put before the Monitor Board, Ericsson and Stimers had a poor relationship. This resulted in the plans being approved and 20 vessels ordered without serious scrutiny of the new design. A total of 14 million U.S. dollars was allocated for the construction of these vessels. It was discovered that Stimers had failed to compensate for the armor his revisions added to the original plan and this resulted in excessive stress on the wooden hull frames and a freeboard of only three inches (76 mm). Stimers was removed from control of the project and Ericsson was called in to undo the damage. He was forced to raise the hulls of the monitors under construction by nearly two feet, and the first few completed vessels had their turrets removed and a single pivot-mount 11 inch Dahlgren cannon mounted. These same few vessels had a retractable spar torpedo added as well.

As a result, *Napa* was converted to a torpedo vessel on June 25, 1864, and turned over to the government upon her completion on May 4, 1865. Never commissioned, she was laid up at League Island, Pennsylvania, until 1875, when she was broken up by John Roach at New York. While at League Island, her name was changed twice: to **Nemesis** on June 15, 1869, and back to *Napa* on August 10, 1869.

USS *Patapsco* was a *Pasaic*-class ironclad monitor. Built in Wilmington at the Harlan and Hollingsworth yards, she was launched on September 27, 1862 and commissioned on January 2, 1863. *Patapsco* was assigned to the South Atlantic blockade, where she took part in a bombardment of Fort McCallister near Savannah on March 3 under Vice Admiral Samuel F. Du Pont. On 7 April *Patapsco* joined eight other ironclads in a vigorous attack on Fort Sumter and received 47 hits from rebel gunfire during that day. Beginning in mid–July, participated in a lengthy bombardment campaign against Charleston's defending fortifications, which led to the capture of Fort Wagner in early September. Fort Sumter was reduced to a pile of rubble, but remained a formidable opponent.

In November 1863 *Patapsco* tested a large obstruction-clearing explosive device that had been devised by *Monitor* designer John Ericsson. Remaining off South Carolina and Georgia during much of 1864 and into 1865, the monitor—or her boat crews—took part in a reconnaissance of the Wilmington River, Georgia, in January 1864 and helped capture or destroy enemy sailing vessels in February and November of that year. On January 14, 1865, while participating in obstruction-clearance operations in Charleston Harbor, *Patapsco* struck a Confederate mine and sank with heavy loss of life.

USS *Saugus* was a single-turreted screw steamer *Canonicus*-class monitor built by Harlan and Hollingsworth in 1864. The vessel was assigned to the James River Flotilla upon completion in April and spent most of her time stationed up the James River, where she could support operations against Richmond and defend against a sortie by Confederate ironclads. She engaged Confederate artillery batteries during the year and later participated in both attacks on Fort Fisher at Wilmington, North Carolina, during December 1864–January 1865. *Saugus* returned to the James River after the capture of Fort Fisher and remained there until Richmond was occupied in early April.

A few days later the monitor was transferred to Washington, D.C., and used to temporarily incarcerate some of the suspected conspirators after the assassination of President Lincoln. She was decommissioned in June and recommissioned in early 1869 for service in the Caribbean and off the coast of Florida. *Saugus* was again recommissioned in late 1872 and generally remained active until late 1877. She was condemned in 1886 and sold for scrap in 1891.

Pusey and Jones served as a subcontractor for the Philadelphia Naval Yard building engines and boilers for the federal side-wheelers *Juniata* (1862), *Mingo*, and *Wyalusing* (1863). They built similarly for the army screw steamers *Stanton*, *Wells*, *Foote*, and *Porter* in 1864 providing engines and boilers.[5] After the war, Pusey and Jones built the revenue cutters *U.S. Grant* (1871) and *Walter Forward* (1882).[6]

Most of the shipyards became idle at the end of the war. International shipping had been disrupted and American commercial hegemony had been eroded to be replaced by foreign commerce. The government sold its large surplus of worn-out vessels at a big discount. American shipping had fallen into a permanent decline and American shipbuilding into a temporary slump.[7]

Confederate Naval Ships Constructed in Delaware

Because so many Wilmington ships were built for southern merchants prior to the Civil War, many of them became blockade-runners. Thanks to the fortunes of war, many of these rebel vessels eventually ended up in the hands of the Federal forces through surrender and capture. Over a dozen Delaware-built vessels are known to have served the Confederacy, and there were probably more, lost to history.

On January 15, 1862, Confederate forces seized the Harlan and Hollingsworth-built **SS *Arizona*** at New Orleans. Her U.S. enrollment was surrendered and replaced by a Confederate register on March 17, 1862. *Arizona* was converted with several other fast steamers to run the blockade to Cuba. On her first voyage to Havana, she was renamed *Caroline*. She served as a blockade-runner for the Confederacy, operating from New Orleans and Mobile to Havana.

On the morning of October 28, 1862, the side-wheeler was steaming from Havana to Mobile with a cargo of munitions when she was sighted by USS *Montgomery*. The Union gunboat immediately set out in pursuit of the stranger, beginning a six-hour chase. When *Montgomery* pulled within range of *Caroline*, she opened fire with her 30-pounder Parrott rifle and expended 17 shells before two hits brought the quarry to heel. Two boats from the blockader rowed out to *Caroline* and one returned with her master, a man named Forbes, who claimed to have been bound for the neutral port of Matamoros, Mexico, not Confederate Mobile. "I do not take you for running the blockade," the flag officer, with tongue in cheek, replied, "but for your damned poor navigation. Any man bound for Matamoros from Havana and coming within twelve miles of Mobile light has no business to have a steamer."

A Pusey and Jones vessel, **A.P. Hurt**, was built in 1860 for the Cape Fear Steamboat Company. She was a sternwheeler of 81 tons. The *A.P. Hurt* took captured Federal troops from the arsenal in Fayetteville to Wilmington after it surrendered to the Confederacy in 1861. When Union troops captured her at Fayetteville (1865), they named prominent African-American mariner Dan Buxton as its pilot and sent it to Chinquapin. Buxton went to the businessmen who had originally owned the *A.P. Hurt* and told them he still considered her their property and promised to return her if he were retained as pilot for life. When she finally sank in 1923 he was still on the job after sixty years and was deemed a master pilot.

The ***Austin***, built in 1860 by Harlan for Charles Morgan of the Southern Steamship Company of New Orleans, became the blockade-runner *Donegal*. She operated out of Mobile before her capture in 1864, when she was sent to Philadelphia as the supply ship USS *Donegal*.[8]

The ***Cecile***, commanded by J.C. Carlin, brought over 200 Enfield rifles for Confederate forces before wrecking on a reef between Nassau and Charleston in 1862 with the loss of 400 barrels of powder.

CSS Beaufort was an iron-hull gunboat that served in North Carolina and Virginia during the Civil War. She was originally called the *Caledonia* and was built at the Pusey and Jones Company of Wilmington, Delaware, in 1854. The *Caledonia* operated out of Edenton, North Carolina. At the outbreak of the war, the *Caledonia*, now renamed *Beaufort*, was put in commission at Norfolk and sailed immediately for New Bern, North Carolina. While en route she engaged the large steamer USS *Albatross* in an inconclusive battle.

She participated in the battles of Roanoke Island in February 1862 and Elizabeth City two days later. She was tender to CSS *Virginia* off Hampton Roads on March 8–9, 1862. In that battle *Beaufort* moved alongside the U.S. frigate *Congress* to accept its surrender. Heavy rifle fire from the shoreline drove her away with several casualties. The *Beaufort* also caused heavy damage to the *Minnesota* before nightfall. *Beaufort* served until the evacuation of Richmond, Virginia, on April 3, 1865, when she was taken into the United States Navy. She was sold September 15, 1865. On October 31, 1865, she was redocumented as the *Roanoke*, and in 1878 she was converted into a barge.

The **CSS *Curlew***, a side-wheel river steamer, was acquired at Norfolk in 1861. She was built at Harlem yards in 1856 for Thomas D. Warren, a doctor and plantation owner from Edenton, North Carolina. After the Civil War broke out, the *Curlew* was initially used as a troop transport, ferrying troops and supplies to various defensive works along the North Carolina coast. She was outfitted with one rifled 32-pounder cannon in the bow and one 12-pounder smoothbore cannon in the stern. Under the command of Thomas T. Hunter (also known as Tornado Hunter), *Curlew* was involved in the capture of the U.S. Army supply boat *Fanny* on October 1, 1861.

On February 7 the *Curlew* and eight other Confederate gunboats attempted to repel the Union invasion of Roanoke Island. During this battle the *Curlew* was holed by a shell and run aground to keep from sinking. The next day she was set on fire when the Confederate forces on Roanoke Island surrendered.

CSS *Ellis* (later **USS *Ellis***) was a gunboat in the Confederate States Navy built in Wilmington, Delaware, by Harlan and Hollingsworth in 1860. She was purchased at Norfolk in 1861. She played an important part in the defense of Forts Hatteras and Clark in August 1861, of Roanoke Island in February 1862, and of Elizabeth City on February 10, 1862. She was captured by the Union army during the latter engagement. Taken into the U.S. Navy and assigned to the North Atlantic Blockading Squadron, she spent her entire U.S. Navy service in the sounds and rivers of North Carolina.

Ellis took part in a combined expedition near Beaufort, North Carolina, on April 25, 1862. On October 14 she was detailed to the blockade of Bogue Inlet and a week later captured and burned the schooner *Adelaide* with a valuable cargo of turpentine, cotton, and tobacco. In November 1862 *Ellis*, under command of Lieutenant William B. Cushing, sailed up the New River Inlet to capture Jacksonville, North Carolina. The steamer captured two schooners, some arms, and mail. On her way downriver, she ran aground and could not be refloated. After dark her commanding officer, with great coolness, moved all the crew except six and all her equipment and supplies except her pivot gun, some ammunition, 2 tons of coal, and a few small arms to one of the captured schooners. While the schooners slipped down the river to wait, Cushing and five of his men remained to fight it out. Early on the morning of November 25 the Confederates opened fire on *Ellis*, and in a short time Cushing was forced to decide between surrender and a pull of a mile and a half to a waiting schooner. Cushing chose not to surrender and before leaving his ship set fire to her in five places, leaving the gun trained on the enemy to let the ship herself carry on the fight when flames would fire the cannon. Cushing and his men reached the schooner and made for the sea, getting the vessel over the bar just in time to escape several companies of cavalry trying to cut off the schooner at the mouth of the inlet. *Ellis* was blown to pieces by the explosion of her magazine on the morning of November 25, 1862.

Flora McDonald was a side-wheel steamer built by Pusey and Jones Shipyards in 1853. She was their first iron steamship built Mississippi River–style with a draft of only 17 inches and a main deck open for freight. She was sold to Cape Fear Shipping and was purchased by the Confederate navy in 1861. The *Flora McDonald*, the second iron-clad steamer on the Cape Fear, catered to first-class passengers. After Wilmington fell to Union forces in February of 1865, most of the remaining steamboats headed upriver and were captured when Union forces occupied Fayetteville, but the *Flora McDonald* went to Elizabethtown. Captain Wynder marched his Confederate company there to prevent enemy gunboats from coming up until General Johnston's army had cleared Fayetteville and burned the steamboat, not only to prevent her capture but to obstruct the waters.

General Rusk, built as a merchantman at Wilmington, Delaware, in 1857, was seized from the Southern Steamship Conpany by the State of Texas at Galveston in 1861. She served as a reconnaissance and signal boat with the Texas Marine Department in and about the waters of Galveston Harbor during the latter half of 1861, trying unsuccessfully on several occasions to slip past the Federal blockade. In early November 1861 she rendered aid to *Royal Yacht* following that vessel's capture and firing by Union forces from USS *Santee* and managed to save her from complete destruction and tow her to safety. In December 1861 *General Rusk* was ordered to take part in the defense of Buffalo Bayou, San Jacinto River. Her most memorable exploit was the capture on April 17, 1861, off Indianola, Texas, of USS *Star of the West*, the first Union transport to make news in the Civil War.

During the early part of 1862 *General Rusk* was placed by General Hebert, commanding Texas Marine Department, under the control of Maj. T.S. Moise, assistant quartermaster, who colluded to transfer the steamer to his associates, authorizing them to place her under the British flag and employ her in blockade-running. After a single successful round-trip under the name *Blanche* she was bound for Havana in October 1862 when pursued by USS *Montgomery*, Comdr. C. Hunter, USN. While attempting to escape, the steamer was run aground near Marianao, Cuba, and seized by a *Montgomery* boat crew. Efforts to get her towed off the bar and underway again ended when fire broke out and consumed both ship and cargo. The incident occasioned strong protest from England, under whose flag she sailed, and Spain, in whose territorial waters she was captured.

Hunter Woodis was a ferry built by Harlan in 1856. She was originally sold to the City of Norfolk and acquired by the Confederacy for use as a transport. She was acquired by the War Department in 1863 for the Department of Virginia for use as a transport.

The capture of the ***St. Mary,*** renamed *Nick King*, off Cuban waters created an international incident when Spanish authorities protested an attack in their waters. Federal forces sank her and then raised and used her under the name USS *Genesee*. After the war she became the *Nick King* again.

CSS *Spray*, built in Wilmington by Pusey and Jones in 1852 (their second iron-hulled vessel), was a side-wheel steamer of 106 tons. She operated at St. Marks, Florida, during 1863–65.

The Harlan-built ***William Hewes,*** an iron side-wheel steamer, operated in commercial service between East Coast and Gulf Coast ports. At the beginning of the Civil War the State of Louisiana seized the ship and made it a blockade runner. She successfully ran the blockade a dozen times. After Union forces captured the lower Mississippi in 1862 she was sold to a North Carolina owner and renamed *Ella and Annie* and remained a blockade-runner. She was captured by USS *Niphon* in 1863 off Wilmington, North Carolina, and sent to Boston to be converted to a gunship of the blockading squadron under Admiral David Dixon Porter. She was renamed USS *Malvern*.

Malvern later returned to the area of Wilmington, North Carolina, which had become the Confederates' principal blockade-running port and was protected by Fort Fisher. Admiral Porter in *Malvern* and a large naval force were required to support two

USS *Malvern* (1863–1865). Watercolor by Erik Heyl, 1952, painted for use in his book *Early American Steamers* (vol. 1). Originally built in 1860 as the steamship *William G. Hewes*, this steamer was the blockade-runner CSS *Ella and Annie* when captured in November 1863. She served for the rest of the Civil War as USS *Malvern*. After sale to civilian owners late in 1865 she again was named *William G. Hewes* and kept that name until wrecked in 1895 (NH 63855, U.S. Naval History and Heritage Command).

assaults there by the army before the fort was taken. In 1865, as war moved to Virginia, *Malvern* was the meeting place for Porter, Grant, and Lincoln on several occasions. She was the Union vessel that carried Lincoln to Richmond. After the war she was renamed *William Hewes* and continued to serve until 1895, when she was wrecked on a reef in a storm off Cuba.

W.W. Hailee served as a troop transport in North Carolina in 1861.

Appendix 3: Post–Civil War, Wilmington-Built Ships, 1871–1917

Below is a representative catalog of ships built in Wilmington in approximately chronological order.[1]

USC&GS *A.D. Bache* (Pusey and Jones, 1871), the second steamer of the U.S. Coast and Geodetic Survey, was named for former superintendent Alexander Bache. She was iron framed and wood sheathed. She was designated for Atlantic and Gulf of Mexico operations with her first mission, being measurements in the Gulf Stream and deep-sea soundings in the Gulf of Mexico during trials of the ship. She dredged the bottom to obtain biological specimens and did many surveys in river approaches, inlets, sounds, and harbors marking shoals and undersea mounts that could be a danger to ships' bottoms. Survey seasons for *Bache* followed much the same pattern, with summer in the north and winter in the south, until 1876, when emphasis shifted to Florida. She mapped new shifting shorelines and undersea crevasses

Between January and June 1898, *Bache* and the steamer *Blake* were assigned temporary duty with the U.S. Navy for special naval surveys at Key West and Dry Tortugas as well as transport and dispatch duties. *Bache* was used to transport divers and salvage workers to Havana in February 1898 after the battleship USS *Maine* was destroyed in an explosion. The *A.D. Bache* was also involved in evacuating the injured. She was condemned as unseaworthy in June 1899. It is unclear whether she was rebuilt or an entirely new hull was constructed, but the second *Bache* made use of the first vessel's salvaged equipment and instruments, along with a new power plant.

USRS *U.S. Grant* (Pusey and Jones, 1872) was an iron-hulled vessel built for the U.S. Revenue Cutter Service for $92,500 and was one of the few three-masted cutters ever in service. She was assigned to the New York station on January 19, 1872. For the next two decades she operated off the East Coast from Block Island Sound to the mouth of the Delaware River.

After a refit in 1893 *U.S. Grant* sailed to Washington via South America for duty in the Pacific Northwest protecting fisheries and lending assistance as far as the Bering Sea. She was placed under navy control on April 11, 1898, as the United States girded for war with Spain. *U.S. Grant* then resumed her peacetime activities, patrolling the same northwest Pacific coastlines of Washington and Alaska. She was removed from service in 1906.

***Five Fathom Bank* Lightship LV-40** (Jackson and Sharp, 1875) was a wooden steamship with fastened iron and copper. She served as a lightship at Pollock Rip, Massachusetts, and at Five Fathom Bank, New Jersey. She was sold at auction in 1905 at Edgemoor Lighthouse Depot.

USS *Ranger* (Harlan and Hollingsworth, 1876), later USS *Rockport* and USS *Nantucket* (PG-23/IX-18), was a screw steamer gunboat with a full-rig auxiliary sail built by Harlan and Hollingsworth (1876) for the U.S. Navy. *Ranger* was destined for a very long—65 years—career, serving first as a U.S. Navy gunboat from 1876 to 1920 and then as a training ship with the U.S. Merchant Marine Academy from 1920 to 1940.

USFC *Fish Hawk* (Pusey and Jones, 1880) was a fisheries research vessel operated by the U.S. Commission of Fish and Fisheries from 1880 to 1926 and manned by a U.S. Navy crew. She was the first large ship purpose-built by any country for the promotion of fisheries and spent her 46-year career operating along the East Coast, the Gulf of Mexico, and the Caribbean. Her home port was Woods Hole, Massachusetts.

Lightship *Trinity Shoal* (LV-43) (Pusey and Jones, 1881) was on station 18 miles offshore in Louisiana south of Vermillion Bay until 1894.

***Northeast End* Lightship (LV 44)** (Pusey and Jones, 1882) was the first iron lightship built in the United States. The *Northeast End* was described as schooner rigged with two cagework towers. Number 44 was stationed on the northeast end of Five Fathom Bank from 1882 until 1926. New Jersey, about 12 miles east of Hereford Inlet and 19.7 miles and 085 degrees from the Cape May Lighthouse.

USS *Nantucket* (PG-23), 1873–1940, formerly USS *Ranger* and USS *Rockport* then loaned to the State of Massachusetts for use at Massachusetts Nautical School, 1933 (NH 500, U.S. Naval History and Heritage Command).

Lighthouse Tender *Wistaria* (Pusey and Jones, 1882) was built as an inspection tender, assigned to the 6th Lighthouse District, and home ported in Charleston, South Carolina. She was transferred to the Public Health and Maritime Hospital in 1911 and used as a floating hospital and later a detention barge at Key West, Florida.

USRS *Walter Forward* (Pusey and Jones, 1882) was an iron-hulled, twin-screw topsail schooner steamer vessel. During her government career *Forward* served along the East Coast and in the Caribbean. The *Forward* was considered a model ship at the time, and one source noted that she was "a fine model for cruising." She was assigned to Mobile, Alabama, where she cruised the Gulf of Mexico and enforced customs laws and assisted mariners in distress. She cruised as far east as Cedar Key, Florida, and made monthly port visits at Key West during her cruising season. She eventually transferred her duty station to Key West. It was during this time, prior to the Spanish-American War, that the U.S. Revenue Cutter Service undertook another mission, preventing the smuggling of men, guns, and ammunition to Cuba. On July 27, 1912, *Forward* was ordered to the depot in South Baltimore, where her crew transferred to the cutter *Miami*, arriving there on August 15. She was then sold on October 24, 1912.

The **USS *Albatross***, another long-lived craft (Pusey and Jones, 1882) was an iron-hulled, twin-screw steamer in the United States Navy and reputedly the first research vessel ever built especially for marine research.

USS *Amphitrite* (Harlan and Hollingsworth, 1883)—the lead ship in her class of iron-hulled, twin-screw monitors—was laid down on June 23, 1874, by order of President Grant's secretary of the navy, George M. Robeson. She was launched on June 7, 1883, and commissioned at the Norfolk Navy Yard on April 23, 1895.

Rapid changes in naval technology and doctrine during the *two decades* she was under construction had repeatedly delayed her progress, and she was redesigned twice while still under construction. Offering a light draft and a steady platform, she joined the North Atlantic Squadron and served primarily in the role of gunnery training prior to the Spanish-American War. At the onset of the war she sailed from Key West under tow due to lack of coal storage space for San Juan. There she bombarded shore positions in May and participated in an invasion operation in the same area in August 1898. Her poor ventilation and other inadequacies caused her to retire to Boston. She continued to serve as a guard and station ship as well as in the training role until she was decommissioned shortly after World War I.

USCGC *Lott M. Morrill* (Pusey and Jones, 1889) was an iron-hulled cutter. She had duty on the southeastern coast and the Great Lakes. Her first homeport was Charleston, South Carolina, where her assigned cruising grounds included the waters between Georgetown, South Carolina, to Beaufort, North Carolina. She was occasionally assigned to temporary duty in the waters off the east coast of Florida. The *Morrill* was taken over by the navy on April 24, 1898, for service in the Spanish-American War. She patrolled between Cuba and Florida during May and for the next 3 months operated along the west coast of Florida. During her tour she captured two ships: a French ship, *Lafayette*, and the Spanish sailing ship *España*. The *Lott M. Morrill* was returned to the Treasury Department on August 11, 1898. She was then assigned to the Great Lakes and was based out of Milwaukee, Wisconsin. Here she served during the open shipping season and was laid up during the winter months. In addition to her regular duties, she also patrolled many regattas, including the T.J. Lipton Cup regatta off Chicago, Illinois, in August of 1904. In 1906 her cruising grounds included the waters between Niagara Falls through Lakes Erie, St. Clair, and Huron to the Straits of Mackinac. On August 4, 1914, she was ordered to "observe neutrality laws" after the outbreak of World War I in Europe. She was transferred to the navy on April 6, 1917. The *Morrill* was in Halifax, Nova Scotia, on December 6, 1917, when the French munitions freighter *Mont-Blanc* exploded, taking the lives of 1,600 people and leveling much of the town. The *Morrill* sent a rescue party and towed other vessels to safety. She was later cited by the secretary of the navy as "the first to render assistance to the ... inhabitants of" Halifax. After the war she returned to the Great Lakes for duty. She was decommissioned on October 19, 1928, and sold to Antonio Di Domenico of New York City.

USCGC *Winona* (Pusey and Jones, 1890) was an iron-hulled, twin-screw cutter. On December 30, 1890, she was ordered to New Bern, North Carolina, for duty. Her assigned cruising grounds were the Pamlico and Albemarle sounds, but during the next years she saw service on waters throughout the southeast over to Galveston, Texas. Other duties included hurricane relief in the Florida Keys in 1906 and working with the Public Health and Marine Hospital Service during quarantines. She patrolled regattas, transported dignitaries, and enforced neutrality laws at sea. She was placed out of commission at Mobile, Alabama, in 1915.

USS *Stringham* (Torpedo Boat No. 19/TB-19) (Harlan and Hollingsworth, 1899) was a steel torpedo boat for the United States Navy. *Stringham* was placed in full commission on October 30, 1906, and assigned to the 3d Torpedo Flotilla, Atlantic Fleet. Assigned to temporary duty with the 1st Torpedo Division on April 1, 1910, *Stringham* was transferred to the Engineering Experimental Station at Annapolis on September 14. She served as a practice ship and training vessel for midshipmen at the United States Naval Academy from 1911 to 1913.

Stringham is especially noteworthy for successfully receiving the first radio signal transmitted from an aircraft to a surface ship, on July 26, 1912, near Annapolis. Ensign Charles H. Maddox, USN, transmitted the words "We are off the water, going ahead full speed on a course for the Naval Academy" from an altitude of 300 feet to the *Stringham*, distance three nautical miles. Later test messages from Maddox's "Wright flyer style" aircraft were received by *Stringham* at distances of up to 15 miles. Maddox later wrote, "These were the first radio messages ever received from an airplane radio transmitting set in the United States and probably in the world."

Rocket (Pusey and Jones, 1900) went to the U.S. Navy as YT-22 in 1911.

USS *Hopkins* (DD-6) (Harlan and Hollingsworth, 1902) was a *Hopkins*-class destroyer. *Hopkins* joined the Atlantic Fleet at Norfolk in 1904. That summer the destroyer deployed with the Coast Squadron for the midshipmen at sea training. In the following years she would serve in the Caribbean and South America en route to the Pacific, sailing from Mexico to Alaskan waters. On February 14, 1910, *Hopkins* suffered a boiler accident. Two sailors were awarded the Medal of Honor for their actions during the incident.

USS *Hull* (DD-7) (Harlan and Hollingsworth, 1902) was a sister ship to the USS *Hopkins*. During her first two years of service *Hull* engaged in patrol and training maneuvers off the Eastern Seaboard. In 1906 she took part in winter exercises with fleet units in Cuban waters. She sailed with the Great White Fleet as an escort vessel on their voyage around South America in 1907. She was detached from the fleet on the West Coast and later did a South Pacific cruise.

Henry Wilson and *Sprigg Caroll* (Pusey and Jones, 1903) were cargo ships for the U.S. Army.

General Nathaniel Greene and *General Thomas S. Jessup* (Pusey and Jones, 1904) were cargo ships for the U.S. Army.

U.S. C&GS *Explorer* (Pusey and Jones, 1904) was a U.S. C&GS Research vessel acquired by the navy on May 22, 1918. She was commissioned **USS** *Explorer* June 3, 1918, and returned to the Coast and Geodetic Survey on March 31, 1919, then went to the U.S. Army in 1942 as *Atkins* (FS 237).

Ellis Island (1904) and *Immigrant* (1905) were both Harlan and Hollingsworth vessels. The first was a passenger ferry and the second was a boarding vessel for use by the U.S. Bureau of Immigration.

Ordnance (Pusey and Jones, 1905) was a U.S. Army cargo ship.

Barge No. 14 (Pusey and Jones, 1905) was a U.S. Navy water barge (later YW 14).

USLHS *Sunflower* (Pusey and Jones, 1906) was a lighthouse tender until World War I and then was acquired by the navy. After the war she returned to service with the Department of Commerce and later the coast guard as USCGC *Sunflower* (WAGJ 247).

Major Albert G. Forse, Capt. A. W. Morrison, and *Capt. Chas. W. Powell* (Pusey and Jones, 1906) were U.S. Army cargo ships and were sold in 1922.

USRCS *Pamlico* (Pusey and Jones, 1907) was a U.S. Revenue Service Cutter designated **CG-15** in 1915. Acquired by the navy on April 6, 1917, she was then ordered to the Chesapeake Bay, where she made short training cruises in the bay for the many naval reserve officer trainees being prepared for duty overseas—a role she carried out for the remainder of the war. She returned to the Treasury Department August 28, 1919, was reclassified as a river gunboat, **WPR-57**, in 1942, and was decommissioned September 6, 1946.

USRCS *Snohomish* (Pusey and Jones, 1908) was a 152-foot (46 m) seagoing tug built at the specific direction of Congress for service on the Pacific Northwest coast. Originally costing $189,000, she was fitted with the latest lifesaving and property-saving equipment available at the time of her construction. She was commissioned by the U.S. Revenue Cutter Service on November 15, 1908, and arrived at her homeport of Neah Bay, Washington, by way of passage around Cape Horn in 1909. *Snohomish* was a regular part of the Bering Sea Patrol and enforced international sealing regulations. Her duties included search and rescue, law enforcement, fisheries patrol, mail delivery to light ships and remote stations, patrolling regattas, and towing disabled vessels. She served her entire career in the Pacific Northwest and was decommissioned and sold December 1, 1934.

USRCS *Androscoggin* (Pusey and Jones, 1908) was the last wooden-hulled cutter to see service with the U.S. Revenue Cutter Service and was designed especially for icebreaking duties. She carried out the work of the USRCS, cruising waters off the northeastern seaboard from Eastport, Maine, to Cape Ann, Massachusetts. Each winter—by virtue of her special construction and her iron-strengthened bow—she would assist ships and craft when needed and destroy menaces to navigation in her assigned waters besides performing icebreaking chores in the ports in her cruising area. During World War I she served as an escort vessel for the navy.

Sonittep (Pusey and Jones, 1907) was a U.S. Coast Guard tug.

USCG *Davey* (CG 19) (Pusey and Jones, 1908) was a U.S. Coast Guard tug—later WYT 81—and was decommissioned in 1945.

U.S. Army *Gen. E.O.C. Ord* (Pusey and Jones, 1908) was a mineplanter scrapped in 1948.

U.S. Army ***General Otis*** (Pusey and Jones, 1909) was a ferry sold to Sunrise Ferries in 1940 as *Nancy Helen*. She was later *Resolute* and was scrapped in 1957.

John A. Palmer, Jr., (Jackson and Sharp, 1911) was a trawler sold to the U.S. Navy in 1919 as SP-319. She was later USS *Pequot* (sold in 1944).

LV 101 *Overfalls* (Pusey and Jones, 1916) was a U.S. Coast Guard lightship that first served as *Charles* in the Chesapeake Bay at Cape Charles, Virginia, from 1916 until 1924. After that assignment she served just over a year as the relief ship for other lightships in her district. She was then moved to Overfalls, Delaware, where she was stationed from 1926 to 1951 as *Overfalls*. In 1939, when the U.S. Lighthouse Service was absorbed into the U.S. Coast Guard, she was reclassified WAL-524 but still kept a station name on her hull. During World War II the vessel was not armed; however, many other lightships were. In 1951 LV-101/WAL 524 was reassigned to Stonehorse Shoal, Massachusetts, where she served until decommissioned in 1963. On September 3, 1964, LV-101 was given to the City of Portsmouth, Virginia, to become a part of the Portsmouth Naval Shipyard Museum. She was renamed *Portsmouth* and was dry-docked at the London Pier in Portsmouth. Although she was never stationed there, she has taken on the city's name.

LV 102 *Brenton Reef* (Pusey and Jones, 1917) was a U.S. Coast Guard lightship. On January 10, 1917, she departed Edgemoor (DE) Lighthouse Depot for New Orleans, and on February 24 she was placed on Southwest Pass (LA). In 1918 she moved to South Pass. During April 18–21, 1926, while docked at Pensacola during a hurricane, her stern was stove in and her plating severely damaged by colliding repeatedly against the bow of LV 81, which was tied up astern. Both vessels were hauled and repaired. In 1933 she was transferred to the 2d District and assigned as relief while being overhauled. In 1935 she was placed on Brenton Reef (RI) until 1962 then moved to Cross Rip (MA) and retired in 1963.

Appendix 4: Ships of World War I from Delaware Shipyards

The following offers a representative catalog of Delaware built ships destined for the United States Shipping Board (in order of construction).[1]

Harlan and Hollingsworth (Bethlehem Steel)

Saetia—United Fruit/U.S. Shipping Board Cargo Ship, February 1918; sunk by a mine, 1918.

Guaro—United Fruit/U.S. Shipping Board, Cargo Ship, April 1918. Later *Isabel Weems*, 1926, *Guaro*, 1936; scrapped, 1937.

Biran—United Fruit/U.S. Shipping Board Cargo Ship, June 1918. Later *Dorothy*, 1924; in collision and sank, 1929.

Pilon/Garibaldi—United Fruit/U.S. Shipping Board Cargo Ship, June 1918. Later *Catherine Weems*, 1926, *Fairfield*, 1928, *Hallfried*, 1939; torpedoed and lost, 1943.

J.A. Bostwick—Standard Oil/U.S. Shipping Board Tanker, August 5, 1918. Later *Cities Service Toledo*, 1929; torpedoed and lost, 1942.

O.T. Waring—Standard Oil/U.S. Shipping Board Tanker, September 24, 1918. Later *Maturines*, 1935; scrapped, 1949.

Tipton—United Fruit/U.S. Shipping Board Cargo Ship, November 1918. Later *Esther Weems*, 1923, *Admiral Benson*, 1927; wrecked, 1930.

Charles M. Everest—Vacuum Oil/U.S. Shipping Board Tanker, December 13, 1918. Later *Naeco*, 1933; torpedoed and lost, 1942.

Norma—United Fruit/U.S. Shipping Board Cargo Ship, December 1918. Later *Northern Sword*, 1942; in collision and lost, 1943.

Cabrille—U.S. Shipping Board Tanker, July 1919. Later *Chilbar*, 1927; scrapped, 1947.

Romulus—U.S. Shipping Board Tanker, July 1919. Later *Spencer Kellog*, 1929, *Rawleigh Warner*, 1945; scrapped, 1955.

Benwood/Gold Star—U.S. Shipping Board Cargo Ship, July 1919. Later *Arcturus* (AK 12), 1921. Later *Gold Star* (AG 12), 1922; scrapped, 1947.

Benclair/Glenora—U.S. Shipping Board Cargo Ship, September 1919. Later *Regulus* (AK 14), 1921; scrapped, 1947.

Muskegot/Delco—U.S. Shipping Board Cargo Ship, September 1919. Later *Domino*, 1922; scrapped, 1950.

Benbrook/Salem County—U.S. Shipping Board Tanker, October 1919. Later Galena, 1923, *Arizona*, 1929; scrapped, 1950.

Siasconset/Bethnor—U.S. Shipping Board Cargo Ship, November 1919. Later *Irene*, 1922, *Nidarholm*, 1939; torpedoed and lost, 1942.

Bencarnot/Natirar—U.S. Shipping Board Cargo Ship, December 1919; torpedoed and lost, 1943.

Macomet—U.S. Shipping Board Cargo Ship, December 1919. Later *Elizabeth*, 1922; wrecked, 1935.

Weweantic/Liberty Minquas—U.S. Shipping Board Tanker, March 1920. Later *Republic*, 1923; torpedoed and lost, 1942.

Sames/Mason City—U.S. Shipping Board Cargo Ship, April 1920. Later *Ellenor*, 1922, *Marcella*, 1946; wrecked, 1958.

Maddequet—U.S. Shipping Board Cargo Ship, May 1920. Later *Lillian*, 1922; in collision and sank, 1939.

Nanquitt—U.S. Shipping Board Cargo Ship, Transferred to Elizabethport.

Nanshun—U.S. Shipping Board Cargo Ship, Transferred to Elizabethport.

Kehuku—U.S. Shipping Board Tanker, June 1920. Later *Chiloil*, 1926; scrapped 1947.

Kekoskee—U.S. Shipping Board Tanker, October 1920. Later *Santa Rita*, 1948; scrapped, 1955.

Eugene V.R. Thayer—U.S. Shipping Board Tanker, December 1920; shelled and lost, 1942.

Pusey and Jones

War Nurse/Piqua—U.S. Shipping Board Cargo Ship, May 1918. Later *Marconier*, 1920, *Ganda*, 1930, *Helle*, 1932; torpedoed and lost, 1941.

War Heroine/Waukesha—U.S. Shipping Board Cargo Ship, May 1918; abandoned, 1948.

War Metal/Middlebury—U.S. Shipping Board Cargo Ship, July 1918; scrapped, 1929.

War Compass/Aurora—U.S. Shipping Board Cargo Ship, September 1918. Later *Carabinier*, 1920, *Yzerhandel*, 1925, *Belgica*, 1928; scrapped, 1960.

War Platoon/Lynchburg—U.S. Shipping Board Cargo Ship, November 1918. Later *Fusilier*, 1920, *Ersthandel*, 1925, *Skrunda*, 1928; bombed and lost, 1941.

War Crater/Marshall—U.S. Shipping Board Cargo Ship, January 1919. Later *Torny*, 1923; torpedoed and lost, 1942.

Eider—U.S. Navy Minesweeper, January 23, 1919. Later YN 20, YNG 20; struck, 1945.

War Dart/Moline—U.S. Shipping Board Cargo Ship, May 1919. Later *Lara*, 1925; scrapped, 1948.

War Shield/Rock Island—U.S. Shipping Board Cargo Ship, July 1919. Later *Falcon*, 1925; scrapped, 1948.

Knights Island—U.S. Shipping Board Cargo Ship, August 1919. Later *Devonier*, 1920; wrecked, 1923.

Fire Island—U.S. Shipping Board Cargo Ship, October 1919. Later *Solhaug*, 1920, *Belgion*, 1935, *Scharlachberger*, 1940; scuttled, 1944.

USS *Eider* (AM-17) launching, at the Pusey and Jones Company, Wilmington, Delaware, on May 26, 1918 (NH 54350, U.S. Naval History and Heritage Command).

Long Island—U.S. Shipping Board Cargo Ship, February 1920. Later *Argentinier*, 1920, *Tourny*, 1928; torpedoed and lost, 1940.

Staten Island/Spartier—U.S. Shipping Board Cargo Ship, March 1920. Later *Nil*, 1925; wrecked, 1927.

Fishers Island—U.S. Shipping Board Cargo Ship, May 1920. Later *Ionier*, 1920, *Favorite* 1930; bombed and lost, 1941.

Shelter Island/Livonier—U.S. Shipping Board Cargo Ship, July 1920. Later *Montaigne*, 1928, *Vella*, 1953, *Annellen*, 1955; scrapped, 1958.

Norwalk—U.S. Shipping Board Cargo Ship, 1920; in collision and sank, 1943.

In addition to the hulls above, constructed for the United States Shipping Board, Pusey and Jones laid down two warships during World War I that launched after the war.

Thrush—U.S. Navy Minesweeper 25-April 19. Later AVP 3; struck, 1945.

Vinyard Shipbuilding, Milford, Delaware

Lightning—U.S. Shipping Board Tug, 1919. Later *Card Boys*.

Chapter Notes

Chapter 1

1. John Thomas Scharf, *History of Delaware*, 2 vols. (Philadelphia: L.J. Richards, 1888), vol. 1, 26–27.
2. John A. Monroe, *History of Delaware* (Newark: University of Delaware Press, 1984), 16–18.
3. Mey arrived in 1614 before Hendrickson. The Dutch followed Hudson's naming and called the bay South River. Their 1655 map by Nicholas Visscher retained the name Cape Cornelius for the southern cape and named a headland, or "false cape," in the vicinity of today's Fenwick Island Cape Hinlopen. Later, when the English drove the Dutch from New Netherlands and William Penn got this grant from James, Duke of York, the southern cape of Delaware Bay was named Cape James. In settling the long dispute between the Calverts and Penns over whose grant covered the upper portion of the peninsula bordered by the Delaware and Chesapeake bays, in 1685 the English Committee for Foreign Trade and Plantations used the Visscher 1655 map to decide that the land north of Cape Hinlopen (shown at Fenwick Island) was granted to Penn and the privy council so granted, giving what is today Delaware to the Penns. The south cape continued to be called Cape James, with Cape Henlopen farther south even on Joshua Fisher's 1756 chart in order to substantiate the Penn claim until it was finally established by the Mason-Dixon survey and an English court ruling in 1760. By then geographers had already begun calling the southern cape Cape Henlopen (Randy J. Holland, *Delaware's Destiny Determined by Lewes* [Dover: Delaware Heritage Press, 2013]).
4. Scharf, *History of Delaware*, vol. 1, 29–30.
5. Hon. Hampton L. Carson, "Dutch and Swedish Settlements on the Delaware," *Pennsylvania Magazine of History and Biography* 33, no. 1 (1909), 12.
6. Ibid., 6.
7. C.A. Weslager, *Delaware's Forgotten River* (Wilmington: Hambleton Company, 1947), 4.
8. Swedish Colonial Society, "A Brief History of New Sweden in America," http://colonialswedes.net/History/History.html.
9. Federal Writers' Project, "Delaware, a Guide to the First State," *The American Guide Series* (New York: Viking, 1938), 26–27.
10. Scharf, *History of Delaware*, vol. 1, 32–34.
11. Warren McDonald, "Duke of York Patent on Pilottown Rd: A Study of How Lewes Happened," *Lewes History* 5 (November 2002), 20–45.
12. Hazel D. Brittingham, "Blockhouse Pond," *Lewes History* 4 (November 2001), 13–14.
13. Leon deValinger, Jr., "The Burning of the Whorekill, 1673," *Pennsylvania Magazine of History and Biography* 74, no. 4 (October 1950), 473–487.
14. Carson, "Dutch and Swedish Settlements on the Delaware," 21.
15. Tracey L. Bryant and Jonathan R. Pennock, *The Delaware Estuary* (Newark: University of Delaware Press, 1988), 19.
16. Scharf, *History of Delaware*, vol. 1, 99–100.
17. William M. Mervine, "Pirates and Privateers in the Delaware Bay and River," *Pennsylvania Magazine of History and Biography* 32, no. 4 (1908), 459–470.
18. John Thomas Scharf, "Pirates and Privateers," *History of Delaware*, vol. 1, 99–107; deValinger, Jr., "The Burning of the Whorekill, 1673," 473–487; Pennock Pusey, "History of Lewes: Read Before the Historical Society of Delaware, Nov. 17, 1902," *Papers of the Historical Society of Delaware* 38 (Wilmington: Historical Society of Delaware, 1903).
19. Scharf, *History of Delaware*, vol. 1, 199–101.
20. Ibid., 129–130.
21. Mervine, "Pirates and Privateers in the Delaware Bay and River," 463–464.
22. Scharf, *History of Delaware*, vol. 1, 95n, 99–108.
23. Mervine, "Pirates and Privateers in the Delaware Bay and River," 464.
24. Federal Writers' Project, *Delaware*, 91–92.
25. Richard Urban, *The City That Launched a Thousand Ships: Shipbuilding in Wilmington, 1644–1997* (Wilmington: Cedar Tree Books, 1999), 3.
26. David B. Tyler, *The Bay and River Delaware: A Pictorial History* (Centreville, MD: Cornell Maritime Press, 1955), 14–15.
27. John L. Cotter, Daniel G. Roberts, and Michael Parrington, *The Buried Past: An Archaeological History of Philadelphia* (Philadelphia: University of Pennsylvania Press 1993), 227.
28. Benjamin Bullivant, *Travel Diary 1697*, ed. Wayne Andres, http://www.nc-chap.org/resources/bullivant.pdf, 71.
29. Dean A. Doerrfeld, et al., *The Delaware Ship and Boat Building Industry, 1830–1940: An Historic Context* (Newark: Center for Historic Architecture and Engineering College of Urban Affairs and Public Policy, University of Delaware, 1994), 10.
30. Theodore Thayer, "Town into City: 1746–1765," in Russell F. Weigley, ed., *Philadelphia: A 300-Year History* (New York: W.W. Norton, 1982), 198. Philadelphia by 1770 led the other seaports (Boston, New York, Charleston) in both shipbuilding and volume of exports.

In a good year, some 700–800 ships visited the Quaker City. Between 1750 and 1775 tonnage of ships registered in Philadelphia by merchants rose from 7,092 to 16,809 (Kevin Phillips, *1775: A Good Year for Revolution* [New York: Viking, 2012]).

31. William Fairburn Armstrong, *Merchant Sail* (Center Lovell, ME: Fairburn Marine Educational Foundation, 1945–1955), 264–266.

32. David B. Tyler, "Shipbuilding in Delaware," *Delaware History* 7 (1957), 207–210.

33. Sussex County, DE, Historic Markers, Ships and Men, Delaware Public Archives, http://archives.delaware.gov/markers/sc/SHIPS%20AND%20MEN%20SC-144.shtml.

34. Federal Writers Project, *Delaware*, 93.

35. Jeffrey Dorwart, *The Philadelphia Navy Yard* (Philadelphia: University of Pennsylvania Press 2001), 16.

36. Ibid., 9–11.

37. *The Delaware Estuary: Rediscovering a Forgotten Resource* (Newark: Sea Grant College Program, University of Delaware, 1988), 20.

38. Weslager, *Delaware's Forgotten River*, 68–70.

39. *The Delaware Estuary*, 18.

40. Judith Roales, *Delaware Lighthouses and Range Lights* (Charleston: Arcadia, 2007), 7.

41. Andrew Knopp, *One Hundred-Year History of the Pilot's Association Bay and River Delaware, 1896–1996* (Dover: Delaware Heritage Press, 1996), 2–3.

42. James E. Marvil, *Pilots of the Bay and River Delaware* (Laurel, DE: Sussex Press, 1965), 30.

43. Knopp, *One Hundred-Year History*, 2–3.

44. Lawrence C. Wroth, "Joshua Fisher's Chart of the Delaware Bay and River," *Pennsylvania Magazine of History and Biography* (January 1950), 99.

45. William Manthorpe, "Establishing the Basis for the Safe Navigation of Delaware Bay, 1756–1856," *Lewes History* 16 (2013).

46. Ibid.

47. *The Delaware Estuary*, 40–41.

48. The first step in the defense of Lewes against an arriving British force, however, was probably the disabling of the lighthouse by Henry Fisher and his guards to hamper the navigation of any ships bringing troops to Delaware Bay. While the cause and perpetrator of the fire have never been determined, local lore has blamed the fire on a confrontation between the British and the keeper. It has been retold often, and generally believed, that sometime during the second week in April 1777, the Roebuck anchored off the cape and sent a long boat ashore.

The British crewmen walked to the lighthouse and asked the keeper to supply their ship with fresh cattle which were grazing on the cape. The lighthouse keeper, whose name was Hedgecock [the lighthouse keeper was Elizabeth Hitchcock, who had succeeded her husband John when he died in early 1776] did not fear the Roebuck's cannon because she was over a half mile away and unable to come closer because of shallow water, and the lighthouse walls were over six feet thick.

So he [she] is reputed to have said, 'I'll give you no cows, but if you don't get out of here, I'll give you some bullets.' The British officer was angry as he returned to his longboat and instead of expected bombardment he sent back several longboats and a landing party. Over a mile of beach separated the lighthouse from the landing, so after seeing them land, keeper Hedgecock had time to round up the cattle and drive them into the pine forest.

Perhaps fearing the arrival of the militia, the British landing party did not follow into the woods but instead took their anger out on the abandoned lighthouse and reportedly set the interior wooden stairway on fire" [John W. Beach, *Cape Henlopen Lighthouse and Delaware Breakwater* (Dover: Dover Litho and Printing, 1970), 35].

The attribution of the British burning the lighthouse starts with Scharf (vol. 2, pp. 1225–1236) and has been cited by others. There are a number of flaws in the story. First of all, if the British had done it, Henry Fisher would surely have reported it as he did other landings, even minor ones. He didn't. Geographically it doesn't make sense. The lighthouse was atop the Great Dune. Cattle normally grazed in the marsh almost a mile away rather than in the sand of the cape and the pine woods. The lighthouse served as a watchtower and the first stage of Fisher's warning system, and it was guarded by Lewes militia. Having been warned of the possible move of the British from Staten Island, they would have been alert at the time. The militia from town routinely was called out when British boats came ashore. If the British party had come ashore, especially the second time in force, a militia force would have been on hand—and even a smaller militia force at the lighthouse was in a superior position to fire down on the British onshore. Even if the lighthouse were undefended, would the British been willing to trudge up the great dune to light the fire? And what had they brought with them to light it?

Not only did Henry Fisher not report the confrontation, neither did William Adair mention such an incident in his diary. Then there is this: "Assistant Director of Naval History, F. Kent Loomis, Captain USN (Ret.) has reported, after a study of the microfilmed log of the *Roebuck*, that no mention was made of the landing or the lighthouse burning" (Beach, 35–36). Such events would normally appear in a ship's log (William Manthorpe, "Lewes in the Revolutionary War," unfinished article).

49. Manthorpe, "Establishing the Basis for the Safe Navigation of Delaware Bay, 1756–1856," 10.

Chapter Two

1. John Monroe, *History of Delaware* (Newark: University of Delaware Press, 2006), 61–73.

2. Tyler, *The Bay and River Delaware*, 23.

3. "Pennsylvania Committee of Safety, September 16, 1775," Peter Force Collection, American Archives: Documents of the American Revolutionary Period, 1774–1776, 3:745 (Northern Illinois University, http://amarch.lib.niu.edu/islandora/object/niu-amarch%3A83426).

4. Molly Murray, "The Lewes Shipwreck Site: A Window into 1770s Economy of Delaware" (October 9, 2010), https://archaeologynewsnetwork.blogspot.com/2010/10/lewes-shipwreck-site-window-into-1770s.html#WIm6DcE3ClQCabZI.97.

5. Pennsylvania Historical and Museum Commission, http://www.phmc.pa.gov/Archives/Research-Online/Pages/Revolutionary-War-Militia-Overview.aspx.

6. Christopher Ward, *The Delaware Continentals* (Wilmington: Historical Society of Delaware, 1941), 4–10.

7. On This Day in History, Delaware Declares Independence, http://www.history.com/this-day-in-history/delaware-declares-independence.

8. Ibid.

9. E.B. Potter, *Illustrated History of the United States Navy* (New York: Thomas Crowell, 1971), 10.

10. Continental Congress, "Resolution of July 18, 1775," *Journals of the Continental Congress* 2 (Washington, D.C.: Government Printing Office, 1905), 189 (http://memory.loc.gov).

11. Charles Oscar Paullin, *The Navy of the American Revolution: Its Administration, Its Policy and Its Achieve-

ments (Chicago: Burrows Brothers, 1906), 374. This work contains summary information on each of the various state navies.

12. John W. Jackson, *The Pennsylvania Navy, 1775–1781* (New Brunswick: Rutgers University Press, 1974), 136.

13. Pennsylvania State Navy, http://panavy.org/history-2/.

14. Paullin, *The Navy of the American Revolution*, 385.

15. Ibid., 391.

16. Ibid.

17. Pennsylvania Navy, https://en.wikipedia.org/wiki/Pennsylvania_Navy.

18. Scharf, *History of Delaware*, vol. 1, 186–187.

19. Ibid.

20. Ibid., 189–190.

21. Ibid.

22. "To Benjamin Franklin from Thomas Read, 8 September 1780," Founders Online, National Archives (http://founders.archives.gov/documents/Franklin/01-33-02-0221 [last update: September 29, 2015]). Source: *The Papers of Benjamin Franklin*, vol. 33, *July 1 through November 15, 1780*, ed. Barbara B. Oberg (New Haven: Yale University Press, 1997), 270.

23. Ibid.

24. James Grant Wilson and John Fiske, eds., *Appletons' Cyclopaedia of American Biography*, vol. 5 (New York: Appleton, 1898), 198.

25. "Continental Naval Committee in Account with James Read," *Naval Documents of the American Revolution* 2, part 3, p. 408.

26. William Manthorpe, "The Read Brothers of New Castle and the Creation of the American Navy."

27. "Continental Naval Committee in Account with James Read," *Naval Documents of the American Revolution* 3, part 5, pp. 961–962.

28. *Pennsylvania Journal* (Wednesday, October 11, 1775), *NDAR* 2, part 3, p. 408.

29. William Manthorpe, "The United States Navy, Revolution through Civil War," unpublished manuscript (n.d.), 1.

30. Potter, *Illustrated History of the United States Navy*, 10–12.

31. Manthorpe, "The Read Brothers."

32. Military History Now, "The Battle for Nassau—The First Mission for America's Marines" (May 17, 2013), http://militaryhistorynow.com/2013/03/17/invasion-of-nassau-the-first-mission-for-americas-marines/.

33. "Letter from Henry Fisher to Pennsylvania Committee of Safety, April 1, 1776," American Archives: Documents of the Revolutionary Period, 1774–1776 (Northern Illinois University Libraries, http://amarch.lib.niu.edu).

34. "Instructions of the Committee of Safety at Philadelphia to Mr. Henry Fisher at Lewis Town, September 16, 1775," *Colonial Records of Pennsylvania* 10 (Harrisburg: Published by the State, printed by Theo. Fenn, 1852), 337.

35. Michael Morgan, *Pilots and Patriots* (New York: Algora, 2005), 27.

36. "Letter from Henry Fisher," 2–3.

37. Morgan, *Pirates and Patriots*, 2.

38. Kim Burdick, "Rolling on the River: Delaware in the American Revolution," *Journal of the American Revolution* (2017), https://allthingsliberty.com/2017/01/rolling-river-delaware-american-revolution/.

39. Scharf, *History of Delaware*, 227.

40. Ibid.

41. Ibid.

42. George C. Daughan, *If by Sea: The Forging of the American Navy, from the Revolution to the War of 1812* (New York: Basic Books, 2011), 89.

43. Naval History and Heritage Command, *Wasp I*, ship's history, https://www.history.navy.mil/research/histories/ship-histories/danfs/w/wasp-i.html.

44. Naval History and Heritage Command, *Andrew Doria*, ship's history, https://www.history.navy.mil/research/histories/ship-histories/danfs/a/andrew-doria-i.html.

45. John Barry Kelly, "Commodore Barry, Father of the American Navy," UShistory.org, http://www.ushistory.org/people/commodorebarry.htm.

46. *Dictionary of American Naval Fighting Ships*, vol. 4 (Washington, D.C.: Navy Department, 1969).

47. Gar Olsen, *Blood Spilled for Freedom: America's Struggle for Survival, 1776–1815* (Bloomington: Author House, 2014), 29

48. Tim McGrath, *John Barry: An American Hero in the Age of Sail* (Yardley, PA: Westholme, 2010), 43–45.

49. Ibid., 99–101.

50. *Dictionary of American Naval Fighting Ships*, vol. 4.

51. McGrath, *John Barry*, 156–159.

52. Ibid., 204.

53. Ibid., 229–230.

54. Ibid., 251–265.

55. Ibid., 321–329.

56. Ibid., 476.

57. Charles E. Green, *The Story of Delaware in the Revolution* (Wilmington: Cann Printing 1975), 74–82.

58. Tim McGrath, *Give Me a Fast Ship* (New York: NAL Caliber, 2014), 165.

59. Scharf, *History of Delaware*, 246–247.

60. Thomas J. McGuire, *The Philadelphia Campaign*, vol. 2 (Mechanicsburg, PA: Stackpole Books, 2007), 182.

61. AmericanRevolution.org, "The Battle of the Kegs, 1778," http://www.americanrevolution.org/war_songs/warsongs55.php.

62. McGrath, *Give Me a Fast Ship*, 165–167.

63. "History of Ships Named 'Delaware'" (Washington, D.C.: Navy Department, Office of Chief of Naval Operations, 1960).

64. "British Fleet Suffers Defeat at Fort Mifflin, Pennsylvania," http://www.freerepublic.com/focus/f-news/2796984/posts.

65. McGuire, *The Philadelphia Campaign*, vol. 2, pp. 207–208.

66. McGrath, *John Barry*, 127–132.

67. Ibid., 203–204.

68. Manthorpe, "The United States Navy, Revolution through Civil War," 5–8.

69. Potter, *Illustrated History of the United States Navy*, 10.

70. Nathan Miller, *The U.S. Navy: A History*, 3d ed. (Annapolis: Naval Institute Press, 1997), 11.

71. Chappelle, *The American Sailing Navy*, 75, 78, 90.

72. "History of Ships Named 'Delaware.'"

73. Ibid.

74. Ibid., 24.

75. Ibid., 26–27.

76. Charles E. Green, *The Story of Delaware in the Revolution* (Wilmington: Cann Press, 1975), 172.

77. Delaware Public Archives, *Military and Naval Records* (Wilmington: Mercantile Printing Company, by authority of Public Records Commission of Delaware, 1912), vol. 2, 919–920.

78. "Letter of Charles Pope to President of Delaware,"

in Delaware Public Archives, *Military and Naval Records* (Wilmington: Mercantile Printing Company, by authority of Public Records Commission of Delaware, 1912), vol. 2, 919-939, 949.
 79. "History of Ships Named 'Delaware,'" 34-36.
 80. Martin Ignatius Joseph Griffin, *Commodore John Barry: The Father of the American Navy* (Philadelphia, 1903), 109.
 81. Ibid., 110-111.
 82. Scharf, *History of Delaware*, vol. 1, 263.
 83. Bob Ruppert, "Joshua Barney's Victory in Delaware Bay," *Journal of the American Revolution* (June, 7, 2016), https://allthingsliberty.com/2016/06/joshua-barney-victory-delaware-bay/.
 84. Ibid.
 85. Joshua Barney, Biography, Naval History and Heritage Command, https://www.history.navy.mil/research/library/research-guides/z-files/zb-files/zb-files-b/barney-joshua.html.
 86. James M. Volo, *Blue Water Patriots: The American Revolution Afloat* (Westport, CT: Greenwood Publishing Group, 2007), 55.
 87. James A. Lewis, *Neptune's Militia: The Frigate South Carolina During the American Revolution* (Kent, OH: Kent State University Press. 1999), 92-94.
 88. Frank Moore, *Songs and Ballads of the American Revolution Papers of George Washington: Revolutionary War Revolutionary War Series* (Carlisle, PA: Applewood Books, 2009), 375.
 89. "Coast Guard History" (Washington, D.C.: USCG Public Information Division CG-213, 1958), 1.

Chapter Three

 1. Stephen H. Evans, *The United States Coast Guard, 1790-1915: A Definitive History* (Annapolis: Naval Institute Press, 1949), 9.
 2. "The First Ten Cutters: The First Commissioned U.S. Revenue Cutters" (United States Coast Guard, U.S. Department of Homeland Security).
 3. Upon its return, the *Alliance* went through several owners and was finally abandoned on the mud flats of the Delaware, where it stayed until the early 1900s when she was destroyed during dredging—a sad end for a proud ship.
 4. Tyler, *Bay and River Delaware*, 37-38.
 5. Potter, *The Naval Academy Illustrated History of the United States Navy*, 29.
 6. Stephen Howarth, *To Shining Sea: A History of the United States Navy* (New York: Random House 1991), 55.
 7. Joseph F. Callo, "William Jones—Secretary Who?" *Military History* (August 28, 2017), http://www.historynet.com/william-jones-secretary.htm.
 8. McGrath, *John Barry*, 423-424.
 9. Potter, *Illustrated History of the United States Navy*, 29.
 10. Howard I. Chappelle, *The American Sailing Navy: The Ships and Their Development* (New York: Bonanza Books, 1949), 56-58.
 11. *Encyclopedia Britannica*, "Joshua Humphreys, American Ship Designer," https://www.britannica.com/biography/Joshua-Humphreys.
 12. Chappelle, *The American Sailing Navy*, 129-130.
 13. Nathaniel Conley, "Quasi-War," *The Encyclopedia of Greater Philadelphia*, http://philadelphiaencyclopedia.org/archive/quasi-war/.
 14. Ibid.

 15. "History of Ships Named 'Delaware,'" 2-3.
 16. William H.J. Manthorpe, Jr., *A History of American Naval Ships Named "Delaware"* (Dover: Delaware Heritage Press, 2017), 46-48.
 17. Ibid.
 18. Robert W. Neeser, "The Ships of the United States Navy: An Historical Record of Those Now in Service and Their Predecessors of the Same Name, 'Delaware'" *Naval Institute Proceedings* 41(United States Naval Institute, 1915, 1982).
 19. Emerson Wilson, "6 Navy Ships Bore Name of 'Delaware,'" *Evening Journal*, April 17, 1965, p. 15.
 20. Ibid.
 21. "History of Ships Named 'Delaware,'" 3.
 22. Jeffrey M. Dorwart, *The Philadelphia Navy Yard* (Philadelphia: University of Pennsylvania Press, 2001), 1-2.
 23. Daughen, *If by Sea*.
 24. V. Chapman-Smith, "Philadelphia and the Slave Trade: The Ganges Africans," *Pennsylvania Legacies* (Historical Society of Pennsylvania) (November 2005).
 25. Mark M. Cleaver, *The Life, Character, and Public Services of Commodore Jacob Jones* (Wilmington: Historical Society of Delaware, 1906), 3-5.
 26. Ibid.
 27. Nathan Miller, *The U.S. Navy: A History*, 3rd ed. (Annapolis: Naval Institute Press, 1997), 45-46.
 28. *Charles Lee Lewis: Famous American Naval Officers* (Boston: L.C. Page, 1924), 100-101.
 29. George Daughan, *The Shining Sea: David Porter and the Epic Voyage of the USS "Essex"* (Philadelphia: Basic Books, 2013), 21.
 30. Virtual American Biographies, David Porter, http://www.virtualology.com/davidporter1/.
 31. Naval History and Heritage Command, Adapted from "William Jones" (biography, dated September 3, 1918) in Navy Department Library Rare Book Room, ZB Files, https://www.history.navy.mil/research/library/research-guides/z-files/zb-files/zb-files-j/william-jones.html.
 32. Ibid.
 33. Ian W. Toll, *Six Frigates: The Epic History of the Founding of the U.S Navy* (New York: W.W. Norton, 2006), 165-168.
 34. Addison Whipple, *To the Shores of Tripoli* (Annapolis: Naval Institute Press, 1991), 80.
 35. Potter, *Illustrated History of the United States Navy*, 33.
 36. Chappelle, *The American Sailing Navy*, 161-164.
 37. Toll, *Six Frigates*, 206-211.
 38. Ibid.
 39. Three warships of the Navy have been named *Reuben James* in his honor: *Reuben James* (DD-245), a four-stack *Clemson*-class destroyer; *Reuben James* (DE-153), a *Buckley*-class destroyer; and *Reuben James* (FFG-57), an *Oliver Hazard Perry*-class frigate.
 40. Potter, *Illustrated History of the United States Navy*, 35.
 41. Ibid.
 42. *Dictionary of American Naval Fighting Ships*, Department of the Navy, https://web.archive.org/web/20050226121548/http://www.history.navy.mil/danfs/m9/meredith-i.htm.
 43. USS *O'Bannon* DD450, http://destroyerhistory.org/fletcherclass/ns_obannon/.
 44. Chappelle, *The American Sailing Navy*, 189-209.
 45. Ibid., 184.
 46. Ibid., 212-214.
 47. Miller, *The U.S. Navy*, 58.

48. Potter, *Illustrated History of the United States Navy*, 38.
49. Mathew Carey, *The Olive Branch; Or, Faults on Both Sides Federal and Democratic: A Serious Appeal on the Necessity of Mutual Forgiveness and Harmony* (Philadelphia, 1815), 111.
50. Scharf, *History of Delaware*, vol. 1, 277.
51. Potter, *Illustrated History of the United States Navy*, 39.
52. Samuel Woodsworth, "By the President of the United States of America: A Proclamation," July 4, 1812, https://archive.org/stream/warv1n2wood#page/1/mode/1up.
53. Eugene Rachlis, *The Story of the U.S. Coast Guard* (New York: Random House, 1961), 26.
54. Callo, "William Jones—Secretary Who?"
55. Ibid.
56. Potter, *Illustrated History of the United States Navy*, 39.
57. Callo, "William Jones—Secretary Who?"
58. Ibid.
59. Ibid.
60. Stephen Budiansky, *Perilous Fight* (New York: Knopf Doubleday, 2011), xiv.
61. Toll, *Six Frigates*, 48–51.
62. Callo, "William Jones—Secretary Who?"
63. Ibid.
64. Paul A. Gilje, "Free Trade and Sailors' Rights: The Rhetoric of the War of 1812," *Journal of the Early Republic*, https://www.questia.com/library/journal/1P3-2867809501/free-trade-and-sailors-rights-the-rhetoric-of.
65. Virtual American Biographies, David Porter, http://www.virtualology.com/davidporter1/.
66. Potter, *Illustrated History of the United States Navy*, 49–50.
67. Two destroyers in the U.S. Navy have been named after Bush. The first, USS *Bush* (DD-166), was a *Wickes*-class destroyer that served from 1919 to 1922 and was scrapped in 1936. The second, USS *Bush* (DD-529), was a *Fletcher*-class destroyer that served from 1943 to 1945. She was sunk in April 1945 off Okinawa after being struck by three Japanese kamikaze aircraft during the naval invasion of Okinawa. http://www.ussbush.com/shrthist.htm.
68. Potter, *Illustrated History of the United States Navy*, 42.
69. Ibid.
70. Scharf, *History of Delaware*, vole. 283.
71. Ibid., 284.
72. During the Civil War a New York ferryboat was acquired by the U.S. Navy and named *Commodore Jones*. She was the first of an ill-starred line of naval ships named for Jacob Jones. *Commodore Jones* served in the evacuation of West Point, Virginia, in 1863 and was on operations along the Mattaponi River, Chickahominy River, and James River. She was sunk by an electric torpedo (mine) in 1864 with the loss of about 40 sailors.

The next U.S. naval ship named for Jacob Jones was one of the famous pre–World War I four-pipers. In 1917 she was with the first group of destroyers sent to England, arriving in May 1917. USS *Jacob Jones* operated in British waters escorting convoys, sighting and attacking submarines, and rescuing survivors of sunken ships all summer. Off Queenstown on December 17 she sighted a torpedo and couldn't avoid it. It hit the stern fuel tank, and as the stern went down depth charges exploded and the ship sank in 8 minutes. Lost were 68 men. Commander Worth Bagley and 38 others survived. The submarine surfaced and took two prisoners but radioed the location of sinking so rescue ops could begin. One of the survivors was Lieutenant Norman Scott, who rose to admiral only to be killed at Guadalcanal. This was the only U.S. major combat ship sunk in Europe in World War I. Another *Jacob Jones* was immediately built. But she was commissioned too late for the war. In the 1920s she operated in the Pacific, and in the 1930s she patrolled in Atlantic waters. Prior to World War II she operated in the Mediterranean evacuating Americans during the Spanish Civil War and in 1940 and 1941 served on neutrality patrol off the U.S. coast. Starting in July 1941, the U.S. began convoying ships via Newfoundland and Iceland, where the British would pick up the convoy. *Jacob Jones* was on that duty until February 1942. In January 1942 German submarine Operation Drumroll began on the U.S. coast and sank 14 ships in January and 17 in February. To combat this, ten of the oldest destroyers were recalled from convoy duty to establish anti-submarine patrols off the coast. *Jacob Jones* was one of the first. On February 22, she sailed from New York and detected and attacked a sub with 57 depth charges off Ambrose light but was unsuccessful. After rearming to shore she departed New York on February 27 with orders to patrol the New Jersey coast to Cape May. Off Barnegat Light, in North Jersey, she came upon flaming wreckage of the tanker *Resor* and searched for survivors; finding none she proceeded south during the night of February 27–28, sailing in radio silence and darkened ship at 15 knots. At dawn on the 28th German sub U-587 fired two torpedoes. The first hit forward of the bridge, exploding a magazine, killing everyone on the bridge, and breaking the forward part of the ship off, which sank. The second torpedo hit aft and sank that portion of the ship. Only 25–30 men amidships were able to abandon ship. As the stern sank, depth charges exploded and killed more men. When remaining survivors were sighted by an army patrol plane only 12 were found and one died en route to Cape May. This was the first U.S. ship sunk after Pearl Harbor.

A third *Jacob Jones* was commissioned in time to convoy troop and supply ships to North Africa for Operation Torch and then later convoyed troop and supply ships to Britain for the Normandy invasions, crossing the Atlantic 20 times. After the German surrender she was sent to the Pacific but arrived at Pearl Harbor just as the Japanese surrendered. She returned to the Gulf Reserve Fleet after the war.

73. Potter, *Illustrated History of the United States Navy*, 42–43.
74. Ibid., 44–45.
75. Scharf, *History of Delaware*, vol. 282.
76. Potter, *Illustrated History of the United States Navy*, 50.
77. Francis Beirne, *The War of 1812* (New York: E.P. Dutton, 1949), 124.
78. Scharf, *History of Delaware*, vol. 1, 283.
79. Ibid., 286.
80. "Cedar Creek," *Niles Weekly Register* 4 (1813), Events of the War, 69.
81. Scharf, *History of Delaware*, vol. 1, 288.
82. William Marine, *The Bombardment of Lewes* (Historical Society of Delaware, 1901), 14–15.
83. Marine, *The Bombardment of Lewes*, 16.
84. Ibid., 19–22.
85. C.H.B. Turner, *Some Records of Sussex County, Delaware* (Philadelphia: Allen, Lane and Scott, 1919), 290.

86. Marine, *The Bombardment of Lewes.*
87. Scharf, *History of Delaware*, vol. 1, 286.
88. Ibid., 296.
89. William S. Dudley, "James Biddle and the Delaware Flotilla," *The Naval War of 181: A Documentary History*, vol. 2 (Washington, D.C.: Government Printing Office, 1985), 83.
90. Ibid.,199.
91. Ibid., 201.
92. Scharf, *History of Delaware*, vol. 1, 298.
93. Robert Fulton, *Torpedo War and Submarine Explosions* (New York: Wm. Elliott, 1810).
94. Potter, *Illustrated History of the U.S. Navy*, 51.
95. Chappelle, *The American Sailing Navy*, 54–55.
96. Ibid., 54–55
97. Ibid., 55–56.
98. Ibid.
99. Theodore Roosevelt, *The Naval War of 1812* (New York: Modern Library), 215–217.
100. Ibid., 207.
101. Stephen Cassin, http://www.arlingtoncemetery.net/scassin.htm. Stephen Cassin (February 16, 1783– August 29, 1857) was an officer in the United States Navy. Born in Philadelphia, the son of naval officer John Cassin, he entered the navy as a midshipman in 1800 and served in Philadelphia and the West Indies during the latter part of the war with France. In the War of 1812 he commanded USS *Ticonderoga* in the Battle of Lake Champlain and was awarded a gold medal for bravery by the United States Congress. He later served in *Peacock* during the Second Barbary War.
102. Rodney Macdonough, *Life of Commodore Thomas Macdonough, U.S. Navy* (Boston: Fort Hill, 1909), 30–31.
103. Ibid., 249–251.
104. The first USS *Macdonough* (DD-9) was a *Lawrence*-class destroyer, which was a sub-class of the *Bainbridge*-class destroyer, in the United States Navy. She was named for Commodore Thomas Macdonough. *Macdonough* was laid down on April 10, 1899, by the Fore River Ship & Engine Company, Weymouth, Massachusetts. Placed in full commission on November 21, 1908, *Macdonough* became the flagship of the 3rd Torpedo Flotilla and sailed for Pensacola, Florida. She participated in operations out of that port until the following spring, when she returned to the East Coast. During the summer of 1909 she cruised with the Atlantic Torpedo Squadron off New England.

Until January 1918 she performed screening assignments off the East Coast. On January 16, 1918, she departed Philadelphia for Brest, France, arriving February 20. She remained off the coast of France providing escort and patrol services until May 20, 1919. Sailing for the United States, she arrived at Philadelphia on June 24 and remained in that port until decommissioned on September 3. Her name was struck from the Naval Vessel Register on November 7, 1919, and her hulk was sold for scrapping on March 10, 1920.

The second USS *Macdonough* (DD-331) was a *Clemson*-class destroyer and was laid down May 24, 1920, by the Bethlehem Shipbuilding Corporation, San Francisco, California. She was launched December 15, 1920. *Macdonough* operated primarily along the West Coast. Periodic maneuvers and cruises with the fleet off the Pacific coast of Central America, the Hawaiian Islands, and in the Caribbean, as well as special assignments, intervened in her normal operations schedule. Included in her special assignments was a goodwill cruise with the fleet to Samoa, Australia, and New Zealand, from June 20 to September 26, 1925. On March 22, 1929, *Macdonough* returned to San Diego from fleet exercises held off Balboa, Panama Canal Zone, and operated off southern California until decommissioning at San Diego on January 8, 1930. She was sold as scrap on December 20, 1930. The third USS *Macdonough* (DD-351) was a *Farragut*-class destroyer in the United States Navy during World War II. *Macdonough* was laid down May 15, 1933, by the Boston Navy Yard and launched August 22, 1934. Following an extensive shakedown cruise to Europe and western South America, she joined the Pacific Fleet and operated out of San Diego, California, until October 12, 1939. She then shifted to Pearl Harbor as part of Destroyer Squadron 1. In port during the attack on Pearl Harbor, *Macdonough* downed one of the Japanese attack planes before heading out to sea to join others in the search for the Japanese task force. For the next three and a half months, the destroyer performed scouting assignments southwest of Oahu. Before returning to Pearl Harbor to escort convoys to and from West Coast ports, she steamed as far as New Guinea, supporting airstrikes on Bougainville, Salamaua, and Lae.

She served for the entire war in the Pacific campaign from Pearl Harbor to Guadalcanal, the Aleutians, the Marshall Islands, the Mariana Islands, and the Philippines. She shelled enemy positions, served as a fighter director ship, escorted convoys, and served on screening and radar picket duty and patrolled for Japanese submarines. *Macdonough*, with *Monterey* and *Stephen Potter*, sank Japanese submarine RO-45 on April 30, 1944. At Guam when hostilities ended, *Macdonough* soon received orders to return to the United States. She arrived at San Diego on September 3, continuing on the next week to the New York Navy Yard, where she was decommissioned October 22, 1945.

The fourth USS *MacDonough* (DLG-8/DDG-39) was a *Farragut*-class guided-missile destroyer in the United States Navy. The fourth *Macdonough* was projected as DL-8 but was redesignated DLG-8 prior to keel laying by the Fore River Shipyard, Bethlehem Steel Co., Quincy, Massachusetts, April 16, 1958. She launched July 8, 1959, sponsored by Mrs. Agnes Macdonough Wilson, great-granddaughter of Commodore Thomas Macdonough, and was commissioned November 4, 1961. She was initially rated as a guided-missile frigate.

She reported to her homeport at Charleston, South Carolina, September 23, 1962, and assumed duties as flagship for the commander, Cruiser-Destroyer Flotilla 6, U.S. Atlantic Fleet. A month later she joined other units of the U.S. 2nd Fleet in enforcing the Cuban quarantine. She served from her homeport in Charleston as well as two Mediterranean cruises. USS *Macdonough* was decommissioned April 6, 1973, and recommissioned May 4, 1974. She was decommissioned a second time on October 23, 1992, stricken from the rolls, and finally scrapped in Philadelphia in 2004. The Liberty Ship *SS Thomas Macdonough* was laid down October 21, 1941, and launched January 28, 1942. She was scrapped in 1967.
105. Hancock County Historical Society, "Thomas Shields, 1783–1827," http://www.hancockcountyhistoricalsociety.com/vignettes/thomas-shields-1783–1827/.
106. Stanley Clisby Arthur, *The Story of the Battle of New Orleans* (New Orleans: Louisiana Historical Society, 1915), http://www2.latech.edu/~bmagee/louisiana_anthology/texts/arthur/arthur—battle.html.
107. Potter, *Illustrated History of the U.S. Navy*, 57.
108. Frederic C. Leiner, *The End of Barbary Terror: America's 1815 War Against the Pirates of North Africa* (Oxford: Oxford University Press, 2007), 39–50.

Chapter Four

1. Potter, *Illustrated History of the U.S. Navy*, 57.
2. Ibid.
3. Anonymous (1824), *A View of the Present State of the African Slave Trade* (Philadelphia: Yearly Meeting of the Religious Society of Friends, William Brown), 33.
4. Francis Warriner, *Cruise of the United States Frigate "Potomac" Round the World, During the Years 1831–34* (New York: Leavitt, Lord, 1835), 104.
5. Potter, *Illustrated History of the United States Navy*, 58–61.
6. Tyler, *Bay and River Delaware*, 63.
7. Ralph D. Gray, *The National Waterway: A History of the Chesapeake and Delaware Canal, 1769–1985* (Chicago: University of Illinois Press, 1989), 18.
8. *Ibid.*, 47–48.
9. Ibid., 66.
10. Frank E. Snyder and Brian H. Guss, *The District: A History of the Philadelphia District U.S. Army Corps of Engineer,s 1866–1971* (Philadelphia: U.S. Army Engineer District, 1974), 86–87.
11. Ibid., 5–6.
12. House Documents, 13th Congress, 2nd Session–49th, 1837–38, 5, https://books.google.com/books.
13. Scharf, *History of Delaware*, vol. 2, 752.
14. Dorwart, *The Philadelphia Navy Yard*, 57–60.
15. Chappelle, *The American Sailing Navy*, 371–374.
16. U.S. Naval Historical Center, USS *Pennsylvania*, Online Library of Selected Images, http://www.ibiblio.org/hyperwar/OnlineLibrary/photos/sh-usn/usnsh-p/penna.htm.
17. Ibid.
18. Dorwart, *Philadelphia Navy Yard*, 76.
19. Urban, *The City That Launched a Thousand Ships*, 17–18.
20. Doerrfeld, et al., *The Delaware Ship and Boat Building Industry, 1830–1940: An Historic Context*, 21.
21. David Tyler, *The American Clyde* (Newark: University of Delaware Press, 1958), 16.
22. Ibid., 8.
23. Naval History and Heritage Command, *Scourge III* (https://www.history.navy.mil/research/histories/ship-histories/danfs/s/scourge-iii.html).
24. Kenneth R. Martin, *Delaware Goes Whaling, 1833–1845* (Greenville, DE: Hagley Museum, 1974), 26–27.
25. Scharf, *History of Delaware*, vol. 2, 751.
26. USS *DeHaven* Sailors Association, "Lieutenant Edwin Jesse DeHaven," http://ussdehaven.org/lcdr.htm.
27. Ibid.
28. Scharf, *History of Delaware*, vol. 1, 321–322.
29. Chappelle, *The American Sailing Navy*, 314–315.
30. *Ships Named "Delaware,"* 4.
31. John P. Gillis, "U.S. *Brandywine*, Journal While on Frigate to South America, 1826–1828," *Brandywine, Congress, Constitution and Tampico, 1826–1847*, Manuscript Box 20, 1826–1847, John P. Gillis Papers, Delaware Historical Society, Wilmington.
32. Staff, Virginia Historic Landmarks Commission, James W. Moody, Jr., director (November 18, 1969), "National Register of Historic Places Inventory-Nomination: Dry dock Number One, Norfolk Naval Shipyard" (pdf), National Park Service, and "Accompanying Four Photos of This and Dry Dock Number Four, from 1984 and Undated."
33. John Lloyd Stephens, *Incidents of Travel in Egypt, Arabia, Petrea and the Holy Land*, vol. 1 (New York: Harper, 1837), 33 (cited in Bowers, 16).
34. Manthorpe, *A History of American Naval Ships Named "Delaware,"* 91, 92.
35. Ibid., 93.
36. Ibid., 5.
37. Donald L. Canney, *Sailing Warships of the U.S. Navy* (Annapolis: Naval Institute Press, 2001), 66.
38. Chappelle, *The American Sailing Navy*, 336.
39. James L. Mooney, *Naval History and Heritage Command, "Brandywine,"* December 13, 2005, https://www.history.navy.mil/research/histories/ship-histories/danfs/b/brandywine-i.html.
40. Ibid.
41. Ibid.
42. Ibid.
43. Ibid.
44. Ibid.
45. In October 1830 Ballard took *Brandywine* to the Mediterranean. Then Patterson is sent to the Mediterranean in *United States*. In the spring of 1833 Ballard takes *Brandywine* home. By July Ballard is commanding *Delaware* and in August sails her to the Mediterranean via France. After *Delaware* finally arrives in the Mediterranean in February Patterson transfers his flag from *United States* to *Delaware*. Ballard takes *United States* home.
46. Ibid.
47. Ibid.
48. Ibid.
49. Ibid.
50. Ibid.
51. Ibid.
52. Ibid.
53. *Dictionary of American Naval Fighting Ships*, vol. 1, p. 151.
54. Find a Grave, Henry Hayes Lockwood, https://www.findagrave.com/memorial/5841809.
55. Wilson, *Forgotten Heroes of Delaware*, 149–150.
56. John H. Eicher and David J. Eicher, *Civil War High Commands* (Stanford: Stanford University Press, 2001), 351.
57. Most of the brief biography of Samuel Du Pont that follows is from an unpublished manuscript by William Manthorpe.
58. Samuel Francis Du Pont Papers, Hagley Museum and Library, Manuscripts and Archives Department, http://findingaids.hagley.org/xtf/view?docId=ead/WMSS_IX.xml.
59. *Franklin II* (Ship of the Line) Naval History and Heritage Command, https://www.history.navy.mil/search.html?q=franklin+III.
60. Claude Berube and John Rodgaard, *A Call to the Sea: Captain Charles Stewart of the USS "Constitution"* (Dulles, VA: Potomac Books, 2005).
61. Jacob Jones to Victor du Pont, February 27, 1821, S.F. Du Pont Papers, W3-3274, Hagley Museum and Library.
62. Samuel Francis Du Pont Papers, Hagley Museum and Library, Manuscripts and Archives Department, http://findingaids.hagley.org/xtf/view?docId=ead/WMSS_IX.xml.
63. Ibid.
64. Manthorpe, "Samuel F. Du Pont," unpublished manuscript.
65. Scharf, *History of Delaware*, 358.
66. William H. Meyers, *Journal of a Cruise to California and the Sandwich Islands in the United States Sloop of War "Cyane," 1841–1844* (San Francisco: Book Club of California, 1955).
67. Ibid.

68. Ibid.
69. Ibid.
70. Richard W. Amero, "The Mexican-American War in Baja California," *Journal of San Diego History*, San Diego Historical Society (Winter 1984), https://www.sandiegohistory.org/journal/1984/january/war/.
71. Ibid.
72. Samuel Francis Du Pont Papers, Hagley Museum and Library, Manuscripts and Archives Department, http://findingaids.hagley.org/xtf/view?docId=ead/WMSS_IX.xml.
73. K. Jack Bauer, "Samuel F. Du Pont, Aristocratic Professional in Captains of the Old Steam Navy," *Makers of American Naval Tradition, 1840–1880*, ed. James Bradford (Annapolis: Naval Institute Press, 1986), 147.
74. Scharf, *History of Delaware*, 358.
75. Manthorpe, "Samuel F. Du Pont."
76. Ibid.
77. Ibid.
78. Scharf, *History of Delaware*, 358.
79. Richard S. West, Jr., *The Second Admiral: A Life of David Dixon Porter* (New York: Coward-McCann, 1937), 24–27.
80. Chester G. Hearn, *Admiral David Dixon Porter: The Civil War Years* (Annapolis: Naval Institute Press, 1996), 12–13.
81. West, *Second Admiral*, 29–33.
82. Ibid., 29–35, 310–311.
83. Hearn, *Admiral Porter*, 21–23.
84. West, *Second Admiral*, 46–47.
85. James Russell Soley, *Admiral Porter* (New York: D. Appleton, 1903), 58, 67–75.
86. Hearn, *Admiral Porter*, 28–33, 34.
87. West, *Second Admiral*, 64–68.
88. Ibid., 71.

Chapter Five

1. W. Emerson Wilson, *A Fort Delaware Journal: The Diary of a Yankee Private, A.J. Hamilton, 1862–65* (Wilmington: Fort Delaware Society, 1981).
2. Scharf, *History of Delaware*, vol. 1, 343.
3. Snyder and Guss, *The District*, 24.
4. Ibid.
5. Tyler, *The American Clyde*, 14–16.
6. Ibid., 15.
7. ORA (Official Records, Armies), *War of the Rebellion: A Compilation of the Official Records of the Union and Confederate Armies*, vol. 51/1, pp. 369–370, 387.
8. Potter, *Illustrated History of the United States Navy*, 71–73.
9. Ibid., 73–74.
10. Dorwart, *Philadelphia Navy Yard*, 81–82.
11. Ibid., 84–85.
12. Ibid., 88, 92–98.
13. Manthorpe, "Samuel F. Du Pont."
14. Ibid.
15. Laura June Davis, "Voices from the Past: Gratifying Duty," *Civil War Monitor*, https://www.civilwarmonitor.com/blog/voices-from-the-past-the-gratifying-duty.
16. Manthorpe, "Samuel F. Du Pont."
17. Ibid.
18. Ibid.
19. Ibid.
20. Obituary, "Admiral Samuel Francis Du Pont," June 24, 1865, *New York Times*.
21. "History of Ships Named 'Delaware,'" 5.
22. Ibid.
23. Ibid.
24. Ibid.
25. Stephen Clegg Rowan, "Congratulatory Address to His Men after Capturing Elizabeth City, North Carolina," Gilder Hehrman Institute of American History, http://www.gilderlehrman.org/collections.
26. Ibid.
27. "History of Ships Named 'Delaware.'"
28. Ibid.
29. Ibid., 7.
30. Ibid.
31. Ibid.
32. Ibid.
33. Ibid.
34. McLane was a Delawarean who had a brief service as a midshipman on the USS *Philadelphia* when he was 18. He was a veteran of the War of 1812, serving in the Wilmington Artillery Company. He had a distinguished political career serving in the House of Representatives, the Senate, as minister to England, secretary of the treasury, and secretary of state.
35. Donald L. Canney, *U.S. Coast Guard and Revenue Cutters, 1790–1935* (Annapolis: Naval Institute Press, 1995).
36. Naval History and Heritage Command, *Hatteras I* (Screw Steamer), July 14, 2015, https://www.history.navy.mil/research/histories/ship-histories/danfs/h/hatteras-i.html.
37. Ibid.
38. Ibid.
39. Ibid.
40. Ibid.
41. Ibid.
42. Naval History and Heritage Command, *Arizona I* (Screw Steamer), June 18, 2015, https://www.history.navy.mil/research/histories/ship-histories/danfs/a/arizona-screw-steamer-i.html.
43. Ibid.
44. Hearn, *Admiral Porter*, 37–40.
45. Ibid.
46. Ivan Musicant, *Divided Waters: The Naval History of the Civil War* (New York: HarperCollins, 1995), 19–26.
47. Gideon Welles and Edgar Thaddeus Welles, *Diary of Gideon Welles*, vol. 1 (Boston: Houghton-Mifflin, 1911), 35.
48. Chester G. Hearn, *The Capture of New Orleans, 1862* (Baton Rouge: Louisiana State University Press, 1995) 98–101.
49. Ibid., 181–186; 204–236; 247–248; 252–253.
50. Bern Anderson, *By Sea and by River: The Naval History of the Civil War* (New York: Knopf, 1962; reprint, Da Capo, 1989), 137.
51. Welles, *Diary*, vol. 1, 157.
52. Hearn, *Admiral Porter*, 144–145.
53. John D. Winters, *The Civil War in Louisiana* (Baton Rouge: Louisiana State University Press, 1963), 48, 171.
54. William T. Sherman, *Memoirs*, vol. 1 (New York: D. Appleton, 1891), 297.
55. Hearn, *Admiral Porter*, 223–225.
56. Ibid., 236–237.
57. Musicant, *Divided Waters*, 294; West, *Second Admiral*, 244.
58. West, *Second Admiral*, 254–255, 256–262.
59. Hearn, *Admiral Porter*, 270–271.
60. Ibid., 280–281; 286–288.

61. Ibid., 294–301.
62. David Dixon Porter, *Incidents and Anecdotes of the Civil War* (New York: D. Appleton, 1886), 295–296.
63. Just before this tour of Richmond, Lincoln stayed aboard Porter's flagship. Earlier, Porter had several meetings with Lincoln during the war. The first one was with Seward and Meigs to plan the relief of Fort Pickens. It was Porter who convinced Lincoln to keep it secret from Welles. The second time was at the beginning of the Civil War, when Porter convinced Lincoln and Welles to trust Farragut, even though he was married to a Virginia woman and had spent most of his life living in Norfolk. He advocated giving Farragut command of the Gulf Squadron. Later, Porter met with Lincoln to propose a plan for taking New Orleans. It was at that time that he advocated the use of the mortar ships on the forts and received the command. There were probably other meetings as well. Even after Vicksburg in September 1863 Lincoln considered Porter "a busy schemer, bold but not of high qualities as a chief." He evidently changed his mind before the end of the war (Craig L. Symonds, *Lincoln and His Admirals* [New York: Oxford University Press, 2008], 254, 330, Kindle ed., citing Gideon Welles Diary of September 21, 1863 and September 27, 1863).
64. Porter, *Incidents and Anecdotes of the Civil War*, 318–320.
65. West, *Second Admiral*, 303–314; Melia, "David Dixon Porter," 237–238.
66. Melia, "David Dixon Porter," 240–241; West, *Second Admiral*, 317–326.
67. West, *Second Admiral*, 335–345.
68. Steven Hill, "Commodore John P. Gillis, Delaware's 'Other' Civil War Naval Hero," *Delaware History* (1987), 187.
69. Scharf, *History of Delaware*, vol. 1, 343.
70. Ibid.
71. Ibid.
72. Ibid.
73. Ibid.
74. Ibid.
75. Dr. Robert Girard Carroon, *Rear Admiral Purnell Frederick Harrington*, Military Order of the Loyal Legion of the United States, Commander's in Chief Biographies, http://suvcw.org/mollus/pcinc/pfharrington.htm.
76. Ibid.
77. Scharf, *History of Delaware*, vol. 1, 344.
78. Ibid.
79. Ibid., 344–345.
80. https://www.findagrave.com/cgi-bin/fg.cgi?page=gr&GRid=45915349.
81. Morgan, *Pirates and Patriots*, 117.
82. Emerson Wilson, *Forgotten Heroes of Delaware* (Cambridge, MA: Deltos, 1969), 146.
83. When Liverpool Was Dixie, "Quartermaster Russell Baker Hobbs CSS *Alabama*," http://www.csa-dixie.com/liverpool_dixie/hobbs.htm.
84. Wilson, *Forgotten Heroes*, 146.
85. Ibid.
86. Ibid.
87. 290 Foundation, "Russell Baker Hobbs," https://sites.google.com/site/290foundation/ancestors-page/russel-baker-hobbs.
88. Citizens of Delaware Who Served the Confederacy, http://www.descv.org/DelawareConfederates.html.
89. Raphael Waldburg, "The Case of David H. White and the First Emancipation Proclamation," http://www.southernheritage411.com/bc.php?nw=060.
90. Ibid.

Chapter Six

1. Paul H. Silverstone, *Civil War Navies, 1855–1883* (Annapolis: Naval Institute Press, 2001), ix.
2. Potter, *Illustrated History of the United States Navy*, 113.
3. Carroll S. Alden and Allen Westcott, *The United States Navy: A History* (Chicago: H.P. Lippincott, 1945), 282.
4. Ship-rigged is a sail plan of three masts with square sails.
5. Geo. Henry Preble, *History of the United States Navy Yard, Portsmouth, New Hampshire* (Washington, D.C.: U.S. Navy Bureau of Yards and Docks, Government Printing Office, 1892), 98. The "old" measure of a ship's size had long been the ship's internal volume for cargo, stores, provisions, etc., expressed as tonnage. In the British and U.S. sailing navies it was calculated by the "Builders Old Measure." With the advent of steamships much of the internal volume was taken up with machinery. Thus, in 1864 the U.S. Navy joined the Royal Navy in calculating a ship's size by a "new" measure in which size was expressed in tonnage by the Moorsom System, which excluded those spaces, giving a lower tonnage figure. Eventually the U.S. Navy began using "displacement" as the tonnage measure of a ship's size. She was listed in the 1867 Naval Register as a 1st rate screw ship of 21 guns with "old tonnage 3177" and "new tonnage 2490," 312-foot, single-screw ship. The Naval History and Heritage Command, *DANFS*, gives the tonnage of *Piscataqua* as "2354."
6. Robert W. Neeser, "An Historical Record of Those Now in Service and of Their Predecessors of the Same Name," *Proceedings, U.S. Naval Institute*, 1915, p. 1977.
7. "History of Ships Named 'Delaware,'" 7.
8. Ibid., 7–8.
9. Ibid., 8.
10. Ibid.
11. Ibid.
12. "History of Ships Named 'Delaware,'" 7–8.
13. James B. Rentfrew, *Home Squadron: The U.S. Navy on the North Atlantic Station* (Annapolis: Naval Institute Press, 2014).
14. Alden and Westcott, *The United States Navy*, 285.
15. Howarth, *To Shining Sea*, 223.
16. Ibid., 386.
17. Independence Seaport Museum, "Steering a Course: A Short History of the Pennsylvania Nautical School and Pennsylvania Maritime Academy," http://www.phillyseaport.org/pennsylvania-nautical-school/.
18. The Pennsylvania State Nautical School, Bulletin, 1932, J. Henderson Welles Archives and Library, Pennsylvania Nautical School Collection (print material).
19. Ibid.
20. Ibid.
21. Phillip Chadwick Foster Smith, *Philadelphia on the River* (Philadelphia: University of Pennsylvania Press, 1986), 112, 113.
22. The New Jersey Naval Militia, originally called the Naval Reserve of New Jersey, was founded in 1895 for the purpose of protecting the coast, harbors, and waterfront property. After the passage of the Federal Naval Reserve Law of 1916, the name was changed to the Naval Militia of New Jersey. The NJNM first saw combat during the Spanish–American War and also fought in World War I and World War II. After reaching a peak strength of 3,590 during the Korean War, the NJNM was absorbed by the United States Naval Reserve in 1963, after which it ceased to exist as an independent organization.

23. Smith, *Philadelphia on the River*, 112–113.
24. (Captain) Lewis E. Davis, "The Grounding of PNS/PMA: A Story of What Was and What Might Have Been," *The Lookout* 50, no. 1 (Autumn 2015), 30–32.
25. William H.J. Manthorpe, Jr., *A Century of Service* (Wilmington: Cedar Tree Press, 2014) 3–4.
26. Ibid.
27. Ibid.
28. https://en.wikipedia.org/wiki/Naval_Force_of_Pennsylvania.
29. Manthorpe, *A Century of Service*, 8.
30. Ibid.
31. Snyder and Guss, *The District*, 132.
32. Potter, *Illustrated History of the U.S. Navy*, 116–118.
33. Benjamin Franklin Cooling, *USS "Olympia": Herald of Empire* (Annapolis: Naval Institute Press, 2007), 14–15.
34. Ibid., 2.
35. "Olympia," *Dictionary of American Naval Fighting Ships*.
36. Ibid.
37. Tyler, *Bay and River Delaware*, 97.
38. Tyler, *The American Clyde*, 33.
39. Tyler, *Bay and River Delaware*, 114.
40. Ibid.
41. Tyler, *The American Clyde*, 33.
42. Gail E. Farr and Brett F. Bostwick with Merville Willis, *Shipbuilding at Cramp and Sons* (Philadelphia Maritime Museum, 1991), 7–12.
43. William C. Emerson, "USS *New Ironsides*: America's First Broadside Ironclad," Robert Gardiner, *Warship, 1993* (London: Conway Maritime Press, 1993), 7–11.
44. William H. Roberts, *USS New Ironsides in the Civil War* (Annapolis: Naval Institute Press, 1999), 92–106.
45. Farr and Bostwick with Willis, *Shipbuilding at Cramp and Sons*, 7–12.
46. Ibid.
47. Dorwart, *The Philadelphia Navy Yard*, 2.
48. Ibid., 117.
49. NavSource Online, Patrol Gunboat Photo Archives, "Wilmington (PG 8)," *Dictionary of American Naval Fighting Ships*, http://www.navsource.org/achives/12/09008d.htm.
50. Ibid.
51. Ibid.
52. Ibid.
53. Ibid.
54. Ibid.
55. Ibid.
56. Ibid.
57. Ibid.
58. Captain John Moore, RN, *Jane's Fighting Ships of World War I* (London: Random House, 2001), 143.
59. Snyder and Guss, *The District*, 130–131.
60. Ibid., 130.
61. Roales, *Delaware Light Houses and Range Lights*, 24–25.
62. Snyder and Guss, *The District*, 72–73.
63. Gray, *The National Waterway*, 157.
64. Ibid., 192.
65. Rae Tyson, "Cape Henlopen Quarantine First Stop for Many Immigrants," *Delaware Online*, December 3, 2014, http://www.delawareonline.com/story/life/2014/12/03/cape-henlopen-quarantine-first-stop-many-immigrants/19711353/.
66. Frank H. Taylor, *The Hand Book of the Lower Delaware River* (Philadelphia: Maritime Exchange, 1895), 24–27.
67. Ibid.
68. Taylor, *The Hand Book of the Lower Delaware River*, 28–36.
69. Ibid.
70. Ibid.
71. Carroon, *Rear Admiral Purnell Frederick Harrington*.
72. Wilson, *Forgotten Heroes*, 175.
73. Ibid.
74. Carroon, *Rear Admiral Purnell Frederick Harrington*.
75. Wilson, *Forgotten Heroes*, 175.
76. Military Times, Hall of Honor, Leonard B. Chadwick, https://valor.militarytimes.com/recipient.php?recipientid=2200.
77. Roger A. Martin, *Delaware's Medal of Honor Winners* (self-published, 1991), 50–54.
78. Ibid.
79. Ibid.
80. Ibid.
81. Ibid.
82. Ibid.
83. Ibid.
84. Bart Armstrong, "Gets Medal of Honor, Almost a VC, Then Gets Queen's Scarf," March 6, 2013, http://www.canadianmedalofhonor.com/sunday-evenings-blogs/gets-medal-of-honor-almost-a-vc-then-gets-queens-scarf.
85. Ibid.
86. Ibid.
87. Ibid.
88. Ibid.
89. Ibid.
90. Ibid.
91. Ibid.
92. Ibid.
93. Robert Trapani, Jr., *Journey Along the Sands: The U.S. Life-Saving Service, Years 1876–1915* (Virginia Beach: Donning, 2002), 15.
94. Taylor, *Handbook of Lower Delaware*, 66.
95. Pam George, *Shipwrecks of the Delaware Coast* (Charleston, SC: History Press, 2010), 48–50.
96. Trapani, *Journey Among the Sands*, 7–15.
97. Washington A. Vickers, Station log, Indian River Inlet Station.
98. Trapani, *Journey Among the Sands*, 22–32.
99. Ibid., 27–29.
100. Ibid., 60.
101. George, *Shipwrecks*, 52.
102. Trapani, *Journey Among the Sands*, 56–60.
103. Ibid.
104. Ibid., 57.
105. Potter, *Illustrated History of the United States Navy*, 118–120.
106. Manthorpe, *Century of Service*, 4–5.
107. Ibid., 5.
108. Ibid., 4–5.
109. Ibid., 6.
110. Ibid.
111. Ibid., 7
112. Ibid.
113. Ibid., 5–7
114. Manthorpe, *Century of Service*, 9.
115. Ibid., 8–9.
116. Ibid., 13–15.
117. William Manthorpe, "U.S. Naval Wireless Station, Cape Henlopen," *Lewes History: Journal of the Lewes Historical Society* 17 (November 2014), 29–47.
118. Manthorpe, *Century of Service*, 17–18.
119. Ibid., 16–19.
120. Ibid., 21–22.

Chapter Seven

1. Pratt, *The Compact History of the United States Navy*, 199.
2. Potter, *Illustrated History of the United States Navy*, 134–136.
3. John Howard Morrow, *The Great War: An Imperial History* (New York: Routledge, 2005), 202.
4. Potter, *Illustrated History of the United States Navy*, 138.
5. Alden, *The United States Navy*, 341.
6. "Subchasers of World War I," http://www.splinterfleet.org/sfww1.php.
7. Howarth, *To Shining Sea*, 309–311.
8. Potter, *Illustrated History of the United States Navy*, 142–143.
9. Alden, 360–364.
10. Potter, *Illustrated History of the United States Navy*, 134–145.
11. DANFS Delaware (BB-28).
12. Pratt, *Compact History of the United States Navy*, 204.
13. U.S. Military Bases, "USCG Training Center Cape May," http://www.militarybases.us/coast-guard/uscg-training-center-cape-may/.
14. Dorwart, *Philadelphia Navy Yard*, 137–138.
15. Alden, 364.
16. "A Brief History of U.S. Marine Corps Action in Europe During World War I," Reference Branch Marine Corps History Division, 2007, http://www.worldwar1centennial.org/index.php/usmc-in-ww1/850-a-brief-history-of-u-s-marine-corps-action-in-europe-during-world-war-i.html.
17. Public Information Division, CG 213, *Coast Guard History*, 12.
18. 1914 Annual Report WDF, Boosting Port of Philadelphia, papers of Independence Seaport Museum Library.
19. Jacob Downs, "World War I," *The Encyclopedia of Greater Philadelphia*, http://philadelphiaencyclopedia.org/archive/world-war-i/.
20. Snyder and Guss, *The District*, 133–134.
21. Dorwart, *Philadelphia Navy Yard*, 2–3.
22. Peter Hernon, *The Great Rescue* (New York: HarperCollins, 2017), 138, 211.
23. Kennard R. Wiggins, Jr., *Delaware in World War I* (Charleston, SC: History Press, 2016), 130–131.
24. Philip Smith, *Philadelphia on the River*, 148–150.
25. Ibid.
26. John W. Lawrence, "Hog Island," *The Encyclopedia of Greater Philadelphia*, http://philadelphiaencyclopedia.org/archive/hog-island/.
27. Daniel H. Jones, "The Hog Islanders", https://web.archive.org/web/20150419131808/http://smmlonline.com/articles/hogislanders/hogislanders.html.
28. Farr and Bostwick with Willis, *Shipbuilding at Cramp and Sons*, 12–13.
29. *Delaware's Port of Wilmington: 75 Years of Personal Service, 1923-1998*, 1–8.
30. Thompson and O'Byrne, *Wilmington's Waterfront*, 20.
31. Wiggins, *Delaware in World War I*, 2–56.
32. Ibid., 52–53.
33. Ibid., 53–54.
34. Ibid., 54–56.
35. Richard Elliott, *Last of the Steamboats* (Cambridge, MD: Tidewater, 1970), 34–36.
36. Manthorpe, *A Century of Service*, 27.
37. Ibid., 28–30.
38. Ibid.
39. Ibid., 31.
40. Ibid., 27–33.
41. Ibid., 36.
42. Ibid., 37.
43. Ibid., 38.
44. George, *Shipwrecks of the Delaware Coast*, 105–108.
45. Manthorpe, *A Century of Service*, 36–42.
46. Robert K. Massie, *Dreadnought* (New York: Random House, 1991), 470.
47. Ibid., 472.
48. Ibid., 471–474.
49. JO2 (Journalist Second Class) Mike McKinley, Naval History and Heritage Command, "Cruise of the Great White Fleet," 2017, https://www.history.navy.mil/research/library/online-reading-room/title-list-alphabetically/c/cruise-great-white-fleet-mckinley.html.
50. USS *South Carolina*, Naval History and Heritage Command, DANFS, 2016, https://www.history.navy.mil/research/histories/ship-histories/danfs/s/south-carolina-iv.html.
51. Norman Friedman, *U.S. Battleships: An Illustrated Design History* (Annapolis: Naval Institute Press, 1985), 63–65.
52. "Bonaparte Is Deluged by Advice on Warship," *Washington Times*, March 29, 1906, p. 8.
53. *Delaware* was dropped from the active list in 1923. In 1944 the Delaware State Society requested that the navy assign the name Delaware to a new battleship; however, they were unsuccessful and remained so until 2012 when the Navy Department announced that a new submarine would assume the name *Delaware* (SSN-791) a *Virginia*-class vessel. Her sponsor is Dr. Jill Biden, wife of Vice President Joseph Biden. Scheduled to deploy in 2018, the new submarine will be the seventh ship of the fleet to bear the name *Delaware*.
54. "First American Dreadnaught, the Delaware Launched," *Los Angeles Herald*, February 7, 1909, p. 2.
55. Christopher B. Havern, Sr., Naval History and Heritage Command, DANFS, "*Delaware VI* (Battleship No. 28), 1910–1923," 2017, https://www.history.navy.mil/content/history/nhhc/research/histories/ship-histories/danfs/d/delaware-vi.html.
56. Ibid.
57. Ibid.
58. Ibid.
59. Ibid.
60. "Giant Battleship Delaware, Most Powerful of All Modern Fighting Craft Afloat," *Newport News Daily Press*, December 12, 1909, p. 2.
61. "Our Dreadnought's Great Speed: Planning Still Larger Battleships," *New York Tribune*, October 24, 1909, p. 1.
62. "Silver Service, Portraits and Flags Presented to Battleship Delaware," *Ogden* (UT) *Evening Journal*, October 5, 1910.
63. "Scouting Ships to Try to Locate the 'Enemy's' Battleships Approaching Cuba form England," *Ogden* (UT) *Evening Standard*, December 30, 1910, p. 8.
64. "The Battleship Delaware and Her Great Cruise," *Caldwell Watchman*, February 3, 1911.
65. "Famous Battleship Delaware Which Will Represent the United States at Coronation," *Bismarck Daily Tribune*, June 20, 1911.
66. Undated and uncredited "Chronology of the USS *Delaware*," Research Library, Washington Navy Yard, Naval History and Heritage Command.
67. Havern, "*Delaware VI*."
68. Ibid.

69. "Vera Cruz Taken After Bombardment," *Medford Mail Tribune* April 22, 1914.
70. "Five Serious Charges of Inefficiency of Our Navy," *Richmond* (VA) *Times Dispatch*, November 15, 1914.
71. "The Truth About the Condition of Our Navy," *New York Tribune*, February 27, 1916.
72. Paul Halpern, "The U.S. Navy in the Great War," *Relevance: The Journal of the Great War Society* (Spring 2004), http://www.worldwar1.com/tgws/usnwwone.htm.
73. Captain Dudley W. Knox, Naval History and Heritage Command, "American Naval Participation in the Great War," 2017, https, //www.history.navy.mil/research/library/online-reading-room/title-list-alphabetically/a/american-naval-participation-in-the-great-war-with-special-reference-to-the-european-theater-of-operations.html.
74. At the British base coal was in plentiful supply but fuel oil was not.
75. Potter, *Illustrated History of the United States Navy*, 141.
76. Alden and Westcott, *The United States Navy: A History* (Chicago, J.B. Lippincott, 1945), 359–361.
77. Paul G. Halpern, *A Naval History of World War I* (Annapolis: Naval Institute Press, 1995), 418–420.
78. Havern, "*Delaware VI.*"
79. Ibid.
80. Ibid.
81. There is a video on YouTube that purports to show the *Delaware* transiting the canal. The time period may be right, but the three guns on the turrets belie the identity of the ship. The *Delaware* had only two guns per turret.
82. Havern, "*Delaware VI.*"
83. From the archives of the Delaware Historical Society Research Library.
84. Havern, "*Delaware VI.*"

Chapter Eight

1. Washington Naval Treaty also known as the Five-Power Treaty, *League of Nations Treaty Series* 25, pp. 202–227.
2. Naval History and Heritage Command, "U.S. Ship Force Levels, 1886–Present," https://www.history.navy.mil/research/histories/ship-histories/us-ship-force-levels.html.
3. Potter, *Illustrated History of the United States Navy*, 146–155.
4. Michael Gannon, *Operation Drumbeat: The Dramatic True Story of Germany's First U-boat Attacks Along the American Coast in World War II* (New York: Harper and Row, 1990), 292.
5. Winston Churchill, *The Hinge of Fate* (Boston: Houghton Mifflin, 1950), 111.
6. American Merchant Marine at War, "U.S. Ships Sunk or Damaged on East Coast of U.S. and Gulf of Mexico During World War II," http://www.usmm.org/eastgulf.html#anchor473040.
7. Snyder and Guss, *The District*, 99–101.
8. William Grayson, *Delaware's Ghost Towers: The Coast Artillery's Forgotten Last Stand During the Darkest Days of World War II* (Bloomington: Author's House, 2005), 3.
9. Named for the Delaware naval hero of the War of 1812.
10. USS *Jacob Jones*, DD 130, Destroyer History Foundation, http://destroyerhistory.org/flushdeck/ussjacobjones/.
11. Ibid.
12. Naval History and Heritage Command, *Jacob Jones II* (Destroyer No. 130), https://www.history.navy.mil/research/histories/ship-histories/danfs/j/jacob-jones-ii.html.
13. "Francis E. Powell," Ships Hit by U-Boats, https://uboat.net/allies/merchants/ship/1299.html.
14. "*San Gil*," Ships Hit by U-Boats, https://uboat.net/allies/merchants/ship/1311.html.
15. "*India Arrow*," Ships Hit by U-Boats, https://uboat.net/allies/merchants/ship/1314.html.
16. Wrecksite, SS *Gypsum Prince*, 1942, https://www.wrecksite.eu/wreck.aspx?20090.
17. "*Hvoslef*," Ships Hit by U-Boats, https://uboat.net/allies/merchants/ship/1421.html.
18. Warrington, *Delaware's Coastal Defenses*, 82.
19. Delaware Public Archives, Sussex County markers, Civil Air Patrol, https://archives.delaware.gov/markers/sc/SC-205.shtml.
20. Manthorpe, *A Century of Service*, 52.
21. Ibid., 58.
22. John deRosier, "How a German Submarine Attack Forever Changed Cape May," *Cape May County*, July 6, 2017, http://www.pressofatlanticcity.com/news/press/cape_may/how-a-german-submarine-attack-forever-changed-cape-may/article_10872806–2fb2–5907-abee-c07880ac94dd.html.
23. 261st Coast Artillery (Harbor Defense), http://www.fortmiles.org/intel/units/261st.html.
24. Manthorpe, *A Century of Service*, 53.
25. Grayson, *Delaware's Ghost Towers*, 41–42.
26. Manthorpe, *A Century of Service*, 55.
27. Ibid.
28. Ibid., 67.
29. Ibid., 65–66.
30. Ibid.
31. Dr. Gary D. Wray, "Two Submarines Brought WWII to Delaware," http://fortmilesha.org/two-submarines/.
32. Ibid.
33. Wray, "Two Submarines."
34. Tyler, *Bay and River Delaware*, 199.
35. Joseph-James Ahern, *Philadelphia Naval Shipyard* (Dover, NH: Arcadia, 1997), 8.
36. Dorwart, *The Philadelphia Navy Yard*, 172.
37. Ibid., 176–178.
38. Manthorpe, *A Century of Service*, 52.
39. Dorwart, *The Philadelphia Navy Yard*, 183.
40. Ibid., 166–190.
41. Naval History and Heritage Command, DANFS, *New Jersey II* (BB-62), https://www.history.navy.mil/research/histories/ship-histories/danfs/n/new-jersey-ii.html
42. Ibid.
43. Farr, Bostwick and Willis, *Shipbuilding at Cramp and Sons*, 14, 15, 56.
44. Naval History and Heritage Command, DANFS, "*Indianapolis II*" (CA-35), https://www.history.navy.mil/research/histories/ship-histories/danfs/i/indianapolis-ii.html.
45. New York Shipbuilding, Camden, New Jersey, 2014, http://shipbuildinghistory.com/shipyards/large/newyorkship.htm.
46. Sun Shipbuilding, Chester, Pennsylvania, 2014, http://www.shipbuildinghistory.com/shipyards/large/sun.htm.
47. Sun Shipbuilding and Drydock Company, Historical Marker, http://explorepahistory.com/hmarker.php?markerId=1-A-2EB.
48. William H. Conner and Leon deValinger, Jr., *Delaware's Role in World War II* (Dover: Public Archives Commission, 1955), vol. 2, pp. 182–183.
49. Ibid.

50. Ibid.
51. Conner and deValinger, 181–182.
52. American Car & Foundry, Wilmington, Delaware (formerly Jackson & Sharp) 2017, http://shipbuildinghistory.com/shipyards/small/americancar.htm.
53. Conner and deValinger, 184–185.
54. *Delaware's Port of Wilmington*, 9–12.
55. Conner and deValinger, 73.
56. Military Times Hall of Valor, Navy Cross, Edgar Bassett, https://valor.militarytimes.com/recipient.php?recipientid=19733.
57. Naval History and Heritage Command, Bassett, https://www.history.navy.mil/research/histories/ship-histories/danfs/b/bassett-i.html.
58. Military Times Hall of Valor, Navy Cross, Howard Bayers, https://valor.militarytimes.com/recipient.php?recipientid=19746.
59. Ibid.
60. Ibid.
61. Naval History and Heritage Command, J. Douglas Blackwood (DE 219), https://www.history.navy.mil/research/histories/ship-histories/danfs/j/j-douglas-blackwood-de-219.html.
62. Ibid.
63. Naval History and Heritage Command, Howard F. Clark, https://www.history.navy.mil/research/histories/ship-histories/danfs/h/howard-f-clark-de-533.html.
64. Military Times Hall of Valor, Navy Cross, Arthur Laurence Dowling, https://valor.militarytimes.com/recipient.php?recipientid=19083.
65. Military Times Hall of Valor, Navy Cross, Wilmer Earl Gallaher, https://valor.militarytimes.com/recipient.php?recipientid=21244.
66. Find a Grave, Adm. Wilmer Earl Gallaher, https://www.findagrave.com/memorial/98410255.
67. Military Times Hall of Valor, Frank Lesher Johnson, https://valor.militarytimes.com/recipient.php?recipientid=20566.
68. Ibid.
69. Naval History and Heritage Command, Kline, https://www.history.navy.mil/research/histories/ship-histories/danfs/k/kline.html.
70. 1930 Submariner, Rear Admiral John "Jack" Elwood Lee, USN http://delaware.usnachapters.com/Documents/AdmLee/RearAdmiralLeeUSN.html.
71. Ibid.
72. Ibid.
73. Ibid.
74. Ibid.
75. Military Times Hall of Valor, Lewis Smith Parks, https://valor.militarytimes.com/recipient.php?recipientid=20757.
76. Ibid.
77. Ibid.
78. Ibid.
79. Ibid.
80. Naval History and Heritage Command, *Pennewill* (DE 175), https://www.history.navy.mil/research/histories/ship-histories/danfs/p/pennewill.html.
81. Ibid.
82. Delaware Aviation Hall of Fame, Louis W. Prost, http://www.dahf.org/prost.html.
83. Ibid.
84. Naval History and Heritage Command, *Reybold I* (DE-275), https://www.history.navy.mil/content/history/nhhc/research/histories/ship-histories/danfs/r/reybold-i.html.
85. Ibid.
86. Military Times Hall of Valor, LeRoy Coard Simpler, https://valor.militarytimes.com/recipient.php?recipientid=20933.
87. Ibid.
88. Ibid.
89. Ibid.

Appendix 1

1. U.S. Senate Committee on Veterans Affairs Report, *Medal of Honor Recipients, 1863–1978* (Washington, D.C.: Government Printing Office, 1979), https://history.army.mil/moh/index.html; C. Douglas Sterner, *United States Navy Heroes*, vol. 1: *Medal of Honor and Distinguished Service Medals*, 2015; additional biographic material at http://www.homeofheroes.com/moh/states/1_states.html/.
2. Paul Silverstone, *Civil War Navies*, 62.
3. Martin, *Delaware's Medal of Honor Winners*, 1–3.

Appendix 2

1. Paul Silverstone, *Civil War Navies, 1855–1883* (Annapolis: Naval Institute Press, 2001), *Official Records of the Union and Confederate Navies in the War of the Rebellion*, especially Series II, Vol. 1 (Washington, D.C.: Naval Records and Library, 1901); *The Dictionary of American Naval Fighting Ships*, http://www.shipbuildinghistory.com/history/shipbuilders.htm.
2. http://www.shipbuildinghistory.com/history/shipyards/2large/inactive/pusey.htm.
3. This compendium of Wilmington-built ships for both the Union and the Confederacy comes from these principle sources: (1) Paul Silverstone's *Civil War Navies, 1855–1883*; (2) *Official Records of the Union and Confederate Navies in the War of the Rebellion*, especially Series II, Vol. 1 (3); *The Dictionary of American Fighting Ships*, Naval Department; and (4) a listing of Wilmington-built shipyards and vessels at http://www.shipbuildinghistory.com/history/shipbuilders.htm.
4. Taylor, *The American Clyde*, 21.
5. http://www.shipbuildinghistory.com/history/shipyards/2large/inactive/pusey.htm.
6. This compendium of Wilmington-built ships for both the Union and the Confederacy comes from these principle sources: (1) Paul Silverstone, *Civil War Navies, 1855–1883*; (2) *Official Records of the Union and Confederate Navies in the War of the Rebellion*, especially Series II, Vol. 1; (3) *The Dictionary of American Fighting Ships*, Naval Department; and (4) a listing of Wilmington-built shipyards and vessels at http://www.shipbuildinghistory.com/history/shipbuilders.htm.
7. Tyler, *Bay and River Delaware*, 96–97.
8. Urban, *The City That Launched a Thousand Ships*, 19–20.

Appendix 3

1. *The Dictionary of American Naval Fighting Ships*, Navy Department; listing of Wilmington-built shipyards and vessels at http://www.shipbuildinghistory.com/history/shipbuilders.htm.

Appendix 4

1. A listing of Wilmington-built shipyards and vessels at http://www.shipbuildinghistory.com/history/shipbuilders.htm; National Archives, *Records of the United States Shipping Board (Record Group 32), 1914–38*, https://www.archives.gov/research/guide-fed-records/groups/032.html.

Bibliography

Ahern, Joseph-James. *Philadelphia Naval Shipyard.* Dover, NH: Arcadia, 1997.

Alden, Carroll S., and Allen Westcott. *The United States Navy: A History.* Chicago: H.P. Lippincott, 1945.

Anderson, Bern. *By Sea and by River: The Naval History of the Civil War.* New York: Knopf, 1962.

Beach, John W. *Cape Henlopen Lighthouse and Delaware Breakwater.* Dover: Dover Graphic, 1970.

Bellas, Henry Hobart. "A History of the Delaware State Society of the Cincinnati." *Papers of the Historical Society of Delaware,* Issue XIII, 1895.

Berube, Claude, and John Rodgaard. *A Call to the Sea: Captain Charles Stewart of the USS "Constitution."* Dulles, VA: Potomac, 2005.

Bryant, Tracey L., and, Jonathan R. Pennock, eds. *The Delaware Estuary: Rediscovering a Forgotten Resource.* Newark: Sea Grant College Program, University of Delaware, 1988.

Budiansky, Stephen. *Perilous Fight.* New York: Knopf Doubleday, 2011.

Burdick, Kim Rogers. *Revolutionary Delaware: Independence in the First State.* Charleston, SC: History Press, 2016.

Canney, Donald L. *Sailing Warships of the U.S. Navy.* Annapolis: Naval Institute Press, 2001.

Carey, Mathew. *The Olive Branch; Or, Faults on Both Sides Federal and Democratic: A Serious Appeal on the Necessity of Mutual Forgiveness and Harmony.* Philadelphia, 1815.

Chappelle, Howard I. *The History of the American Sailing Navy: The Ships and Their Development.* New York: Bonanza, 1949.

Churchill, Winston. *The Hinge of Fate.* Boston: Houghton Mifflin, 1950.

Clark, William Bell. *Gallant John Barry, 1775–1803: The Story of a Naval Hero of Two Wars.* New York: Macmillan, 1938.

Cleaver, Mark M. *The Life Character and Public Services of Commodore Jacob Jones.* Wilmington: Historical Society of Delaware, 1906.

Conner, William H., and Leon deValinger, Jr. *Delaware's Role in World War II.* Dover: Public Archives Commission, 1955.

Cooling, Benjamin Franklin. *USS "Olympia": Herald of Empire.* Annapolis: Naval Institute Press 2007.

Dale, Frank. *Delaware Diary: Episodes in the Life of a River.* New Brunswick: Rutgers University Press, 1997.

Daughan, George C. *If by Sea: The Forging of the American Navy from the Revolution to the War of 1812.* New York: Basic Books, 2008.

Delaware Public Archives. Military and Naval Records, Vol. 2. Wilmington: Mercantile Printing, by authority of Public Records Commission of Delaware, 1912.

Doerrfeld, Dean A., with David L. Ames, Bernard L. Herman, and Rebecca J. Siders. *The Delaware Ship and Boat Building Industry, 1830–1940: An Historic Context.* Newark, DE: Center for Historic Architecture and Engineering, College of Urban Affairs and Public Policy, University of Delaware, 1994.

Dorwart, Jeffrey M., with Jean K. Wolf. *The Philadelphia Navy Yard: From the Birth of the U.S. Navy to the Nuclear Age.* Philadelphia: University of Pennsylvania Press, 2001.

Dudley, William S. *The Naval War of 1812: A Documentary History.* Vol. 2, *James Biddle and the Delaware Flotilla.* Washington, D.C.: Government Printing Office, 1985.

Dunlap, G.D. *America's Cup Defenders.* New York: American Heritage Press, 1970.

Eicher, John H., and David J. Eicher. *Civil War High Commands.* Stanford: Stanford University Press, 2001.

Evans, Stephen H. *The United States Coast Guard, 1790–1915: A Definitive History.* Annapolis: Naval Institute Press, 1949.

Fairburn, William Armstrong. *Merchant Sail.* Center Lovell, ME: Fairburn Marine Educational Foundation, 1945–1955.

Farr, Gail E., and Brett F. Bostwick, with Melville Willis. *Shipbuilding at Cramp and Sons: A History and Guide to Collections of the William Cramp and Sons Ship and Engine Building Company.* Philadelphia: Philadelphia Maritime Museum, 1991.

Federal Writers' Project. *Delaware: A Guide to the First State.* New York: Viking, 1938.

Feuer, A.B. *The U.S. Navy in World War I.* Westport, CT: Praeger, 1999.

Forester and Company. *Delaware Port of Wilmington: 75 Years of Personal Service, 1923–1998.* Wilmington: Diamond State Port, 1998.

Frank, William P. *Stories and Legends of the Delaware Capes*. Wilmington: Miles Frederick, 197?.
Friedman, Norman. *U.S. Battleships: An Illustrated Design History*. Annapolis: Naval Institute Press, 1985.
Gannon, Michael. *Operation Drumbeat: The Dramatic True Story of Germany's First U-boat Attacks Along the American Coast in World War II*. New York: Harper and Row, 1990.
George, Pam. *Shipwrecks of the Delaware Coast*. Charleston, SC: History Press, 2010.
Gray, Ralph D. *The National Waterway: A History of the Chesapeake and Delaware Canal, 1769–1985*. Chicago: University of Illinois Press, 1967.
Grayson, William C. *Delaware's Ghost Towers: The Coast Artillery's Forgotten Last Stand During the Darkest Days of World War II*. Bloomington: Author's House, 2005.
Green, Charles E. *Delaware Heritage: The Story of the Diamond State in the Revolution*. Wilmington: Press of William Cann, 1975.
Griffin, Martin Ignatius Joseph. *Commodore John Barry: The Father of the American Navy*. Philadelphia, 1903.
Halpern, Paul G. *A Naval History of World War I*. Annapolis: Naval Institute Press, 1995.
Hearn, Chester G. *Admiral David Dixon Porter: The Civil War Years*. Annapolis: Naval Institute Press, 1996.
_____. *The Capture of New Orleans, 1862*. Baton Rouge: Louisiana State University Press, 1995.
Hernon, Peter. *The Great Rescue*. New York: HarperCollins, 2017.
Hill, Steven. "Commodore John P. Gillis: Delaware's 'Other' Civil War Naval Hero." *Delaware History* (1987).
"History of Ships Named 'Delaware.'" Washington, D.C.: Navy Department, Office of Chief of Naval Operations, 1960.
Holland, Randy J. *Delaware's Destiny Determined by Lewes*. Dover: Delaware Heritage, 2013.
Howarth, Stephen. *To Shining Sea: A History of the United States Navy, 1775–1991*. New York: Random House, 1991.
Jackson, John W. *The Pennsylvania Navy, 1775–1781*. New Brunswick: Rutgers University Press, 1974.
Jones, Jerry W. *United States Battleship Operations in World War One*. Annapolis: Naval Institute Press, 1998.
Knopp, Andrew. *One Hundred Year History of the Pilot's Association Bay and River Delaware, 1896–1996*. Dover: Delaware Heritage, 1996.
Kotowski, Bob. "Finding Their Way: Early Delaware Bay Charts in Lewes History." *Journal of the Lewes Historical Society* 16 (2013).
Leiner, Frederic C. *The End of Barbary Terror: America's 1815 War Against the Pirates of North Africa*. Oxford: Oxford University Press, 2007.
Lewis, Charles Lee. *Famous American Naval Officers*. Boston: L.C. Page, 1924.
Lewis, James A. *Neptune's Militia: The Frigate "South Carolina" During the American Revolution*. Kent, OH: Kent State University Press, 1999.

Macdonough, Rodney. *Life of Commodore Thomas Macdonough, U.S. Navy*. Boston: Fort Hill, 1909.
Manthorpe, William H.J., Jr. *A Century of Service: The U.S. Navy on Cape Henlopen, Lewes, Delaware, 1898–1996*. Wilmington: Cedar Tree, 2014.
_____. "Establishing the Basis for the Safe Navigation of Delaware Bay, 1756–1856." *Lewes History* 16 (2013).
_____. "U.S. Naval Wireless Station, Cape Henlopen." *Lewes History: Journal of the Lewes Historical Society* 17 (November 2014).
Marine, William. *The Bombardment of Lewes*. Historical Society of Delaware, 1901.
Martin, Kenneth R. *Delaware Goes Whaling, 1833–1845*. Wilmington: Hagley Museum 1974.
Martin, Roger A. *Delaware's Medal of Honor Winners*. Self-published, 1993.
Marvil, James E. *Pilots of the Bay and River Delaware*. Laurel, DE: Sussex Press, 1965.
Massie, Robert K. *Castles of Steel: Britain, Germany, and the Winning of the Great War at Sea*. New York: Random House, 2003.
_____. *Dreadnought*. New York: Random House, 1991.
McGrath, Tim. *Give Me a Fast Ship: The Continental Navy and America's Revolution at Sea*. New York: NAL Caliber, 2014.
_____. *John Barry: An American Hero in the Age of Sail*. Yardley, PA: Westholme, 2010.
Meyers, William H. *Journal of a Cruise to California and the Sandwich Islands in the United States Sloop of War "Cyane," 1841–1844*. San Francisco: Book Club of California, 1955.
Miller, Nathan. *The U.S. Navy: A History*, 3rd ed. Annapolis: Naval Institute Press. 1997.
Monroe, John. *History of Delaware*. Newark: University of Delaware Press, 1976.
Moore, Frank. *Songs and Ballads of the American Revolution Papers of George Washington*. Revolutionary War Revolutionary War Series. Carlisle, PA: Applewood Books, 2009.
Morgan, Michael. *Pirates and Patriots: Tales of the Delaware Coast*. New York: Algora, 2005.
Morrow, John Howard. *The Great War: An Imperial History*. New York: Routledge, 2005.
Musicant, Ivan. *Divided Waters: The Naval History of the Civil War*. New York: HarperCollins, 1995.
Neeser, Robert W. "The Ships of the United States Navy: An Historical Record of Those Now in Service and Their Predecessors of the Same Name, Delaware." *Naval Institute Proceedings* 41 (1915).
Paullin, Charles Oscar. *The Navy of the American Revolution: Its Administration, Policy, and Its Achievements*. Cleveland: Borroughs Brothers, 1906.
Porter, David Dixon. *Incidents and Anecdotes of the Civil War*. New York: D. Appleton, 1886.
Potter, E.B. *The Naval Academy Illustrated History of the United States Navy*. New York: Thomas Y. Crowell, 1971.
Pratt, Fletcher. *The Compact History of the United States Navy*. New York: Hawthorne Books, 1957.
Preble, Geo. Henry. *History of the United States Navy*

Yard, Portsmouth, New Hampshire. Washington, D.C.: U.S. Navy Bureau of Yards and Docks, Government Printing Office, 1892.

Preston, Anthony, David Lyon, and John H. Batchelor. *Navies of the American Revolution*. Englewood Cliffs, NJ: Prentice Hall, 1975.

Rachlis, Eugene. *The Story of the U.S. Coast Guard*. New York: Random House, 1961.

Roales, Judith. *Delaware Lighthouses and Range Lights*. Charleston, SC: Arcadia, 2007.

"Rolling on the River: Delaware in the American Revolution." *Journal of the American Revolution*. (2017).

Roosevelt, Theodore. *The Naval War of 1812*. New York: Modern Library.

Seibold, David J., and Charles J. Adams. *Shipwrecks, Sea Stories and Legends of the Delaware Coast*. Barnegat Light, NJ: Exeter Books, 1989.

Silverstone, Paul H. *Civil War Navies, 1855–1883*. Annapolis: Naval Institute Press, 2001.

Smith, Philip Chadwick Foster. *Philadelphia on the River*. Philadelphia: University of Pennsylvania Press, 1986.

Snyder, Frank E., and Brian H. Guss. *The District: A History of the Philadelphia District U.S. Army Corps of Engineers, 1866–1971*. Philadelphia, U.S. Army Engineer District, 1974.

Stephens, John Lloyd. *Incidents of Travel in Egypt, Arabia, Petrea and the Holy Land*, Vol. 1. New York: Harper, 1837.

Thompson, Priscilla M., and Sally O'Byrne. *Wilmington's Waterfront*. Charleston, SC: Arcadia, 1999.

Toll, Ian W. *Six Frigates: The Epic History of the Founding of the U.S. Navy*. New York: W.W. Norton, 2006.

Trapani, Robert, Jr. *Indian River Life-Saving Station: Journey Among the Sands, the U.S. Life-Saving Service, Years 1876–1915*. Virginia Beach: Donning, 2002.

Tuchman, Barbara. *The First Salute: A View of the American Revolution*. New York: Alfred A. Knopf, 1988.

Tyler, David B. *The American Clyde: A History of Iron and Steel Shipbuilding on the Delaware from 1840 to World War I*. Wilmington: University of Delaware Press, 1958.

_____. *Bay and River Delaware: A Pictorial History*. Centreville, MD: Cornell Maritime Press, 1955.

United States Coast Guard Public Information Division, CG 213. *Coast Guard History*. Washington, D.C.: Government Printing Office, 1958.

Urban, Richard. *The City That Launched a Thousand Ships*. Wilmington: Cedar Tree, 1999.

Utt, Ronald D. *Ships of Oak, Guns of Iron: The War of 1812 and the Forging of the American Navy*. Washington, D.C.: Regnery, 2012.

Volo, James M. *Blue Water Patriots: The American Revolution Afloat*. Westport, CT: Greenwood, 2007.

Ward, Christopher. *The Delaware Continentals*. Wilmington: Historical Society of Delaware, 1941.

Warriner, Francis. *Cruise of the United States Frigate "Potomac" Round the World, During the Years 1831–34*. New York: Leavitt, Lord, 1835.

Warrington, C.W. *Delaware's Coastal Defenses: Fort Saulsbury and a Mighty Fort Called Miles*. Wilmington: Delaware Heritage Commission, 1991.

Welles, Gideon, and Edgar Thaddeus Welles. *Diary of Gideon Welles*, Vol. 1. Boston: Houghton-Mifflin, 1911.

West, Richard S., Jr. *The Second Admiral: A Life of David Dixon Porter*. New York: Coward-McCann, 1937.

Wiggins, Kennard R., Jr. *Delaware in World War I*. Charleston, SC: History Press, 2015.

Willis, Sam. *The Struggle for Sea Power: A Naval History of the American Revolution*. New York: W.W. Norton, 2015.

Wilson, W. Emerson. *Forgotten Heroes of Delaware*. Cambridge, MA: Deltos, 1969.

_____. *A Fort Delaware Journal: The Diary of a Yankee Private: A.J. Hamilton, 1862–65*. Wilmington: Fort Delaware Society, 1981.

Index

Numbers in **_bold italics_** indicate pages with illustrations

A, B, C, D ships 133, 142
Abbott, William G. (shipbuilder, Milford DE) 172
Abrams Offhandle (Dutch vessel) 8
USC&GS *A. D. Bache* (survey steamer) 249
Ada (schooner) 242
USS *Adams*: frigate 56; school ship 134
Adams, John (Confederate sailor) 128
Adams, President John 53–54
Adams, President John Quincy 93–94
Addie (shipwreck) 156
Adelaide (schooner) 246
Admiral (British tanker) 176
USS *Admiral* transport steamer 115
Advance (exploration vessel) 88
Africa 13, 59–60, 81, 128–129, 134, 151–153, 195, 207, 214, 245, 262–265, 274
CSS *Alabama* (raider) 117, ***118***, 119, 126, 128–130, 240, 267
USS *Alaska* 224, 235
USS *Albatross* (steamer) 245, 251
CSS *Albemarle* (steamer) 115
USS *Albion* (schooner) 125
Alert (12 gun sloop) 33, 34, 40, 69
Alexander, Captain Charles 27, 29
Alexander Hamilton (merchantman) 55
Alfred (Continental Navy frigate) ***22***
Alice L. Webb (schooner) 241
Allee, Senator James 180
USS *Allegheny* 230
USS *Allegheny* (AT-9) (fleet tug) 198
Allen, Captain Noah 72
USS *Alliance* 151
Alliance (Continental Navy frigate) 26, 33, ***34***, 35, 51
Allie H. Belden (shipwreck) 156
Amalia (Spanish brig) 104
USS *Amaranthus (Christiana)* (screw tug) 239
American Car and Foundry Company 208
"American Clyde" 140, 203, 220, 268, 271, 275
American International Shipbuilding Co. 169
Ammen, Captain Daniel 132
USS *Amphitrite* (monitor) 251
Anaconda Plan ***108***, 110, 117
Andrew Doria (Continental Navy frigate) 22, 27, ***30***, 31, 37, 40
USRCS *Androscoggin* (cutter) 253–254
Angus, Captain Samuel 74

Anna Murray (shipwreck) 156
USS *Annapolis* (gunboat, school ship) 134
Annapolis MD 89, 92, 97,101,107, 110, 134, 185–186, 191–192, 252
A.P. Hurt (sternwheeler) 245
Appleby (British steamer) 174
USS *Arctic* 138
Argal, Samuel 5
Argentina 92, 146
USS *Argus* (brig) 65
Aries, John 13
USS *Arizona* (battleship) 40, 213
CSS *Arizona (Caroline)* (steamer) 119–120, 240, 244, 266
USS *Arkansas* (BB-33) (battleship) 185, 191–192
Arnold (floating battery) 23
Ashland (steam freighter) 86
USS *Aster (Alice)* (steamer tug) 239
HMS *Astrea* (frigate) 49
HMS *Atalanta* (frigate) ***34***
USS *Atlanta* (protected cruiser) 133, 142
Atlantic Blockading Squadron 97, 109, 112, 114–115, 117–118, 123, 126–127, 131, 150, 239–242, 246
Atlantic Marine Corps Advance Base Headquarters 143
Atlas (privateer) 72
HMS *Augusta* (ship of the line) 35, ***38***, ***39***
Austin (Donegal) (blockade runner) 245
Avery (pirate) 12
Ayers, Captain 20

Back Creek 82
USS *Bainbridge* 229
Bainbridge, William 55, 63, 69, 78–80
Baker, Captain Thomas 56–57
USS *Baldwin* (DD-624) (destroyer) 223
Baldwin, Charles (MOH) 223
Baldwin Locomotive Works 198
Ball, Senator L. Heisler 192
Ballard, Captain Henry E. 90, 95, 98
Baltimore 6, 15, 28, 33, 48, 53, 57, 73, 74, 77, 81, 83, 87, 103, 107, 116, 117, 134, 196, 231, 251
Baltimore (Continental Navy frigate) 25
Bangor (USS *Scourge*) (steamer) ***86***, 87
Banks, General Nathaniel P. 122–123
Barbary pirates 50, 52, 61–62, 64, 78, 80, 91, 264, 274
Barge No. 14 (YW-14) 253

277

Barnegat Lighthouse 162, 174–176, 197, 263, 275
USS *Barney* (gunboat) 114
Barney, Captain Joshua 24, 45, **46**, 47, 48, 262
USS *Baron De Kalb* 233
Barrett, Edward (MOH) 225
Barron, Captain James 65
Barry, Commodore John 27, 28, 31–**32**, 33–35, 39–41, 43–45, 53, 56, 60, 63, 133, 261, 262, 273, 274
Bassett, Ensign Edgar Rees 209–210
Battle of Brandywine 26, 35, 70
Battle of Bull Run 128
Battle of Cape May 45
Battle of Coral Sea 209, 211
Battle of Delaware Bay 45
Battle of Dogger Bank 163
Battle of Fajardo 151
Battle of Jutland 163, 165
Battle of Lake Champlain 67,75–**77**
Battle of Lake Erie 67
Battle of Midway 209–210, **212**
Battle of Mobile Bay 127
Battle of Philadelphia 35
Battle of Plattsburg 75–76
Battle of Princeton 33, 61
Battle of Savo Island 211
Battle of the Atlantic 201
Battle of the Delaware Capes (Third battle of Delaware Bay) 49–50
battle of the kegs 36
Battle of Trenton 23, 33, 61
Battle of Tsushima Straits 178
Battle of Turtle Gut 33
Battle of Valparaiso 69–**70**
Baxter, Thomas 11
Bayers, Captain Edward H. 210
Bayly, Vice Admiral Lewis 164
Beatty, Admiral Sir David 189
Beatty, J.F. 158
CSS *Beaufort (Caledonia)* (gunboat) 245
USS *Becuna* (submarine) 3
Bedford, Gunning, Sr. (governor) 25
Bellanca Aircraft Company 198
Belleau Wood, Marines 168
HMS *Belvidera* (frigate) 72
Benbrook (Salem County, Galena, Arizona) (tanker) 256
Bencarnot (Natirar) (cargo ship) 256
Benclair (Glenora, Regulus) (cargo ship) 255
Benfold, Edward C. (MOH) 224
Benwood (Gold Star, Arcturus) (cargo ship) 255
Beresford, Commodore John de la Poer 73
Bermuda 71, 74, 218
Bethany Beach DE 154, 156, 210
HMS *Betsy* (British brig) 29, 33, 47
Biddle, Commodore James 70, 74, 80, 95, 101, 104, 264, 273
Biddle, Nicholas 27, 31, 40
Billings Fort 37

Billings Island 37
Biran (Dorothy) (cargo ship) 255
Bismarck, Emperor Otto von 177
Black, Lieutenant Commander 197
Black Point (collier) 201
Black Prince (Alfred) (Continental Navy frigate) 22, 26–27, 32
"Black Sunday" 174
CSS *Black Warrior* (schooner) 114
Blackjack Maru (LST number) 21, 207
Blackwood, Dr. J. Douglas 211
USC&GS *Blake* (survey steamer) 249
Blimp (airship) 167, 198, **202**–203, 218; (K-23) **219**
Blue Anchor Tavern 10
Blyde Boodschap (Glad Tydings) 6
Board of Wardens, Port of Philadelphia 15
Boer War 152–153
Bolton, Captain William C. 96
Bombay Hook DE 12, 43, 161, 168
Bonaparte, Charles (Secretary of the Navy) 179
Bonaparte, Joseph 95
Bonaparte, Emperor Napoleon 57,65–66, 72, 77–78, 90, 95, 164, 177
Boone, Joel Thompson (MOH) 224
Booth, John Wilkes 117
Bordentown NJ 6, 40
Borie, Adoph E. (Secretary of the Navy) 124–125
Boston (Continental Navy frigate) 40
USS *Boston* (cruiser) 142
USS *Boston* (frigate) 95
Boston MA 33, 42, 48, 53, 55, 59, 61, 87, 103, 127, 128, 134, 145, 161, 184,-185, 189, 191–192, 236,247, 251, 259
Boston Iron and Metal Company 192
Bourbon (frigate) 25
Bouteille, Jean 42
Bradhurst, Captain Benjamin 49
USS *Brandywine (Susquehanna)* (frigate) 85, 89, **92**–96, 115, 125, 230, 265
Brandywine River 13, 15, 171
Brazell, John (MOH) 224–225
Brazil 72, 91–92, 96, 99, 126, 145–146
Brenton Reef (LV102) (lightship) 254
Brewington, Myron V. 47
Broadkill River 15
Bronze Star 216, 220
USS *Brooklyn* (cruiser) 119, 151, 225, 234, 240
Brooklyn Navy Yard 99, 161
Brown, Lieutenant Robert (translator) 201
Brutsche, Henry (MOH) 225
Buchanan, David M. (MOH) 225
Buchanan, Commodore Franklin (USNA Superintendent) 97

Buchanan, James (Secretary of State) 105
Buffalo (sloop) 74
Bulldog (armed galley) 23
Bullivant, Dr. Benjamin 14
Burke (armed galley) 23
Burlington NJ 6, 23, 25
Burnside, General Ambrose E. 114–115, 230
Burton, Representative Hiram 180
Burton, Captain Joseph Hughes 43
Bush, Captain John 70
Bush, Major Lewis 70
Bush, Lieutenant William Sharp 70
Bushnell, David (inventor) 36
Butler, General Benjamin F. 123–124, 241
Butler, Darlington Smedley (MOH) 225

Cabot, John 5
Cabrille (Chilbar) (tanker) 255
Cahall, Anne P. (sponsor) **180**
Cahall, Dr. Lawrence M. 180
Caldwell, Thomas 23, 25
USS *Calena* 234
USS *California* 150
California gold rush 81
Camden (NJ) 3
Camden (armed galley) 23
Camel (sloop) 74
Campbell, Charles H. 105
Canada 19, 66, 75, 77, 88, 153
USM *Canonicus* (militia ship) 137–138
Canoot (French pirate) 12
Cape Clear 68
Cape Cornelius 6
Cape Henlopen 1, 6, 16, 20, 28–29, 31, 35, 44, 46, 56, 148–149, 154, 156, 158–161, 168, 173, 174, 198, 199, **202**, 203, 259, 260, 268, 273, 274; lighthouse 18, **19**, 22, 51, 148, 158
Cape Henlopen Quarantine Hospital 148–150, 161, 173
Cape Horn 69
Cape May 20, 33, 44–46, 49, 72, 74, 84, **155**, **167**, 168, 172–174, 176, 197- 201, 203, 236, 250, 263, 269, 270
Cape of Good Hope 68
Captain A. Morrison (Army cargo ship) 253
Captain Chas. A. Powell (Army cargo ship) 253
Caribbean Sea 52, 54, 80, 105, 118, 143, 152, 191,192, 240, 244, 250–252, 264
USS *Carter* (DE-112) (destroyer escort) 201
Carter, Richard 158
USS *Cassin* (destroyer) 203
Cassin, Captain Stephen 76
USS *Castine* (Gunboat #6) 161
Cecil County MD 25
Cecile 245
Cedar Creek DE 73, 263

Index

A Century of Service: The U.S. Navy on Cape Henlopen 1
Ceres (whaleship) 87
USS *Ceres* (side-wheel steamer) 230
Chadwick, Leonard (MOH) 143, 151–154, 225–226
Charles M. Everest (Narco) (tanker) 255
USS *Charleston* (protected cruiser) 133
Charleston SC 32, 42, 59, 61, 73, 109, 110–112, 120, 126, 133, 140–141, 145, 161, 185, 241–245, 251, 259, 264
Charming Sally (privateer sloop) 46
Chateau-Thierry, Marines 168
Chatham (armed galley) 23
Chauncey, Lieutenant Charles W. 96
Chauncy, Commodore Isaac 67, 75
USS *Cherokee* (naval tug) 176
HMS *Cherub* (sloop) 69–**70**
Cholister, George Robert (MOH) 226
Civil Air Patrol 198
USS *Chesapeake* (frigate) 53, 54, 65–**66**
Chesapeake and Delaware Canal 81–**82**, 83, 107, 148, 196, 265, 274
Chesapeake Bay 14, 15, 24, 33, 35, 48, 51, 81, **82**, 83, 94,103, 107, 110, 115, 116, 117, 128, 186, 188, 196, 254
Chester PA 6, 10, 20–21, 35, 37, 41, 44, 61, 84, 103, 141, 170, 198, 206, 270
USS *Chestnut Hill* 236
chevaux-de-frise **36**, **37**, 38
USS *Chicago* (CA-29) (heavy cruiser) 218
USS *Chicago* (protected cruiser) **136**, 142
China 26, 51–52, 81, 96, 99, 102, 132, 146, 195, 210, 215, 216, 229, 231, 235
SS *China Arrow* (tanker) 197–198
Chincoteague VA 44
Ch'i-ying 96
Christina Ferry Lines 173
Christina River 6, 7, 8, 13, 14, 15, 29, 83, 141, 171, 173, 207, 208
HMS *Chubb* (sloop of war) 76
Churchill, Winston 153
USS *Cincinnati* 151
City of Athens (passenger liner) 176–177
Claason, Claas (shipbuilder) 13
Clark, Howard Franklin 211
Clark, Commodore Dr. Robert Hill 127
USS *Claxton* 218
USS *Cleveland* (light cruiser) 206
Clifford, Tobert T. (MOH) 226
USS *Clinton* (tugboat) 239
coal 83, 110, 128, 130–131, 138, 142, 144, 165, 168, 170, 177, 179, 183, 185, 188, 246, 251, 270
Coast Signal Service 157–159

Cockburn, Admiral Sir George 73
Cohansey (river packet) 84
USS *Colorado* (BB-45) (battleship) 192
USS *Columbia* 84
Columbus (Continental Navy frigate) 22
USS *Commodore Jones* (ferryship) 116
Conan Doyle, Arthur 153
USS *Concord* (brig) 73, 95
Confederacy (Continental Navy frigate) 44
HMS *Confiance* (frigate) 76
Congress (armed galley) 23
Congress (Continental Navy frigate) 40, 99
USS *Congress* (frigate) 53, 78, 99–101, 126, 245
Congreve rockets 73
USS *Connecticut* 225, 229
Constance (Continental Navy brig) 9
USS *Constellation* (frigate) 53–55, 59, 61, 91–92, 95, 99, 125, 151
USS *Constitution* (Old Ironsides) (frigate) 53, 63, **68**–69, 72, 77–78, 91, 93, 99, 110, 179, 181, 265
Constitution of the United States 21, 25, 52
Continental Congress 21, 22, 25, 26, 32, 40, 53, 260
Continental Navy 26–28, 32
Convention (brig) 24, 39
Cooch's Bridge 35
Cooper's Island (Vandever's Island) 13
Corunda (steamship) 146
Coward, Penelope Holt 60
Crabbe, Captain Thomas 96
Cramp, Charles H. 141
Cramp, William 141
Cramp and Sons (shipbuilders) 141–**142**, 171, 203, 206, 268–270, 273
Crane, Commodore William M. 89
Cranston, Simon 15
Crilley, Frank William (MOH) 226
Cripps, Thomas (MOH) 227
USS *Croaker* (SS-246) (submarine) 216
La Croyable (Retaliation) (French privateer) 55, **57**
Cruz, Anibal (Chilean minister) 185
Cuba 56, 59,104, 119, 133, 143–144, 151, 157, 176, 184–186, 188, 191–192, 226, 228, 233,-234, 245, 247,-248, 251, 253, 264, 269
USS *Cumberland* 242
Curacao 56–57
CSS *Curlew* (side-wheel steamer) 114, 246
Curtis H-16 flying boats 167
Cushing, Caleb (envoy) 96
Cutter, George W. (MOH) 227
USS *Cyane* (corvette) 81, 91, 100–101, 265, 274

D. Ellis (schooner shipwreck) 157
Dan (schooner) 155
USCG *Davey* (tug) 254
Davis, Jefferson 106
Davis, John (printer) 17
Davis, Colonel Samuel Boyer 73
Deacon, Captain David 95
Deakin, Charles (MOH) 227
Decatur (sloop of war) 126
Decatur, Captain Stephen, Sr. 54–**56**, **58**, 63
Decatur, Commodore Stephen II 54, 60, 63–64, 67, 69, 72, 75, 78, 80, 91
Declaration of Independence 25
DeHaven, Edwin Jesse (explorer) 87–88
Delavue, John (shipbuilder) 63, 138, 147–150, 155160
Delaware (brig) 85
Delaware (privateer brig) 33, 35, 40, 43–45
Delaware (schooner) 23
Delaware (sloop) 39
USS *Delaware* (SP-467) (minesweeper) 174
Delaware (state ship) 42–43
USRC *Delaware* (USRC *Louis McLane, Lois Dolive*) 117
Delaware (I): Continental Navy frigate 27, 37, **41**; *Le Dauphin*, French privateer 42; *United States*, whaler/trader 42
Delaware (II) (converted merchantman *Hamburg Packet* 1798) 54–**55**, **57**
USS *Delaware* (III) (ship-of-the-line) **88**, 89–**91**, **92**, 93, 99
USS *Delaware* (IV) (*Edenton, Virginia Dare*) (side-wheel steamer) **113**–117
USS Delaware (V) (Piscataqua) (screw steamer frigate) 131, **132**, 133
USS *Delaware* (VI) (BB-28) (battleship) 1, 160, **176**–177, 179 **182**–186, 188–**189**, 190–193
Delaware and Raritan Canal 83, 86
Delaware Bay and River chart **17**
Delaware Breakwater 83, 138, **147**, 150, 155, 160–161
Delaware Breakwater Quarantine Hospital 173
Delaware capes 1, 13, 26, 28, 32–33, 49, 71–73, 154, 157, 168, 173, 195, 197, 200–201, 274
Delaware Fish Oil Company 174
Delaware in World War I 1
Delaware Iron Ship and Engine works 141
Delaware Navy 42–43
Delaware Regiment, Continental Army 21
Delaware River Shipbuilding Baseball League 172
Delaware state seal 5
Delgado Perrado (Spanish gunboat) 144
Dempster, John (MOH) 227

De Vries, David 161
De Vries, Peter 6
Dewey, Admiral George 140, 158, 179
Dey of Algiers 78, 80
Dias, Ralph E. (MOH) 228
Dickenson, Jonathan 14
USS *Dickerson* (DD-157) (destroyer) 218
Dickinson (armed galley) 23
Di Domenico, Anthony 252
HMS *Diomede* (frigate) 48–50
Discovery (English pinnace) 5
Distinguished Conduct Medal 153–154
Distinguished Flying Cross 210–211, 218, 220
Distinguished Service Medal 225, 235, 271
USS *Dixie* (destroyer) 161
Doenitz, Admiral Karl 196
USS *Dolphin* 94, 142
Dolphin (Dutch vessel) 8
Doolen, William (MOH) 228
Dougherty, Captain Henry 29
Doughty, William (designer) 89
Douglas SBD-3 Dauntless scout bomber) *212*–213
Dove, Marmaduke (sailing master) 94
Dover DE 6, 21, 60, 84, 127, 129, 150, 217, 259–260
Dowling, Lieutenant Commander Arthur 211–212
Downs, Captain John 89
Dravo Corporation (shipyards) 203, 207
HMS *Dreadnought* (battleship) 171, 177–181, 183, 186, 269, 274
USS *Drusilla* (SP-372) (patrol boat) 174
Duc de Lauzane 34
Duck Creek 43
Duke, pirate vessel 12
Duke of York 8, 9
Duke of Wellington 77
Du Moulin, Frank (MOH) 228
Du Pont, Rear Admiral Samuel Francis 97–*98*, 100–103, 109–112, 125–126, 184, 242–243, 265–266
Du Pont Company powder works 171–173, 198
Durney, Austin J. (MOH) 228
Dury, Andrew 17
Dutch colonists 6, 7, 8, 9, 13
Dutch West India Company 6

USRCS *Eagle* (cutter) 56
USS *Eagle* 54, 75
Eagle boats 164
HMS *Edward* (sloop) 31, 32, 33
Edward (whaleship) 101
Edwards, Walter Atlee (MOH) 229
Edwin (merchant brig) 78
Effingham (Continental Navy frigate) 23, 27, 28, 35, 39, 40
USS *Eider* (minesweeper) 256, *257*
Eldridge, Acting Master J.H. 116
Eliza and Mary (sloop) 73

Elizabeth (sloop) 118
Elk River 35, 82
CSS *Ellis* (steamer) 114
Ellis Island (ferry) 253
CSS/USS *Ellis* (gunboat) 246
Emma (blockade runner) 242
English, Captain Earl 132
English Channel 166, 297
USS *Enterprise* (CV-6) (aircraft carrier) 210, 212
USS *Enterprise* (frigate) 54, 61–62
Ericsson, John (*Monitor* designer) 242–244
USS *Erie* (sloop of war) 94
Esmeralda (Mexican merchantman) 104
Espana (Spanish sailing ship) 251
USS *Essex* 61, 69–*70*, 72, 262
Esso Gettysburg (T-2 tanker) 206
Estedio (Algerian brig) 78
Estrella (Spanish gunboat) 144
Eugene V. R. Thayer (tanker) 256
Exhibition of the Industry of All Nations 102
USS *Experiment* 54
Experiment (armed galley) 23
Exploration 5–6
USC&GS *Explorer* (research vessel) 53
Eyre, Manuel (shipbuilder) 15

USS *F-4* 226
Fair American (privateer, formerly *General Washington*) 45
Faithful Steward (shipwreck) 154
Falconer, Nathaniel 27
USS *Falmouth* (sloop of war) 126
CSS *Fanny* (steamer supply boat) 114, 246
Farragut, Admiral David G. 91, 103, 109, 118, 121, 123, 125–127, 237, 240,2 64, 267
Fenwick Island 197–198, 201, 259
Fenwick Light 176
Ferry Lines 173
Field, Captain Nehemiah 29
Fire Island (Solhaug, Belgion, Scharlachberger) (cargo ship) 2, 56
USFC *Fish Hawk* (fisheries research vessel) 250
Fisher, Henry (pilot) 18, 28–29, 35
Fisher, Admiral John A. "Jacky" 177–178
Fisher, Joshua (chartmaker) *17*, 18
Fishers Island (Ionier, Favorite) (cargo ship) 257
Five Fathom Bank (lightship LV-40) 250
USS *Fletcher* (DD-445) (destroyer) 213
Flora McDonald (side wheel steamer) 108, 246–247
USS *Florida* (BB-30) (battleship) 165, *189*, 192
Fly, Continental Navy 28, 37
USS *Foote* 242
Foote, Captain Andrew 99
Ford Motor Company 164

CSS *Forrest* (steamer) 114
Fort Barlow 230
Fort Beauregard 110, 237
Fort Casimir 7, *8*
Fort Christina (Wilmington) *9*, *10*, 13
Fort Delaware 107, 146, 199
Fort DuPont 112, 146–147, 199
Fort Fisher *123*, 138, 141, 227, 229–230, 233, 236–238, 241, 244, 247
Fort Jackson 121, 225
Fort Jefferson 120
Fort McAllister 111
Fort Mercer 23, 35, *36*, 38, 39
Fort Mifflin 23, *24*, 35, *36*, 38, *39*, 55, 56
Fort Miles 156, 199, 270, 275
Fort Monroe 97, 114–116
Fort Morgan 225, 227, 232
Fort Mott 146–147, 199, 201
Fort Nassau 6
Fort Pickens 120
Fort St. Philip 121
Fort Saulsbury 199
Fort Sumter 111–112, 120, 126–127, 243–244
Fort Walker 110, 126, 237
Fort Zachary Taylor 120
Forward (revenue schooner) 88–89
Foster, Lieutenant Amos P. 15
Fourth Naval District 137, 162, 173, 198, 200, 203
HMS *Fowey* 28
HMS *Fox* 43
Fox, Gustavus Vasa (Assistant Secretary of the Navy) 111, 142
Fox, Josiah (ship designer) 63
France 25, 33–34, 48–49, 52–54, 57, 59, 61–62, 65, 74, 76, 79, 90, 92, 94, 119, 135, 140, 151, 164, 166, 169, 172, 174, 180, 184, 186–187, 195, 207, 224, 236, 240, 264–265
Francis, Charles Robert (MOH) 229
Francis E. Powell (tanker) 197
Frankford Arsenal 198
Franklin (armed galley) 23
USS *Franklin* (ship of the line) 80, 98
Franklin, Benjamin 25
Frederick, Captain Thomas 49
Fremont, Captain John C. 100
French, Daniel (sculptor) 112
Friendship (Salem trader) 81
HMS *Frolic* (sloop of war) 70–*71*
USS *Frolic* 237
Fry, Isaac N. (MOH) 229
Fullam, George T. 128
USS *Fulton* (steamship) 127
Fulton the First (Demologos) (steam frigate) 74
Fulton, Robert 75
HMS *Furious* 203

Gallaher, Rear Admiral Wilmer Earl 212–213
USS *Ganges* 59
Gen. E.O.C. Ord (Coast Guard tug) 254

General Greene 24, 46–47, 253
General Greene (schooner cutter) 51, 56
HMS *General Monk* (*General Washington*) 24, **45**–48
General Nathaniel Greene (Army cargo ship) 253
General Otis (Nancy Helen, Resolute) (ferry) 254
General Rusk (Blanche) (merchantman) 247
General Thomas Jessup (Army cargo ship) 253
George Washington (privateer) 46
George Washington (brig) 52
Germany 163, 177–178, 180, 187, 191, 194–195, 201, 270, 274
Gibraltar 54, 63, 78, 90, 94–95, 146, 164, 192
USS *Gillis* (destroyer; DD-260) 126
Gillis, Commodore John P. 90, 111, **125**–126, 265, 267, 274
Gleaves, Rear Admiral Albert 165
La Gloire (French destroyer) 176–177
Gloria (Spanish transport) 144
Glouchester NJ 6
Godfrey, Thomas (scientist) 17
Godyn, Samuel 6
Goellet (British merchantman) 72
Golden Age (Confederate steamer) 233
Goodrich, Captain C.F. 157
Gosnell, Paul G. 209
Gosport Navy Yard 91, 93
Governor A. Mouton (steamer) 118
Governor Jay (cutter) 56
USS *Grampus* (schooner) 99
Grand Fleet, British 163, 165, 187–193
USRC *Grant* (revenue cutter) 242, 244
Grant, General Ulysses S. 122, 124
Gray, Anne B. (ship's sponsor) 143
USS *Grayling* (SS-209) (submarine) **215**
Great Blizzard of 1888 147, 155
Great Britain 13, 7, 15, 49, 52–53, 65–66, 82, 85, 128, 163–164, 177–180, 187–188, 203, 274
Great Britain (iron ship) 85
Great White Fleet 78–179
USS *Greer* (destroyer) 195
Gregory, Lieutenant 44–45
Greisinger, Captain David 96
Grice, Francis (naval constructor) 89
Gross, Samual (aka Samuel Marguiles) (MOH) 229
Grumman F4F-4 (*Wildcat* fighter) **209**–210, 219
Grumman F6F-5 (*Hellcat* fighter) 210–211
Grumman F8f-1 (*Bearcat* fighter) 211
Guantanamo (Spanish gunboat) 144
Guardian (Spanish gunboat) 144
Guaro (Isabel Weems) (cargo ship) 55

HMS *Guerriere* (frigate) 68–69
USS *Guerriere* (frigate) 77, 91, 94
Guerrero (Mexican brig) 104
Gulf Blockading Squadron 109, 117–118, 121, 126–127, 239, 240
Gulf of Mexico 85, 87–88, 95, 99, 117, 196, 249, 251
Gypsum Prince (British freighter) 198

Haffee, Edmund (MOH) 230
Haiti 55, 105, 191, 211, 225, 229
Half Moon 5
Hall, Dr. David 156
Hamilton, Alexander 51–52
Hamilton, Richard (MOH) 230
Hammerhead Crane, Philadelphia Naval Yard **204**
Hammond, Andrew Snape 28, 30
Hampton Roads VA 91, 93, 95, 97, 109, 115–116, 121, 145, 157, 184–186, 191–192, 241–242, 245
Hancock (armed galley) 23
Hancock (Continental Navy frigate) 40
USS *Hancock* (AP-4) (transport) 174
Hancock, John 33
Hand, Alexander (MOH) 230–231
Harbor Defense Command Posts (HDCP) 199
Harbor Entrance Control Post (HECP) 156, 198–201
Harbor of Refuge 148, 201
Hard Times (Confederate steamer) 242
Harding, Commander Jesse 49
Harford (schooner) 242
Harlan and Hollingsworth (Wilmington shipbuilders) 85–86, 108,111, 113, 117, 119, 140–141, 171–172, 239, 241–2444, 246, 250, 253, 255
HMS *Harlem* (British sloop) 33, 44
Harrington, Rear Admiral Purnell Frederick 127, 143, **149**, 150–151, 267
Harrington, Captain Purnell F. **149**
Harrington, Samuel M. 127
Harrington, Colonel Samuel M., USMC 151
Harris, John 42
Hart, James 12
USS *Hartford* 150
HMS *Hartland* 214
Haslet, Colonel John 21
Haslet, Governor Joseph 73
USS *Hatteras* (side-wheel steamer) 117, **118**, 119, 239
Havre de Grace, MD 73
Hawkins, Rush 114
Haydon, William 17
Hayley, Mary 42
USS *Haynsworth* 220
Hazard (privateer barge) 43
Hazelwood, Captain John 23, 24, 37, 41
Head of Elk (MD) 15, 35
USS *Helena* (gunboat) 144

Hendrickson, Cornelius 5
Henley, Captain Robert 76
Henry Brinker 116
Henry Wilson (Army cargo ship) 253
Herbert L. Pratt (torpedoed tanker) 174–**175**
Herman, Augustine 81
Hero (frigate) 15
USS *Hertzel* 116
Heyes, Peter 6
Higgins boats 208
High Seas Fleet, German 165–166, 187, 191
Hill, Joseph Edwin (MOH) 231
USS *Hist* 144
Hitler, Adolf 194–195
Hobbs, Russell Baker (Confederate sailor) 128
Hobson, Admiral Richard Pearson 180
Hoffman, Halbert 231
Hog Island 37, 156, 169–**170**, 171, 203, 269
USS *Holland* (SS-1) (submarine) 160
Hollanse Tuijn (Dutch vessel) 8
Holt, Rhyves 60
Hoop (Dutch vessel) 8
Hooper, John 156
Hope (Continental Navy brig) 49
USS *Hopkins* (DD-6) (destroyer) 252
Hopkins, Commodore Esek 28, 47
USS *Hornet* 33, 47, 74, 144
USS *Hornet* (CV-12) (aircraft carrier) 210
Horton, William Charlie (MOH) 231
USS *Howard F. Clark* (DE-533) (destroyer escort) 211
Howe, Admiral Richard 35
Howe, General Sir William 23, 35, 36, 39
Hudson, Henry 5, 161
Hudson Palisades 83
Hudson River 5
USS *Hull* (DD-7) (destroyer) 252–253
Hull, Captain Isaac 69, 77, 91, 94, 100
Humphreys, Charles 53
Humphreys, Joshua 15, 27, 53, 58, 262
Humphreys, Samuel 58, 63, 84
USS *Hunchback* (gunboat) 114
Hunter, Thomas T. "Tornado" 246
Hunter Woodis (ferry) 247
Hurion, Miles 43
Hutton, Nathaniel (shipbuilder) 63
SS *Hvoslep* (Norwegian freighter) 198
Hyder Ally (Continental Navy frigate) 24, **47**–48

Ice Boat, Philadelphia 110, 137
USS *Idaho* (BB-24) (battleship) 142, 161, 218
Immigrant (boarding vessel) 253

USS *Independence* (light carrier) 206
USS *Independence* (ship of the line, frigate raze) 80, 100–101
Independence Seaport Museum 3
SS *India Arrow* (tanker) 197–198
Indian No. 2 (steamer) 118
Indian River 74, 154–156, 268, 275
USS *Indiana* (BB-1) (battleship) **142**
USS *Indianapolis* (CA-35) (cruiser) 206
L'Insurgente (French vessel) 54, 59
Intrepid (captured ketch) 63–**64**
Intrepid (Delaware schooner) 42
USS *Iowa* (battleship) 205
Ira D. Sturgis (shipwreck) 156
Ireland 15, 32, 52, 164, 166, 191, 228, 234
Iron Pier, Lewes DE 147–150
USS *Iroquois* 127
Irwin and Co., Thomas and Mathew, Philadelphia 40, 43
HMS *Isis* (50-gun) 35, 38

USS *J. Douglas Blackwood* (DE219) (destroyer escort) 211
J. A. Bostwick (Cities Service Toledo) (tanker) 255
Jackson, President Andrew 90, 95
Jackson and Sharp (Wilmington shipbuilders) 172, 203, 271
USS *Jacob Jones* (DD-130) (destroyer) **196**–197, 199, 201, 263, 269–270
La Jaloux (French privateer) 56
James, James Hemphill, USMC 127–128
James, Reuben 64, 262
James River 114
Japan 81, 103, 126,132, 134, 177–178, 180, 188, 194, 197, 208–213, 216, 220, 231, 263–264
HMS *Java* (frigate) **68**, 72
Jay, John 43
Jay Treaty (1794) 53
Jefferson (whaler) 87
USRCS *Jefferson* (cutter) 66
Jefferson, Thomas 50, 52–53, 61–62, 65, 67, 98
John A. Palmer, Jr. (trawler) 254
USS *John Adams* 95
John R. Williams (tug) 200–201
John Walsh (Confederate steamer) 233
Johnson, President Andrew 129
Johnson, Rear Admiral Frank Lesher 213–214
Johnson, John (MOH) 231–232
Jones, Jacob 59, **60**–63, 65, 70–72, 75, 77–78, 90, 94, 98–99, 116, 262, 265, 273
USS *Jacob Jones* 60, 116, 184, 196, 197, 199, 201, 263, 269–270
Jones, John Paul 22, **27**
Jones, William (MOH) 232
Jones, William (Secretary of the Navy) 61–62, 67, 74
Jones Creek 43

USS *Jonquil (J.K. Kirkman)* (steam tug) 240
Jose Garcia (Spanish transport) 144
Josephine (sloop) 118
Joyner, Captain John 49–50
Juanita (Mexican brig) 100
USS *Juanita* 150, 174, 242
Juniata (screw sloop) 110
HMS *Junon* (frigate) 74
J.W. Somers (shipwreck) 156

Kaga (Japanese aircraft carrier) 212
Kaiser Wilhelm II 177
Kalmar Nyckel (Key of Kalmar) 6
USS *Kansas* 231
USS *Kearney* (destroyer) 195
Kearney, General 100
USS *Kearsarge* 119, 128, 130, 240
Kehuku (tanker) 256
Kekoskee (tanker) 256
Kelly, John D. (MOH) 232
USS *Keokuk* (ironclad) 112
Kessler, John 44
Keystone State 110, 135, 137
Kidd, Captain (pirate) 12
Kimball, Sumner Increase 154
King, Admiral Ernest J. (fleet commander) 196
King Albert, Belgium 191
King Ferdinand II 95
King George V 185
HMS *Kingfisher* 28, 33
USS *Kingfisher* (AM-25) (minesweeper) 175
Kitts Hummock 43
USS *Kline* (DE-687) (destroyer escort) 214
Kline, Stanly Fly 214
Knights Island (Devonier) (cargo ship) 256

HMS *Lady Susan* 33
Lafayette (French vessel) 251
Lafayette, General Marquis de 92–94
Lake Champlain 59, 67, 75, 77, 264
Lake Erie 75
Lake Ontario 75–77
Lakehurst Naval Air Station, NJ 198, 203, 218
HMS *LaPaz* 72
USS *Larkspur (Pontiac)* (tugboat) 240–241
Latrobe, Benjamin 81
Laurens, John 33
Lawrence, Captain James 69
Lawson, John (MOH) 232
League Island (Philadelphia Navy Yard) 110, 137–138, 142–143, 158, 161–162, 167, 169, 190, 203–204, 243
Lealtad (Spanish frigate) 104
Lear, Nicholas (MOH) 232–233
Lee, Rear Admiral John "Jack" Elwood 215–216
Legion of Merit 213, 217, 220
Leon, Pierre (MOH) 233

HMS *Leopard* 28, 65–**66**
Levery, William (MOH) 233
SS *Leviathan (Vaterland)* (troopship) 165
Lewes DE 6, 12, 13, 15, 16, 17, 18, 21, 28–29, 35, 43, 60, 72–75, 83, 138, **147**–148, 154–159, 161, 172–175, 197–198, 200–201, 219, 259–260, 263–264, 268, 274
Lewes-Rehoboth Canal 200
Lexington (Continental Navy brig) 30, **31**, 32, 33, 35
Lexington (sloop of war) 100
USS *Lexington* (CV-2) (aircraft carrier) 211
SS *Liberator* (merchantman) 218
Libertad (Mexican frigate) 204
Liefde (Dutch vessel) 8
Lightning (Card Boys) (tug) 257
Lincoln, President Abraham 103, 112, 117, 120, 122, 124, 129, 239, 244, 248, 267
HMS *Linnet* (brig) 76
Liston, Edmund 12
Livingston, Edward (minister to France) 90
Lloyd, Benjamin (MOH) 233
USS *Lockwood* (gunboat) 114
Lockwood, Henry Hayes 87, 97–98, 138, 265
Lockwood, James (booth, Arctic explorer) 98
Lockwood, John (surgeon) 97
Logan, Rear Admiral Leavitt Curtis 104
Long, Austin H. 158
Long Island (Argentinier, Tourny) (cargo ship) 257
Lord Baltimore 9
Lord de La Warr 5
Lord Dunmore 33
Lord Robert's Horse 153
USCGC *Lott M. Morrill* (cutter) 251–252
Louisa (privateer) 54
USS *Louisiana* (gunboat) 114, 124, 241
LSM (landing ship medium) 207
LST (landing ship tank) 207
Lucy Ann (whaleship) 87
Lusitania (liner) 163
Luxembourg, Chevalier 48
CSS *Lyn Haven* (schooner) 114

MacArthur, Lieutenant Arthur 161
MacArthur, Douglas 161
Macdonough, James 59
Macdonough, Thomas **59**, 61–65, 69, 75–78, 98, 184, 264, 274
Macedonian 75
HMS *Macedonian* (frigate) 68, 71–72
MacNeal, Harry Lewis (MOH) 233–234
Macomet (Elizabeth) (cargo ship) 256
USS *Macon* (airship) 219

Index

Maddequet (Lillian) (cargo ship) 256
Maddox, Ensign Charles H. 252
Madison, President James 65–69, 75, 98
Maffet, Captain David 72
Magnolia (schooner) 118
Magnolia (whaleship) 101
Mahan, Caotin Alfred T. 102, **137**–138, 188
Mahoney, F. (Confederate sailor) 128
USM *Mahopac* (militia ship) 137–138
Maier, Louis P. 158
Maine 14, 57, 65, 87, 200, 253
USS *Maine* (armored cruiser) 133, 143, 157, 249
Major Albert G. Forse (Army cargo ship) 253
Maling, Nicholas (Confederate sailor) 128
Maltby and Company, Norfolk 97
USS *Malvern (William G. Hewes, Ella and Annie)* 247–**248**
Manaiung (Manyunk) 6
HMS *Manchester* 203
USS *Manchester* (cruiser) 217
USM *Manhattan* (militia ship) 137–138
Manila, Battle of 3
Manthorpe, William H.J., Jr. 1, 173, 175, 260–262, 265, 268–270, 274
USS *Marblehead* 143, 151–152, 225–226, 233
Marconi, Guglierlmo 158
Margery (schooner) 72
Marham (governor) 12
Maria Ponton (Spanish gunboat) 144
Marine Eagle (C4 cargo ship) 207
Marsouin (French privateer) 56
Marte (Spanish brig) 104
Martha Washington (schooner) 242
HMS *Martin* (sloop of war) 74
Martin, Edward S. (MOH) 234
Mary Ann (schooner) 72
Mary E. Banks (schooner) 116
Mason, Captain Christopher 48
Massie Telephone and Telegraph Co. 160
Mastico (Tripoli ketch) 63
Matilda (privateer) 72
Maury, Matthew F. 94
Mausert, Frederick W. III (MOH) 234
USS *Mayflower* 185
McCauley, Captain Charles S. 91, 93
McClellan, General George B. 112, 115, 121
McClernand, General John A. 122
McDonald, Commander William B. 199
McKean, Thomas 21
McKee, Christopher 67
Medal of Honor 130, 143, 151–154, 216, **223**, 225, 227, 229, 231, 233, 235, 237, 252, 268, 271, 274

Mediterranean Sea 54, 62–65, 77–80, 89–91, 93–96, 98–99, 125, 127, 140, 146, 186, 195, 263–265
Meigs, Captain Montgomery C. 120
Meigs, John (engineer) 171
Merchant Marine Academy 135
Merchant Shipbuilding Corporation, Bristol 171
Meredith, Jonathan 64–65
HMS *Merlin* (sloop) 35, **38**
CSS *Merrimac* (Virginia) 242, 245
Meshuda (Algerian flagship) 78
Mexican-American War 81, 85, 99, 101, 266
Mexico 88, 95, 99, 100–101, 104–105, 117, 120, 126, 186, 193, 196, 249, 251–252
Mey, Cornelius 6
Michael, Commander Willard D. **202**
USS *Michigan* (battleship) 179
Milford DE 6, 84
Miller, Hugh (MOH) 234
Milner, Captain 83
Milton DE 15
USS *Mingo* 242
USS *Minneapolis* 169
USS *Minnesota* (BB-22) (battleship) 176
USS *Minnesota* (steam frigate) 102, 116, 245
Mirboka (Tunisian ship) 63
USS *Mississippi* 127, 142
Mississippi River 108–109, 117, 120–122, 127, 131, 142, 186, 237, 246–247
Mitchell, Joseph (MOH) 235
Mitsubishi A6M (*Zero* fighter) 210, 220
Mitsubishi F1M2 (*Pete* floatplane) 209
CSS *Mobile* (blockade runner) 117
Mohawk (frigate) 75
USS *Mohican* 237
USS *Monadnock* (monitor) **123**
USS *Monitor* 138, 242
HMS *Monk (Washington)* (frigate) 24
Monongahela (screw sloop) 110, 127, 150
USS *Montana* (ACR-13) (armored cruiser) 161
Montesquieu (merchantman) 73
USS *Montgomery* (cruiser) 146
USS *Montgomery* (gunboat) 120, 245, 247
Montgomery (Pennsylvania Navy flagship) 23, 28, 39–41
Montgomery, Elizabeth 15
Montgomery, Captain James 24, 51
USS *Monticello* (screw steamer) 126
Montresor, John (engineer) 36
Moore, Charles (designer) 86
Moore, John (shipbuilder, Bethel DE) 172
Morris Commodore Charles 92, 94

Morris, Captain Richard 56
Moran Towing and Transportation Company 200
Morris, Robert 25, 26, 51
USS *Morse* (gunboat) 114
Morse, Commodore Charles 72, 91
Moshulu 3
Mount Vernon (steamboat) 94
USS *Mount Washington* 116
Muckle, Lieutenant J.S. 138
Mudd Island 35
USS *Muir* (DE770) (destroyer escort) 201
USS *Mullany* (DD-528) (destroyer) 213
Murray, Commander 116
Muskegot (Delco, Domino) (cargo ship) 256
Mussolini, Benito 195

Nancy (Pennsylvania Navy brig) 33
Nanquitt (cargo ship) 256
Nanshun (cargo ship) 256
Nanticoke River 15
USS *Nantucket (PG-23)* (USS *Ranger,* USS *Rockport*) 250
USS *Napa (Nemesis)* (monitor) 243
Napoleon (river packet) 84
USS *Nashville* 152, 228
National Harbor of Refuge, Lewes DE 148
USS *Nautilus* 78
USS *Nautilus* (SSN-571) (nuclear submarine) 216
Naval Act of 1916 163
Naval Aircraft Factory, Philadelphia **166**–167, 169, 203–204, 207
Naval Efficiency Board 102
Naval Section Base 173
Naval War College **137**–138
Navigational Aids 16–18
Navy Cross 209–211, 213, 215–220, 223, 226, 228, 229, 271
Navy Department, creation by Congress 51, 54
Neill, Colonel Henry 43
Nelson, Lord Admiral Horatio 64, 177
Nelson, John (Congressman) 95
Nereyda (Peruvian vessel) 69
Neuse River 115–116
USS *Nevada* (battleship) 166, 191
New Amsterdam 7
New Bern NC 115–116, 245, 252
New Castle DE 6–**8**, 9–10, 12, 14, 21, 23, 25, 28, 29, 37, 41, 52, 55–57, 59, 65, 70, 72, 74, 83–84, 105, 138, 148, 155, 168, 198, 233, 237, 261, 274
USS *New Constitution (Delaware)* (battleship) 179, 181
USS *New Hampshire* 158
USS *New Ironsides* **123**, 141, 227, 230, 233, 237–238, 268
USS *New Jersey* (BB-62) (battleship) 3, 204–**205**, 206
New Jersey (sloop) 73
New Jersey Naval Militia 134

Index

New Jersey Shipbuilding Company 172
New Netherlands *7*, 16
New York 23–24, 35–36, 43, 46, 50, 59, 61,69, 71–72, 74–75, 77–78, 81, 83, 86–88, 90, 94–96, 102, 106–107, 116, 120, 127–128, 132–135,139, 141, 150–151, 158, 165,168, 174, 176, 183, 185–187, 189, 191, 196–197, 203, 206, 224–225, 227, 243, 249, 252, 259
USS *New York* (armored cruiser) 151
USS *New York* (BB-34) (battleship) 165, **189**
New York Shipbuilding Corporation, Camden NJ 196, 203, 206, 270
Newark DE 35
Newport News 116, 126, 143, 181, 184, 269
Newport News Shipbuilding 180
USS *Niagara* 127
Nicholson, Captain John B. 90
HMS *Nieman* (frigate) 74
USCG *Nike* (cutter) 197–198
Nimitz, Chester W. 161, 215
USS *Niphon* 247
Nones, Captain Henry Benjamin 88–89
Norfolk VA 57, 59, 84, 89–93, 96–97, 101, 109, 116, 125, 134, 145, 151, 161, 184–186, 191–192, 196, 218, 227, 239, 245–247, 251–252, 265, 267
Norma (Northern Sword) (cargo ship) 255
North America (whaler) 87
North Atlantic Blockading Squadron 97, 109, 114,115, 117, 123, 127, 239, 241–242, 246
USS *North Carolina* (ship-of-the-line) 94, 99
USS *North Dakota* (battleship) 179, 181, 184, 192
North River 5
North Sea 163–164, 190, 195
Northeast End (LV-44) (lightship) 250
Norwalk (cargo ship) 257
Norway 190, 201

O'Bannon, Lieutenant Presley Neville 65
Ocean (steam freighter) 96
L'Ocean (French brig) 56
USS *Ohio* (battleship) 173
USS *Ohio* (ship of the line) 77, 99
USS *Oklahoma* (battleship) 166, 191, 203
CSS *Old North State* (steamer) 115
Old Swede's Church (Wilmington) 15
Oliver Cromwell, Connecticut State Navy 42
USS *Olympia* (protected cruiser) 3, 133, *139*–140, 268, 273
Onrust 5
USS *Ontario* (sloop) 99

Operation Neuland 195
Operation Paukenschlag (Drumbeat) 195
Ordnance (Army cargo ship) 253
USS *Osceola* 143
USS *Ossipee* (steam sloop) 126
O.T. Waring (Maturines) (tanker) 255
HMS *Otter* 28
Overfalls (LV101) (lightship) 156, 254

Pacific Mail Steamship Company 106
Pacific Squadron 90, 95, 97, 100, 126
USRCS *Pamlico* (CG-15) (WPR-57) (cutter) 253
Pamlico River 116
Panama Canal 138, 163–164, 185, 191–192, 197, 264
USS *Para* (schooner) 241–242
USS *Parche* (SS-384) (submarine) 216
Paris, Mary 128
Parker, Sir Peter 31
Parks, Rear Admiral Lewis Smith 216–217
USS *Patapsco* (monitor) 111, **243**–244
CSS *Patrick Henry* 241
HMS *Patriot* (brig) 66
Patterson, Commodore Daniel T. 90, 104
Patterson, George Ann 104
Patty (Continental Navy brig) 25
Paul Jones (privateer) 72
Paulding, Admiral Hiram 93
USS *PCE(R)855* (rescue vessel) 211
HMS *Pearl* (frigate) 33, 35
Pearl Harbor HI 40,194, 196, 198, 203–204, 209, 213, 215–216, 231
Pedricktown Ordnance 198
Pedro, Dom (emperor of Brazil) 92
Penn, William 9, *11*
Pennewill, Governor Simeon 161, 180
Pennewill, Lieutenant Commander William Ellison 217–218
USS *Pennewill* (DE-175) (destroyer escort) 218
Penn's Grove NJ 84
USS *Pennsylvania* 84–**85**
USS *Pennsylvania* (battleship) 203
Pennsylvania Abolition Society 60
Pennsylvania Committee of Safety 20, 22
Pennsylvania Nautical School 134–**135**
Pennsylvania Naval Militia 135–137
Pennsylvania State Nautical School 134–135
Pennsylvania State Navy 22–26, 41
Pennsylvania state seal 5
Penrose, James and Thomas (shipbuilders) 15
USS *Pensacola* (flagship) 150
Penuel, George A. 209
USS *Peoria* (gunboat) 157

USS *Pequot (John A. Palmer)* (trawler) 254
USS *Perry* (brig) 96, 99, 114
Perry, Commodore Matthew 81, 87, 105, 126, 134, 263–264
Perry, Oliver Hazard 69, 75
Peru 69, 94, 145, 191, 224
Petition to the King of the Congress of 1774 25
USS *Petrel* 235
Pfeifer, Louis Fred (aka Louis F. Theis) (MOH) 235
Philadelphia PA 1, 3, 6–7, 10–*11*, 12–*14*, 15–18, 20–22, 24–29, 31–45, 49–54, 58–65, 67, 72–73, 76,80–81, 83–88, 91, 98, 103, 109–110, 112, 114–115, 117, 124–129, 134–135, 137–138, 140–143, 147–151, 155, 157–159, 161–162, 166–160, 171–172, 174–176, 191, 196, 198–199, 201, 203–204, 207, 209, 211, 224–225, 227–232, 234–237, 239, 241–242, 244–245, 259–270, 273, 275
USS *Philadelphia* (frigate) **58**, 61, 63, **64**, 84, 91, 115, 266
Philadelphia Maritime Exchange 147, 158, 268
Philadelphia Navy Yard 3, 40, **58**–59, 80, 84, 85, 98, 103, 109–110, 117, 127, 129, 137, 142, 143, 161–162, 167, 169, 174, 198–199, 203–**204**, 207, 239, 242,260,-262, 264–270, 273, 275
Philadelphia No. 1 (Peoria) (pilot boat) 157
Philadelphia No. 2 (pilot boat) 157, 174
Philadelphia Quartermaster Terminal 169
Phineas Sprague (merchant steamer) 110
HMS *Phoebe* (frigate) 69–**70**
Phoebe (slave ship) 59
Pickett Boat Number No. 1 230
USS *Pilgrim* (screw steamer tug) 242
USS *Pillsbury* (DE-113) (destroyer escort) 201
Pilon (Garibaldi) (cargo ship) 255
pirates and privateers 11–13
Plattsburg NY 76
USS *Plunger* (A-1) (submarine) 161
USS *Pocahontas* (steamer) 126
HMS *Poictiers* (frigate) 71–73
Polly (tea ship) 20
USS *Pompano* (SS-181) (submarine) 216–**217**
Poody (USS *Hatteras Jr.*) 118
USS *Pope* (DE-134) (destroyer escort) 201
Pope, Colonel Charles 42
USS *Porpoise* (schooner) 94, 99
Port Mahon, Minorca 89, 90, 94–95
Port Penn DE 33, 40
Port Royal, SC 109–*111*, 126, 241–242
USS *Porter* (steamer) 242

Porter, Colonel Carlile Patterson 104
Porter, Commodore David **61**, 63, 69–70, 72, 80
Porter, Admiral David Dixon 97, **103**–104, 120–121,123, 125, 138, 241, 247 262–263, 266–267, 274, 275
Porter, Major General David Dixon II 104
Porter, Major David Essex 104
Porter, David Henry 104
Porter, Evalina 106
Porter, Georgianne 106
Porter, Richard Bache 105
Porter, Captain Theodoric 104
Porter, Thomas 104
USS *Portsmouth* 100
Potomac River 94, 107, 117, 131, 242
USS *Potomac* (frigate) 81, 265, 275
USS *Powhatan* (steam frigate) 120, 126–127, 227
Preble (sloop of war) 76, 126
Preble, Commodore Edward 63–65, 76
USS *President* (frigate) 53
USS *President Lincoln* (troop transport) 211
Presidential Unit Citation 216
Prince Albert 185
USS *Princeton* (armed steamer) 85, 127–128
Prinses Royael (Dutch vessel) 8
Printz, Governor 13
prisoners of war (POW) 44, 50, 57, 65, 69, 76, 78, 107, 114, 207, 230, 233, 263
privateers 1, 11–12, 23–24, 33–35, 40, 42–43, 45–46, 48–49, 51, 54–**57**, 61, 66, 68, 72, 79–81, 241, 259
Prole, John 49
Prost, Louis William 218
Providence (Continental Navy frigate) 40
Prudent (slave ship) 59
USS *Purdy* (DD-734) (destroyer) 213–**214**
Purissiam Conception (Spanish supply steamer) 144
USS *Puritan* (monitor) 143, 150
Purvis, Hugh (MOH) 235
Pusey and Jones (Wilmington shipbuilders) 85–86, 108, 140–141, 172, 203, 208, 242, 244–247, 249–254, 256–**257**
Putnam (floating battery) 23

Quackenbush, Lieutenant S.P. 113, 115
quasi-war with France 53–55, 57
MS *Quay* (patrol vessel) 169
HMS *Quebec* **45**, 46, **48**
Queen Anne's War 12
HMS *Queen Elizabeth* **189**
Queen Victoria 153, 177
USS *Quinnebaug* 234
SS *Quistconck*, Hog Islander 170

HMS *Racehorse* (sloop) 31, 37

Raleigh (Continental Navy, 32 guns) 33, 35, 40
Randolph (Continental Navy frigate) 27, 40, 53
Ranger (armed galley) 23
USS *Ranger* (CV-4) (aircraft carrier) 218
Ranger (privateer) 72
USS *Ranger* (*Rockport, Nantucket*) (gunboat, training ship) **250**
USS *Raritan* (frigate) 93, 126–127
Ray, Richard (Confederate sailor) 128
Read, George 21, 25, 28
Read, James 25
Read, Thomas 23, 25–28, 52
Reanie, Neafie and Company (Philadelphia shipbuilders) 86
Red Bank NJ 35, 37
Red Wing (shipwreck) 156
Reedy Island 149–150
Reedy Point DE 43
Rehoboth Beach DE 154, 156, 198, 200–201, 220
Reprisal 33, 37
Rescue (exploration vessel) 88
USS *Rescue* (steamer) 242
USS *Resolute* 242
HMS *Resolution* 203
HMS *Restless* (destroyer) 191
Retaliation 55
USS *Reuben James* (destroyer) 195, 206, 262
Revenge (Delaware privateer) 42
Reybold, Lieutenant Commander John Keane 218–219
USS *Reybold* (DE-177) (destroyer escort) 219
Reynard (French sloop) 56
USS *Richmond* 151, 225, 227, 232, 237
Rising, John 7
River and Bay Pilots 16
R.J. Locklan (Confederate steamer) 233
Roach, John (ship builder) 141
Roanoke Island 114
Robeson, George (Secretary of the Navy) 125
Robinson, Captain Isaiah 31
Rocket (YT-22) 252
Rodger, Rear Admiral Thomas S. 166, 191
Rodgers, Captain Josiah 46, 47
Rodgers, Commander William L. 246
Rodman, Rear Admiral Hugh 165, 185, 189–**190**, 191
Rodney, Caesar 21, 42
USS *Roe* (DD-24) destroyer 161
HMS *Roebuck* (frigate) 23, **24**, 28, 29–31, 35, **38**, 260
Romulus (*Spencer Kellog, Rawleigh Warner*) (tanker) 255
Roosevelt, President Franklin Delano 161, 194, 198, 203
Roosevelt, President Theodore 78,137, 148, 160, 161, 163, 178, 179, 264, 275

R.P. Resor (tanker) 197
Ross, George 26
Rowan, Captain Stephen C. 114–115, 132
HMS *Rowena* (destroyer) 191
Royal Yacht 247
Ruan, Mia N. 151
Ruby (schooner) 74
Rush, Captain William Rees (MOH) 235
Russell, John (Confederate sailor) 128

USS *Sabine* 228
USS *Saetia* (cargo ship) 176, 254
St. Eustatius 31
St. Kitts 57
USRS St. Louis (Keystone State) 136–138
St. Mary (*Nick King*, USS *Genesee*) 247
St. Mihiel, Marines 168
St. Peter's Church, Lewes DE 174
Salem NJ 6
Salter, Thomas (shipbuilder) 43
Saltonstall, Dudley 27
Sames (*Mason City, Ellenor*) (cargo ship) 256
San Gill (fruit transport) 197
Sanderson, Aaron (MOH) 235
Sans Pareil (French privateer) 56
USS *Santee* 247
Santo Domingo 105, 191–192
Sapp, Isaac (MOH) 236
Sarah (schooner) 118
USS *Saranac* 127
USS *Saratoga* (CV-43) aircraft carrier 219
USS *Saratoga* (flagship) 76, 134–**135**, 225
USS *Sassacus* 241
USS *Saugus* (monitor) 244
USS *Savannah* 100, 241
Savannah GA 109–110, 127,176 218, 241, 243
Scapa Flow, Orkney Islands 165, **189**–191, 193
Schmidt, Oscar, Jr. (MOH) 236
Schuylkill River PA 10
Scotland 189, 192, 227, 233
Scotland (Confederate steamer) 233
Scott, General Winfield 105, 108, 110
USS *Scourge* (*Bangor*) (gunboat) **86**, 87
USS *Scourge* (sloop) 75
USS *Sea Gull* (receiving ship) 125
CSS *Seabird* (steamer) 114
Seagrove (Continental Navy schooner) 49
Second Vincent Act of 1938 194
USS *Selinur* (Keystone State II) 135
USS *Seminole* 111, 126
Semmes, Captain Raphael 128–130
USS *Seneca* (*Keystone State*) 135
Senegalais (Free French destroyer escort) 207
Settlement 6–11

Seven Day's Battle 116
Seven Years War 40
Severn (British ship) 20
Seward, William H. (Secretary of State) 120
Shackamaxon (Kensington PA) 6
shallop 13
Sharpe, H. Rodney 200
USS *Shaw* (destroyer) 203, 209
Shelter Island (Livonier, Montaigne, Annellen) (cargo ship) 257
USS *Shenandoah* 236
Shields, Thomas (purser) 78
shipbuilding on the Delaware 13–15
Shipley, William 15
Shoho (Japanese aircraft carrier) 210
USS *Shokokon* 226
Shubrick, Commodore William B. 100–101
Siasconset (Bethnor, Irene, Nidarholm) (cargo ship) 256
Sikorski HNS-1 (helicopter) **202**
Silver Star 70, 213–214, 216
Simpler, Rear Admiral LeRoy Cord 219–220
USS *Simpson* 218
Sinclair, Lieutenant Arthur 128
USS *Siren* 64
Sixth Battle Squadron 189–191
USS *Skipjack* (E-1) (submarine) 161
Slave Trade Act of 1794 60
slaves 13, 52, 59–60, 81, 107, 124, 129, 134, 262, 265
Sloat, Commodore 99–100
Smith, Captain William 40
Smith and Terry Company, Bethel DE (shipbuilders) 172
Smyrna DE 84, 223
USRCS *Snohomish* (seagoing tug) 253
Solebay (French warship) 56
Sonittep (tug) 254
USS *South Carolina* (BB-26) (battleship) 171, 179, 181
USS *South Carolina* (formerly *L'Indien*) (Continental Navy frigate) **48**–50
USS *South Dakota* (BB-57) (battleship) 206
South River 5, **7**, 16
HMS *Southhampton* (frigate) 72
Southwark (Philadelphia Navy Yard) 3, **58**, 80, 85, 110, 142
Spanish-American War 3, 133,-134,137,-138, 140, 143–144, 149–150, 157, 159, 161, 179, 251
Spanish influenza epidemic **166**, 169
HMS *Spartan* (frigate) 74
Speedwell (Continental Navy sloop) 39
Spence, Walter H. 158
Spencer (privateer) 72
USS *Spitfire* (gunboat) 105
Spotswood, John A. 57
CSS *Spray* (side wheel steamer) 247

Sprigg Caroll (Army cargo ship) 243
Squier, Captain Matthew 48
S.T. Carrison (schooner) 241
Stackpole, Commodore 74
Stanton, Edwin (Secretary of War) 122
USS *Star of the West* (Union transport) 247
Staten Island 83, 86
Staten Island (Spartier, Nil) (cargo ship) 257
HMS *Statira* (frigate) 74
Stewart, James A. (MOH) 236
Stimers, Alban B. (engineer) 243
Stockton, Commodore Robert 99–100
Stoner, Dr. George W. 148
Strickland, William 83
USS *Stringham* (torpedo boat No. 19/TB-19) 252
Stuyvesant, Peter 8
submarine 1, 3, 36, 160–161, 163–**165**, 166, 168–172, 174–176, 187–188, 190, 192–**202**, 206, 213, **215**–216, 218, 236, 263–264, 269–271
submarine chasers 164, 172, 208, 269
Sully, Thomas, painter 72
CSS *Sumter* (steamship) 127
Sun Shipbuilding 203, 206–207, 270
USLHS *Sunflower* (lighthouse tender) 253
Superior (whaleship) 87
USS *Supply* (storeship) 106
USS *Susquehanna* (side-wheel steamer) 85
Swedesboro NJ 6
Swedish colonists 6, 7, 8, 13
Sweepstakes (brigantine) 12
Sweetman, Jack 52
HMS *Sybylle* (man of war) 34

T2 tankers 206–207
USS *Tacony* 225
Taft, President William H, 185
Talbot, Captain Silas 46
USS *Tampa* (cutter) 168
USS *Tarantula* (B-3) (submarine) 161
Task Force 17 210
Tattnal, Captain Josiah 105
Taussig, Commander 164
Taylor, General Richard 123
Taylor, William G. (MOH) 236
Teach, Edward (Blackbeard the pirate) **12**, 13
USS *Teal* (AM-23) (minesweeper) 175
CSS *Tennessee* (ram) 227
USS *Terror* 142, 150
Terry, General Alfred H. 124
USS *Texas* (battleship) 151, 165, 190
Thatcher, Admiral Henry Knox 128
Thirty Years War 7
Thompson, Commodore Charles 94

Thompson, Launt (sculptor) 112
Thompson, William (MOH) 236–237
Three Brothers (shipwreck) 154
three lower counties 5, 9, 11
Three Sisters (sloop) 74
Thrush (minesweeper) 257
USS *Ticonderoga* 76, 229, 236
Tingey, Captain Thomas 56
Tipton (Esther Weems, Admiral Benson) (cargo ship) 255
Todd, Captain Chapman C. 143
Togo (Japanese admiral) 178
Tonawanda (schooner) 129
Tory Jack 42
Totten, Commander Benjamin J. 97
trade 15–16
Treaty of Alliance (1778) 53
Treaty of Amity, Commerce and Navigation (1794) 53
Treaty of Cahuenga 100
Treaty of Ghent 80
Treaty of Guadalupe-Hidalgo 101
Treaty of Mortefontaine (1800) 57
Treaty of Paris (1783) 51–52
Treaty of Wang Hsia 96
Treaty of Westphalia (1648) 7
Trench Coxe (steamer) 148
USS *Trenton* 226
HMS *Trespassy* (brig) **34**
Trewlow, Strickland 220
Trinidad 145
Trinity Shoal (LV-43) (lightship) 250
Tripoli 61–65, 90–91, 262
Tripoli (Barbary cruiser) 62
Trippe, Lieutenant John 64–65
Trout, James M. (MOH) 237
Trumble (Continental Navy frigate) 40
Truxton, Captain Thomas 59
Turner, James (engraver) 17
Tuscarora (screw sloop) 110
Two Sisters (sloop) 74
Tyler, President John 92

U-117 (submarine) 175
U-130 (submarine) 197
U-140 (submarine) 175
U-151 *Deutschland* (submarine) 174
U-373 (submarine) 201
U-578 (submarine) 197
U-652 (submarine) 195
U-853 (submarine) 201
U-858 (submarine) 201–**202**
U-Boat 164–**165**, 174–175, 190, 192, 195–198, 201, 206–207, 221, 270, 274
HMS *Ulysses* 72
USS *Union* 242
Union (steam packet) 110
Unknown Soldier 140
Uruguay 92, 145
USS *United States* 35, 53, 56, 94–95, 97, 104
U.S. Auxiliary Naval Force 137–138
U.S. Coast Guard 1, 50, 51, 135, 156, 168, 173–174, 198–200, 206–207,

253–254, 262, 263, 266, 269, 273, 275
USS *U.S. Grant* (revenue cutter) 242, 249
U.S. Life-saving Service 154–158, 161, 268, 275
U.S. Lighthouse Service 51, 101–102, 150, **155**, 158, 251, 254
U.S. Naval Academy 71, 97–99, 101, 124,127, 134–135, 138,150, 211–213, 215, 219
U.S. Naval Air Station, Cape May **167**
U.S. Naval Institute 151
U.S. Naval Reserve Force 137, 159, 161, 211, 214, 218, 253
U.S. Naval Observatory 88, 97
U.S. Revenue Cutter Service (USRCS) 1, 50–51,54, 56, 89, 117, 140, 156, 244, 249, 251, 253, 262
Upland (Chester PA) 6, 10
Urbana (storage ship) 242
USS *Utah* (battleship) 166, 191, 203, 218

USS *Valley City* 116
Valley Forge PA 25
van Buren, Vice President Martin 90
USS *Vanderbilt* (steamer) **123**
Vantine, Joseph E. (MOH) 237
Venezuela 145
la Vengeance (French vessel) 54
USS *Vermont* 151
Vestal (steam packet) 84
Vickers, Elizabeth Hooper 156
Vickers, Nathan 156
Vickers, Washington A. (surf man) 156
Vicksburg MI 121–122, 225, 267
HMS *Vigilant* (bombardment vessel) 39
Vigilant (Delaware schooner) 42–43
USS *Vincennes* (CA-44) (cruiser) 211
USS *Vincennes* (flagship) 95
Vinyard Shipbuilding Co., Milford DE 172, 208
USS *Viper* (B-1) (submarine) 161
Virginia (Continental Navy frigate) 40
CSS *Virginia (Merrimac)* 245
USS *Virginia (Merrimac)* 242
Virginia Capes 65, 84, 184–186
Virginius (gunrunner) 133
Voco (British tanker) 198
Vogel Grip (Bird Grip) 6
Volans, Samuel (Confederate sailor) 128
Von Dunlop, Carl 23, 38
Vreeland, Admiral Charles E. 185

Waag (Dutch vessel) 8
USS *Wabash* (steam frigate) 110
Wadsworth Commodore Alexander S. 95–96
Wake Island 216
Walsh, Robert 92

USRS *Walter Forward* (revenue cutter) 242, 251
Walvis (whale) 6
War Compass (Aurora, Carabinier, Yzerhandel, Belgica) (cargo ship) 256
War Crater (Marshall, Torny) (cargo ship) 256
War Dart (Moline, Lara) (cargo ship) 256
War Heroine (Waukesha) (cargo ship) 256
War Metal (Middlebury) (cargo ship) 256
War Nurse (Piqua, Marconier, Ganda, Helle) (cargo ship) 256
War of Independence 15, 18–19, 21–22, 25, 27, 41
War Platoon (Lynchburg, Fusilier, Ersthandel, Skrunda) (cargo ship) 256
War Shield (Rock Island, Falcon) (cargo ship) 256
Warren (armed galley) 23
Warren (Continental Navy frigate) 40
USS *Warren* (sloop of war) 100
Warrington, Captain Lewis 80
USS *Washington* (battleship) 203
Washington (frigate) 23, 25, 27, 28, 39, 40–41, 45
Washington (galley) 29
Washington Naval Treaty 192, 194, 270
Washington Navy Yard 92, 93, 115, 117, 230
Washington (ship of the line) 80
Washington, General George 21, 23, 25, 33, 34, 35, 36, 40, 52, 53
Washington, DC 48, 91, 97, 103, 105, 106, 107, 110, 112, 115, 122, 126, 140, 150, 188, 192, 201, 237, 242, 244, 249
Washington Naval Treaty 192
Washington, NC 116
Wasp (Continental Navy sloop) 27–30, 33, 37, 47, 65, 70–**71**, 74, 261
Watson, Rear Admiral Adolphus E. 198
SS *Waukegan* 196
Welcome 10
Welles, Gideon (Secretary of the Navy) 111, 126, 129, 266–267, 275
USS *Wells* (steamer) 242
Welsh, James (Confederate sailor) 128
West, James (shipwright) 13
USS *West Virginia* (BB-48) (battleship) 192
Weweantic (Liberty, Minquas) (tanker) 256
whaling 4, 6, 16, 42, 83, 87, 265
Wharton, P. (Confederate sailor) 128
Wharton and Humphrey shipyard 40
Wharton family (shipbuilders) 15
White, David Henry (Confederate slave) 129–130

White, Joseph (MOH) 237
White Jacket, H. Melville 97
USS *Whitehead* (gunboat) 114
Whorekill (Horekill) Creek 8
Wiccacoa (Passyunk) PA 6
USS *Widgeon* (AM-22) (minesweeper) 175
Wilcocks, John 45
USS *Wilderness* 241
William G. Hewes (Ella and Annie, USS Malvern) (side wheel steamer) 247–**248**
Willing, Morris and Cadwalader (shipping firm) 32
Willis, Richard (MOH) 238
Wilmington DE 6–9, 15, 29, 37, 41–43, 52, 65, 70, 72–74, 83–90, 108–109, 111–113, 123, 125, 127, 138, 140–141, 148, 171–173, 184, 198, 201, 207–209, 211–212, 215–216, 218, 226, 239–241, 243–247, 249, 251, 253, 257, 259–262, 265–266, 268–269, 271, 273–275
Wilmington (first trading vessel built in Wilmington) 15
USS *Wilmington* (PG-8) (gunboat) 143, **144**–146
Wilmington and Penn's Grove Transportation Company 173
Wilmington Marine Terminal 208
Wilmon Whillden (sidewheel steamer) 84, 242
Wilson, Dr. B.F. 150
Wilson, Edith Bolling (first lady) 171
Wilson, Elizabeth 128
Wilson, President Woodrow 163, 171, 186
Wilson Line ferries 173
USCGC *Winona* (cutter) 252
Winslow, Lieutenant Cameron 152
Winslow, Captain John A. 128–129
Winters, John D. (historian) 122
Wireless Telegraphy 159–160
USS *Wisconsin* (battleship) 205
Wistaria (lighthouse tender) 251
Wm. H. Davidson (shipwreck) 156
USS *Wolverine* (IX-31) 137
Women's Christian Temperance Union 180
USS *Wompatuck* 144
Woodburn (schooner) 72
Woodbury, Levi (Secretary of the Navy) 90
Woodruff and Beach (Hartford shipbuilders) 131
World War I 1, 163,167–169, 171, 178–181, 185–188, 190, 255–257, 268, 270
World War II 3, 194–197, 199, 201, 203, 205–221, 251–255, 257, 263–264
W.W. Hailee (troop transport) 248
USS *Wyalusing* 223, 233, 242
USS *Wyandank* 235
USS *Wyoming* (BB-32) (battleship) 165, **189**

XYZ Affair 54

HMS *Yarmouth* (ship-of-the-line) 40
Yeo, Sir James 72
USS *Yorktown* (CV-5) (aircraft carrier) 209, 212
USS *Yorktown* (CV-10) (aircraft carrier) 210
USS *Yorktown* (gunboat) 150
USS *YP-334* (patrol boat) 201
Yuzuki (Japanese destroyer) 210

Zabiaka (Russian cruiser) 142

CSS *Zenith* (schooner) 114
Zephyr (river packet) 84
Zimmerman telegram 163
Zwaanendael 6

www.ingramcontent.com/pod-product-compliance
Lightning Source LLC
Chambersburg PA
CBHW080801300426
44114CB00020B/2786